Good Housekeeping

THE
ULTIMATE
CHRISTMAS
Collection

WHEN USING KITCHEN APPLIANCES PLEASE ALWAYS
FOLLOW THE MANUFACTURER'S INSTRUCTIONS

HarperCollins*Publishers*
1 London Bridge Street
London SE1 9GF

www.harpercollins.co.uk

HarperCollins*Publishers*
Macken House, 39/40 Mayor Street Upper
Dublin 1, D01 C9W8, Ireland

First published by HarperCollins*Publishers* 2023

1 3 5 7 9 10 8 6 4 2

Text and photography © Good Housekeeping 2023

Project editor: Tracy Müller-King

Recipe writers: Meike Beck, Emma Franklin, Alice Shields,
Grace Evans, Georgie D'Arcy Coles, Lucy Jessop, Suzannah Butcher,
Elizabeth Fox, Sophie Austen-Smith, Monaz Dumasia, Charlotte Watson,
Madeline Burkitt, Gabriella English, Zoe Garner, Olivia Spurrell

Photographers: Alex Luck, Gareth Morgans, Myles New,
Kate Whitaker, Charlie Richards, Kris Kirkham, Mike English,
Sam Stowell, Maja Smend, Stuart West, Tom Regester, Emma Lee,
Peter Cassidy, Jon Whitaker, Dan Jones, James Everett, Mike Garten,
Will Heap, Adrian Lawrence, Steve Baxter, Martin Thompson,
Philip Webb, Elisabeth Zeschin, Stephen Conroy

Good Housekeeping asserts the moral right to be identified as the
author of this work

A catalogue record of this book is available from the British Library

ISBN 978-0-00-848785-0
Printed and bound by GPS Group

MIX
Paper | Supporting
responsible forestry
FSC™ C007454

This book is produced from independently certified FSC™ paper
to ensure responsible forest management.

For more information visit: www.harpercollins.co.uk/green

Good Housekeeping

THE ULTIMATE CHRISTMAS

Collection

400 FOOLPROOF RECIPES TO SEE YOU THROUGH THE FESTIVE SEASON

HarperCollinsPublishers

Contents

Introduction

Christmas may only come once a year but, I know you'll agree, we live and breathe that day for many, many more days than that! And, if you're the one doing the catering for friends and family, no other occasion comes with higher expectations.

Everyone looks forward to indulging in great food, and we want the festive dishes we serve to be perfect – which is no easy feat! Of course, what matters most is getting together with loved ones, but we can't help but want our Christmas celebrations to go smoothly, too. Who doesn't love the glory of a few 'oohs' and 'aahs' when they present the turkey, flame the Christmas pudding or pass round the mince pies?

It's five years since we brought you our bestselling *Christmas with Good Housekeeping* cookbook, and I know *Good Housekeeping* readers love it because they've told me so. They've also shared with me their desire for more, and I'm happy to oblige.

The need for Yuletide culinary inspiration runs deep, and as much as we love traditional dishes, we also want to try new twists on old favourites to surprise family and friends. Moreover, with so many of us now needing to cater for a variety of dietary requirements in our gathered crowds, there's a demand for more vegetarian, vegan and free-from recipes, too.

So, I'm so very pleased to introduce you to what I can proudly claim is the *Ultimate Christmas* cookbook – 500 pages literally crammed to bursting with wonders from the *Good Housekeeping* kitchen. From novel ideas for Christmas breakfast to beautiful bakes and fabulous foodie gifts, I promise there's no dish you won't find within this mighty tome.

I hope you'll enjoy using it this year and for many more Christmases to come – I know I will.

Wishing you and your families a magical season full of comfort, joy and deliciousness...

Gaby

Gaby Huddart, Editor-in-chief, Good Housekeeping

DIETARY INDEX

For those following a vegetarian, vegan, gluten-free or dairy-free diet, you'll find recipes throughout the cookbook where you see these symbols.

VN Vegan recipes

GF Gluten-free recipes

DF Dairy-free recipes

V Vegetarian recipes

- Check all packaging if following a specific diet, as brands vary.
- Not all cheese is vegetarian, though vegetarian cheeses (and dairy-free cheese suitable for vegans) are widely available. Read the label and look for the Vegetarian Society Approved symbol.
- Stock can contain gluten or dairy, and vegetable stock won't necessarily be suitable for vegans – always check the label.
- Wine can contain animal protein, so check to ensure it is suitable for vegetarians or vegans.

Tips for a stress-free Christmas

HOW TO GET THE TURKEY JUST RIGHT

The sheer size of a turkey can make many cooks quite nervous, but these simple hints will help you achieve perfect results.

What size do you need?

See our Timed to Perfection chart below, which will show you how many portions you should get from a particular size bird.

If your bird is frozen

Using our chart as a guide, leave your frozen turkey in its bag and thaw it at room temperature, removing the giblets as soon as they are loose. When there are no ice crystals inside the cavity and the legs are flexible, cover the turkey and put it in the fridge – check the chart for approximate thawing times. After thawing, cook the turkey within 24hr. Remember never to refreeze defrosted meat.

Get the stuffing right

Just before cooking, loosely stuff the neck end of the turkey only so that heat can circulate and cook the inside of the bird properly. Allow 225g stuffing for each 2.3kg dressed weight of bird. Secure the neck skin with skewers or cocktail sticks, or sew using a trussing needle threaded with fine string.

Cooking to perfection

Weigh the bird after stuffing, coat with butter, then season and cover it in foil (or follow the instructions for your chosen recipe), using our guide below for timings. Aim for your bird to be ready at least 30min before you plan to eat, so it has time to rest after cooking. During resting, the residual heat should remedy any pinkness. For golden skin, remove the foil about 1hr before the end of cooking time, basting regularly.

TIMED TO PERFECTION: PORTIONING, THAWING AND COOKING YOUR TURKEY

Calculated for an oven temperature of 190°C (170°C fan) mark 5.

Oven-ready weight (at room temp)	Approx number of servings	Approx thawing time	Cooking time
550g–1.4kg	2–3	4–10hr	1–1hr 30min
1.4–2.3kg	4–6	10–15hr	1hr 30min–2hr
2.3–3.6kg	6–10	15–18hr	2–3hr
3.6–5kg	10–15	18–20hr	3–3hr 15min
5–6.8kg	15–20	20–24hr	3hr 15min–4hr

How to tell if it's cooked through

Pierce the thickest part of the leg with a skewer. The juices should run golden and clear with no trace of pink. Using a cooking thermometer is another failsafe method – a meat thermometer should read at least 72°C when inserted into the thickest part of the breast (not leg). Once the turkey is ready, cover with foil and keep in a warm place for up to an hour until you're ready to carve.

FAILSAFE TURKEY CARVING GUIDE

- For neat slices, make sure your carving knife is properly sharp. No carving knife? Use a long, thin-bladed knife instead (not a serrated knife as this will rip the meat).
- Once the turkey has rested, transfer it to a large board, ideally one with small spikes to secure the bird as you carve.
- Remove and discard the string used to tie the legs.
- Hold one of the legs by the knuckle, then slice between the leg and body (the hip joint), pulling the leg away from the body as you cut. The leg should come away quite easily. Repeat with the other leg.
- Either carve each leg between the thigh and drumstick to create 2 pieces, or slice the meat straight off the legs and discard the bones. (Or freeze the bones for later, to use in stock.)
- To carve the breast meat, the traditional method is to hold your knife flat against the breast (securing the bird with a carving fork) and cut the meat along the length of the breast. The second method is to cut the whole breast off the carcass by slicing down one side of the backbone, then cutting under the breast, following the line of the ribcage. Then just slice the breast on the board. Repeat with the other side.
- If you want to serve the wings, lift up each wing to find the joint, then cut through this joint between the wing and breast. Repeat with other wing.
- Remember to pick over your carved and cooled bird for any leftovers.

ENTERTAINING ON A BUDGET

Being a good host doesn't need to cost a fortune. Here are some GH Save tips and tricks to ensure your season sparkles – no matter how much you spend.

Pick your favourites

Before you write your shopping list, ask your family and guests what they really like to eat at Christmas and, more importantly, what they don't. It sounds obvious, but it's easy to feel pressured into serving certain things (sprouts, say, or red cabbage). It's a waste of money, though, if nobody actually enjoys eating them.

The early bird

Seek out multi-buy offers on high-value items such as wine, and start buying early. This helps spread the cost, and you're more likely to get good deals earlier in the season. Search online to find bargains – and not just in supermarkets. Check out online wine merchants too.

Crown it

If serving smaller numbers, a turkey crown is a far more economical option. A bone-in crown still looks magnificent as a centrepiece, or choose a boneless one and make it go even further with a tasty sausage and breadcrumb stuffing. Visit goodhousekeeping. com/uk for recipe inspiration.

Meaty mains

For the confirmed carnivores looking for a festive roast, it's easy to overbuy to impress. Be guided by how much you'll actually need per person to minimise overspending. Aim to buy the highest-welfare poultry or meat you can afford, and make up those costs by choosing cheaper and fewer sides. Alternatively, make those sides work harder and serve smaller portions of meat.

Food-waste warrior

Be on the lookout for avoidable waste – this often gets overlooked during times of feasting. Citrus fruit looking a bit sad? Slice it and open-freeze, then keep it frozen, ready to use as cocktail garnishes. Whizz stale bread into breadcrumbs, then freeze and use as needed. Stir limp leaves and herbs into soups. Sign up to food-waste apps to share what you can't use.

Twice as nice

We all know leftovers make for great, easy meals, but their volume can get overwhelming when you're entertaining. Arm yourself with freezer-safe containers and portion, label, date and freeze as you go so you can enjoy them at a later date rather than binning them.

Go veggie

It's no secret that eating plant-based meals can significantly cut costs but, understandably, not everyone wants a turkey-free Christmas. You can cut out meat in other areas of your menu and go veggie with your starter, sides or stuffing. See goodhousekeeping.com/uk for some meat-free inspiration that will help save you money.

Bring a dish

An easy way to cut costs is to ask everyone to bring a dish, but remember to oversee what people are planning to avoid an unbalanced spread or repetition. Friends and family will want to help reduce stress and to feel they have contributed, so doing this ticks that box, too.

Be drink aware

Don't go overboard on your drinks selection. Alcohol is a major expense when entertaining and quickly adds up. You really don't need to offer a cocktail cabinet full of options – plus guests will usually bring a bottle or two as well. See p58 for our top tipple recipes.

Plan for success

It's no surprise that planning meals helps you stick to a budget. Write a list of what you'll need to prevent impulse buying at the supermarket and putting unnecessary festive fare into your shopping basket. Don't just include suppers either – plan your

breakfasts and lunches, and shop accordingly to avoid last-minute panic buying and splurging. Don't forget to factor in using up leftover ingredients.

RSVPs

If you're planning on hosting a larger party, get an accurate headcount so that you can gauge the drinks and food accordingly, otherwise the temptation will be to over-cater and overspend.

Rent, don't spend

Hosting a canapé party? Look into renting not only the glassware but also serving platters and dishes. Buying more quickly racks up costs and it can be hard to find somewhere to store them afterwards.

Be energy efficient

Keep the use of multiple cooking appliances to a minimum to cut down on energy costs. Better yet, pick recipes that use only one pan, as this will cut down on the washing-up, too!

THE THOUGHT THAT COUNTS

Planning to give homemade food gift such as chutney, biscuits or mincemeat? You'll find some great ideas on p270–303. Follow these tips to make sure they're prepared – and stored – perfectly.

Keep it clean

It's vital that all equipment is thoroughly clean – check your bowls, pans and utensils before use and always sterilise bottles or jars before filling.

Sterilising bottles and jars

An easy way to sterilise glass bottles, jars and lids is to run them through a hot dishwasher cycle. You can also wash them in hot, soapy water, rinsing well, then drying in an oven preheated to 130°C (110°C fan) mark ½ for 10min.

Hot or cold?

Cold liquids should be decanted into cool sterilised containers, but hot foods like jams and chutneys should be decanted into hot sterilised containers to avoid the glass cracking from sudden temperature

shocks. Put the hot jars on a tea towel to protect your work surface and catch spills.

A perfect set

The setting point for marmalades and jams is achieved when the mixture reaches 104.5°C on a kitchen thermometer. Or chill 2 or 3 saucers in the freezer. When the jam has boiled for 15min, take the pan off the heat and spoon a blob on to a chilled saucer. Leave for a few minutes, then push the surface with your finger. If it wrinkles and doesn't break to reveal liquid, the setting point has been reached. If it's not ready, boil for 5min more before testing again.

OTHER HANDY HINTS AND SMART-COOK SECRETS

You're bound to be rushed off your feet at this time of year, but these crafty tricks and no-one-will-notice cheats should help ensure minimum stress and maximum enjoyment for you!

Love labels

Prepare and freeze dishes ahead from the Fill Your Freezer chapter (p468). Label and date containers so you aren't left baffled by an anonymous icy block a few months down the line.

Be prepared

Keep a sweet pastry case in the freezer and ingredients for your favourite filling in the cupboard and you will always be able to knock together a tasty dessert for unexpected guests.

Numbers game

If making canapés (there are lots of ideas on p30–57), allow 10 per person for an evening party without dinner, and aim to make the last round a sweet bite. If you're serving drinks and nibbles before a meal, 4–5 savoury canapés per person will be plenty.

Not drinking? No problem!

If you're having a party, don't forget about the guests who are driving or those who don't drink – be sure to have a non-alcoholic cocktail on offer. There are lots of interesting 0% alcohol drinks available right now, or try our mocktail recipes on p72–75.

Glaze of glory

After boiling and before roasting your ham, brush over a mixture of 50g dark brown sugar, 1 tbsp thin-cut marmalade, 2 tsp English mustard powder and 1 tbsp brandy. Use any spare mixture to re-glaze once during cooking.

It's a carve-up

To carve a rack of pork easily, remove the bones in one go by slicing down just above them, then simply slice the meat.

Crispy crackling

If your pork crackling isn't as crispy as you'd like, you can still rescue it. Remove the crackling and preheat the grill to medium-high. Put the whole piece of crackling on a baking tray and grill until crisp and puffed (watch carefully to prevent scorching, turning the tray to avoid hot spots).

It's OK to cheat

If planning to serve some dishes out of a packet, stock up on fresh herbs, such as rosemary and parsley, along with key Christmas spices and condiments, such as cinnamon. Adding these to shop-bought items as a garnish or for flavour, where appropriate, can make things taste (and look) more homemade.

New use for old pies

If you have any stale leftover mince pies, crumble them into vanilla ice cream and serve with a tot of brandy for an instant pud.

Cream with a kick

If you want something indulgent with your festive dessert, whip 150ml double cream with 2 tbsp icing sugar and 1½ tbsp Cointreau until the mixture forms soft peaks.

Firm royal icing

To make a firm royal icing, in a medium bowl, whisk 10g egg white until frothy. Sift in 65g icing sugar and whisk to combine. You're looking for a very stiff but still pipeable consistency – you may need to add up to 10g more sifted icing sugar or, if it's too stiff, whisk in a drop of water. Use immediately.

Colouring in

Dye your own ready-to-roll icing by whizzing it in a food processor with a little food colouring paste (available from cake shops) – avoid liquid colourings, as these will make the icing too wet. Knead the icing until smooth.

Berry nice

To crystalise berries or leaves for decorating a cake or pud, pat dry fresh berries with kitchen paper, then dip in egg white. Roll in caster sugar and leave to dry overnight in a warm place on a tray lined with baking parchment.

1

Rise
& Shine

Egg and Chorizo Croissant Brunch Sandwich

Simple, indulgent and oh-so-delicious. The spring onion relish takes this to the next level, but you could easily just add some finely chopped chives to the sandwich instead.

FOR THE SPRING ONION RELISH
1 tbsp vegetable oil
1 tsp finely grated fresh root ginger
2 spring onions, finely chopped
1 tsp toasted sesame oil

FOR THE SANDWICHES
1 tsp vegetable oil
60g diced chorizo
4 large croissants
4 medium eggs
4 slices Jarlsberg cheese, or similar

1. For the spring onion relish, in a small frying pan, heat the vegetable oil over medium heat and cook the ginger for 1min 30sec or until sizzling. Reduce heat to low, add the spring onions and cook, stirring, for 1min. Remove from heat, stir in the sesame oil and a pinch of salt. Set aside.

2. Preheat oven to 180°C (160°C fan) mark 4. For the sandwiches, heat the oil in a large non-stick frying pan over medium heat and cook the chorizo for 3–4min, or until crisp and the chorizo has released some of its oil. Pour the chorizo and most of the oil into a small bowl.

3. Split the croissants horizontally, place on a baking tray (cut-side up) and warm in the oven for 3–4min, or according to pack instructions.

4. Meanwhile, return the frying pan to medium heat, crack in the eggs and cook for 3–4min, or until the whites are set but the yolks are still a little runny.

5. To serve, place a slice of cheese on the bottom half of each croissant, top with a fried egg and spoon over a quarter of the chorizo and oil. Top with spring onion relish and serve immediately.

Hands-on time: 20min
Cooking time: about 15min
Makes 4

PER BRUNCH SANDWICH 593cals, 27g protein, 38g fat (17g saturates), 34g carbs (5g total sugars), 3g fibre

Orange Pancakes with Cinnamon Butter and Bacon

These pancakes are super-soft and fluffy – the ideal partner for the sweet-savoury combo of bacon, orange and cinnamon.

200g plain flour
1 tbsp baking powder
2 tbsp caster sugar
2 large eggs, separated
175ml milk
40g butter, melted, plus extra to cook
2 oranges
8 streaky bacon rashers

FOR THE CINNAMON BUTTER
75g butter, softened
3 tbsp maple syrup, plus extra to serve
2½ tsp ground cinnamon

★ GET AHEAD
Make the cinnamon butter up to 2 days ahead. Cover and chill. Allow to come up to room temperature before serving.

1. To make the cinnamon butter, whisk all the ingredients together in a bowl until smooth and fluffy. Set aside.

2. Mix the flour, baking powder, sugar and ½ tsp salt in a bowl. In a jug, whisk the egg yolks, milk and butter together. Finely zest the oranges and stir the zest into the jug. Pour into the flour mixture and stir gently until just combined. In a separate bowl (with a clean whisk), beat the egg whites to soft peaks and fold gently into the batter.

3. Heat a large non-stick frying pan over medium heat and brush with a little butter. Spoon tablespoons of the batter into the pan (spacing apart), spreading slightly with the back of the spoon – you'll need to cook in batches. Cook for 1–2min until bubbles appear on the surface, then flip and cook for another minute until golden. Remove to a plate, cover and keep warm while you cook the remaining pancakes, wiping the pan and re-buttering between batches.

4. Fry or grill the bacon until crisp. Cut the skin and pith off the oranges and slice thinly. Serve the pancakes with the bacon, cinnamon butter, orange slices and extra maple syrup, to drizzle.

Hands-on time: 25min
Cooking time: about 15min
Serves 4

PER SERVING 657cals, 17g protein, 37g fat (20g saturates), 61g carbs (22g total sugars), 3g fibre

Swirled Cinnamon Rolls

Multiple risings are the secret to these soft, fluffy buns.

FOR THE DOUGH
600g strong white flour, plus extra to dust
7g sachet fast-action dried yeast
100g caster sugar
275ml milk
1 medium egg
50g unsalted butter, melted, plus extra to grease

FOR THE FILLING AND TOPPING
40g unsalted butter, very soft
60g caster sugar
2 tsp ground cinnamon
50g pecans or walnuts, roughly chopped
50g sultanas
125g icing sugar

1. Start by making the dough. Sift the flour into a large bowl and stir though the yeast, sugar and 1 tsp salt. Heat the milk until it's just warm, whisk in the egg and melted butter, then add it to the flour bowl in one go. Quickly mix to a soft but not sticky dough (adjust with a little more flour/milk if needed).

2. Scrape out the dough on to a lightly floured surface and knead for 5min until elastic and smooth. Transfer to a large, greased bowl, cover with clingfilm and leave to rise in a warm place until well risen (about 1hr 30min).

Hands-on time: 35min, plus rising and setting
Cooking time: about 35min
Makes 12 rolls

PER BUN 377cals, 8g protein, 11g fat (5g saturates), 67g carbs (30g total sugars), 2g fibre

3. Take the dough out of the bowl, knead it to burst any air bubbles, then return it to the bowl. Cover and leave to rise for a further 30min (this will help develop the flavour).

4. Line a large baking sheet with baking parchment. Lightly dust a work surface and roll out the dough to a rectangle roughly 23cm x 38cm. Arrange so a long edge is in front of you, then spread butter over the rectangle (right to the edges). Scatter over the sugar, cinnamon, nuts and sultanas.

5. Brush the long edge furthest away from you with water (to help it stick). Roll up the dough tightly starting from the nearest edge – keeping it as round as possible, and pressing lightly to seal it along the watered edge.

6. Cut the roll into 2.5cm slices and arrange them swirl-side up on the baking sheet (leaving space between the rolls to allow for expansion). Loosely cover with greased clingfilm and leave to rise in a warm place for 30min.

7. Preheat oven to 190°C (170°C fan) mark 5. Remove the clingfilm and bake the buns for 25-30min until nicely golden and well risen. Five minutes before the buns are finished baking, sift the icing sugar into a bowl and mix in just enough water to make an icing with a smooth, thick, spoonable consistency.

8. As soon as the buns come out of the oven, spoon over the icing and leave to set. Serve warm or at room temperature.

Panettone French Toast Bake

Prepare this special breakfast treat to the end of step 2 ahead of time and chill.

Butter, to grease
500g panettone, thickly sliced
500ml milk
200ml double cream
50g caster sugar
3 medium eggs
1 tbsp vanilla bean paste
2 tsp ground cinnamon
½ tsp freshly grated nutmeg
2 tbsp icing sugar

1. Grease a 2.6 litre ovenproof dish with butter. Cut the panettone slices in half widthways and arrange in the dish, overlapping them slightly.

2. In a large jug, whisk the milk, cream, sugar, eggs, vanilla and spices. Pour over the panettone. Cover and leave to soak in the fridge for up to 12hr, or for 1hr at room temperature.

3. Preheat oven to 160°C (140°C fan) mark 3. Uncover the dish and bake for 35–40min, or until the custard has just set. Remove from oven and preheat grill to high.

4. Dust top with icing sugar and grill until just golden and caramelised (watch carefully, as it catches quickly). Allow to sit for a couple of minutes before serving.

Hands-on time: 15min, plus (overnight) soaking
Cooking time: about 40min
Serves 6

PER SERVING 597cals, 12g protein, 32g fat (19g saturates), 65g carbs (40g total sugars), 2g fibre

Buck's Fizz Curd

We've taken everyone's favourite festive cocktail and put it in a zesty curd. Serve it slathered on toast or stirred into porridge.

3 large oranges
150ml cava
200g caster sugar
3 medium egg yolks
2 tbsp cornflour
100g unsalted butter, cubed

1. Finely grate the zest from the oranges and set aside. Halve the oranges and squeeze the juice into a large pan. Add the cava and half the sugar. Heat gently, stirring, to dissolve the sugar. Increase heat and bubble for 15min until slightly reduced.

2. In a bowl, whisk the egg yolks, remaining sugar and cornflour to combine. Carefully whisk in the hot orange liquid. Return the liquid to the pan and whisk in the zest and butter. Bring the mixture to the boil, whisking constantly – it will start to thicken. Bubble for 1min, then remove from the heat. Transfer to a clean bowl, cover with clingfilm and leave to cool. The curd will continue to thicken.

3. Decant into a sterilised jar (see p10) and keep in the fridge for up to 1 week.

Hands-on time: 15min, plus cooling
Cooking time: about 20min
Makes 500g (20 servings)

PER 25G SERVING 51cals, 0g protein, 1g fat (0g saturates), 10g carbs (9g total sugars), 0g fibre

Baked Shakshuka

This warming, spiced dish will set you up on a chilly Christmas morning.

1 tbsp olive oil
6 spring onions, finely sliced
2 garlic cloves, crushed
1 green chilli, deseeded and finely chopped
1 tsp cumin seeds
2 tsp harissa paste
2 x 400g tins cherry tomatoes
500g spinach
25g pack flat-leaf parsley, roughly chopped
25g pack coriander, roughly chopped
8 medium eggs
100g feta, crumbled
1 tsp sumac (optional)
Flatbreads, warmed, to serve

1. Preheat oven to 180°C (160°C fan) mark 4. Heat the oil in a large pan over medium heat and fry the spring onions until softened (about 5–6min). Stir in the garlic, chilli and cumin seeds and cook for 1min. Add the harissa and tomatoes. Bring to the boil and simmer for 15–20min until reduced.

2. Gradually add the spinach, stirring, until incorporated and wilted. Stir through most of the herbs and check the seasoning. Transfer to an ovenproof serving dish or roasting tin roughly 25.5 x 35.5cm. Make 8 wells in the sauce and crack in the eggs, spacing apart. Cook in a preheated oven for 10–12min, until the egg whites are set. Scatter over the feta, remaining herbs and sumac, if using. Serve with warmed flatbreads.

Hands-on time: 20min
Cooking time: about 40min
Serves 4

PER SERVING 280cals, 23g protein, 16g fat (6g saturates), 9g carbs (9g total sugars), 4g fibre

Luxe Chocolate Granola

Make this fruity, nutty granola ahead of time for a stress-free start to the day.

175g apple sauce
100g golden syrup
100g light brown soft sugar
400g rolled oats
50g good-quality cocoa powder
50g sunflower seeds
75g pecans, roughly chopped
75g dark chocolate, finely chopped
75g dried cranberries
Yogurt, to serve (optional)
Raspberries or blueberries, to serve (optional)

1. Preheat oven to 170°C (150°C fan) mark 3 and line a large baking sheet with baking parchment. Heat the apple sauce, golden syrup and sugar in a large pan until melted. Add the oats, cocoa powder and sunflower seeds and mix well. Spread evenly on the lined baking sheet.

2. Bake for 20min, then stir (it should begin to clump). Bake for 15min more. Stir through the pecans and bake for a further 8–10min until the pecans are lightly toasted and the granola clumps are crispy. Allow to cool completely, then stir through the chocolate and cranberries.

3. Serve layered with yogurt and raspberries or blueberries, if you like. Keep in an airtight container at cool room temperature for 1 month.

Hands-on time: 15min, plus cooling
Cooking time: about 45min
Makes 900g (about 18 servings)

PER 50G SERVING 187cals, 4g protein, 7g fat (1g saturates), 27g carbs (14g total sugars), 3g fibre

Pancetta Breakfast Cups

Substitute ketchup for the brown sauce in these tasty little frittatas, if you prefer.

Vegetable oil, to grease
12 pancetta rashers
3 medium eggs, beaten
50g crème fraîche
50g mature Cheddar, grated
Small handful chives, finely chopped
6 cherry tomatoes, halved
50ml brown sauce

1. Preheat oven to 180°C (160°C fan) mark 4. Grease a 12-hole mini muffin tin with a little oil. Slice the pancetta rashers in half widthways. Lay 2 pieces into each hole of the tin, so they cover the base and come up the sides a little.

2. In a bowl, whisk the eggs, crème fraîche, cheese, most of the chives and plenty of seasoning. Spoon into the lined holes. Put a tomato half into each hole, cut-side up. Cook for 15min, or until golden brown and set. Cool slightly in the tin before gently transferring to a serving plate.

3. To serve, mix the brown sauce with 1 tbsp water to loosen. Drizzle over the breakfast cups, scatter over the remaining chives and serve just-warm.

★ GET AHEAD
Make to the end of step 2 up to 1 day ahead. Transfer to a baking tray, then cover and chill. To serve, reheat for 5min in an oven preheated to 180°C (160°C fan) mark 4. Complete the recipe.

Hands-on time: 20min
Cooking time: about 15min
Makes 12 cups

PER CUP 91cals, 4g protein, 8g fat (4g saturates), 2g carbs (1g total sugars), 0g fibre

Breakfast Cobbler

Classic English breakfast ingredients are combined with a cheesy cobbler topping.

4 smoked streaky bacon rashers, roughly chopped
6 pork sausages, roughly chopped
2 x 415g tins baked beans in tomato sauce
2 tsp dried mixed herbs
4 large tomatoes, roughly chopped

FOR THE COBBLER
175g self-raising flour
½ tbsp baking powder
75g mature Cheddar, coarsely grated
100ml milk
2 medium eggs

1. Heat a casserole or deep ovenproof frying pan over medium heat and cook the bacon for 5min, stirring regularly, until starting to crisp up. Add the sausages and cook for 10min until browned.

2. Stir through the baked beans, dried herbs and plenty of seasoning. Bubble for 5min. Remove from the heat and stir through the tomatoes.

3. Preheat oven to 200°C (180°C fan) mark 6. In a large bowl, mix the flour, baking powder, Cheddar and some seasoning. Add the milk and 1 beaten egg, then stir until just combined. Dollop heaped spoonfuls of the mixture on to the bean mixture.

4. Beat the remaining egg and brush it over the cobbler to glaze. Cook in the oven for 25min or until piping hot and golden. Serve.

Hands-on time: 20min
Cooking time: about 45min
Serves 6

PER SERVING 532cals, 29g protein, 25g fat (10g saturates), 44g carbs (11g total sugars), 8g fibre

Truffled Ham and Eggs en Cocotte

A simple and luxurious way to cook eggs, made even more special when served with buttery brioche soldiers.

25g butter, melted, plus extra to grease
4 large slices thick-cut ham
100ml double cream
8 medium eggs
2 tsp truffle oil
4 chunky brioche slices, cut from a loaf
1 tbsp finely chopped chives, to garnish (optional)

1. Preheat oven to 170°C (150°C fan) mark 3. Grease 4 x 200ml ramekins with butter and lay a slice of ham in each to line the base and sides.

2. Divide the cream among the ramekins, season, then crack 2 eggs into each. Drizzle ½ tsp truffle oil over each and finish with a little extra freshly ground black pepper.

3. Trim the side crusts from the brioche slices, then cut each slice into 4 strips. Put on a baking sheet and brush all over with the melted butter.

4. Put the ramekins into a small roasting tin and carefully pour enough hot water into the tin to come halfway up the sides of the ramekins. Bake the eggs and brioche for 12–15min, or until the eggs are just set and the bread has turned golden.

5. Sprinkle the chives, if using, over the eggs and serve hot with the brioche soldiers to dip.

Hands-on time: 10min
Cooking time: about 15min
Serves 4

PER SERVING 582cals, 29g protein, 39g fat (20g saturates), 27g carbs (7g total sugars), 1g fibre

Raspberry and Yogurt Breakfast Muffins

Add more honey if you like a sweeter muffin.

1 ripe, yellow banana (not speckled or black)
200g natural yogurt
50ml vegetable oil
2 medium eggs
6 tbsp runny honey
200g self-raising flour
75g ground almonds
1 orange, zested and juiced
200g raspberries or blackberries

FOR THE TOPPING
100g icing sugar, sifted
2 tbsp freeze-dried raspberry pieces (optional)

1. Preheat oven to 190°C (170°C fan) mark 5. Line a 12-hole muffin tin with cases. In a bowl, mash the banana, then mix in yogurt, oil, eggs and honey.

2. Sift over the flour, add the ground almonds, orange zest and raspberries. Using a large metal spoon, gently fold until just combined.

3. Divide among muffin cases; bake for 25–30min, or until golden. Cool in the tin for 5min, then transfer to a wire rack to cool completely.

4. For the topping, mix the icing sugar with 1 tbsp orange juice. Drizzle over the muffins and sprinkle over the freeze-dried raspberry pieces, if using. Leave to set before serving.

Hands-on time: 20min, plus cooling and setting
Cooking time: about 30min
Makes 12 muffins

PER MUFFIN 230cals, 6g protein, 8g fat (1g saturates), 32g carbs (20g total sugars), 1g fibre

Brown Butter, Hazelnut and Chocolate Banana Bread

Take your banana bread to the next level with our hazelnut and dark chocolate version. Browning the butter adds a lovely nutty flavour.

75g butter, plus extra to grease and serve (optional)
3 large very ripe bananas, about 350g peeled weight
175g light brown soft sugar
1 large egg, beaten
1 tbsp vanilla bean paste
175g plain flour
1 tsp baking powder
50g toasted hazelnuts, roughly chopped
100g dark chocolate, roughly chopped

1. Preheat oven to 180°C (160°C fan) mark 4. Grease and line a 900g loaf tin with baking parchment. Melt the butter in a medium pan over low heat. Increase the heat to medium-high and cook, swirling the pan occasionally, until the butter is golden brown. Pour into a large heatproof bowl and set aside to cool slightly.

2. Pulse the bananas in a food processor until smooth. Alternatively, mash well with a fork. Tip into the butter bowl and add the sugar, egg and vanilla. Mix until combined. Next, mix in the flour and baking powder, followed by the hazelnuts and chocolate.

3. Scrape into the lined tin and smooth to level. Bake for 1hr 5min, or until a skewer inserted into the centre comes out clean. Leave to cool completely in the tin. Serve in slices with a little butter, if you like.

★ TO STORE
Once the banana bread is cool, store in an airtight container at room temperature for up to 3 days.

Hands-on time: 20min, plus cooling
Cooking time: about 1hr 10min
Serves 10

PER SERVING (without butter) 314cals, 5g protein, 13g fat (6g saturates), 44g carbs (29g total sugars), 2g fibre

Caramelised Onion Scrambled Egg Brioche

Slowly scrambling the eggs using a spatula creates a wonderfully velvety texture.

1 tbsp olive oil
2 red onions, finely sliced
2 tsp caster sugar
1 tbsp balsamic vinegar
1½ tbsp sriracha
4 tbsp mayonnaise
8 large eggs
50g butter
Small handful chives, finely chopped
50g vegetarian Italian-style hard cheese (or Parmesan
    if you don't need it to be veggie), finely grated
4 brioche buns

1. Heat the oil in a medium non-stick frying pan over low-medium heat. Add the onions and a pinch of salt and fry, stirring occasionally, for 10–12min until softened. Stir in the sugar, vinegar and a pinch of salt, then increase heat to high and bubble for 1–2min until reduced and sticky. Empty into a bowl and wipe the pan clean with kitchen paper.

2. In a small bowl, mix together the sriracha and mayonnaise, then set aside.

3. Crack the eggs into a large bowl and whisk with some seasoning until combined. Reheat the pan over low heat and add the butter to melt. Pour in the eggs and cook, folding them over one another with a spatula when they start to set, until just cooked through (about 10–15min). Fold in most of the chives and the cheese. Check the seasoning.

4. Meanwhile, preheat oven to 150°C (130°C fan) mark 2. Put the buns on a baking tray and warm through for 5min.

5. To serve, slice the brioche buns in half (if not pre-sliced) and spread the sriracha mixture over the cut sides. Divide the onions among the bottoms of the buns and top with the scrambled eggs, reserved chives and the brioche lids. Serve.

Hands-on time: 25min
Cooking time: about 30min
Serves 4

PER SERVING 726cals, 30g protein, 48g fat (18g saturates), 42g carbs (13g total sugars), 3g fibre

Cardamom Babka

As this recipe uses a lot of ground cardamom, you can opt to buy it ready-ground online or from specialist retailers. Alternatively, make your own by grinding the seeds of roughly 25 green cardamom pods, which will make enough for the dough and filling.

FOR THE DOUGH
450g strong white flour, plus extra to dust
7g sachet fast-action dried yeast
½ tbsp ground cardamom (see intro)
1 tsp ground cinnamon
75g unsalted butter, melted, plus extra to grease
250ml milk

FOR THE FILLING
100g unsalted butter, softened
50g caster sugar
1½ tbsp ground cardamom

FOR THE GLAZE
50g caster sugar
½ tbsp pearl sugar

1. In a freestanding mixer fitted with a dough hook or in a large bowl, mix the flour, yeast, spices and ½ tsp fine salt. Add the butter and milk and mix to form a dough. If making by hand, tip on to a lightly floured work surface. Knead by hand or on medium speed for 5–10min until smooth and elastic. Return to the bowl, cover and leave to rise in a warm place until doubled in size, about 1hr 30min.

2. Lightly grease a 900g loaf tin. For the filling, in a small bowl combine all the ingredients.

Hands-on time: 40min, plus rising and cooling
Cooking time: about 50min
Serves 8

PER SERVING 448cals, 7g protein, 20g fat (12g saturates), 59g carbs (16g total sugars), 2g fibre

3. Tip the dough on to a lightly floured work surface and roll into a roughly 30 x 40cm rectangle. Spread the filling over the top of the dough. Roll up tightly from a long edge, then slice in half lengthways to make 2 long pieces with the filling exposed.

4. Lay the pieces side-by-side, with the filling facing upwards. Lightly press 2 of the ends together, then twist the lengths into each other by lifting 1 piece over the other repeatedly, making sure you keep the filling exposed.

5. Once you have a long, twisted length, push both ends simultaneously into the centre to shorten the length. Lift and squeeze it into the greased tin.

6. Loosely cover with greased clingfilm (butter-side down) and leave to rise again in a warm place for 1hr 30min–2hr, or until noticeably puffed.

7. Preheat oven to 180°C (160°C fan) mark 4. Bake the babka for 45–50min, or until deep golden, loosely covering it with foil if it's getting too dark.

8. When almost baked, make the glaze. In a small pan over low heat, mix the caster sugar and 50ml water, stirring until the sugar dissolves. Bring to the boil and remove from the heat.

9. Brush all the glaze over the top of hot babka as soon as it comes out of the oven, then sprinkle over the pearl sugar. Cool completely in the tin before transferring to a board. Serve in slices.

★ GET AHEAD
Make, knead and cover the dough up to 1 day ahead. Chill (no need to rise). To serve, allow the dough to come to room temperature and rise. Complete the recipe.

★ TO STORE
Once cool, wrap the babka well in foil and keep at room temperature for up to 2 days.

Charred Corn Fritters

Charring the corn adds a wonderful smokiness to these fritters.

3 tbsp olive oil
2 tsp hot smoked paprika
3 corn cobs
150g gluten-free self-raising flour
100g quick-cook/instant polenta
2 medium eggs
275ml milk
4 spring onions, finely chopped

TO SERVE
4 fried eggs
Sliced avocado
Fresh tomato salsa

1. Rub 1 tbsp oil and the paprika all over the corn cobs. Heat a large frying pan over high heat and fry the cobs for 10min, turning regularly, or until charred. Leave to cool completely.

2. Slice the kernels off the cobs: hold a cob upright (on its end) on a board and shave off the kernels with a large knife. Repeat with all the cobs.

3. In a large bowl, whisk together the flour and polenta. Whisk in the eggs, then gradually whisk in the milk to make a batter. Stir through the spring onions, corn kernels and some seasoning.

4. Heat 1 tbsp oil in a large non-stick frying pan over medium heat. Add 2½ tbsp of batter to the pan to make fritters, spacing apart. Cook for 2min per side, or until golden and cooked. Repeat with the rest of the mixture (you should have 12 fritters), adding more oil as needed.

5. Divide the fritters among 4 plates. Top with a fried egg and serve with avocado and salsa.

Hands-on time: 30min, plus cooling
Cooking time: about 20min
Serves 4

PER SERVING 664cals, 26g protein, 34g fat (8g saturates), 60g carbs (9g total sugars), 6g fibre

Breakfast Trifle

This is delicious served immediately, when the granola still has a crunch to it.

FOR THE GRANOLA
350g giant oats
125g pecans, roughly chopped
½ tsp ground cinnamon
1 tsp ground ginger
100ml vegetable oil
175ml maple syrup, plus extra to drizzle
1 tsp vanilla essence
100g sultanas

FOR THE COMPOTE
250g sugar
400g rhubarb, roughly chopped
3 Bramley apples, peeled and diced
Zest and juice 1 orange
3 x 450ml tubs Greek yogurt, to serve

1. Preheat oven to 180°C (160°C fan) mark 4 and line a large baking sheet with parchment paper.

2. In a large bowl, stir together the oats, pecans and spices. In a large mixing bowl, combine the oil, maple syrup and vanilla.

3. Stir the wet ingredients into the dry to combine. Spread out the granola in a single layer on the baking tray and cook for 30min, shaking once.

4. When the granola is still warm, stir through the sultanas. Allow to cool completely before transferring to an airtight container.

5. Meanwhile, make the compote. Put all the ingredients into a large pan with 200ml water, bring to the boil, then simmer for 15–20min until soft and the liquid has reduced. Set aside to cool completely.

6. To assemble the trifle, spoon a layer of compote into a trifle dish or glass bowl, top with a layer of yogurt, then one of granola. Repeat until you fill the dish. Top with a dollop of yogurt and a drizzle of maple syrup. Serve immediately or store in the fridge for up to 5hr.

Hands-on time: 30min, plus cooling
Cooking time: about 30min
Serves 10–12

PER SERVING (for 12) 521cals, 11g protein, 23g fat (6g saturates), 66g carbs (44g total sugars), 5g fibre

Dahl Baked Eggs

An Indian-inspired twist on shakshuka. The slow-cooked lentils break down into something creamy and hearty, rather like a savoury porridge, and get flavoured at the last minute with mellow spices and a hint of sugar.

200g chana dal (yellow split lentils)
2 medium-large ripe tomatoes, roughly chopped
1 tsp turmeric
40g ghee or butter
2 tsp black/brown mustard seeds
¼ tsp dried chilli flakes
Small handful dried curry leaves
1 tbsp demerara or palm sugar
100g baby spinach
Juice ½ lemon
4 medium eggs
Flatbreads, to serve (optional – gluten-free, if required)

1. In a large wide pan (that has a lid), mix the lentils, tomatoes, turmeric and 1 litre water. Bring to the boil over medium heat. Cover with the lid, then reduce heat to low and cook for 1hr, stirring occasionally, until the lentils are tender.

2. Remove the lid, increase the heat to high and bubble for 15–20min, or until most of the water has evaporated and the dahl is soupy.

3. Meanwhile, in a small frying pan over medium heat, melt the ghee/butter. Add the mustard seeds, chilli flakes and curry leaves. Fry for 1–2min, until the spices start to pop and smell nutty. Add the spice mixture to the lentil pan, along with the sugar, spinach, lemon juice and plenty of salt, stirring until the spinach starts to wilt.

4. Make 4 wells in the lentil mixture and crack an egg into each. Cover and cook over low heat for 10–12min, or until the whites are set but the yolks are still runny. Serve with flatbreads, if you like.

★ GET AHEAD
Prepare to end of step 1 up to a day ahead. Cool, cover and chill. Complete recipe to serve.

Hands-on time: 20min
Cooking time: about 1hr 35min
Serves 4

PER SERVING 388cals, 21g protein, 17g fat (8g saturates), 34g carbs (8g total sugars), 6g fibre

Mushroom Molletes

This Mexican-inspired vegetarian breakfast is full of flavour and looks pretty, too.

FOR THE MOLLETES
2 part-baked baguettes
430g pouch or tin refried beans
100g Cheddar, grated
1 tbsp olive oil
300g portabellini mushrooms, sliced
½ tsp ground cumin
½ tsp paprika
½ tsp ground coriander

FOR THE PICO DE GALLO
150g cherry tomatoes, roughly chopped
½ onion, finely chopped
1 fresh jalapeño or green chilli, deseeded and finely
    chopped
Small handful coriander, finely chopped
Juice 1 lime

1. For the molletes, bake the baguettes according to packet instructions. Set aside to cool. Adjust the oven temperature to 200°C (180°C fan) mark 6.

2. Meanwhile, make the pico de gallo. In a bowl, mix all the ingredients with some seasoning, then set aside.

3. When the baguettes are cool, cut in half lengthways and scrape out a little of the soft bread centre (see GH Tip). Put the bread halves on a baking tray, cut-side up, and spread over the refried beans. Sprinkle over the Cheddar. Cook in the oven for 7min, or until the cheese has melted.

4. Meanwhile, heat the oil in a large frying pan over high heat. Cook the mushrooms for 7–8min, or until tender and any moisture has evaporated. Stir through the spices and cook for 1min.

5. To serve, top the baguettes with the mushrooms and serve with the pico de gallo.

★ GH TIP
Whizz the scraped-out bread to make breadcrumbs and freeze for future use.

Hands-on time: 25min, plus cooling
Cooking time: about 25min
Serves 4

PER SERVING 385cals, 19g protein, 13g fat
(6g saturates), 42g carbs (4g total sugars), 9g fibre

Canapés
& Light Bites

Beetroot Bloody Mary Soup Shots

A colourful, wintry twist on a classic.
These shots can be enjoyed hot or cold,
and you can serve them in small coffee
cups if you don't have shot glasses.
To serve cold, transfer the juice mixture
to a jug, cool, cover and chill for at least
1 hour, or until ready to serve.

250ml beetroot juice
60ml vodka
1 tbsp vegan horseradish sauce
1 tsp Henderson's Relish or vegan Worcestershire Sauce
    (see GH tip)
2–3 tsp lemon juice, to taste
Pinch celery salt, plus 1 tsp to serve
Tabasco, to taste

TO SERVE
2 lemon slices
6 cocktail beetroot

1. Whisk the beetroot juice, vodka, horseradish,
   Henderson's Relish/Worcestershire Sauce, 2 tsp
   lemon juice, pinch celery salt and a few dashes
   of Tabasco together in a small pan and heat
   gently, stirring. Taste and adjust the seasoning
   and spices to your taste. Keep warm.

2. Put the 1 tsp celery salt on a small saucer or
   plate. Rub the rims of 6 large shot glasses
   (or similar) with one of the lemon slices, then
   dip into the celery salt to coat the edges.

3. Slice the remaining lemon slice into 6 small
   wedges. Make a small vertical slit in the bottom
   half of each cocktail beetroot and lemon wedge
   and arrange a beetroot and lemon wedge on the
   edge of each glass. Carefully pour the cocktail
   into the glasses and serve.

★ GH TIP
Worcestershire Sauce is a key ingredient of
traditional Bloody Marys, but is unsuitable for
vegetarians as it contains anchovies. Vegetarians
should try Henderson's Relish instead.

Hands-on time: 10min
Cooking time: about 5min
Serves 6

PER SERVING 51cals, 1g protein, 0g fat (0g saturates),
6g carbs (6g total sugars), 1g fibre

Spiced Crispy Chickpeas

A simple, lower-fat alternative to nuts that's distinctly moreish.

1 tsp cornflour
1 tsp olive oil
2 tsp sweet smoked paprika
400g tin chickpeas, drained and rinsed

1. Preheat oven to 220°C (200°C fan) mark 7 and line a large baking tray with baking parchment.

2. In a medium bowl, mix the cornflour, oil, paprika and ½ tsp fine salt. Pat the chickpeas dry with kitchen paper and add to the bowl. Toss to coat.

3. Tip the chickpeas on to the lined tray and spread to a single layer. Cook for 25–30min, shaking halfway through, or until crisp. Leave to cool on the tray before transferring to a bowl. Serve.

★ GET AHEAD
Make up to 12hr ahead. Cool completely, then store in an airtight container.

Hands-on time: 5min, plus cooling
Cooking time: about 30min
Serves 10

PER SERVING 36cals, 2g protein, 1g fat (0g saturates), 4g carbs (0g total sugars), 1g fibre

Whipped Feta Dip with Marinated Olives and Tomatoes

A wonderfully easy and impressive looking make-ahead dish.

125g mixed colour baby tomatoes, halved
100g mixed olives, pitted
1–2 garlic cloves, finely chopped
2 tsp thyme leaves
4 tbsp extra virgin olive oil
Crispbreads, bread sticks or pitta chips, to serve

FOR THE WHIPPED FETA
250g good-quality feta, crumbled
1 small garlic clove, crushed
1 tbsp extra virgin olive oil
150g Greek yogurt

1. In a bowl, combine the tomatoes, olives, garlic (to taste), thyme, oil and some freshly ground black pepper. Stir well, cover and chill overnight.

2. Put the feta, garlic and oil in a small processor with half the yogurt and whizz until smooth, scraping down the sides. Scrape into a serving bowl, mix in the remaining yogurt, cover and chill.

3. To serve, spoon the tomato mix over the feta, drizzle with a little of the marinating oil. Serve with crispbreads, bread sticks or pitta chips for dipping.

★ GET AHEAD
Prepare to the end of step 2 up to 2 days ahead.

Hands-on time: 10min, plus (overnight) marinating
Serves 20

PER SERVING 71cals, 3g protein, 6g fat (3g saturates), 1g carbs (1g total sugars), 0g fibre

Pomegranate, Brie and Cranberry Crostini

A simple canapé that showcases why this classic pairing works so well.

---

1 small part-baked baguette
Oil, to brush
75g smooth cranberry sauce
Finely grated zest ½ orange, plus pared zest to serve
30g pomegranate seeds
150g brie, cut into 16 even slices

1. Preheat oven to 200°C (180°C fan) mark 6. Slice the baguette into 20 x 1cm-thick slices, on a slight diagonal. Discard the ends. Brush the slices on both sides with oil and arrange on a baking tray lined with baking parchment. Sprinkle over some salt. Cook for 5min, then turn and cook for 5–7min more until golden and crisp.

2. Meanwhile, heat the cranberry sauce in a small pan with the orange zest until bubbling. Season lightly and stir in the pomegranate seeds.

3. Add a slice of brie to each baguette slice, bake for 1–2min, until just starting to melt. Spoon on the warm compote, sprinkle over pared zest and serve.

★ GET AHEAD
Toast the bread slices 1 day ahead, cool, then store in an airtight container. Complete recipe to serve.

Hands-on time: 10min
Cooking time: about 12min
Makes 20 crostini

PER CROSTINI 60cals, 3g protein, 2g fat (1g saturates), 7g carbs (2g total sugars), 0g fibre

Gin-infused Cucumber 'Blini' with Smoked Salmon Cream Cheese

You only need a small amount of gin here, and a little caviar would make a luxurious alternative to the capers.

---

1 small cucumber
1½ tbsp gin
100g smoked salmon trimmings
75g full-fat cream cheese
1 tbsp finely chopped dill, plus extra fronds to garnish
Finely grated zest ½ lemon
2 tsp baby (non-pareille) capers, drained

1. Trim the ends from the cucumber, cut into 16 x 1cm rounds and arrange on a large plate in a single layer. Brush over 1 tbsp gin, cover with clingfilm and chill while you make the topping.

2. In a food processor, pulse the salmon trimmings, cream cheese and remaining ½ tbsp gin until smooth. Transfer to a bowl, then stir in the chopped dill, lemon zest and some seasoning.

3. To serve, pipe or spoon the smoked salmon mixture on to the cucumber slices. Top each with a few baby capers and a dill frond. Serve.

★ GET AHEAD
Make the salmon-cream cheese mixture up to 2 days ahead. then close-cover and chill.

Hands-on time: 15min
Makes 16 blinis

PER BLINI 29cals, 2g protein, 2g fat (1g saturates), 0g carbs (0g total sugars), 0g fibre

Mulled Wine Glazed Devils on Horseback

As canapés go, these are hard to beat. We've given them a boozy makeover with mulled wine — buy it ready-made, or make it yourself by infusing red wine with a couple of mulling spice sachets.

20 pitted prunes
150ml mulled wine
10 unsmoked streaky bacon rashers
½ tbsp Dijon mustard
2 tbsp runny honey

1. Put the prunes into a small bowl and pour over the wine. Cover and leave to soak overnight.

2. Preheat oven to 200°C (180°C fan) mark 6. Lay the bacon rashers on a board and brush one side with the mustard. Cut each rasher into 2 shorter lengths.

3. Drain the prunes (reserving the wine) and wrap each in a bacon strip. Arrange the prunes, seam-down, on a baking tray lined with baking parchment. Cook in the oven for 10min.

4. Meanwhile, transfer the wine to a small pan and bubble until reduced to about 3 tbsp. Whisk in the honey and some seasoning and bubble for another minute.

5. Remove the devils from the oven and brush with the glaze. Return to oven and cook for a further 10–15min, or until the bacon is just crisp at the edges. Remove from the oven and spoon over any glaze that has run off on to the baking tray. Allow to cool for a few minutes before serving with cocktail sticks.

★ GET AHEAD
Soak prunes up to 1 week ahead in an airtight container.

Hands-on time: 10min, plus (overnight) soaking and cooling
Cooking time: about 25min
Makes 20 canapés

PER CANAPÉ 65cals, 2g protein, 3g fat (1g saturates), 6g carbs (6g total sugars), 1g fibre

Pea and Mint Fritters

These are also fabulous for brunch — make the fritters twice the size and serve with a poached egg on top.

1½ tbsp olive oil
2 spring onions, finely chopped
175g frozen petits pois peas
4 tbsp chopped mint
40g plain flour
1 medium egg, beaten
Soured cream

TOPPINGS (optional)
Cooked quails' eggs, halved
Shredded ham hock
Sliced crispy chorizo
Mint leaves, shredded

1. Heat ½ tbsp oil in a frying pan, add the spring onions and fry on low heat for 2–3min until tender. Set aside.

2. Put the peas in a sieve in the sink and pour a kettleful of boiling water over them. Drain thoroughly, then crush well with a fork or potato masher. Stir in the fried spring onions, mint, flour, egg and some seasoning.

3. Heat the remaining oil in the frying pan over medium heat. Add heaped tablespoons of the pea mixture, spacing a little apart, and fry for 1–2min per side until firm. Transfer to a serving platter, cool slightly and top with a little soured cream and your topping of choice.

★ GET AHEAD
Cook the fritters up to 2hr ahead. Leave covered at room temperature. Complete the recipe to serve.

Hands-on time: 15min
Cooking time: about 10min
Makes 12 fritters

PER FRITTER (with 1 tsp soured cream – no topping)
53cals, 2g protein, 3g fat (1g saturates), 4g carbs
(1g total sugars), 1g fibre

Sweet Onion Sausage Rolls

Home-made sausage rolls are much more delicious than the ready-made variety — and you can customise them by adding ingredients such as the marmalade we've used here.

300g sausage meat
Small handful parsley, finely chopped
375g pack ready-rolled shortcrust pastry (in a rectangular sheet)
2 tbsp onion marmalade
1 large egg, lightly beaten
Poppy seeds to sprinkle

1. Put the sausage meat in a large bowl and stir in the parsley. Unroll the pastry sheet and cut lengthways into 4 equal strips. Thinly spread 1 tbsp of the onion marmalade lengthways down the middle of one of the strips, then repeat with another strip.

2. Divide the sausage mixture in half. Shape one half into a thin cylinder as long as the pastry strips, then position it on top of one of the marmalade strips. Repeat with the remaining sausage mixture. Brush the visible pastry around the sausage cylinders with the beaten egg, then top with the remaining pastry strips. Press down on the edges to seal. Transfer to a baking sheet and chill for 30min.

3. Preheat the oven to 200°C (180°C fan) mark 6. Line 2 baking trays with baking parchment. Brush both rolls with beaten egg and sprinkle over some poppy seeds. Cut into 4cm pieces and arrange on the baking trays. Cook for 15min or until golden. Serve warm or at room temperature.

Hands-on time: 20min, plus chilling
Cooking time: about 15min
Makes about 22 rolls

PER ROLL 125cals, 4g protein, 9g fat (3g saturates), 7g carbs (1g total sugars), 1g fibre

Pork Belly Bites

These can be prepared hours in advance and reheated when you're ready to serve.

600g pork belly
200ml bourbon whiskey
4 tbsp muscovado sugar
¼ tsp dried chilli flakes
½ cucumber

1. Preheat oven to 220°C (200°C fan) mark 7. Pat the pork dry with kitchen paper. Sprinkle the skin with fine salt and rub in. Place skin-side up on a wire rack over a roasting tin. Add water (avoid getting the pork wet) to come 2.5cm up the sides of the tin. Cook for 1hr 30min, or until the meat is tender and crackling is crisp.

2. Heat the bourbon, sugar and chilli in a pan, stir to dissolve, then boil until syrupy. Set aside.

3. Leave the pork, uncovered, until cool. Place skin-side down on a board; cut into 16 bite-sized cubes (a serrated knife is best). Peel the cucumber into 16 thin ribbons; discard the seedy core.

4. Dip each pork cube in glaze. Thread a cucumber ribbon and pork cube on to 16 cocktail sticks. Serve.

★ GET AHEAD
Cook the pork up to 3hr ahead. Leave uncovered at room temperature. Put in a hot oven for 5min and complete recipe to serve. Glaze can be made 2hr ahead; leave at room temperature.

Hands-on time: 30min, plus cooling
Cooking time: about 1hr 30min
Makes 16 canapés

PER CANAPÉ 140cals, 7g protein, 8g fat (3g saturates), 4g carbs (4g total sugars), 0g fibre

Spiced Baked Nuts

A wonderful mix of spice and crunch, this is a recipe you'll turn to again and again.

---

1 medium egg white
¼ tsp cayenne pepper
½ tsp mixed spice
400g mixed unsalted nuts (we used cashews, almonds, pistachios, pecans and walnuts)
25g sunflower seeds
1 tbsp sesame seeds

1. Preheat oven to 180°C (160°C fan) mark 4 and line a baking tray with baking parchment. In a medium bowl, mix the egg white, cayenne and mixed spice, ½ tsp fine salt and some freshly ground black pepper.

2. Stir in the nuts and seeds; make sure everything is coated. Scrape the mixture on to the lined baking tray and spread to an even thickness.

3. Cook for about 15min, until golden. Leave to cool, then serve.

★ GET AHEAD
Make up to 1 week ahead. Once cool, store in a sealed jar or airtight container.

Hands on time: 10min, plus cooling
Cooking time: about 15min
Makes about 450g (serves 18)

PER 25G SERVING 152cals, 5g protein, 13g fat (2g saturates), 3g carbs (1g total sugars), 2g fibre

Pecan Shortbreads with Cheesy Cream

These savoury shortbreads make a modern, melt-in-your-mouth canapé.

125g plain flour, plus extra to dust
100g butter, chilled and cubed
50g Parmesan, finely grated
40g pecans, finely chopped

FOR THE FILLING
50g Dolcelatte
50g cream cheese

1. In a food processor, pulse the flour and butter until the mixture resembles fine breadcrumbs. Alternatively, rub the butter into the flour using your fingertips.

2. Pulse/stir in the Parmesan, followed by the pecans and some freshly ground black pepper. Tip the mixture on to a work surface and briefly knead to bring together into a disc. Wrap the dough in clingfilm and chill for 30min.

3. Lightly flour a work surface and roll out the shortbread to 3mm thick. Cut rounds using a 5cm round cutter, re-rolling trimmings. Arrange on a baking tray, spacing apart. Chill for 20min.

4. Preheat oven to 190°C (170°C fan) mark 5. Cook the shortbreads for 10–12min, until lightly golden. Cool for 5min on tray before transferring to a wire rack to cool completely.

5. Beat together the filling ingredients. Gently sandwich the shortbreads together with the cheese mixture and serve.

★ GET AHEAD
Make the shortbreads up to 2 days ahead. Once cool, store in an airtight container at room temperature. Complete the recipe up to 1hr ahead.

Hands-on time: 25min, plus chilling and cooling
Cooking time: about 10min
Makes about 30 sandwiches

PER SANDWICH 68cals, 2g protein, 5g fat (3g saturates), 3g carbs (0g total sugars), 0g fibre

Coronation Chicken Bites

Make these veggie-friendly by swapping the chicken for a 400g tin drained and rinsed chickpeas – they're also tasty with leftover turkey. If you prefer a heartier canapé, serve on gluten-free oat cakes.

50g mayonnaise
50g Greek-style yogurt
½–1 tsp mild curry powder, to taste
1 tbsp mango chutney (check it's gluten-free)
Few dashes Worcestershire sauce (check it's gluten-free),
    to taste
2 cooked skinless chicken breasts, cut into 1cm pieces
1 celery stick, finely chopped
25g dried ready-to-eat apricots, finely chopped
15g sultanas
2 Little Gem lettuces, leaves separated
15g flaked almonds, toasted
Small handful coriander, finely chopped

1. In a large bowl, mix the mayonnaise, yogurt, curry powder, mango chutney and Worcestershire sauce. Stir in the chicken, celery, apricots, sultanas and some seasoning.

2. Arrange the lettuce leaves on a large platter. Spoon in the chicken mixture and garnish with flaked almonds and coriander. Serve.

★ GET AHEAD
Make the chicken mixture up to 2 days ahead, then cover and chill. Complete the recipe to serve.

Hands-on time: 15min
Makes 12 bites

PER BITE 76cals, 5g protein, 5g fat (1g saturates), 3g carbs (3g total sugars), 1g fibre

Polenta, Grape and Gorgonzola Bites

Try Brie instead of Gorgonzola, if you like.

1 tbsp vegetable oil, plus extra to grease
250ml gluten-free vegetable stock
250ml milk
140g quick-cook/instant polenta
25g butter
25g Parmesan, finely grated
13 red seedless grapes, halved
75g Gorgonzola, cut into small pieces

1. Grease a 20.5cm square tin; set aside. Pour the stock and milk into a medium pan. Bring to the boil. When bubbling, whisk in the polenta, reduce heat to low and whisk until thickened, about 3min.

2. Remove from heat and whisk in the butter, Parmesan and some seasoning. Pour into the greased tin and press to an even layer using a spatula. Set aside to cool and set, about 4hr.

3. Preheat oven to 200°C (180°C fan) mark 6. Tip the polenta out on to a board. Cut into 25 squares or stamp out 25 small shapes. Put on a baking tray lined with baking parchment and brush with 1 tbsp oil. Cook for 10–12min, or until slightly crisp on top. Set aside to cool.

4. Arrange on a large platter and top each with half a grape and a piece of blue cheese, securing with a cocktail stick, if needed. Serve.

Hands-on time: 25min, plus cooling and setting
Cooking time: about 20min
Makes 25 bites

PER BITE 49cals, 2g protein, 3g fat (1g saturates), 5g carbs (1g total sugars), <1g fibre

★ GET AHEAD
Prepare to the end of step 2 up to 3 days ahead. Cool, cover and chill. Complete the recipe up to 4hr ahead.

Spicy Crab Mini Filo Triangles

Delicious served with a dipping sauce of soy, spring onions, chilli and ginger.

Melted butter, to grease and brush
150g white crabmeat, fresh or tinned
4 spring onions, trimmed and finely chopped, plus extra to garnish
1 red chilli, deseeded and finely chopped
5cm piece fresh root ginger, finely grated
Finely grated zest and juice 1 lime
4 sheets filo pastry
Dipping sauce, to serve (optional)

1. Preheat the oven to 200°C (180°C fan) mark 6 and lightly grease 2 large baking trays. To make the filling, in a medium bowl mix together crabmeat, spring onions, chilli, ginger, lime zest and juice, and some seasoning. Set aside.

2. Lay 1 sheet of filo on a board, with a long edge facing you, and cut it vertically into strips, roughly 7.5cm wide. Working with 1 strip at a time, spoon 1 tbsp crab mixture on to the bottom corner, then fold up to form a triangle. Continue rolling the triangle up the length of the pastry strip, retaining the triangle shape, and brushing the last part of the strip with butter so it sticks together. Put on a baking tray.

3. Repeat with the remaining filo and crab filling (you should have about 20 triangles). Brush the tops of the triangles with melted butter.

4. Cook in the oven for 20min or until crisp and golden. Leave to cool on a wire rack and serve just warm, garnished with spring onions and with a dipping sauce on the side, if you like.

★ GET AHEAD
Prepare to end of step 3 up to 5hr ahead. Cover the baking trays with foil and chill. To serve, uncover the trays and complete the recipe.

Hands-on time: 30min, plus cooling
Cooking time: about 20min
Makes about 20 triangles

PER SERVING Per serving 38cals, 2g protein, 1g fat (1g saturates), 5g carbs (0.4g total sugars), 0.3g fibre

Mixed Pinwheels

These are so simple, yet very effective!

100g roasted red peppers, from a jar
Flour, to dust
500g block puff pastry
75g soft goat's cheese, at room temperature
2 thyme sprigs, leaves picked
100g black olive tapenade
1 egg, beaten

1. Dry red peppers thoroughly with kitchen paper, then whizz them to a purée in a food processor.

2. Lightly dust a work surface with flour. Halve the pastry and roll out one of the halves into a 20.5cm x 25.5cm rectangle. If not already soft, beat the goat's cheese to soften, then spread it over the rolled-out pastry. Next, spread over the red pepper purée and sprinkle over the thyme leaves. Season with freshly ground black pepper.

3. Starting from one of the long edges, roll up the pastry as tightly as you can. Wrap in clingfilm and chill for 1hr.

4. Roll out the remaining pastry as before. Spread with olive tapenade and roll it up tightly from one of the long edges. Wrap in clingfilm and chill for 1hr.

5. Preheat the oven to 200°C (180°C fan) mark 6. Line 2 or more large baking sheets with baking parchment. Unwrap the pastry rolls and trim the edges. Slice each roll into 1cm-thick rounds and arrange on baking sheets, swirl-side up – spacing them at least 2cm apart. Chill for 20min.

6. Brush the the pastry swirls with egg and bake for 15–20min until golden. Transfer to a wire rack and serve warm or at room temperature.

★ GET AHEAD
Make up to 1 day ahead. Once cool, pack into an airtight container and store at room temperature. Reheat in a single layer on baking sheets in an preheated 200°C (180°C fan) mark 6 oven for 10min.

Hands-on time: 25min, plus chilling
Cooking time: about 20min
Makes about 40 pinwheels

PER SERVING 60cals, 1g protein, 4g fat (2g saturates), 4g carbs (0.2g total sugars), 0.3g fibre

Easy Beetroot, Walnut and Stilton Blinis

If you are short on time, you can use ready-made blinis instead of making your own.

FOR THE BLINIS
100g plain flour
1 tsp caster sugar
1 medium egg
75ml milk, at room temperature
25ml vegetable oil, plus extra to fry

FOR THE BEETROOT AND WALNUT TOPPING
25g walnut pieces, plus extra to garnish
150g cooked beetroot (not in vinegar), drained
    and chopped
2 tbsp double cream
1½ tsp English mustard

TO SERVE
25 small chunks vegetarian Stilton or similar vegetarian
    blue cheese (approx 60g total)

★ GET AHEAD
Make the blinis and topping up to a day ahead. Cool, cover and keep the blinis at room temperature. Chill the topping in a piping/sandwich bag. To serve, allow to come up to room temperature. Assemble up to 1hr ahead.

1. To make the blini batter, sift the flour into a medium bowl and stir in the sugar and a large pinch of fine salt. Make a well in the centre and crack in the egg. Start whisking the egg, then gradually add the milk. Still whisking, draw in the flour to make a smooth batter (push through a sieve if not smooth). Whisk in the oil. Cover and set aside to rest for 30min.

2. Meanwhile, make the topping. Whizz the walnuts in the small bowl of a food processor until finely chopped. Add the beetroot, cream, mustard and seasoning, then whizz again until fairly smooth. Transfer to a piping or plastic sandwich bag.

3. Heat a little oil in a large heavy-based frying pan over medium heat. Spoon or pipe in the batter, spacing a little apart, to make 4cm round blinis. Cook for 2–3min until bases are golden. Flip and cook for a further 2min. Set aside on a wire rack. Continue until all batter is used, adding more oil as needed. You should have about 25 blinis.

4. To serve, snip the corner of a piping/plastic bag and pipe on beetroot topping. Add a chunk of Stilton and garnish with extra walnut pieces. Arrange on a serving platter.

Hands-on time: 30min, plus resting
Cooking time: about 20min
Makes about 25 blinis

PER BLINI 58cals, 2g protein, 4g fat (1g saturates), 4g carbs (1g total sugars), 0g fibre

Stuffed Cheese and Pistachio Dates

More of an assembly job than a recipe, but oh-so tasty. To serve warm, make up to the end of step 1, then arrange on a baking tray and pop into an oven preheated to 180°C (160°C fan) mark 4 for 5min.

200g soft goat's cheese
2 tbsp double cream
24 pitted medjool dates
25g pistachio kernels, roughly chopped

1. Mix the goat's cheese and double cream with plenty of seasoning. Cut a slit lengthways in each date and stuff with the cheese mixture.

2. Sprinkle over the pistachios and serve.

★ GET AHEAD
Stuff the dates 1 day ahead; cover and chill. To serve, allow to come to room temperature and sprinkle over the pistachios.

Hands-on time: 15min
Makes 24 dates

PER DATE 95cals, 2g protein, 4g fat (2g saturates), 13g carbs (12g total sugars), 1g fibre

Cheesy Bread Twists

Best eaten within a few hours of baking, these substantial canapés are a delight served with dips or just as they are.

150ml milk
125g butter, chopped
2 medium eggs
350g strong white flour, plus extra to dust
1 tsp fast-action dried yeast
Oil, to grease
125g Gruyère cheese, finely grated
Poppy and/or sesame seeds

★ GET AHEAD
Complete the recipe up to 1 day ahead. Cool completely. Store at room temperature in an airtight container. To serve, refresh in a single layer on baking sheets for 15min at 200°C (180°C fan) mark 6.

1. Heat the milk in a small pan until you see steam rising, then pour into a jug and stir in the butter to melt. Leave to cool until just warm, then beat in 1 egg until combined.

2. Put the flour, yeast and 1 tsp salt into a large bowl. Make a well in the centre, add the warm milk mixture and mix to combine. Tip out on to a work surface dusted with flour and knead until smooth and elastic – about 5min. Put into a lightly greased bowl, cover with clingfilm and leave to rise in a warm place for 1hr, or until doubled in size.

3. Lightly grease 4 baking sheets with oil and preheat oven to 220°C (200°C fan) mark 7. Re-flour your work surface. Knead the risen dough briefly, then roll out into a rectangle measuring 15 x 60cm – it should be about 5mm thick.

4. Lightly beat the remaining egg. Brush some of it over the top of the dough, then sprinkle the cheese over the left half of the rectangle. Fold over the empty dough to cover the cheese. Roll out again to 15 x 60cm.

5. Cut into strips about 1cm wide and 15cm long. Twist each strip several times and position on the baking sheets, spacing a little apart. Brush with egg and sprinkle over poppy/sesame seeds.

6. Bake for 10–12min or until golden. Serve warm or at room temperature.

Hands-on time: 40min, plus rising
Cooking time: about 15min
Makes about 28 twists

PER TWIST 110cals, 4g protein, 6g fat (4g saturates), 10g carbs (0.3g total sugars), 0.4g fibre

Mini BLTs

We've shrunk the sandwich classic for this quick and easy canapé recipe. Perfect for a dinner or drinks party.

40g butter, melted
8 slices white bread (medium cut)
1 Little Gem lettuce
6 slices Parma ham
2 tbsp mayonnaise
12 cherry tomatoes, halved

YOU'LL ALSO NEED
24 cocktail sticks

1. Preheat the grill to medium. Brush melted butter over both sides of each slice of bread. Grill (in batches if necessary) on a baking sheet until golden and toasted on each side.

2. Using a 3.5cm round cutter, stamp out 48 toast circles (or cut into crustless squares if you prefer). Set aside.

3. Cut the lettuce into roughly 4cm pieces – you need 24. Next cut each Parma ham slice into quarters.

4. To assemble, lay a piece of lettuce on top of 24 of the bread rounds, then pipe/spread on the mayonnaise. Top each stack with a folded piece of Parma ham, a cherry tomato half and a final round of toast. Secure in place with a cocktail stick.

★ GET AHEAD
Assemble up to 30min before serving.

Hands-on time: 25min
Cooking time: about 5min
Makes 24 sandwiches

PER SANDWICH 63cals, 2g protein, 3g fat (1g saturates), 7g carbs (1g total sugars), 0.5g fibre

Pork Satay Sticks

Serve the satay sauce either at room temperature or gently warmed through.

450g pork fillet
1 tsp mild curry paste
2 tsp toasted sesame oil

FOR THE SATAY SAUCE
125g salted peanuts
½ tbsp caster sugar
160ml tin coconut cream
1 tsp mild curry paste
1 tbsp sweet chilli sauce

YOU'LL ALSO NEED
Cocktail sticks

1. Cut the pork fillet into finger-sized strips and put into a non-metallic bowl. Add the curry paste and sesame oil. Mix well. Cover, chill and leave to marinate for about 1hr.

2. To make the satay sauce, whizz the peanuts and sugar in a food processor until finely chopped. Add the coconut cream, curry paste and sweet chilli sauce and blend again until smooth. Spoon into a serving bowl, cover and set aside.

3. Preheat the grill to medium. Arrange the pork in a single layer on a baking sheet and grill for 5min, turning occasionally, until cooked through and golden. Serve warm or at room temperature with the satay sauce and cocktail sticks.

Hands-on time: 20min, plus marinating
Cooking time: about 5min
Makes about 24 sticks

PER STICK 77cals, 6g protein, 5g fat (2g saturates), 2g carbs (1g total sugars), 0.1g fibre

Smoked Pâté Bites

You can use your favourite smoked fish for different flavours in these simple but always popular nibbles.

100g full-fat cream cheese
100g hot smoked salmon, skinned
Finely grated zest of 1 lemon
3 slices rye bread, about 200g
Chopped dill, to garnish

1. Put the cream cheese into a food processor. Add the skinned smoked salmon, lemon zest and some seasoning. Pulse briefly until well combined but still with some texture. Empty into a bowl.

2. Cut each slice of rye bread into equal bite-sized pieces. Dollop or spread some fish pâté on to each piece of bread.

3. Garnish with freshly cracked black pepper and dill and serve.

★ GET AHEAD
Prepare to end of step 1 up to 1 day ahead. Cover with clingfilm and chill. Complete recipe up to 1hr ahead.

Hands-on time: 15min
Makes about 30 bites

PER BITE 31cals, 2g protein, 1g fat (1g saturates), 3g carbs (0.3g total sugars), 0.4g fibre

Roast Beef and Yorkshire Puddings

A guaranteed crowd-pleaser.

1 tbsp olive oil
2 x 180g beef fillet steaks
6 ready-made Yorkshire puddings
Creamed horseradish, to serve
Chopped parsley, to garnish (optional)

1. Heat the oil in a pan over medium-high heat, then fry the steaks for 2–3min per side (for medium), but cook for longer or shorter if you prefer. Set aside to rest until just warm or room temperature.

2. Meanwhile, heat the Yorkshire puds according to the pack instructions. Set aside to cool slightly.

3. When ready, cut each pud into 6 equal pieces and slice the beef into 36 thin slices.

4. Spoon a little horseradish on to each piece of pudding, top with a beef strip, ground black pepper and parsley, if you like. Serve.

★ GET AHEAD
Prepare to end of step 1 up to 2hr ahead and cover the cooked beef with foil. Complete recipe up to 30min ahead.

Hands-on time: 25min, plus resting
Cooking time: about 10min
Makes 36 canapés

PER CANAPÉ 31cals, 3g protein, 1g fat (0.4g saturates), 2g carbs (0.1g total sugars), 0.1g fibre

Brie and Cranberry Moneybags

Crisp filo, sweet cranberry and oozing Brie – what could be better?

9 sheets filo pastry
75g unsalted butter, melted
150–175g Brie, cut into 1cm cubes
2 tbsp cranberry sauce

1. Preheat oven to 200°C (180°C fan) mark 6. Brush a sheet of filo with some melted butter. Keep layering filo/butter until you have 3 layers (keep filo you are not working with covered with a damp tea towel), then cut into 8 x 9cm squares.

2. Put 3 cubes of Brie in the centre of each filo square and top with a little cranberry sauce. Working one square at a time, bring the filo sides up over the filling and pinch together firmly to create a moneybag shape. Repeat with the remaining squares and filling.

3. Repeat the buttering, filling and shaping process twice more to end up with 24 moneybags.

4. Put the filo bags on baking sheets and cook in the oven for 8–10min until golden and crisp. Allow to cool for 10min before serving warm.

★ GET AHEAD
Complete the recipe up to 4hr ahead. To serve, arrange on a baking sheet and reheat for 5–8min at 200°C (180°C fan) mark 6.

Hands-on time: 45min, plus cooling
Cooking time: about 10min
Makes 24 parcels

PER PARCEL 94cals, 3g protein, 5g fat (3g saturates), 9g carbs (1g total sugars), 0.5g fibre

Goat's Cheese Truffles

These no-fuss cheese bites look super pretty, and can easily be made a day ahead.

250g rindless soft goat's cheese log

FOR THE TOPPINGS (each will cover 250g cheese)
1½ tbsp each finely chopped pistachios, finely chopped
   dried cranberries and crushed pink peppercorns
   mixed together
OR
4 tbsp finely chopped chives
OR
4 tbsp mixed black and white sesame seeds, toasted
   and cooled

1. Mash the goat's cheese in a bowl with a pinch of
   salt. Roll the cheese into walnut-sized balls and
   put on a tray lined with baking parchment.

2. Put your topping of choice into a small bowl.
   Roll the goat's cheese balls in the topping, then
   return to the tray. Cover with clingfilm and chill
   for up to 24hr or until ready to serve. Remove
   from the fridge 30min before serving.

Hands-on time: 15min
Makes about 18 truffles

PER TRUFFLE (without topping) 50cals, 3g protein,
4g fat (3g saturates), 0.1g carbs (0.1g total sugars),
0g fibre

Chicken Taco Bites

A moreish combination of ingredients served in cute home-made mini taco shells.

5 large flour tortilla wraps
2 tbsp sunflower oil
300g chicken thigh fillets, about 4
2 tsp sweet smoked paprika
2 garlic cloves, crushed
250g passata
1½ tbsp tomato ketchup
2 tsp soy sauce
1 tsp English mustard
2 tsp white wine vinegar

FOR THE GUACAMOLE
2 ripe avocados
Finely grated zest and juice 1 lime

TO SERVE
50g Cheddar, finely grated

★ GET AHEAD
Make to the end of step 6 up to 1 day ahead.
Store the shells in an airtight container at room temperature. Cover and chill the guacamole and, separately, the cooled chicken mixture. To serve, reheat the chicken gently in a covered pan. Re-crisp the shells in rungs of the rack for 3–4min in an oven preheated to 200°C (180°C fan) mark 6, then cool.

Hands-on time: 35min
Cooking time: about 45min
Makes 34 bites

PER BITE 63cals, 3g protein, 4g fat (1g saturates),
4g carbs (0g total sugars), 1g fibre

1. Preheat oven to 200°C (180°C fan) mark 6. Using a 7.5cm cutter, stamp out 34 rounds from the tortillas. Using 1 tbsp of the oil, brush both sides of rounds. Set a wire rack (not cross-hatched) on a baking tray. Gently fold rounds to form a taco shape and arrange between rungs of the rack (with fold at bottom).

2. Transfer tray/rack to oven and cook the shells for 5–7min until starting to crisp and turn golden. Remove from the oven and quickly but gently prise open any that have closed. Arrange upside down on a board to cool.

3. Meanwhile, heat the remaining oil in a medium pan over medium heat. Brown the chicken on both sides (about 5min). Add the paprika and garlic. Cook for 1min, then add the remaining sauce ingredients. Bring to the boil, cover and simmer for 20min until cooked.

4. Lift the chicken out on to a board. Bring the sauce back up to the boil. Cook for 10–12min until reduced and thickened.

5. Finely shred the chicken. Return to the sauce, check the seasoning and transfer to a bowl.

6. To make the guacamole, halve and destone the avocados. Whizz the flesh in a food processor with lime zest and juice and seasoning (or mash in a bowl with a fork). Transfer to a serving bowl.

7. Serve the shells with chicken, guacamole and grated Cheddar.

Meatball Subs

This miniature version of an American classic is well worth the effort, and guests will love assembling them. Any leftover sauce is delicious with pasta.

FOR THE BREAD ROLLS
150ml milk
15g unsalted butter
225g strong white flour, plus extra to dust
1 tsp fast-action dried yeast
Oil, to grease

FOR THE MEATBALLS
250g beef mince
25g Parmesan cheese, finely grated
25g fresh breadcrumbs
1 garlic clove, crushed
1 medium egg, beaten
1 tbsp olive oil

1. Heat the milk in a small pan until small bubbles appear around the edge. Take off heat, add the butter to melt, then set aside until lukewarm. In a large bowl, mix the flour, yeast and ½ tsp fine salt. Make a well in the centre and quickly mix in milk mixture. Scrape on to a lightly floured surface and knead until smooth and elastic (about 10min). Form into a ball. Transfer to a lightly greased medium bowl and cover with clingfilm. Leave to rise in a warm place for 1hr or until well risen.

2. Punch dough down in bowl and divide into 34 equal pieces on a work surface (it's easiest to weigh the dough and divide by 34). Shape each piece into a submarine shape, about 5cm long. Arrange on baking trays lined with parchment paper, spacing at least 2.5cm apart. Cover with greased clingfilm (oil-side down) and leave to rise in a warm place until well risen (about 30–45min).

3. Meanwhile, make the meatballs. Preheat oven to 220°C (200°C fan) mark 7. In a medium bowl, mix together all the ingredients (except the oil). Roll into 34 small balls, each about 2.5cm in diameter. Transfer to a roasting tin lined with baking parchment and drizzle with oil.

4. Uncover the bread rolls and make a lengthways slash in the top of each with a sharp knife. Dust lightly with flour. Put the rolls and meatballs into the oven. Cook rolls for 8–10min until light golden but still soft – transfer to a wire rack to cool. Cook meatballs for 15–20min, shaking the tin occasionally, until browned.

5. To serve, cut the bread rolls open – we did ours through the top. Serve with meatballs and the Marinara and Easy Cheesy sauces.

Hands-on time: 1hr, plus rising and cooling
Cooking time: about 25min
Makes 34 subs

PER SUB (with sauces) 81cals, 4g protein, 4g fat (2g saturates), 7g carbs (1g total sugars), 1g fibre

The dipping sauces

Marinara Sauce

In a pan, gently fry ½ **finely chopped onion** in ½ **tbsp olive oil** for 5–8min. Add **1 crushed garlic clove**, **400g tin chopped tomatoes**, **1 tsp caster sugar** and **a pinch of cayenne pepper**. Simmer for 15–20min, stirring often, until reduced. Add **a handful chopped basil leaves** and season to taste. Transfer to a serving bowl. Serve warm.

Easy Cheesy Sauce

In a small pan, heat **200ml milk**, **25g unsalted butter**, **25g plain flour** and **75g grated red Leicester cheese**. Whisk continuously over a medium heat until the sauce thickens and the cheese has melted – about 3–5min. Stir in **25ml milk**. Season and transfer to a serving bowl. Serve warm.

★ GET AHEAD
Make the rolls and meatballs up to 1 day ahead. Once cool, keep unsliced rolls in an airtight container at room temperature. Store cooled meatballs covered in the fridge. To serve, reheat the meatballs in an oven preheated to 150°C (130°C fan) mark 2, covered with foil for 15min. Slice open the rolls.

Doughnut Dippers

This yeast-free doughnut recipe means these can be on the table in no time at all.

150ml milk
75g unsalted butter
200g self-raising flour, plus extra to dust
1 tsp baking powder
1 medium egg
Vegetable oil, to fry
75g caster sugar
½ tsp ground cinnamon (optional)

★ GET AHEAD
Fry the doughnuts and coat in the sugar mixture up to 4hr ahead. To serve, refresh in a single layer on a baking sheet in an oven preheated to 200°C (180°C fan) mark 6 for 5min. Serve warm.

1. In a medium pan, heat the milk, 100ml water and butter until almost boiling. Take off the heat, then add the flour and baking powder. Mix until the dough is smooth. Set aside to cool for 10min, then beat in the egg.

2. Lightly dust a work surface with flour and roll/pat out the dough to a rough 18 x 23cm rectangle. Slice in half lengthways then, working across the rectangles, cut into 1.5cm strips (you should have about 28).

3. Pour enough oil into a large pan (with a lid, for safety) to come a third of the way up the sides. Heat over medium heat to 180°C, using a cook's thermometer to measure the temperature. Mix the sugar and cinnamon, if using, in a large shallow bowl.

4. Fry the doughnuts in batches for about 3–4min, turning occasionally with a slotted metal spoon, until deep golden. Lift on to kitchen paper to drain before coating in the sugar mixture. Serve warm as they are, or with our suggestions of dips if you like.

Hands-on time: 30min, plus cooling
Cooking time: about 15min
Makes about 28 doughnuts

PER DOUGHNUT 85cals, 1g protein, 6g fat (2g saturates), 7g carbs (2g total sugars), 0g fibre

The dipping sauces

Hot Chocolate

In a medium pan, gently heat **150g chopped dark chocolate**, **15g unsalted butter**, **40g golden syrup** and **150ml double cream** until melted and smooth. Pour into a heatproof bowl and serve warm with the doughnuts.

PER 1 TBSP 63cals, 0g protein, 5g fat (3g saturates), 4g carbs (4g total sugars), 0g fibre

Passion Fruit

Halve **6 ripe passion fruits** and scrape the pulp into a food processor. Pulse to loosen, then push through a sieve into a medium pan. Reserve ½ tbsp seeds and discard the rest. To the fruit juice, add **2 medium eggs**, **100g diced unsalted butter**, **200g caster sugar** and **1½ tbsp cornflour**. Cook over medium heat, whisking constantly, until thickened (the mixture will need to bubble). Stir through the reserved seeds. Cool and serve with the doughnuts.

PER 1 TBSP 65cals, 1g protein, 3g fat (2g saturates), 8g carbs (7g total sugars), 0g fibre

Raspberry

In a blender, whizz **250g raspberries** with **25g icing sugar**. Strain through a fine sieve into a medium bowl, discarding the seeds. Serve with the doughnuts.

PER 1 TBSP 6cals, 0g protein, 0g fat (0g saturates), 1g carbs (1g total sugars), 0g fibre

Mini Meringue Mince Pies

Our revamped version of this Christmas classic lifts mince pies to new heights.

325g plain flour, plus extra to dust
100g Trex, chilled and cubed
100g Stork baking block, chilled and cubed
600g mincemeat (check it's dairy free)

FOR THE MERINGUE
150g caster sugar
2 large egg whites
Edible gold glitter spray (optional)

YOU'LL ALSO NEED
Sugar thermometer

1. To make the pastry, put the flour, Trex and Stork into a food processor with a pinch of salt and pulse until the mixture resembles fine breadcrumbs (or rub the fats into the flour and salt with fingertips if you don't have a food processor). Tip into a bowl, make a well in the centre and add 2 tbsp chilled water. Stir quickly with a cutlery knife until the pastry starts to come together. Bring together with your hands and knead gently to form a smooth ball. Halve, shape into 2 discs, wrap in clingfilm and chill for 30min.

2. Preheat oven to 190°C (170°C fan) mark 5. Roll out half of the chilled pastry on a lightly floured surface to the thickness of a £1 coin. Stamp out 24 rounds using a 5cm round cutter (re-rolling the trimmings as necessary). Use the rounds to line a 24-hole mini muffin tin, then fill the cases with half of the mincemeat and chill for 15min.

3. Bake the pies for 20-25min until the pastry is sandy to touch and the mincemeat is bubbling. Repeat with the remaining pastry and mincemeat until you have 48 mini pies.

4. To make the meringue, put the sugar in a saucepan with 3 tbsp water and dissolve over a gentle heat. Once the sugar is dissolved, turn up heat and, using a sugar thermometer, bring the mixture up to 120°C.

5. Meanwhile, whisk the egg whites to stiff peaks. Once the sugar syrup has come up to temperature, carefully pour over the egg whites in a steady stream, whisking constantly. When all of the syrup has been incorporated, continue to whisk for another 15-20min, or until the mixture is cool. Transfer to a piping bag fitted with a 1cm nozzle and pipe a swirl on top of each pie. Use a blowtorch, if you have one, to gently toast the meringue, or flash under a hot grill for 1-2min until golden. Spritz with a little gold glitter, if you like, and serve.

Hands-on time: 45min, plus chilling
Cooking time: about 45min
Makes 48 pies

PER PIE 106cals, 1g protein, 5g fat (2g saturates), 14g carbs (8g total sugars), 1g fibre

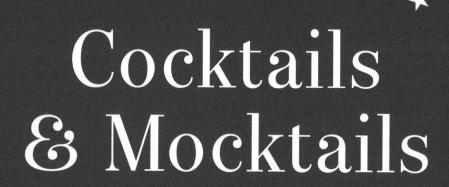

Cocktails
& Mocktails

Cranberry Sangria

Don't let the colour fool you, this is actually a white wine spin on sangria. Using cava instead of red wine makes it deliciously refreshing.

250ml cranberry juice
150ml brandy
1 lime, sliced into thin rounds
1 orange, sliced into thin rounds
75cl bottle cava, chilled
250ml sparkling lemonade, chilled
100g frozen cranberries
Ice, to serve

1. Mix the cranberry juice, brandy, lime and orange slices in a jug. Cover and chill for at least 2hr (or up to 24hr).

2. To serve, decant the cranberry mixture into a punch bowl or large pitcher and slowly stir in the cava and lemonade. Add the cranberries and a couple of handfuls of ice. Serve, making sure each glass has some ice and a few cranberries.

Hands-on time: 5min, plus chilling
Serves 8

PER SERVING 137cals, 0g protein, 0g fat (0g saturates), 7g carbs (7g total sugars), 0g fibre

Honey and Pear Brandy Old-fashioned

A twist on a classic short and strong cocktail – top up with more soda water if you prefer a longer drink.

1 tsp runny honey
50ml brandy
25ml Poire William or pear juice
2 dashes Angostura bitters
Ice, to serve
Soda water (optional)
Pear crisp, to garnish (optional)

1. In a small tumbler, stir the honey, brandy, pear liqueur or juice and the Angostura bitters until the honey is fully dissolved.

2. Add ice and top up with soda water, if using. Garnish with a pear crisp, if you like, and serve.

Hands-on time: 5min
Serves 1

PER SERVING 207cals, 0g protein, 0g fat (0g saturates), 15g carbs (15g total sugars), 0g fibre

Hot Buttered Rum

For an extra seasonal spin, swap the lemon zest for clementine zest. Spices such as clove and star anise would work well, too.

50g unsalted butter
125g light brown soft sugar
Pared zest 1 lemon
1 cinnamon stick, plus extra to serve
400ml dark rum
Nutmeg, for grating
Cinnamon sticks, to garnish (optional)

1. In a medium pan, heat the butter, sugar, lemon zest and 1 cinnamon stick over low heat, stirring occasionally, until the butter and sugar are melted and combined. Remove from heat and stir in the dark rum. Pass through a fine sieve, discarding the cinnamon and lemon.

2. Divide among 8 heatproof glasses or mugs and top up with a little hot water. Grate over some nutmeg and garnish with cinnamon sticks.

Hands-on time: 5min
Cooking time: 5min
Serves 8

PER SERVING 218cals, 0g protein, 5g fat (3g saturates), 15g carbs (15g total sugars), 0g fibre

Winter Spiced Negroni

A fresh take on a trendy classic. Play around with the spices — whole peppercorns or cardamom pods would work rather nicely.

2 cinnamon sticks
2 star anise
5 whole cloves
250ml gin
250ml Campari
250ml red vermouth
8 clementine or orange slices
Vegetable oil, for brushing
Ice, to serve

1. In a small frying pan, toast the cinnamon sticks, star anise and cloves until fragrant, then empty into a large jug. Add the gin, Campari and vermouth, and leave to infuse for at least 4hr (or up to 24hr).

2. To serve, brush the clementine or orange slices with vegetable oil. Heat a non-stick frying pan over medium-high heat and fry the slices until lightly charred on both sides.

3. Fill 8 short glasses with ice and add the clementine or orange slices. Strain in the spiced negroni mixture and serve.

Hands-on time: about 10min, plus infusing
Cooking time: about 5min
Serves 8

PER SERVING 186cals, 0g protein, 0g fat (0g saturates), 11g carbs (11g total sugars), 0g fibre

Clementine and Vanilla Margarita

A seasonal twist on this delicious classic

250ml tequila
125ml triple sec
125ml freshly squeezed clementine juice, plus slices to garnish
75ml freshly squeezed lime juice
2 tsp vanilla bean paste, plus extra to serve
Ice, to shake

1. Put the tequila, triple sec, clementine and lime juices, and vanilla bean paste into a cocktail shaker. Fill with ice and shake.

2. Put ½ tsp fine salt on a small saucer or plate. Rub the rim of 4 margarita or martini glasses with a little extra vanilla bean paste, then dip them into the salt to coat the edges. Strain the margarita mixture into the glasses, garnish each with a clementine slice and serve.

Hands-on time: 5min
Serves 4

PER SERVING 220cals, 0g protein, 0g fat (0g saturates), 3g carbs (3g total sugars), 0g fibre

Pineapple Rum Punch

This tropical drink is fruity and refreshing, but also wonderfully warming. The chilli adds an herbaceous kick that pairs well with the fire of the ginger beer, but you can leave it out if you prefer.

300ml pineapple or spiced rum
500ml pineapple juice, chilled
600ml ginger beer, chilled
Juice 2 limes, plus wedges to garnish
1 green chilli, halved and deseeded, plus slices to garnish (optional)
Handful mint leaves, plus extra sprigs to garnish
Ice, to serve
Maraschino cherries, to garnish (optional)

1. In a large jug, mix together the rum, pineapple juice, ginger beer, lime juice, chilli (if using) and mint leaves.

2. Fill 6 tumblers with ice and some mint sprigs. Divide the punch among the glasses and garnish each with a lime wedge plus a slice of chilli and/or maraschino cherry, if using. Serve.

Hands-on time: 5min
Serves 6

PER SERVING 161cals, 0g protein, 0g fat (0g saturates), 12g carbs (12g total sugars), 0g fibre

Eggnog Latte

A coffee-spiked twist on the classic creamy Yuletide eggnog.

550ml whole milk
2 cinnamon sticks
1 vanilla pod, split lengthways
¼ tsp freshly grated nutmeg, plus extra to garnish
3 medium egg yolks
2 tsp cornflour
100g runny honey
125ml bourbon
Ice, to serve
200ml freshly brewed espresso
Aerosol cream, to garnish

1. In a medium pan, heat the milk, cinnamon sticks, vanilla and nutmeg over medium heat until just simmering.

2. Meanwhile, whisk the egg yolks, cornflour and honey in a bowl until foamy and slightly paler in colour. Gradually whisk in the hot milk mixture (including spices). Return the mixture to the pan and cook, whisking regularly, until just simmering and slightly thickened, about 8–10min (it will continue to thicken as it cools). Remove from heat, lay clingfilm or baking parchment directly on the surface to stop a skin from forming and leave to cool, then chill for at least 1hr (or up to 24hr).

3. To serve, remove and discard the cinnamon and vanilla from the nog mixture and whisk in the bourbon. Fill 6 latte glasses or large tumblers with ice, then divide the espresso among them. Pour over the nog mixture and top with a swirl of cream and some extra freshly grated nutmeg. Serve immediately.

Hands-on time: 15min, plus cooling and chilling
Cooking time: about 15min
Serves 6

PER SERVING 191cals, 5g protein, 6g fat (3g saturates), 18g carbs (16g total sugars), 0g fibre

Chai Mulled Cider

A lovely apple-y twist on mulled wine. This recipe makes more mulling syrup than you need, but it keeps well and makes a lovely gift, decanted into a pretty bottle and tied with a ribbon and tag. You need to start the recipe at least a day ahead to give the syrup time to infuse.

FOR THE CHAI MULLING SYRUP
250g golden caster sugar
2 whole star anise
2 cinnamon sticks
10 green cardamom pods, bruised
1 vanilla pod, split lengthways
4 chai tea bags

FOR THE CIDER
1.5 litre quality cider
125ml Calvados, golden rum or brandy
2 cinnamon sticks
1 red-skinned apple, thinly sliced
1 small orange, thinly sliced

1. Make the syrup at least 1 day ahead. Put the sugar and spices in a medium pan and add 250ml water. Heat gently, stirring, until the sugar dissolves. Increase heat to medium, bring to the boil and bubble gently for 5min. Remove from heat, add the tea bags and set aside to cool completely. Remove the tea bags, pressing lightly to extract the flavour, then discard. Pour the syrup and spices into a jar or food container with a lid. Cover and leave to infuse at room temperature for at least 24hr or up to 1 month, then strain into a jar or bottle.

2. To make the mulled cider, in a large pan stir together the cider, Calvados/rum/brandy, cinnamon sticks and 200ml mulling syrup. Cover the pan with a lid and bring slowly to a simmer (about 10min).

3. Once the cider is bubbling, add the apple and orange slices, re-cover and leave to infuse for 5min. Serve in heatproof glasses or mugs, garnished with the fruit slices and cinnamon sticks, if you like.

Hands-on time: 10min, plus cooling and (overnight) infusing
Cooking time: about 20min
Serves 8

PER SERVING 181cals, 0g protein, 0g fat (0g saturates), 23g carbs (23g total sugars), 0g fibre

Pear and Ginger Spritz

A fruity, refreshing long drink to kick-start any party.

150ml London Dry Gin
4 mint sprigs, plus extra to garnish
Ice, to shake and serve
100ml pear liqueur
Juice 1 lime
750ml chilled ginger beer

1. Shake the gin, mint and a few ice cubes in a sealed cocktail shaker (or mash lightly in a jug, without ice, with the end of a rolling pin).

2. Strain into a large jug, then add the liqueur, lime juice and ginger beer. Fill 6 tall glasses with ice and pour in the cocktail. Garnish with mint sprigs and serve.

Hands-on time: 5min
Serves 6

PER SERVING 147cals, 0g protein, 0g fat (0g saturates), 14g carbs (14g total sugars), 0g fibre

Churchill's Breakfast

With a cinnamon stick cigar, this pays homage to Sir Winston Churchill, who liked a whisky in the morning.

1 small cinnamon stick
60ml blended Scotch whisky
25ml cold brew coffee or cooled espresso
1 tbsp maple syrup
Dash Angostura bitters
Few ice cubes

1. Pop a martini glass in the freezer for 10min. Meanwhile, light one end of a cinnamon stick with a gas flame. When the flame goes out (blow it out if it remains alight), set the stick aside to cool.

2. To serve, remove the glass from the freezer. In a sealed cocktail shaker (or jam jar with a lid), shake the remaining ingredients. Strain into the glass, finely grate over some of the unburnt end of the cinnamon stick, then float the stick in the glass and serve.

Hands-on time: 5min, plus freezing
Serves 1

PER SERVING 172cals, 0g protein, 0g fat (0g saturates), 10g carbs (9g total sugars), 0g fibre

Spiced Orange Fizz

The orange syrup is quick to make, and even easier to drink. Use any fizz you like in this seasonal delight.

25g caster sugar
150ml orange juice
Pared zest 1 orange
1 cinnamon stick
2 star anise
2 cloves
2 bay leaves
75cl bottle Prosecco, chilled

1. Heat the sugar, juice and 150ml water over low heat until the sugar dissolves. Add the zest, spices and bay leaves, then increase the heat and bubble for 10min until reduced by half. Cool, then strain.

2. Divide among 6 Champagne flutes and slowly top up with Prosecco.

★ GET AHEAD
Make and strain the syrup up to 3 days ahead. Store covered in the fridge. Complete the recipe to serve.

Hands-on time: 10min, plus cooling
Cooking time: about 15min
Serves 6

PER SERVING 131cals, 0g protein, 0g fat (0g saturates), 12g carbs (12g total sugars), 0g fibre

Winter Sangria

Our version of the classic has a rosé twist and is perfect for colder days.

75cl bottle rosé wine
150ml Cointreau
250ml pomegranate juice
½ orange, sliced into rounds
2 cinnamon sticks
Ice, to serve
50g pomegranate seeds

1. Mix the rosé, Cointreau, pomegranate juice, orange slices and cinnamon in a jug. Cover and chill for at least 2hr (or up to 24hr).

2. To serve, fill 6 large wine glasses with ice and divide the pomegranate seeds among them. Pour in the cocktail, add the orange slices (discarding the cinnamon), and serve.

★ GET AHEAD
Make to end of step 1 up to 1 day ahead. Complete recipe to serve.

Hands-on time: 10min, plus chilling
Serves 6

PER SERVING 205cals, 0g protein, 0g fat (0g saturates), 15g carbs (15g total sugars), 0g fibre

Festive White Russian

Not actually Russian in origin, this cocktail gets its name from having vodka as the base. Traditionally it's a Black Russian, but it becomes White with the addition of cream.

50ml vodka
35ml coffee liqueur
50ml milk
50ml gingerbread syrup (see right)
Ice, to serve
1 tbsp double cream

1. Measure the vodka, coffee liqueur, milk and gingerbread syrup into a cocktail shaker (or jar with a lid). Add a handful of ice, close and shake well to combine and chill.

2. Strain into a glass, stir in the cream and serve.

Hands-on time: 5min, plus chilling
Serves 1

PER SERVING 460cals, 2g protein, 9g fat (6g saturates), 46g carbs (46g total sugars), 0g fibre

Gingerbread Syrup

Add a drizzle to cocktails, ice cream or even your coffee.

50g golden syrup
3 tbsp treacle
2 cinnamon sticks
2–3cm fresh root ginger, peeled and roughly chopped
1 tsp vanilla extract

1. In a small pan over medium heat, stir together the golden syrup, treacle, cinnamon sticks, ginger and 300ml water. Bring to the boil and bubble for 5min, then remove from heat and stir in the vanilla. Leave to cool completely, then strain. Chill in the fridge for up to 2 weeks.

Hands-on time: 5min, plus cooling and chilling
Cooking time: about 8min
Makes 275ml

PER 1 TBSP SERVING 15cals, 0g protein, 0g fat (0g saturates), 4g carbs (4g total sugars), 0g fibre

Mulled Wine Margarita

This party favourite will leave your house smelling amazing. Add as much (or as little) tequila as you like.

4 whole cloves
8 allspice berries
2 cinnamon sticks
8 black peppercorns
75cl bottle red wine
400ml apple juice
Juice 1 orange
100ml orange liqueur (optional)
200ml tequila
50g agave syrup
75g dark brown soft sugar

TO GARNISH (optional)
½ tbsp granulated sugar
6 orange slices, halved

1. Mix all the ingredients (apart from the garnish) in a medium-large pan with a lid. Cook over medium heat, stirring frequently, until the sugar dissolves. Turn down the heat, cover and gently simmer, stirring occasionally, for 45min.

2. Meanwhile, garnish the glasses, if you like. Mix ½ tbsp fine sea salt and the sugar on a saucer. Using the orange slices, wet the rims of 12 heatproof glasses. Dip the rims into the salt mixture and set aside.

3. Strain the warm margarita into the prepared glasses and garnish with orange slices. Serve.

Hands-on time: 10min
Cooking time: about 50min
Makes about 1.5 litres (serves 12)

PER SERVING 178cals, 0g protein, 0g fat (0g saturates), 19g carbs (19g total sugars), 0g fibre

Dirty Chai Latte Martini

This twist on an espresso martini is guaranteed to impress. Serve as a party cocktail or an after-dinner digestif. Looking to limit the caffeine? Skip the extra coffee shot.

---

1 chai tea bag
25ml coffee liqueur
25ml milk
50ml espresso, cooled
50ml vodka
10ml sugar syrup (see opposite)

TO SERVE
Ice
Ground cinnamon or cocoa powder, to dust

1. Cover the tea bag with 150ml just-boiled water. Set aside to cool.

2. Measure the coffee liqueur, milk, cooled espresso, vodka, sugar syrup and 40ml of the cooled chai tea into a cocktail shaker (or jar with a lid). Add a handful of ice, close and shake well to combine and chill.

3. Strain into 2 martini glasses. Dust with a little cinnamon or cocoa powder. Serve.

Hands-on time: 10min, plus cooling
Serves 2

PER SERVING 141cals, <1g protein, <1g fat (<1g saturates), 14g carbs (14g total sugars), 0g fibre

Merry Mojito

Use a still cider instead of the apple juice for an added kick. Alternatively, make this virgin by leaving out the rum without missing any of the flavour.

---

1 tsp brown sugar
10 mint leaves, plus a sprig to garnish
Juice 1 lime
50ml white rum
100ml fresh apple juice
50–75ml ginger beer

TO SERVE
Ice
Fresh root ginger slices (optional)

1. In a cocktail shaker (or jar with a lid) muddle/crush the sugar, mint leaves and lime juice with a spoon. Add the rum, apple juice and plenty of ice. Close and shake vigorously to combine and chill.

2. Strain into a highball glass filled with ice and top up with ginger beer. Garnish with a sprig of mint and ginger slices, if you like. Serve.

Hands-on time: 5min
Serves 1

PER SERVING 177cals, 0g protein, 0g fat (0g saturates), 16g carbs (16g total sugars), 0g fibre

Sugar Syrup

In a small pan, heat **300g caster sugar** and **150ml water** over low heat, stirring until the sugar dissolves. Turn up the heat, bring to the boil and bubble for 1min. Set aside to cool completely. Cover and chill for up to 1 month.

Mocktails

For designated drivers, expectant mothers, dieters or just those who don't drink at all, mocktails allow your guests to enjoy the festivities with a delicious non-alcoholic cocktail.

Pear Sipper

2 pears, plus extra slices to garnish (see GH Tip)
2 tbsp ground cinnamon
50ml lemon verbena or decaf chai blend tea
Nutmeg, for grating

1. Juice the pears, then mix with the cinnamon in a shallow pan and warm gently over a very low heat. Stir in the tea, then transfer to a heat-resistant glass and serve with a grating of nutmeg and few slices of pear.

★ GH TIP
To make a pear fan garnish, core and quarter a pear. Keeping the stem end intact (so the slices will remain attached to the stem), cut each quarter into fine slices, then fan them out.

Hands-on time: 15min
Cooking time: about 5min
Serves 2

PER SERVING 74cals, 0.5g protein, 0g fat (0g saturates), 16g carbs (16g total sugars), 4g fibre

Warming Ginger Soda

300g unpeeled fresh root ginger
225g caster sugar
6 whole cloves
Zest and juice 1½ lemons
1 litre soda water
Mint leaves, to garnish

1. Finely slice the ginger and put into a pan with the caster sugar, cloves and lemon zest and juice. Add about 600ml cold water to cover and heat gently to dissolve the sugar, then turn up the heat and simmer for 10min.

2. Strain through a fine sieve into a jug. Allow to cool for 10min, then top up with the soda water. Garnish with fresh mint leaves.

★ GET AHEAD
Make the syrup up to 3 days ahead and chill. Add soda to serve.

Hands-on time: 5min, plus cooling
Cooking time: about 10min
Makes about 1.6 litres (serves 6)

PER SERVING 148cals, 0g protein, 0g fat (0g saturates), 38g carbs (38g total sugars), 0g fibre

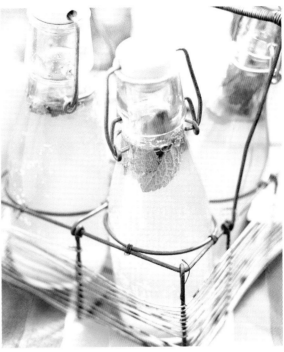

Tropical Teaser

Cucumber Spritz

150ml no added sugar orange and mango drink (or your preferred flavour)
1 litre ginger beer
Zest and juice 1 lime
Ice, to serve
Mint sprigs
6 tsp grenadine (optional)

1. Pour the orange and mango squash into a large jug. Add the ginger beer and lime zest and juice.

2. Fill 6 tall glasses with ice, then add a mint sprig to each glass. Pour in the squash mix, drizzle 1 tsp grenadine, if using, into each glass and serve.

1–2 cucumbers, plus extra slices to serve
Dash watermelon juice
50ml sparkling water
Handful mint

1. Whizz the cucumber in a juicer, then add the watermelon juice and sparkling water and stir together.

2. Pour into a pair of highball glasses and garnish with mint sprigs and cucumber slices.

Hands-on time: 5 min
Makes about 1.6 litres (serves 6)

PER SERVING 95cals, 0.5g protein, 0g fat (0g saturates), 23g carbs (23g total sugars), 0g fibre

Hands-on time: 5min
Serves 2

PER SERVING 35cals, 0g protein, 0g fat (0g saturates), 5g carbs (5g total sugars), 1g fibre

Mulled Cranberry and Raspberry Punch

2 litres cranberry juice
1 cinnamon stick
10 whole cloves
2.5cm piece fresh root ginger, roughly chopped
40g golden caster sugar
200g frozen raspberries
2 oranges

1. Pour the juice into a pan, then add the spices and sugar. Set aside a few raspberries to decorate, then add the rest to the pan. Halve 1 orange and add the halves to the pan. Heat the mixture gently and stir to dissolve the sugar, then simmer for 5min or until the raspberries are soft.

2. Strain through a fine sieve, pressing the raspberries and orange halves gently with the back of a spoon to extract the juice.

3. Return the liquid to the heat and warm through. Slice the remaining orange into thin wedges. Ladle the punch into glasses, garnish with raspberries and orange wedges and serve.

★ GH TIP
To make it a cocktail, add 150ml fruit liqueur.

★ GET AHEAD
Make to the end of step 2 up to 3 days ahead. Cool, cover and chill. To serve, complete the recipe.

Hands-on time: 10min
Cooking time: about 10min
Makes about 2 litres (serves 10)

PER SERVING 167cals, 0.5g protein, 0g fat (0g saturates), 35g carbs (35g total sugars), 1g fibre

Mulled Cranberry and Raspberry Punch

Beetroot Zinger

2cm piece fresh root ginger
4 small beetroot, peeled
Ice, to serve
Soda water
Rosemary sprigs, to garnish

1. Peel the ginger and juice with the beets. Pour into a cocktail shaker and shake well.

2. Add ice to 2 rocks glasses, then pour over the juice. Add a splash of soda water to each and garnish with rosemary sprigs.

Hands-on time: 5min
Serves 2

PER SERVING 51cals, 2g protein, 0g fat (0g saturates), 9g carbs (8g total sugars), 2g fibre

Apple and Ginger Alcohol-free Twist

Apple and Ginger Alcohol-free Twist

1 litre clear apple juice
1.1 litres ginger beer (see GH Tip)
Juice 3 limes
½ tsp each ground cinnamon and freshly grated nutmeg

TO SERVE
Sprigs of mint
Lime slices
Ice cubes

1. In a large jug, mix together the apple juice, ginger beer (see GH Tip) and lime juice.

2. Combine the cinnamon and grated nutmeg in a small bowl.

3. When ready to serve, pour the juice mixture into each glass and top with a pinch of spice, then add a sprig of mint, a slice of lime and ice cubes.

★ GH TIP
For an alcoholic version, replace 150ml of the ginger beer with ginger wine.

Green Power Daiquiri

1 banana
Juice ¼ lime, plus extra slices to serve
25g baby spinach
30ml rice malt syrup

1. Slice the banana and freeze. When ready to serve, juice the lime and add to a blender with the banana.

2. Next add the spinach and rice malt syrup, then blend everything together. Serve in cocktail glasses, each garnished with a slice of lime.

Hands-on time: 5min
Serves 2

PER SERVING 105cals, 1g protein, 0g fat (0g saturates), 24g carbs (22g total sugars), 1g fibre

Hands-on time: 5min
Makes around 2 litres (serves 10)

PER SERVING 87cals, 0.5g protein, 0g fat (0g saturates), 21g carbs (19g total sugars), 0g fibre

4

Starters

Bresaola with Celeriac and Pear Remoulade

A quick-to-make dish that includes an update on a classic remoulade.

2 tbsp caster sugar
2 tbsp red wine vinegar
150g radishes, thinly sliced
1 celeriac (about 500g)
2 pears
Juice 1 lemon
100ml mayonnaise
200ml crème fraîche
1 tbsp wholegrain mustard
Small handful tarragon, chopped
24 slices bresaola
Rocket, to serve

1. In a small bowl, mix the caster sugar, vinegar and ½ tsp sea salt. Add the radishes and leave to pickle for 20min.

2. Peel the celeriac, then slice into thin matchsticks – use a mandoline or a julienne peeler, if you have one. Slice the pears into thin matchsticks and put both into a large bowl with the lemon juice and toss to coat. Mix the mayonnaise, crème fraîche, mustard and tarragon together before combining with the celeriac mixture. Season to taste.

3. Serve a spoonful of remoulade with 3 slices of bresaola per person, a few radishes, a sprinkle of black pepper and rocket, if you like.

★ GET AHEAD
Make the remoulade up to 3hr ahead, cover and chill.

Hands-on time: 15min, plus pickling
Serves 8

PER SERVING 262cals, 9g protein, 20g fat (8g saturates), 9g carbs (9g total sugars), 4g fibre

Wild Mushroom Soup with Cheddar Tuilles

This earthy soup is a perfect winter warmer. If you can't get hold of fresh, wild or exotic mushrooms, simply replace with more chestnut mushrooms. To make it vegan, swap the cream for a dairy-free alternative and serve with croutons.

FOR THE SOUP
15g dried wild mushrooms
1 tbsp olive oil
1 onion, finely chopped
1 garlic clove, crushed
200g mixed wild or exotic mushrooms, roughly chopped
600g chestnut mushrooms, roughly chopped
2 tbsp plain flour
1 tbsp minced black truffle/truffle paste
1.3 litre vegetable stock
100ml double cream, plus extra to garnish
1 tbsp truffle oil, to garnish (optional)

FOR THE TUILLES
½ tsp English mustard powder
15g plain flour
40g mature Cheddar, finely grated
40g butter, melted and cooled slightly
1 medium egg white

★ GET AHEAD
Make the tuilles up to 1 day ahead. Cool, then store in an airtight container at room temperature. Make the soup up to 3 days ahead, then cool, cover and chill. To serve, reheat the soup until piping hot, thinning with a little extra water or stock, if needed.

Hands-on time: 30min
Cooking time: about 40min
Serves 8

PER SERVING 256cals, 7g protein, 20g fat (11g saturates), 11g carbs (4g total sugars), 3g fibre

1. First, make the tuilles. Preheat oven to 190°C (170°C fan) mark 5. Line 2 large baking sheets with baking parchment. In a food processor, pulse the mustard powder, flour and most of the cheese (reserving some to sprinkle) until combined. Add the butter and egg white and pulse to mix.

2. Dollop 8 scant tablespoonfuls on to the baking sheets, spacing apart. Spread each into a 9cm circle with the back of a spoon. Sprinkle over the reserved cheese. Cook in the oven for 12min, until lightly golden. While warm, loosen each tuille with a palette knife and shape over a rolling pin to curl (or you can leave them flat). If they harden before shaping, return to the oven for 30sec to re-soften.

3. For the soup, put the dried mushrooms in a small heatproof bowl, pour over 100ml freshly boiled water from the kettle and soak for 20min. Heat the oil in a large pan over medium heat and cook the onion for 10min until softened. Turn up the heat to high and add the garlic and fresh mushrooms. Strain the soaked mushrooms (reserving the liquid) and add to the pan. Cook for 5min, or until the mushrooms have softened slightly.

4. Stir through the flour and truffle, add the stock and reserved soaking liquid. Bring to the boil, then simmer for 10min until thickened slightly. Blend until smooth; stir in the cream.

5. Divide among 8 warmed bowls, drizzle with cream and truffle oil, if using. Serve with tuilles.

Roast Tomato Soup with Herby Brioche Croutons

Basil is the classic partner for tomatoes in summer, but for a winter version rosemary works wonderfully well.

1.5kg plum tomatoes, halved
2 onions, thinly sliced
3 garlic cloves, crushed
3 rosemary sprigs
3 tbsp olive oil
2 tbsp sundried tomato paste (or 6 sundried tomatoes in oil, drained)
6 tbsp double cream

FOR THE HERBY CROUTONS
3 thick slices brioche
1 tbsp olive oil
1 garlic clove, crushed
1 tbsp finely chopped rosemary leaves

★ GET AHEAD

Prepare to the end of step 3 up to 1 day ahead. Cool, cover and chill the soup. Cool the croutons completely, then transfer to an airtight container. Warm the croutons briefly in a low oven and complete the recipe to serve.

1. Preheat oven to 200°C (180°C fan) mark 6. Put the tomatoes, onions, garlic and rosemary in a large roasting tin, drizzle with the olive oil and some seasoning. Toss gently to coat. Roast for 30min. Stir the vegetables gently and roast for a further 30–40min until tender and slightly charred. Remove and discard the rosemary stalks (don't worry about a few leaves).

2. Put half the vegetables and the sundried tomato paste/tomatoes into a liquidiser or food processor with 300ml freshly boiled water. Whizz until very smooth, then pour into a large pan. Whizz the remaining vegetables with a further 300ml freshly boiled water, then add to pan.

3. Make the croutons. Remove the crusts from the bread and cut into cubes. Toss the bread, oil, garlic, chopped rosemary and plenty of seasoning on a large baking tray. Cook in oven for 10min, or until golden, turning halfway through.

4. To serve, warm the soup through, stirring occasionally. Pour into warmed bowls, add 1 tbsp cream to each, then drag a cocktail stick through the cream to create a swirl. Top with the warm croutons and serve.

Hands-on time: 20min
Cooking time: about 1hr 20min
Serves 6

PER SERVING 314cals, 4g protein, 21g fat (9g saturates), 25g carbs (14g total sugars), 4g fibre

Roquefort, Leek and Walnut Tarts

Using ready-rolled puff pastry saves time, and the results are no less stunning for it.

375g pack ready-rolled puff pastry
40g butter, plus extra to grease
2 medium eggs
400g trimmed leeks, thinly sliced
2 tbsp chopped fresh chives
100g Roquefort, sliced into 6 triangles
75g walnuts, chopped

1. Preheat the oven to 200°C (180°C fan) mark 6. Unroll the pastry and cut in half lengthways, then cut each half into 3 squares. Using the tip of a sharp knife, score a smaller square 1cm in from the edge of each to make a frame.

2. Put the squares on a greased baking tray. Beat 1 egg lightly and brush over each pastry case, then chill for 10min. Bake for 10min or until well risen and lightly golden. Carefully lift off the top layers of each inner square and discard, then use a fork to scoop out any uncooked pastry from each centre.

3. Melt the butter in a frying pan, add the leeks and cook for about 10min or until they're soft. Beat the remaining egg and add to the leeks with the chives. Season. Divide the mixture among the pastry cases.

4. Put a slice of cheese on each tart and top with the walnuts. Return the tarts to the oven and bake for 10–15min or until golden.

Hands-on time: 25min, plus chilling
Cooking time: about 35min
Serves 6

PER SERVING (assuming 125g pastry discarded)
403cals, 11g protein, 31g fat (15g saturates), 18g carbs
(2g total sugars), 3g fibre

Duck and Blackberry Salad

Sliced duck breast, greens and toasted walnuts in a fruity dressing — this is a lovely starter.

4 skin-on duck breasts
40g walnuts
200g Tenderstem broccoli, trimmed
2 echalion shallots, finely sliced
10 juniper berries, crushed
4 tbsp moscatel vinegar or 2 tbsp red wine vinegar
½ tbsp runny honey
200ml chicken stock
150g fresh blackberries, halved or frozen blackberries left whole
100g lamb's lettuce or other leaves

1. Score the skin of the duck breasts in a criss-cross pattern using a sharp knife and making sure not to cut down into the flesh. Season. Place skin-side down in a large heavy-based frying pan. Turn heat on to low-medium and cook for 20min, spooning excess fat out of the pan regularly, until the skin is golden and crisp.

2. Meanwhile, preheat oven to 180°C (160°C fan) mark 4. Put the walnuts in a small roasting tin and toast in the oven for 8min. Set aside to cool. Blanch the broccoli in a large pan of boiling water for 2min, then drain and rinse under cold water and set aside.

3. Turn the duck and cook for 2min. Transfer to a shallow roasting tin (reserve the pan) and cook in oven for 6–8min for pink meat (cook for longer, if you prefer). Set aside to rest.

4. Spoon out all but 1 tbsp fat from the duck frying pan and return the pan to medium heat. Add the shallots and cook for 3–4min until just softened. Stir in the juniper berries, vinegar, honey and stock and simmer for 8min. Add the blackberries and simmer for 2–3min, until syrupy.

5. Divide the broccoli and salad leaves among 6 plates. Slice the duck and arrange on top. Spoon over the dressing and scatter with walnuts.

Hands-on time: 25min
Cooking time: about 35min
Serves 6

PER SERVING 303cals, 35g protein, 16g fat (3g saturates), 4g carbs (4g total sugars), 3g fibre

Layered Chicken and Pork Terrine

The overnight pressing helps make this zesty terrine sliceable. We stamped out festive shapes from our toasts to add a fun factor, but you could just cut into triangles.

½ tbsp olive oil, plus extra to brush
1 onion, finely chopped
1 garlic clove, crushed
2 tbsp brandy (optional)
12 smoked streaky bacon rashers
500g pork mince
50g dried apricots, finely chopped
5 sage leaves, finely sliced
2 skinless chicken breasts
40g pistachio kernals, roughly chopped
Finely grated zest ½ orange

TO SERVE
Fruity chutney or onion marmalade
Toasts

1. Heat the oil in a medium pan and gently cook the onion for 10min until softened. Add the garlic and fry for 1min. Carefully add the brandy, if using, and bubble for 30 seconds, then tip mixture into a large bowl and set aside to cool.

2. Preheat oven to 180°C (160°C fan) mark 4. Lightly stretch about 10 of the bacon rashers lengthways and use to line inside of a 900g loaf tin, leaving excess hanging over the sides (trimming to fit short sides if needed). Spoon a third of the cooled onions into a separate bowl. To the

remaining two thirds, add the pork mince, apricots, sage, ½ teaspoon salt and plenty of freshly ground black pepper. Set aside.

3. Next, whizz the chicken breasts in a food processor until finely ground. Add to the bowl with just onions in it and mix in the pistachios, orange zest and ½ teaspoon salt.

4. Press half the pork mixture into the base of the lined loaf tin, levelling the surface. Top with the chicken mixture in an even layer, then finish with the rest of the pork mixture, pressing to level. Fold any overhanging bacon over the filling, then cover with the remaining rashers. Press down again to make sure the surface is smooth. Lightly oil a small sheet of aluminium foil, then press on top of the loaf tin. Wrap the tin well in a further double layer of foil and put into a roasting tin.

5. Half-fill the roasting tin with boiling water, then carefully transfer to the oven. Cook for 1hr 30min until the terrine feels solid if pressed. Lift the tin out of the water. Unwrap the outer layers of foil (leaving the greased foil layer in place). Carefully discard liquid from the terrine. Leave to cool.

6. Sit the loaf tin on a baking tray, then sit three tins of tomatoes (or similar) on top of the terrine (resting on the foil layer). Chill overnight.

7. To serve, preheat oven to 190°C (170°C fan) mark 5. Unmould the terrine onto a baking tray and lightly brush with oil. Brown in oven for 25min (if you don't want it browned, omit this step). Serve warm or at room temperature with chutney and toasts.

Hands-on time: 40min, plus cooling and overnight chilling
Cooking time: about 2hr 10min
Serves 8

PER SERVING (without chutney/toasts) 305cals, 27g protein, 19g fat (6g saturates), 4g carbs (4g total sugars), 1g fibre

Tomato Sorbet

A surprising palate cleanser that refreshes without being overly sweet.

750g tomatoes on the vine (weight without vine)
½ tsp red wine vinegar

1. Cut a small cross across the top of each tomato, then drop into a bowl of freshly boiled water for 1min until the skins begin to come away. Lift out with a slotted spoon, leave to cool slightly, then peel off and discard the skins.

2. Halve the tomatoes, then whizz in a food processor until completely puréed. Add the vinegar and ¾ tsp salt, then churn in an ice-cream machine until almost frozen. Transfer to a freezerproof container, cover and freeze until solid. Alternatively, pour the tomato mixture into a freezerproof container and freeze until semi-frozen, whisk to break up any ice crystals, then freeze until solid.

3. To serve, soften at room temperature for 15min, then scoop into balls.

★ GET AHEAD
Freeze up to 1 month ahead. Complete the recipe to serve.

Hands-on time: 15min, plus churning and freezing
Serves 8

PER SERVING 19cals, 1g protein, 0g fat (0g saturates), 3g carbs (3g total sugars), 1g fibre

Saffron Prawns with Butternut Ribbon Salad

You will need a butternut squash with a long neck for this dish. Save the base for another recipe, such as soup or mash.

1 tbsp olive oil
2 garlic cloves, crushed
Pinch saffron strands
Pinch dried chilli flakes
3 tbsp runny honey
24 extra-large raw peeled king prawns, defrosted if frozen
Neck end of medium butternut squash, peeled (about 250g)
1 red chilli, deseeded and sliced into rings (optional)
2 handfuls mint leaves

FOR THE DRESSING
Juice 1 orange
1 tbsp olive oil
1 tbsp runny honey

YOU'LL ALSO NEED
8 short (18cm) metal or wooden skewers, soaked in cold
    water if wooden

1. In a bowl, mix the oil, garlic, saffron, chilli, honey, prawns and some black pepper. Thread the prawns on to skewers, arrange on a baking tray lined with foil and brush over any remaining marinade. Cover and chill until needed, up to 4hr ahead.

2. Whisk the dressing ingredients in a bowl with plenty of seasoning. Peel the butternut neck into ribbons using a Y-shaped peeler and add to the dressing bowl with the chilli, if using; toss to coat. Cover and chill for at least 30min, up to 4hr ahead.

3. To serve, remove the butternut from the fridge and preheat grill to high. Sprinkle the prawns with a little salt and grill for 7–9min, turning halfway, until cooked. Add the mint to the butternut and toss to mix, then divide among 4 plates and top with the prawn skewers. Serve.

★ GET AHEAD
Prepare the prawns and butternut to end of step 2 up to 4hr ahead and chill. Complete recipe to serve.

Hands-on time: 25min, plus marinating
Cooking time: about 10min
Serves 4

PER SERVING 162cals, 16g protein, 6g fat (1g saturates), 10g carbs (7g total sugars), 1g fibre

Gnudi with Browned Butter and Sage Pangrattato

Gnudi make a wonderfully light starter, similar to spinach and ricotta ravioli but without the pasta. Prepare them at least 8hr in advance – they're best made the day before you want to eat them.

500g ricotta
200g baby spinach
10 basil leaves
50g vegetarian Italian-style hard cheese, finely grated
¼ whole nutmeg, finely grated
150g semolina
150g unsalted butter
75g fresh white breadcrumbs
18 sage leaves

1. Put the ricotta in a sieve over a bowl and set aside for 20min to drain off excess liquid. Meanwhile, put the spinach into a colander in the sink and pour over a full kettle of just-boiled water to wilt (you may need to do this in batches). When cool enough to handle, lift up handfuls of the spinach and firmly squeeze out excess moisture, then pat dry thoroughly on kitchen towel.

2. Finely chop the spinach and basil and put into a large bowl. Mix in the drained ricotta, grated hard cheese, nutmeg and plenty of seasoning.

3. Sprinkle half the semolina over a baking tray. Dust your hands with some of the semolina, then roll the ricotta mixture into 18 golf ball-sized balls, placing them on the semolina tray as you go. Sprinkle the remaining semolina over the gnudi, and gently roll the gnudi/shake the tray to coat evenly in semolina. Chill, uncovered, for at least 8hr, or ideally overnight.

4. To serve, melt half the butter in a large frying pan over medium-high heat. Add the breadcrumbs, sage leaves and a pinch of salt and fry for 3–4min until the breadcrumbs are golden and the sage leaves starting to crisp. Tip on to a plate lined with kitchen paper.

5. In a large, wide pan of boiling salted water, cook the gnudi for 3–4min or until they start to rise to the surface. Meanwhile, return the frying pan to medium heat, add the remaining 75g butter and cook, swirling occasionally, until the butter is golden brown and smells nutty.

6. Using a slotted spoon, scoop the gnudi out of the pan and divide among 6 warmed plates. Spoon over the browned butter, then scatter with the breadcrumbs and sage. Serve immediately.

Hands-on time: 25min, plus (overnight) chilling
Cooking time: about 10min
Serves 6

PER SERVING 419cals, 14g protein, 33g fat (20g saturates), 17g carbs (2g total sugars), 1g fibre

★ GET AHEAD
Make the gnudi up to 48hr ahead. Chill, uncovered, turning them in the semolina roughly every 12hr.

Beetroot Prawn Cocktail

A colourful twist on a classic starter. Using a mix of cheaper cold-water prawns and larger king prawns helps keep costs down, while still ensuring everyone gets a generous helping of seafood.

FOR THE MELBA TOAST
4 medium slices sandwich bread, we used seeded (see GH Tip)

FOR THE PRAWN COCKTAIL
150g mayonnaise
100g tomato ketchup
1½ tbsp horseradish sauce
Finely grated zest 1 lemon and juice ½, keep separate
Few dashes Tabasco, to taste
200g cooked and peeled cold-water prawns, defrosted if frozen
200g iceberg lettuce, finely shredded
330g pack cooked beetroot (in natural juice)

TO SERVE
150g cooked and peeled king prawns
Few pinches cayenne pepper or paprika (optional)
Lemon wedges

★ GET AHEAD
Make the prawn mixture up to 1 day ahead. Cover and chill. Make the melba toast up to 3hr ahead. Set aside at room temperature. Assemble the cocktail up to 3hr ahead and chill.

1. For the melba toast, preheat grill to medium and arrange the bread on a baking sheet. Toast under the grill until golden on both sides. When cool enough to handle, use a serrated knife to remove the crusts, then slice each toast horizontally through its centre, creating 2 thin sheets. Next, slice each sheet in half diagonally. Return the triangles to the baking sheet, untoasted side up, and grill until golden. Set aside to cool.

2. For the prawn cocktail, in a medium bowl, mix the mayonnaise, ketchup, horseradish sauce, lemon zest and Tabasco to taste. Using kitchen paper, thoroughly pat the prawns dry, then gently stir into the sauce and check the seasoning. In a separate bowl, toss the shredded lettuce with the lemon juice.

3. Drain the beetroot, pat dry with kitchen paper and finely chop. Divide among 8 glasses or small bowls. Spoon over half the prawn cocktail and top with the lettuce, followed by the remaining prawn cocktail.

4. To serve, arrange the king prawns on top and dust with a little cayenne pepper/paprika, if using. Serve with the melba toast and lemon wedges for squeezing over.

Hands-on time: 30min, plus cooling
Cooking time: about 5min
Serves 8

PER SERVING 261cals, 11g protein, 16g fat (1g saturates), 17g carbs (9g total sugars), 3g fibre

★ GH TIP
Using seeded bread to make the melba toast adds extra flavour and crunch, but you could go classic and use white bread or wholemeal, if you prefer.

Smoked Mackerel Pâté with Rye Crackers

This pâté has a lovely green colour from the watercress, but parsley would make a good alternative.

FOR THE RYE CRACKERS
100g wholemeal rye flour
100g plain flour, plus extra to dust
1 medium egg

FOR THE PÂTÉ
100g butter
160g watercress
150g smoked mackerel fillets, skinned
250g Greek-style yogurt
Finely grated zest and juice 1 lemon

★ GH TIP
To make by hand, finely chop the watercress and the mackerel and add to a large bowl. Add the cooled butter, yogurt, most of the lemon zest, the lemon juice and seasoning. Mix well.

★ GET AHEAD
Once cool, store the crackers in an airtight container at room temperature for up to 3 days. Make pâté to end of step 4 up to 1 day ahead. Cover and chill.

Hands-on time: 30min, plus cooling
Cooking time: about 35min
Serves 6

PER SERVING (with 2 crackers) 396cals, 13g protein, 26g fat (13g saturates), 27g carbs (2g total sugars), 4g fibre

1. Preheat oven to 160°C (140°C fan) mark 3 and line 2 baking sheets with baking parchment. For the crackers, in a large bowl mix the rye and plain flours with ½ tsp fine salt. Make a well in the centre. In a jug, whisk the egg and 75ml water until combined. Pour into the flour well, stirring constantly until the dough comes together.

2. Tip on to a lightly floured work surface and knead for 5min, until you have a smooth dough. Re-flour the surface, then roll out the dough as thinly as possible (about 1mm), to a rough rectangle about 24 x 32cm.

3. Trim the edges to neaten, then slice into 12 equal rectangles. Transfer to the lined baking sheets, spacing a little apart. Bake for 25min. Carefully remove the sheets from the oven and flip each cracker over. Return to the oven for 10min more. Set aside to cool.

4. For the pâté, melt the butter in a small pan. Set aside to cool. Put the watercress in a food processor (see GH Tip) and whizz until finely chopped. Add the skinned mackerel, yogurt, most of the lemon zest (reserve some for garnish), the lemon juice, cooled butter and plenty of seasoning. Whizz until fairly smooth. Spoon into 6 individual ramekins or small bowls and spread to level. Chill until ready to serve.

5. To serve, sprinkle over the remaining lemon zest and some freshly ground black pepper. Serve with the rye crackers.

Pear, Candied Pecan and Blue Cheese Salad

A fruity, elegant salad that's sure to impress. Replace the blue cheese with goat's cheese, if you're not a fan.

FOR THE SALAD
4 tbsp runny honey
Large pinch saffron
Pared zest and juice 1 lemon
4 firm but ripe Conference pears, peeled, halved and cored
200g lamb's lettuce or watercress
200g Dolcelatte or other vegetarian soft blue cheese

FOR THE DRESSING
1 garlic clove, crushed
2 tsp Dijon mustard
2 tbsp sherry or cider vinegar
6 tbsp extra virgin olive oil

FOR THE CANDIED PECANS
1 medium egg white
1 tsp caster sugar
½ tsp cayenne pepper
200g pecan halves

★ GET AHEAD
Candy the pecans up to 1 week ahead, then cool and store in an airtight container at room temperature. Poach the pears up to 1 day ahead, then cool and chill in the poaching liquid. To serve, bring the pears back up to room temperature and complete the recipe.

Hands-on time: 20min, plus cooling
Cooking time: about 40min
Serves 8

PER SERVING 407cals, 8g protein, 35g fat
(8g saturates), 34g carbs (13g total sugars), 3g fibre

1. First make the candied pecans. Preheat oven to 190°C (170°C fan) mark 5 and line a baking tray with baking parchment. In a medium bowl, mix the egg white, sugar, cayenne and ½ tsp fine salt. Stir in the pecans to coat. Scrape on to the lined tray and spread to a single layer. Cook for 12–15min, until toasted and crisp. Cool completely on the tray.

2. For the salad, mix the honey, saffron, lemon zest and juice and 500ml water in a pan (that will later hold the pears snugly in a single layer). Heat gently, stirring to dissolve the honey. Add the pears in a single layer and lay a sheet of baking parchment directly on top to keep them submerged. Cook very gently for 15–20min, until just softened. Cool completely in the poaching liquid.

3. To serve, whisk the dressing ingredients with 2 tbsp of the poaching liquid and some seasoning. In a large bowl, toss the salad leaves with half the dressing and divide among 8 plates.

4. Drain the pears and cut each half into 3 wedges. Divide among plates and dot over the blue cheese. Spoon over the remaining dressing, sprinkle over the candied pecans and serve.

Charred Aubergine with Cashew and Red Pepper Sauces

The glaze for the aubergines is sticky, sweet and savoury all at once. If you can't find black rice vinegar, use balsamic vinegar instead.

3 medium aubergines
1 tbsp vegetable oil
3 tbsp black rice vinegar
2 tbsp white wine vinegar or apple cider vinegar
3 tbsp soy sauce
2 tbsp light muscovado sugar
2 tbsp caster sugar
Small handful chives, finely chopped

FOR THE RED PEPPER SAUCE
200g jarred roasted red peppers (drained weight)
½ tsp white wine vinegar or apple cider vinegar
1 tsp paprika

FOR THE CASHEW SAUCE
75g cashews
½ tsp white wine vinegar or apple cider vinegar

1. Preheat oven to 220°C (200°C fan) mark 7. Put the aubergines on a tray and prick each a few times with a fork. Roast for 50min, then carefully wrap each in clingfilm and leave to cool.

2. Meanwhile, whizz all the ingredients for the red pepper sauce and some seasoning in a blender. Empty into a serving bowl and set aside.

3. Next, put the cashews into a small pan, cover with water and bring to the boil, then simmer for 10min until tender. Drain well, then whizz in a clean blender with 75ml water, the vinegar and some seasoning until smooth. Set aside.

4. Heat a large frying/griddle pan over medium heat. Unwrap the aubergines and dry with kitchen paper. Brush with the oil and cook in the pan for 10min, turning frequently, until charred all over. Transfer to a board (reserve the pan).

5. Meanwhile, in a small pan over medium heat, mix both vinegars, soy sauce and both sugars until the sugars dissolve. Increase heat and bubble until reduced by half and thick. Set aside.

6. Slice the aubergines in half lengthways and return to the reserved pan over medium heat. Add the glaze and toss to warm and coat.

7. Place the aubergine halves on to 6 plates. Drizzle over the cashew sauce and garnish with chives. Serve with the red pepper sauce.

★ GET AHEAD
Prepare to end of step 5 up to 3hr ahead. Cover and chill the aubergines and sauces separately. Cover the glaze and set aside at room temperature. To serve, let everything come to room temperature. Melt the glaze in a large frying pan over low heat. Halve the aubergines; complete the recipe to serve.

Hands-on time: 30min, plus cooling
Cooking time: about 1hr 5min
Serves 6

PER SERVING 174cals, 5g protein, 9g fat (2g saturates), 18g carbs (15g total sugars), 4g fibre

Charred Leeks with Caesar Dressing, Crispy Prosciutto and Rye Croutons

A lighter take on a typically indulgent salad, this dressing uses kefir or buttermilk, which not only cuts down the fat without compromising on flavour, but also adds gut-friendly bacteria.

200g dark rye bread, cut or torn into rough 2cm pieces
1 tbsp finely chopped parsley, plus extra to serve
1 tbsp olive oil
4 prosciutto slices
12 baby leeks, trimmed and tough outer leaves removed
125ml kefir or buttermilk
½ small garlic clove, crushed
2 anchovy fillets in oil, drained and finely chopped
15g Parmesan, finely grated, plus extra to serve
1 tsp lemon juice, plus pared zest to serve

⭐ GET AHEAD
Prepare the leeks to the end of step 2 up to 1 day ahead. Cover with damp kitchen paper and chill. Cook the croutons and prosciutto and make dressing a couple of hours in advance. Store cooled croutons and prosciutto in an airtight container until needed. Chill the dressing but bring to room temperature before serving. Complete the recipe to serve.

1. Preheat oven to 200°C (180°C fan) mark 6. Toss the bread, parsley and ½ tbsp oil together with some seasoning on a baking tray. Arrange the prosciutto on top and cook in the oven for 12–15min, until both croutons and prosciutto are crisp. Remove from oven and leave to cool, then break the prosciutto into bite-size shards.

2. Meanwhile, blanch the leeks in a large pan of boiling water for 1–2min until just tender. Drain and transfer to a large bowl of ice-cold water to stop the cooking. Drain again, pat dry with kitchen paper and halve lengthways.

3. Whisk the kefir or buttermilk, garlic, chopped anchovies, Parmesan and lemon juice together in a small bowl. Season with freshly ground pepper.

4. Preheat a large griddle pan over high heat until smoking and brush the leeks with the remaining oil. Griddle the leeks for 2–3min per side until well charred (do this in batches, if needed). Divide the leeks among 6 plates, drizzle with the dressing and scatter over the croutons, prosciutto shards and a little extra Parmesan and parsley. Serve.

Hands-on time: 15min
Cooking time: about 20min
Serves 6

PER SERVING 161cals, 8g protein, 5g fat (2g saturates), 18g carbs (3g total sugars), 5g fibre

⭐ GH TIP
Omit the prosciutto and anchovies and swap the Parmesan for vegetarian Italian-style hard cheese to make this suitable for vegetarians.

Salmon Millefeuille

Cucumber jellies add a modern edge to this salmon terrine.

About 600g smoked salmon in long slices

FOR THE JELLY
1 cucumber, unpeeled
2 tbsp chopped fresh dill, plus extra to sprinkle
5 leaves gelatine
Juice ½ lemon
Oil, to grease

FOR THE FILLING
500g full-fat cream cheese
Finely grated zest and juice 1 lemon
150g hot smoked salmon, skinned and flaked

1. To make the jelly, trim the ends off the cucumber and roughly chop. Whizz in a food processor with the dill and 100ml water until the mixture is as smooth as you can get it, then empty into a pan. Submerge the gelatine in the mixture and leave to soften for 5min.

2. Heat the cucumber mixture, stirring occasionally, until the gelatine dissolves. Meanwhile, sit a sieve over a large jug and line with a layer of kitchen paper. Stir the lemon juice and a large pinch of salt into the cucumber mix. Strain through the sieve, allowing it to drip through. Set aside to cool.

Hands on time: 45min, plus cooling and (overnight) chilling
Cooking time: about 5min
Serves 8

PER SERVING (without toasts) 416cals, 27g protein, 34g fat (19g saturates), 1g carbs (1g total sugars), 0.3g fibre

3. Line a loaf tin or small serving dish with a double layer of clingfilm and lightly grease with oil. Pour in the cucumber mix and sprinkle with a little dill. Chill until set.

4. For the salmon millefeuille, put the filling ingredients into the (cleaned-out) food processor and whizz until smooth. Check the seasoning and set aside.

5. Line a 900g loaf tin with a double layer of clingfilm, making sure there is excess hanging over the sides. Add a layer of smoked salmon slices, overlapping them slightly to cover (leave some excess hanging over the sides of the tin).

6. Spoon in a third of the filling and level. Top the filling with a layer of smoked salmon. Repeat the layers twice more, ending with a smoked salmon layer. Fold the salmon hanging over the edge of the tin into the middle and cover with clingfilm. Chill for at least 5hr or ideally overnight.

7. Remove the top clingfilm from the salmon and invert on to serving plate. Lift off the tin and peel off the clingfilm. Invert the jelly on to a board and cut into 1.5cm cubes, then arrange around the terrine. Sprinkle with dill. Serve the terrine in slices (use a serrated knife), with jellies and toasts, if you like – we cut our toasts into Christmas tree shapes.

★ GET AHEAD
Make to the end of step 6 up to 1 day ahead. Complete the recipe to serve.

Ultimate Easy Chicken Liver Pâté with Cranberry Cointreau Jelly

You'll be amazed how easy a truly delicious and luxurious pâté is to make. This is best made a day ahead to allow the flavours to develop.

FOR THE CRANBERRY JELLY
2 sheets platinum-grade leaf gelatine
125ml cranberry juice
100g frozen cranberries
2 tbsp caster sugar
2 tbsp Cointreau

FOR THE PÂTÉ
50g butter
2 echalion shallots, finely chopped
800g free-range chicken livers
150ml double cream
2 tbsp Cointreau
Finely grated zest 1 orange
Toast, to serve

1. First, make the jelly. Cover gelatine with cold water and leave to soak for 5min. Meanwhile, heat the cranberry juice, cranberries, sugar and Cointreau in a small pan over medium-high heat, stirring until the sugar dissolves and cranberries soften, about 10min. Lift out the gelatine (squeeze out excess water) and stir into the hot cranberry mixture to dissolve. Set aside to cool while you make the pâté.

2. Melt half the butter in a large frying pan. Cook the shallots for 10–12min until soft and translucent. Meanwhile, pat the livers dry with kitchen paper, then trim and discard sinews or discoloured bits.

3. Transfer the shallots to a high-speed blender or food processor. Return the pan to medium-high heat and add half the livers. Cook for 5min, turning once, until browned, just firm to the touch and cooked through. Remove the cooked livers to a processor/blender with a slotted spoon or tongs and pour over the cream. Return the pan to heat and cook the remaining livers as before. Add the Cointreau, orange zest and remaining butter to the pan, bubble for 1min, then scrape into the processor/blender with 1½ tsp salt. Whizz until as smooth as possible, scraping down the sides occasionally (see GH Tip).

4. Divide the pâté mixture among 6 ramekins and smooth the surface to level. Chill for 30min to firm, then gently spoon over the cooled jelly mixture. Chill for at least 4hr, or ideally overnight, before serving with toast on the side.

★ GH TIP
For a completely silky-smooth pâté, push it through a sieve before putting into the ramekins.

★ GET AHEAD
Make up to 2 days ahead. Once the jelly has set, cover the ramekins and chill.

Hands-on time: 35min, plus cooling and (overnight) chilling
Cooking time: about 35min
Serves 6

PER SERVING (without toasts) 367cals, 24g protein, 23g fat (14g saturates), 9g carbs (9g total sugars), 1g fibre

Potted crab

Chilli and a dash of Worcester sauce give this simple starter a delicious kick!

200g white crab meat
½–1 red chilli, deseeded and finely chopped
1½ tbsp chopped chives, plus extra to garnish
Few dashes Worcestershire sauce
Zest and juice ½ lemon, plus lemon wedges to serve
250g unsalted butter
Few gratings fresh nutmeg
Bread and lemon wedges, to serve

1. In a medium bowl, mix the crab with the chilli, chives, Worcestershire sauce, lemon zest and juice. Check the seasoning. Divide equally among 4 ramekins.

2. Melt the butter in a small pan. Take off the heat, then spoon off and discard any surface scum. Pour the clear butter over the crab mixture, dividing it equally among the ramekins, and discard the milky whey in the bottom of the pan.

3. Sprinkle some nutmeg and extra chives on top of each ramekin. Cover and chill for at least 1hr.

4. Take the ramekins out of the fridge 10min before serving. Serve with bread and lemon wedges.

★ GET AHEAD
Make to the end of step 3 up to 2 days in advance. Complete the recipe to serve.

Hands-on time: 15min, plus chilling
Cooking time: about 5min
Serves 4

PER SERVING (without bread) 508cals, 11g protein, 52g fat (33g saturates), <1g carbs (<1g total sugars), 0g fibre

Sizzling Scallops with Pancetta and Sage

This superb starter will have your guests wondering where you've hidden the restaurant chef.

1 tbsp sunflower oil
150g cubed pancetta
6 sage leaves, finely shredded
18 scallops (with or without the coral), cleaned
Balsamic glaze, to garnish
1 punnet cress, to garnish

1. Heat half the oil in a large frying pan over a medium heat and fry the pancetta for 8min, until golden. Add the sage leaves and fry for 1min more. Tip the mixture and any oil into a bowl. Cover with foil to keep warm.

2. Pat the scallops dry with kitchen paper and season well with salt and pepper. Heat the remaining oil in the pancetta pan, turn up the heat to high and fry the scallops for 2-4min (depending on their size), turning halfway during cooking time – they should be lightly golden and feel springy when pressed.

3. Divide the scallops among 6 small plates, then spoon the pancetta mixture and any oil around them. Dot each plate with balsamic glaze and scatter over some cress. Serve immediately.

★ GET AHEAD
Fry the pancetta up to 1 day ahead, but do not add the sage. Tip into a bowl, cover and chill. When ready to serve, fry the pancetta for 2min to reheat, add the sage and complete the recipe.

★ GH TIP
You can fry the scallops as close together as you like – it helps them stay upright rather than tipping on to their sides.

Hands-on time: 15min
Cooking time: about 15min
Serves 6

PER SERVING 174cals, 11g protein, 14g fat (3g saturates), 0g carbs (0g total sugars), 0g fibre

5

The
Main Event

Herby Turkey Crown

Turkey crowns are simple to roast and carve, and delicious to eat. If it is off the bone, it will take longer to cook – allow an extra 20–30min.

4kg free-range turkey crown, on the bone if possible
2 large onions, skin on, thickly sliced
50g butter, softened
Finely grated zest 1 lemon
250g pack smoked streaky bacon
6 rosemary sprigs, broken into shorter lengths

1. One hour before cooking, remove the turkey from the fridge and weigh it, taking a note of its weight. Calculate the cooking time, allowing 30–35min per kg, plus 20–30min if the crown is off the bone. Scatter the onions in a roasting tin that will just fit the crown, then lay the turkey on top (breast up) and allow to come up to room temperature.

2. Preheat oven to 190°C (170°C fan) mark 5. In a small bowl, mix the butter, lemon zest and some seasoning. Spread over the top and sides of the turkey (using your hands is easiest). Next, cover as much of the top and sides as possible with bacon – a lattice pattern is nice (it will shrink on cooking). Tuck in the rosemary sprigs. Loosely cover the tin with foil.

3. Roast for the calculated time, basting occasionally (add a little water to the tin if the base is catching), removing the foil for last 30min of cooking. To check it's cooked, insert a fork into the thickest part of the breast and check the juices run golden and clear. If there's any red tinge, return the crown to the oven and keep checking every 10min. Alternatively, use a meat thermometer – the temperature needs to read at least 72°C when inserted into the thickest part of the breast.

4. Transfer the turkey to a board, cover with foil and then clean tea towels. Leave to rest in a warm place for at least 30min or up to 1hr before transferring to a warmed platter and serving in slices with our Easiest Get-Ahead Gravy (p185).

Hands-on time: 45min, plus coming up to room temperature and resting
Cooking time: about 2hr 20min
Serves 8, with leftovers

PER 125G SERVING (including 20g bacon) 261cals, 36g protein, 13g fat (6g saturates), 0g carbs (0g total sugars), 0g fibre

Thyme and Sherry-Glazed Turkey

If you prefer to stuff your bird, use our Pork, Apricot and Hazelnut Stuffing (p178), remembering to weigh your turkey stuffed to calculate cooking time. If you like, add any resting juices from the turkey to the Onion and Porcini Gravy (p183).

5.4kg free-range turkey, giblets removed
2 carrots, halved lengthways
2 large onions, cut into thick slices
2 clementines or satsumas, plus extra to garnish (optional)
Small handful thyme sprigs
50g butter, softened

FOR THE GLAZE
75ml dry sherry
3 tbsp marmalade
1 tbsp Dijon mustard

1. Remove the turkey from the fridge 1hr before cooking and remove any wrapping, giblets or trussing. Pat dry with kitchen paper and use tweezers to pull out any stray feathers. Allow the turkey to come up to room temperature. Weigh the turkey and calculate the cooking time, allowing 30–35min per kg.

2. Preheat oven to 190°C (170°C fan) mark 5. Put the carrots and onions into the base of a large sturdy roasting tin and sit the turkey on top (breast-side up). Halve 1 clementine and pop both pieces into the turkey cavity with half the thyme sprigs. Loosely tie the legs together with kitchen string.

3. Finely zest and juice the remaining clementine and mix with the softened butter, some seasoning and leaves picked from the remaining thyme sprigs (don't worry, it won't come together well). Rub all over the turkey and loosely cover the bird and tin with foil. Roast for the calculated time.

4. Meanwhile, make the glaze. In a small pan, heat the sherry and bubble for 3–5min to intensify. Add the marmalade and mustard, stirring to dissolve. Bubble for 2min, then set aside.

5. When the turkey has 45min cooking time remaining, remove the foil and brush glaze all over the bird (there should be some glaze left). Return the bird to the oven (without foil) and repeat the glazing after 20min.

6. To make sure the turkey is cooked, insert a fork into the thickest part of the breast and check that the juices run golden and clear. If not, return the bird to the oven and keep checking every 10min. Alternatively, use a meat thermometer – the temperature needs to be at least 72°C when inserted into the thickest part of the breast.

7. Transfer the turkey to a board, cover well with foil and lay over a couple of clean tea towels to help keep the heat in. Leave to rest in a warm place for at least 30min or up to 1hr 15min.

8. To serve, unwrap the turkey and transfer to a warm serving plate. Garnish with fried clementine halves. Serve with gravy and sides.

Hands-on time: 20min, plus coming up to room temperature and resting
Cooking time: about 3hr 15min
Serves 8, with leftovers

PER 125G SERVING (with 50ml gravy) 303cals, 40g protein, 13g fat (5g saturates), 5g carbs (3g total sugars), 1g fibre

★ GH TIP
Fried clementines look beautiful presented
with the turkey, but you could decorate it with
the stuffing balls or fresh herbs instead.

Stuffed Turkey Roll

This is a great alternative to an entire turkey, with a sweet and salty stuffing made from apple and chorizo.

Large skin-on turkey breast, about 2.3kg
25g butter, softened

FOR THE STUFFING
15g butter
2 shallots, finely chopped
125g soft cooking chorizo sausages
1 eating apple, peeled, cored and finely chopped
50g fresh white breadcrumbs
1 medium egg
Small handful parsley, finely chopped

FOR THE GRAVY
2 tbsp plain flour
200ml white wine
300–400ml chicken stock
1 tsp runny honey

1. To make the stuffing, melt the butter in a large frying pan over low heat and fry the shallots until softened, about 5min. Meanwhile, remove and discard the skin from the chorizo sausages and break them into small pieces. Add to the pan and fry for 5min until lightly golden and cooked through.

2. Stir through the chopped apple and fry for 1min, then remove from heat and allow to cool.

3. Preheat oven to 190°C (170°C fan) mark 5. Using your hands, remove the skin from the turkey breast and set aside. To butterfly the breast, put it in front of you on a board. Holding a large knife parallel to the board, make a horizontal cut along the length of the breast about 1cm up from the board – stop cutting just before you reach the opposite edge of the breast so the slices stay attached. Open out the meat, then repeat, cutting and opening it out again in the same way. Flatten the meat as much as possible to a rectangle of even thickness measuring about 30.5 x 33cm. This requires quite a few cuts in the same direction all over the meat; if needed, cut off bits and reposition them. If the meat is not an even thickness when finished, bash with a rolling pin.

4. Stir the breadcrumbs, egg, parsley and some seasoning into the chorizo mixture and press on top of the turkey. Roll up the meat in the same direction as the cuts, then wrap the reserved skin around the roll. Secure in place with lengths of knotted kitchen string. Weigh the rolled breast and calculate the cooking time, allowing 30–35min per kg. Put in a sturdy roasting tin just larger than the roll.

5. Rub the softened butter all over and roast for the calculated cooking time until cooked through – the temperature needs to be at least 72°C on a meat thermometer when inserted into the centre of the roll.

6. Transfer the roll to a board (set aside the roasting tin for the gravy), then loosely cover with foil and leave to rest for about 25min.

Hands-on time: 40min, plus resting
Cooking time: about 1hr 40min
Serves 8

PER SERVING 532cals, 89g protein, 14g fat (6g saturates), 8g carbs (2g total sugars), 2g fibre

7. For the gravy, spoon off most of the fat from the tin, then put the tin over medium hob heat and whisk in the flour. Cook for 1min. Whisk in the wine (scraping up all the sticky bits from the base of the tin) and leave to bubble for a few minutes. Whisk in the stock and leave to simmer, whisking occasionally, for a couple of minutes until thickened. Add the honey, then strain into a serving jug or clean pan to reheat when needed.

8. Serve the turkey roll in slices with the gravy.

★ GET AHEAD
Prepare to the end of step 4 up to 1 day ahead (don't preheat oven). Cover and chill. Complete the recipe to serve, allowing the meat to come up to room temperature for 30min before rubbing it with butter and roasting.

Turducken 3-bird Roast

The juniper and clementine-scented stuffing, together with the trio of meats, gives such delicious flavour to the roasting juices – you could even skip the gravy-making and simply serve it with the strained juices from the roasting tin.

4 boneless duck breasts
6 skinless boneless chicken thigh fillets (about 600g)
3kg boneless skin-on turkey crown
25g butter, softened
Bay leaves, to decorate (optional)

FOR THE STUFFING
400g pork sausages, skinned
75g fresh white breadcrumbs
Finely grated zest 2 clementines
Handful parsley, finely chopped
6 juniper berries, bruised and chopped
2 garlic cloves, crushed

FOR THE GRAVY
2 tbsp plain flour
200ml white wine
4 juniper berries, bruised
1 tsp runny honey

YOU'LL ALSO NEED
Kitchen string

★ GET AHEAD
Prepare to the end of step 5 up to 2 days ahead (do not preheat oven), then cover and chill. To serve, bring to room temperature for 30min before completing the recipe.

Hands-on time: 35min, plus resting
Cooking time: about 2hr 30min
Serves 10

PER SERVING 783cals, 111g protein, 32g fat (11g saturates), 11g carbs (2g total sugars), 1g fibre

1. Preheat oven to 190°C (170°C fan) mark 5. For the stuffing, mix all the ingredients with ½ tsp fine salt and plenty of freshly ground black pepper. Set aside.

2. Pull the skin off the duck breasts and set aside. Use a sharp knife to cut each breast in half through its depth. If the meat is not evenly thick, bash gently with a rolling pin. Trim excess fat and sinew from the chicken thighs, then bash gently with a rolling pin to an even thickness.

3. Lay 6–8 long pieces of kitchen string horizontally in front of you on a large board, spacing them 3cm apart. Lay the turkey crown skin-side down on top, with the breasts vertical. To butterfly the crown, using a sharp knife and, holding it horizontally and starting at the centre, cut into the left breast about halfway through its thickest part, slicing along the length. Stop cutting just before you reach the edge of the breast so that the slice stays attached. Open out the slice. Repeat the butterflying with the right breast.

4. Spread half the stuffing mixture over the turkey. Arrange the duck breasts on top in a single layer, then dot over half the remaining stuffing. Finally, arrange the chicken thighs in 2 parallel lines vertically down the centre and top with the remaining stuffing.

5. Gently roll/fold up the sides of the turkey crown over the stuffing to completely enclose it, using the string to help you. Tie tightly to secure. Weigh the joint and calculate the cooking time,

allowing 35–40min per kg. Arrange, seam-side down, in a sturdy roasting tin just larger than the roll. Add the duck skins to the tin.

6. Rub the softened butter all over the roll and season. Tuck a few bay leaves under the string, if you like. Loosely cover with foil and roast for the calculated cooking time or until cooked through, removing the foil for the final 30min. The temperature needs to read at least 72°C on a meat thermometer when inserted into the centre of the roll.

7. Transfer to a board (set aside the roasting tin for gravy), then loosely cover with foil and leave to rest for about 25min.

8. Meanwhile, make the gravy. Discard the duck skins and pour the contents of the tin into a jug. Allow to settle briefly so the fat rises to the top. Put the tin over medium hob heat, add 1 tbsp fat from the jug and whisk in the flour. Cook for 1min. Whisk in the wine and juniper berries (scraping up all the sticky bits from the base of the tin) and leave to bubble for a few minutes. Skim off any remaining fat from the jug (reserve it for roasting potatoes) and whisk 300ml of the juices into the roasting tin (top up with chicken stock if you don't have enough). Simmer for a couple of minutes, whisking occasionally, until thickened. Taste and add honey, if needed, then strain into a serving jug or pan (to reheat).

9. Serve the 3-bird roast in slices with the gravy.

Roast Goose with Ginger and Orange Stuffing

Roast goose makes a fantastic festive meal and will really wow your guests.

5.5–6kg oven-ready goose with giblets
2 oranges
6 bay leaves, plus extra to garnish

FOR THE GRAVY
2 onions
2 carrots
2 celery sticks, roughly chopped
2 bay leaves
A few thyme sprigs
2 heaped tbsp plain flour
3 tbsp ginger wine

FOR THE STUFFING
1 tbsp sunflower oil
2 onions, finely chopped
4 balls stem ginger in syrup, drained and finely chopped
200g fresh white breadcrumbs
450g good-quality sausage meat
3 tbsp finely chopped thyme leaves

FOR THE GINGER GLAZE
2 balls stem ginger in syrup, drained and finely chopped, plus 4 tbsp syrup from the jar
4 tbsp ginger wine

★ GET AHEAD
Prepare the stuffing, giblet stock and glaze up to 1 day ahead. Chill. Complete the recipe to serve.

Hands-on time: 45min, plus resting
Cooking time: about 3hr 40min
Serves 6

PER SERVING 986cals, 68g protein, 62g fat (20g saturates), 35g carbs (10g total sugars), 4g fibre

1. Set aside the giblets and neck from the bird. Take note of the goose weight. Preheat oven to 180°C (160°C fan) mark 4. Place the goose on a rack over a large, sturdy roasting tin and prick with a skewer a few times down each side just below the wing to help release the fat. Season. Finely grate the zest from the oranges and set aside for later. Cut the oranges into quarters and pop them into the goose cavity with the bay leaves. Cover the goose legs with foil. Roast for 30min per kg, plus an extra 20–30min if you like your goose well done.

2. While the goose is cooking, prepare the gravy, stuffing and glaze. Separate the liver from the rest of the giblets – it will be the large, softer one. Pat dry on kitchen paper and cut into small pieces, discarding any sinew. Set aside. Put the rest of the giblets in a big pan with the neck (roughly chopped), onions, carrots, celery, bay leaves, thyme and seasoning. Add 1 litre water, bring to the boil and simmer for 1hr 30min. Put a lid on the pan for the last 30min so the stock doesn't evaporate too much. Strain through a fine sieve into a jug.

3. For the stuffing, heat the oil in a large non-stick frying pan and fry the onions for 5min until softened. Add the liver and fry for a further 1–2min until browned. Tip into a large bowl, then cool. Add the remaining ingredients and reserved orange zest to the onions and liver. Season and mix well. Shape into 18 balls and place on a baking tray, cover and chill until ready to cook.

A lot of fat renders out of a goose while cooking. When you've finished, strain through a fine sieve, chill and freeze for a later date. Roast potatoes are fantastic cooked in goose fat. If you don't fancy making your own giblet stock, you can use shop-bought chicken stock.

4. To make the ginger glaze, put the stem ginger, syrup and ginger wine into a small pan and bring to the boil, stirring. Remove from the heat and set aside until ready to use.

5. After the goose has been cooking for 1hr 30min (or 2hr if you prefer your goose well done), remove from the oven and put on a board. Carefully drain the fat from the roasting tin into a large heatproof bowl (there will be a lot). Return the goose to the rack (over the roasting tin) and continue cooking for a further 1hr 30min, removing the foil after 30min.

6. To see if the bird is cooked, pierce the thickest part of the thigh with a skewer and check the juices run clear. Brush the goose with glaze and return to the oven for 5min until glossy and browned. Take out of the oven and increase the temperature to 200°C (180°C fan) mark 6.

7. Put the goose on a serving platter and cover loosely with foil and a tea towel and leave to rest for 20–30min. Spoon 3 tbsp of the reserved goose fat over the stuffing balls and cook in the oven for 20–25min, turning once, until golden brown and cooked through.

8. While the stuffing is cooking, make the gravy. Spoon off as much of the fat as possible from the roasting tin into the fat bowl. Place the roasting tin over medium hob heat and stir in the flour until combined. Slowly add 500ml giblet stock and bring to the boil, stirring constantly. Strain

the gravy into a medium pan and stir in the ginger wine. Bring to a simmer and cook for 2–3min, stirring regularly. Season to taste. Place the stuffing balls around the goose with a few bay leaves. Pour gravy into a warm jug and serve.

Spiced Pomegranate-glazed Duck

A delicately spiced and fruity alternative to turkey, ideal for smaller gatherings.

2.5–3kg whole duck with giblets
10 cardamom pods
½ tsp ground ginger
1 small orange, cut into quarters
2 whole star anise
½ pomegranate, seeds only (or 50g pomegranate seeds)
Handful mint leaves, shredded

FOR THE GIBLET STOCK AND GRAVY
2 tsp vegetable oil
1 large onion, cut into large chunks
2 carrots, cut into large chunks
2 celery sticks, cut into large chunks
2 garlic cloves, bruised and peeled
2 bay leaves
1 litre fresh chicken stock
2 tbsp plain flour
50ml pomegranate juice

FOR THE GLAZE
150ml pomegranate juice
2 tbsp runny honey
4 slices fresh root ginger, peeled and bruised (about 15g)

★ GET AHEAD
Make the giblet stock for the gravy up to 2 days ahead, then cool, cover and chill.

Hands-on time: 35min, plus resting
Cooking time: about 2hr 25min
Serves 4

PER SERVING 600cals, 59g protein, 31g fat (10g saturates), 20g carbs (13g total sugars), 2g fibre

1. Preheat oven to 200°C (180°C fan) mark 6. Remove the giblets from the duck and set aside. Weigh the duck and calculate the cooking time, allowing 20min per 500g, plus 15min. Put on a rack over a large, sturdy roasting tin and prick the skin all over with a fork to help release the fat. Pat dry with kitchen paper.

2. Using a pestle and mortar, bash the cardamom pods to break the husks, then pick out the seeds (discard husks). Grind the cardamom until fine, then mix in the ginger and 1 tsp each fine salt and freshly ground black pepper. Rub the spice mix all over the duck, then squeeze the juice from the orange quarters into the cavity. Pop the squeezed quarters and star anise into the cavity. Roast for the calculated cooking time.

3. Meanwhile, make giblet stock for the gravy. Heat the oil in a medium pan over medium heat and fry the giblets until lightly browned (about 3–4min). Add the onion, carrots, celery, garlic and bay leaves and fry for 2min. Pour in the stock and bring to the boil. Reduce heat and simmer gently for 1hr 30min (it should reduce quite a bit). Strain through a fine sieve into a jug.

4. To make the glaze, mix all the ingredients in a small pan and bubble gently over low heat for 10–12min until reduced and sticky. When the duck is nearly cooked, remove from oven, brush with the glaze (leaving the ginger in the pan) and return to the oven for the final 10min.

5. Put the cooked duck on a serving board or platter, loosely cover with foil and a tea towel (to keep the heat in) and leave to rest in a warm place for 20–30min. Spoon off all but 1–2 tbsp fat from the roasting tin into a bowl to discard. Put the roasting tin over medium hob heat and stir in the flour until combined. Slowly add 500ml of the strained giblet stock, stirring to scrape any sticky bits from the base of the tin. Bring to the boil, stirring constantly.

6. Strain the gravy into a medium pan and stir in the pomegranate juice. Bring to a simmer and cook for 2–3min, until thickened. Season to taste.

7. Sprinkle the pomegranate seeds and mint over the duck. Reheat the gravy and serve alongside.

★ GH TIP
Strain and save the fat from roasting the duck to use for roast potatoes.

Lemon, Pancetta and Tarragon Roast Chicken

The crispy pancetta topping will make this simple roast chicken a new favourite.

750g small waxy potatoes, halved
20g tarragon, roughly chopped
2 tbsp olive oil
50g butter, softened
2 cloves garlic, crushed
Zest and juice 1 lemon
1.4kg free-range chicken
12 pancetta slices
400g cherry tomatoes on the vine

1. Preheat oven to 200°C (180°C fan) mark 6. Toss the potatoes, half the tarragon, the oil and some seasoning in roasting tin large enough to hold the chicken with some space around it. Set aside.

2. In a small bowl, mix the butter, garlic, remaining tarragon, some seasoning and the lemon zest. Put the chicken on a board, remove any trussing, and pat dry with kitchen paper. Squeeze the lemon juice into the chicken cavity, then tuck the squeezed halves inside the bird. Lift up the neck flap and use your fingers to ease the skin gently away from the flesh along the length of the breast.

3. Spread half the flavoured butter mixture under the skin, all over the breast. Rub the remaining butter all over the bird. Sit it in the roasting tin, breast-side up, moving the potatoes to the sides. Lay the pancetta over the breast of the chicken and tie the legs together with kitchen string.

4. Roast for 40min, or until the legs are golden and the pancetta is starting to crisp. Turn oven down to 180°C (160°C fan) mark 4 and pour 100ml water into the tin. Roast for a further 40–45min, adding the tomatoes to the tin for the final 20min. A meat thermometer inserted into the thickest part of the thigh should read at least 75°C.

5. Cover the tin with foil and set aside to rest for 20min, before serving with the juices in the tin.

Hands-on time: 20min, plus resting
Cooking time: about 1hr 25min
Serves 4

PER SERVING 869cals, 52g protein, 58g fat (20g saturates), 33g carbs (6g total sugars), 5g fibre

Sloe Gin Ham

Fruity sloe gin adds a sticky sweetness to this glazed ham – a delicious, contemporary spin on the classic. If your gammon is tied, keep it this way during boiling for neatness. Remove the string for scoring and re-tie for glazing and roasting.

4kg whole boneless smoked/unsmoked gammon
1 litre apple juice
1 onion, sliced
2 bay leaves
1 cinnamon stick
20 or so peppercorns
40–50 whole cloves

FOR THE GLAZE
100g damson plum jam
50g granulated sugar
75ml sloe gin

1. Weigh the gammon, then put it into a large deep pan with the apple juice. Top up with cold water to cover, then add the onion, bay, cinnamon and peppercorns. Bring to the boil, then reduce the heat, cover and simmer for 25min per 450g until cooked through, skimming off the surface scum regularly (to reduce saltiness) if you'll be using the cooking liquor for stock at a later date.

2. Remove the ham from the cooking liquid and put on a board. Leave to cool for 15min.

3. Preheat oven to 220°C (200°C fan) mark 7. Untie the ham and use a knife to remove the skin, leaving a good layer of fat on the ham. Score a diamond pattern into the fat (not cutting down into the meat). Re-tie the ham (to maintain a better shape) and stud a clove into each diamond.

4. Line a roasting tin that will just fit the ham with a double layer of foil. Add the ham (fat-side up). In a small bowl, mix the glaze ingredients. Brush roughly a third over the meat and into the fat. Roast for 25–30min, basting with the rest of the glaze every 10min until the skin is caramelised. Serve warm or at room temperature in slices.

★ GET AHEAD
Finish up to 2 days ahead, then cool and chill (loosely wrapped in foil). Any leftovers will keep well in the fridge for up to 4 days.

Hands-on time: 25min, plus cooling
Cooking time: about 4hr 30min
Serves 8, with leftovers

PER 125G SERVING 283cals, 29g protein, 15g fat (5g saturates), 5g carbs (5g total sugars), 0g fibre

★ GH TIP
To serve, joint the birds into 8 as you would a chicken.

Hands-on time: 30min
Cooking time: about 2hr 30min
Serves 8

PER SERVING 368cals, 40g protein, 21g fat
(7g saturates), 6g carbs (5g total sugars), 3g fibre

Braised Guinea Fowl

The guinea fowl is cooked on top of red cabbage, which imparts a wonderful flavour.

2 tbsp rapeseed oil
2 oven-ready guinea fowl
150g smoked lardons
400g whole shallots, peeled
1 small red cabbage, cored and finely sliced
12 juniper berries, crushed
2 tsp dark brown sugar
1 tbsp red wine vinegar
2 fresh thyme sprigs
150ml hot chicken stock

1. Preheat the oven to 180°C (160°C fan) mark 4. Heat 1 tbsp of the oil in a hob-proof casserole large enough for both birds and brown the guinea fowl over a medium to high heat. Remove from the casserole and set aside.

2. Add the remaining oil and the lardons to the casserole. Fry gently to release the fat from the lardons, then add the shallots and cook over a medium heat until browned.

3. Add the cabbage and cook for 5min, stirring, until it has softened slightly. Add the juniper berries, sugar, vinegar, thyme and hot stock. Season.

4. Put the guinea fowl on top of the cabbage, then cover the casserole with a lid or double thickness of foil and braise in the oven for 1hr 30min. Remove the lid and continue cooking for 30min until cooked through – the juices should run clear when you pierce the thighs with a skewer.

5. Transfer the guinea fowl to a board and spoon the cabbage and juices on to a serving platter. Arrange the birds on top of the cabbage and serve.

Garlic Lamb with Chestnut and Tomato Relish

An impressive looking roast that cooks in under 30mins.

3 garlic cloves, crushed
3 racks of lamb, trimmed (around 900g; ask your butcher to do this for you)
1 tbsp Dijon mustard
75g pancetta, chopped
100ml extra virgin olive oil
175g cooked chestnuts, roughly chopped
75g sunblush tomatoes
2 tsp caster sugar
2 tbsp balsamic vinegar
4 tbsp chopped flat-leaf parsley

1. Preheat the oven to its highest setting – around 240°C (220°C fan) mark 9. Rub the garlic all over the lamb and spread the upper fat side with 2 tsp mustard.

2. Put the lamb racks into a shallow flameproof roasting tin just big enough to hold them and press the pancetta into the mustard – don't worry if a few bits fall off. Drizzle the lamb with 1–2 tbsp olive oil, then cook for 15–20min for medium, 20–25min for well done.

3. Remove the lamb from the oven, take out of the roasting tin and leave to rest in a warm place for 5min. Put the tin over gentle heat on the hob and stir in the chestnuts, tomatoes, caster sugar, balsamic vinegar and remaining mustard and olive oil. Stir briskly until mixed and heated through. Season to taste. Carve the lamb into cutlets and stir the parsley into the pan juices. Serve the lamb and sauce with mashed potato and green beans, if you like.

★ GET AHEAD
Prepare the lamb up to the end of step 1 up to 1 day ahead. Cover and chill. To serve, remove the lamb from the fridge 20min before cooking. Complete the recipe.

Hands-on time: 15min
Cooking time: about 25min
Serves 6

PER SERVING 429cals, 29g protein, 28g fat (8g saturates), 14g carbs (7g total sugars), 2g fibre

Lamb Crown with Couscous Stuffing

This is a roast with wow factor – a brilliant choice if you fancy a change from the traditional. Remember to order this crown roast in advance and ask your butcher to prepare it for you.

3-rack crown roast of lamb, at room temperature, fat removed
25ml olive oil
25g parsley
4 thyme sprigs, leaves picked
2 garlic cloves
1 tbsp wholegrain mustard

FOR THE STUFFING
Couple of pinches saffron (optional)
100g couscous
40g pine nuts
50g butter
1 small onion, finely chopped
2 garlic cloves, crushed
1 tsp dried mint
1 medium egg, beaten
50g dried figs, finely chopped
75g feta, crumbled
Pomegranate seeds, to garnish

★ GET AHEAD
Complete steps 2–4 up to 1 day ahead, but don't mix in the egg. Cover and chill. To serve, complete step 1, allow the stuffing to come up to room temperature before mixing in the egg, then complete the recipe.

Hands-on time: 45min, plus resting
Cooking time: about 40min
Serves 8

PER SERVING 571cals, 28g protein, 46g fat (21g saturates), 11g carbs (4g total sugars), 1g fibre

1. Preheat oven to 200°C (180°C fan) mark 6. Put the lamb on a baking tray. Into the small bowl of a food processor, put the oil, parsley (stalks and all), thyme leaves, garlic, mustard and some seasoning. Whizz until well mixed. Alternatively, bash the oil, herbs, garlic and seasoning in a pestle and mortar, then mix in the mustard. Rub over the lamb and roast for 25min.

2. Meanwhile, make the stuffing. Put the saffron, if using, into a bowl and cover with a little boiling water. Leave to soak for 5min. Put the couscous and saffron mix, if made, into a heatproof bowl and just cover with boiling water. Cover tightly with clingfilm and leave for 5min.

3. Dry heat a frying pan and toast the pine nuts until golden (watch them – they brown suddenly). Empty on to a plate. Return the pan to the heat with butter and onion and gently fry for 5min to soften. Add the garlic and fry for a further minute. Take the pan off the heat.

4. Fluff up the couscous with a fork. Mix in the onion, pine nuts, mint, egg, figs, feta and seasoning.

5. Carefully take the lamb out of oven and spoon the stuffing into the central cavity. Return to the oven for 15min for pink meat (longer if you like).

6. Carefully transfer the lamb to a board using a fish slice. Cover with a few layers of foil, leave to rest 20min. Sprinkle over the pomegranate seeds. To carve, slice between the bones to create cutlets.

Stuffed Lamb Saddle

The freshness of the salsa verde complements the rich lamb.

1.5kg boned saddle of lamb (ask your butcher to do this)
1 tbsp olive oil
Few thyme sprigs

FOR THE STUFFING
25g butter
1 small onion, finely chopped
2 garlic cloves, crushed
75g fresh white breadcrumbs
½ tbsp wholegrain mustard
100g goat's cheese round, crumbled
1 medium egg yolk
1 tbsp thyme leaves

FOR THE SALSA VERDE
2 tbsp capers, rinsed
25g mint, leaves picked
25g parsley
2 tbsp red wine vinegar
½ tbsp Dijon mustard
2 tbsp olive oil
Juice ½ lemon

YOU'LL ALSO NEED
Kitchen string

★ GET AHEAD
Prepare to the end of step 2 up to 1 day ahead (do not preheat oven). To serve, allow to come to room temperature for 30min, then complete the recipe.

Hands-on time: 20min, plus cooling and resting
Cooking time: about 1hr 5min
Serves 6

**PER SERVING 605cals, 58g protein, 36g fat
(15g saturates), 12g carbs (2g total sugars), 2g fibre**

1. First, make the stuffing. Heat the butter in a small pan over low heat and fry the onion for 10min until softened. Stir in the garlic and fry for 1min. Empty into a medium bowl and allow to cool. Stir in the remaining stuffing ingredients and some seasoning.

2. Preheat oven to 200°C (180°C fan) mark 6. Lay the lamb saddle on a board in front of you, fat-side down and with the fillets running vertically. Shape the stuffing into a sausage and lay vertically down the centre. Bring the sides of the lamb up and roll into a fat sausage. Tie along the length with kitchen string to secure in place.

3. Heat the 1 tbsp oil in a large frying pan over medium-high heat. Fry the rolled lamb until browned all over. Put into a roasting tin just large enough to hold it and slip a few thyme sprigs under the string.

4. Roast for 50min for pink meat (cook for longer if you prefer it more well done). Transfer to a board and loosely cover with foil, then leave to rest for 20min. Meanwhile, make the salsa. Whizz all the salsa verde ingredients with some seasoning in a food processor to make a chunky sauce.

5. Serve the lamb in slices with the salsa verde on the side.

Stilton and Thyme Stuffed Beef Rib

For sheer impressiveness, few things beat a magnificent rib of beef.

3-bone rib of beef, about 3.4–4kg, chine bone removed
Flaked sea salt, to sprinkle
3 red onions, cut into chunky wedges

FOR THE STUFFING
4 large echalion shallots (about 250g), finely chopped
3 tbsp thyme leaves, chopped
2 garlic cloves, crushed
1½ tbsp mixed peppercorns, crushed
1 tbsp Dijon mustard
125g Stilton, crumbled
75g fresh breadcrumbs
1 medium egg yolk

YOU'LL ALSO NEED
Kitchen string

★ GET AHEAD
Prepare to end of step 4 up to 1 day ahead (do not preheat the oven), put into the roasting tin, cover and chill. To serve, uncover and allow the beef to come to room temperature for 1hr before completing the recipe.

Hands-on time: 25min, plus cooling and resting
Cooking time: about 2hr 35min–3hr
Serves 8–10

PER SERVING (if serving 10) 965cals, 69g protein, 73g fat (33g saturates), 8g carbs (4g total sugars), 2g fibre

1. Heat a large frying pan over medium-high heat. Once hot, add the beef, fat-side down, and sear the outside for 5min until well browned. Set aside to cool slightly.

2. Meanwhile, make the stuffing. Pour off all but 2 tsp fat from the pan into a small bowl (reserve the fat) and return the pan to medium heat. Add the shallots and fry for 8–10min until softened and lightly golden. Stir in the thyme, garlic and crushed pepper and fry for 2min. Tip into a bowl, stir in the mustard and leave to cool.

3. Stir the Stilton, breadcrumbs, egg yolk and some seasoning into the stuffing mixture. Preheat oven to 220°C (200°C fan) mark 7.

4. Put the beef on a board with the ribs on the right-hand side and remove any string. Starting from the bone side, cut along the fat line that's about 3cm in from the outside edge of the meat, slicing around the central eye of the meat to make a flap for the stuffing (making sure to keep the flap attached at the base edge). Press the stuffing evenly over the eye of the meat. Lay the flap back over the stuffing and secure in place with string. Brush all over with a little of the reserved beef fat and sprinkle over some flaked sea salt and freshly ground black pepper. Weigh the stuffed joint.

5. Put the beef in a roasting tin just large enough to hold it and roast for 25min. Turn down temperature to 180°C (160°C fan) mark 4 and continue roasting for 15min per 500g plus 15min for rare beef (the internal temperature should reach 50–53°C on a meat thermometer) or a further 25min if you prefer it medium rare (internal temperature 54–57°C). Add onion wedges to the tin for the final 30min, turning gently in the fat before returning to the oven.

6. Once cooked, remove the beef from the oven, loosely cover with foil and leave to rest for at least 20min (or up to 45min). Sprinkle with a little extra flaked sea salt and serve with the roasted onions.

Rolled Stuffed Loin of Pork with Gravy

This showstopper is a bit fiddly but is worth it. The stuffing is filled with the festive flavours of dried cranberries, cloves, cinnamon and garlic.

3.8kg fillet end loin of pork, rind and bones removed and reserved (to give approx 2.2kg loin; see GH Tip)
450g thickly sliced streaky bacon

FOR THE MARINADE
250ml olive oil
125ml white wine or vermouth
2 tbsp Worcestershire sauce

FOR THE STUFFING
125g streaky bacon
2 onions, quartered
4 garlic cloves
1 tsp ground ginger
1 tsp ground cinnamon
½ tsp ground cloves
Handful parsley
1 tbsp olive oil
200g dried cranberries

FOR THE RUBIED GRAVY
200g cranberry sauce
1 tsp Dijon mustard
½ tsp Worcestershire sauce
250ml chicken stock
60ml ruby port

Hands-on time: 35min, plus (overnight) marinating and resting
Cooking time: about 2hr 35min
Serves 8–10

PER SERVING (for 10) 800cals, 49g protein, 54g fat (19g saturates), 26g carbs (23g total sugars), 2g fibre

1. To butterfly the pork, lay it on a board in front of you. Holding a knife parallel to the board, make a horizontal cut along the length of the fillet about 1.5cm up from the board – stop just before you reach the opposite edge of the pork, so it remains in one piece. Open out the fillet, then make further slices to flatten it (keeping it an even thickness). Put the marinade ingredients into a large freezer bag with ½ tsp salt and the pork. Chill overnight.

2. For the stuffing, put the bacon in a food processor with the onions, garlic, spices and parsley, then whizz. Heat the oil in a pan and fry the spiced mixture gently for 10min. Add the cranberries and cook for a further 5min. Cool completely.

3. Preheat oven to 200°C (180°C) mark 6. Vertically lay long pieces of string spaced 4cm apart on a sheet of baking parchment. Lay the bacon on top (overlapping the slices slightly) in a rectangle the same length as the pork. Shake the excess marinade off the pork and lay it, de-rinded-side down, on to the bacon. Spread the stuffing over the pork, leaving a 2.5cm border around the edge. Roll up the pork from a long side then, holding it in place and using the baking parchment to help, wrap the bacon around it. Secure with the string. Tuck in any meat or stuffing that pokes out.

4. Arrange the bones in a roasting tin and sit the pork on top. Cook for 2hr–2hr 15min until cooked through and a thermometer inserted in the centre reads at least 71°C. Halfway through cooking, place the scored rind in a separate shallow tin and sprinkle with salt. Cook alongside the pork on a separate shelf for 1hr.

5. Once the pork is cooked, rest it out of the oven, but leave the crackling in while you make your gravy. Put all the ingredients in a pan and bring to a boil, stirring to dissolve everything. Let it bubble for 5min until glossy but still runny.

6. Remove the string and cut pork into thick slices, about 2.5cm. Serve with the gravy and crackling.

★ GH TIP
Be sure to keep the bones and rind and ask the butcher to score it for you. You can also ask the butcher to butterfly the pork.

★ GET AHEAD
Stuff and tie the loin 1 day ahead, cover and chill. Rest for 20min at room temperature before cooking. Make the gravy up to 3 days ahead and keep covered in the fridge. Reheat in the pan to serve.

Perfect Roast Pork Belly and Apple Sauce

Guests will all want some of the crisp crackling on this rich pork, which is perfectly offset by the tart fruity sauce.

1.5kg piece pork belly
3 Bramley apples (about 350g), peeled, cored and roughly chopped
1½ tsp cider vinegar
1 sprig of thyme, leaves stripped
1½ tbsp caster sugar

★ GH TIP
If your crackling isn't as crispy as you'd like, remove the whole piece of crackling and preheat the grill to medium-high. Put the cracking on a baking tray and grill until crisp and puffed (watch carefully to avoid scorching, turning the tray to avoid any hot spots). Complete the recipe to serve.

★ GET AHEAD
Make the apple sauce up to 1 day ahead, then transfer to a bowl, cover and chill. Allow to come up to room temperature before serving.

Hands-on time: 15min, plus drying and resting
Cooking time: about 3h 30min
Serves 6

PER SERVING 684cals, 48g protein, 51g fat (18g saturates), 9g carbs (9g total sugars), 1g fibre

1. Using a small sharp knife, score lines into the skin of the pork (cutting into the fat) about 1cm apart, but not so deep that you cut into the meat. Pat the pork completely dry, then leave uncovered at room temperature to air-dry for about 45min.

2. Preheat oven to 220°C (200°C fan) mark 7. Rub lots of salt over the pork skin. Rest a wire rack above a deep roasting tin and put the pork skin-side up on the rack. Roast for 30min, then turn down the oven temperature to 170°C (150°C fan) mark 3 and continue cooking for 3hr – by this stage the crackling should be crisp and golden (if not, don't panic, see GH Tip).

3. Transfer the pork to a board and use a sharp knife to slice off the crackling in one piece (about the outer 2cm). Cover the pork meat loosely with foil and leave to rest for 30–40min.

4. Meanwhile make the apple sauce. Put the chopped apples in a medium pan with the cider vinegar, 3 tbsp water, thyme leaves and caster sugar. Bring to the boil, then cover and cook for 5–8min until the apples have softened completely. Mash with a wooden spoon to make a thick sauce, then season to taste (adding more sugar if you wish).

5. To serve, cut the crackling into 6 long strips, then cut the pork belly into 6 neat squares. Serve each square topped with a strip of crackling, the apple sauce and a selection of seasonal veg.

Fennel and Lemon Rack of Pork

This pork joint is special enough for experienced cooks, yet simple to master for those new to making a roast dinner.

Large handful curly parsley
1 garlic clove, roughly chopped
Finely grated zest 1 lemon
2 tsp fennel seeds
1 bay leaf
3 tbsp olive oil
8-rib pork rack (around 2kg; ask your butcher to scrape the bones and remove the fat for you)
1 onion, sliced thickly into rings
Sea salt

FOR THE GRAVY
1 tbsp plain flour
200ml cider
500ml hot chicken stock
1 tbsp quince or redcurrant jelly
1 tsp Dijon mustard

1. Preheat the oven to 240°C (220°C fan) mark 9. Put the parsley, garlic, lemon zest, fennel seeds, bay leaf and 2 tbsp oil into a food processor and whizz to make a paste.

2. Remove the butcher's string from the pork rack and, using a sharp knife, carefully cut away the rind in one piece, leaving behind the fat on the pork. Set aside. Rub the fennel paste over the fat, then replace the rind. Tie in place with 6–8 pieces of string. Weigh the pork and calculate the cooking time; allow 25min per 450g.

DF

Hands-on time: 20min, plus resting
Cooking time: about 2hr 30min
Serves 8

PER SERVING 320cals, 26g protein, 21g fat (7g saturates), 5g carbs (3g total sugars), 0.5g fibre

3. Keeping the onion rings intact, arrange them in the base of a roasting dish just large enough to hold the meat. Put the pork on top. Rub the rind with the remaining oil and sprinkle generously with sea salt. Roast for 30min, then turn down to 180°C (160°C fan) mark 4. Continue cooking for the calculated time until the juices run clear when you pierce the meat with a knife. Put the pork on a board, cover loosely with foil and set aside to rest – it will keep warm for up to 1 hour.

4. To make the gravy, discard the onion from the pan. Tip away all but 1 tbsp of the fat and put the pan on the hob over a medium heat. Sprinkle in the flour and stir, scraping up all the meaty bits stuck to the bottom – they contain lots of flavour. Take off the heat and slowly blend in the cider. Return to the heat and bubble for 2min, then add the stock. Simmer for 15min.

5. Stir in the jelly, mustard and any juices from the pork, then strain and check the seasoning. Pour into a warmed jug and take to the table.

6. Remove the string from the pork and slice between the bones with the crackling still attached. Divide among 8 plates and serve.

★ GH TIPS
• If the crackling softens under the foil, pop it under a high grill for 1–2min to crisp up – watch it closely.
• If you don't want to rest the pork for more than 30min, you can still make a gravy ahead of time. Transfer the joint to a clean pan 30min before the end of its cooking time, then put it back in the oven.

Wrapped Roast Monkfish with Champagne Sauce

Roasted on a bed of confit onions with a creamy Champagne sauce on the side, this is a luxurious main for fish lovers.

1 large monkfish tail (1.25–1.5kg), skinned and filleted
   to give 2 x 400–500g fillets (see GH Tip)
2 tbsp olive oil, plus extra to drizzle
2 tbsp finely chopped dill, plus extra to scatter
Finely grated zest ½ lemon
6–8 Parma ham slices
2 onions, halved and thinly sliced
2 garlic cloves
2 bay leaves
300ml hot chicken or vegetable stock
25g butter
1 echalion shallot, finely chopped
400ml Champagne
200ml double cream
2 tbsp baby (non-pareille) capers, drained
½–1 tsp sugar, to taste

YOU'LL ALSO NEED
Kitchen string

★ GH TIP
You'll need to go to a fishmonger for the monkfish, or order from one of the excellent suppliers online, many of whom will do the prep work for you.

Hands-on time: 35min, plus chilling
Cooking time: about 45min
Serves 4

PER SERVING 611cals, 43g protein, 41g fat (22g saturates), 8g carbs (7g total sugars), 2g fibre

1. Pat the monkfish dry with kitchen paper. Drizzle with a little olive oil, then scatter over the dill, lemon zest and some seasoning and rub to coat. Put a large piece of clingfilm horizontally on a work surface. Lay the ham slices vertically and side-by-side, overlapping the edges slightly, to make a rectangle just longer than 1 of the fillets.

2. Place the fillets across the bottom of the ham 'top to tail', so that there is a thick fillet end and a thin end together on both sides (adjust the ham if needed). Starting from the fish end and using the clingfilm to help you, roll up the fillets tightly in the ham, keeping the fillets together. Secure in place along the length with kitchen string. Wrap tightly in the clingfilm, twisting the ends like a cracker to seal and give a good shape. Chill until needed.

3. Preheat oven to 180°C (160°C fan) mark 4. Heat the oil in a large ovenproof frying pan or shallow casserole dish over low-medium heat. Add the onions and a pinch of salt and cook for 10min, stirring occasionally, until softened. Finely slice 1 garlic clove, add to the onions with the bay leaves and cook for 2min. Add 200ml stock, cover and bring to a simmer. Bubble gently for 10min, then remove from heat and season.

4. Melt the butter in a separate large non-stick frying pan over medium heat. Carefully remove the clingfilm from the monkfish. Fry the monkfish for 1–2min, turning gently, until lightly

browned. Transfer to the onion pan/casserole and roast for 12–15min, until the fish is cooked through and opaque. Remove and keep warm.

5. While the monkfish is cooking, make the sauce. Return the frying pan to low heat, crush the remaining garlic and add to the pan with the shallot. Cook gently for 5min until softened. Add the Champagne and remaining 100ml stock, bring to the boil and bubble until reduced by

half. Stir in the cream and bubble until reduced and the sauce coats the back of a spoon. Stir in the capers, some seasoning and the sugar, if needed.

6. Scatter some dill over the monkfish and onions and serve with the sauce on the side.

★ GET AHEAD
Prepare to the end of step 2 up to 1 day ahead and keep chilled. Complete the recipe to serve.

Salmon Coulibiac

This twist on the classic salmon en croûte makes an excellent prepare-ahead main. Fans of kedgeree will love the lightly spiced, herby rice.

5 medium eggs
Flour, to dust
750g all-butter puff pastry
750g skinless, boneless salmon fillet in one piece

FOR THE RICE
1½ tsp each cumin, coriander and fennel seeds
25g butter
2 echalion shallots, finely chopped
2 garlic cloves, finely chopped
1 star anise
5 cardamom pods, bashed
1 cinnamon stick
1 bay leaf
200g wild and basmati rice mix
Pinch of turmeric (optional)
500ml vegetable stock
Finely grated zest and juice 1 lemon
Small handful parsley, chopped
50g flaked almonds, toasted
1 tbsp capers, drained and roughly chopped

1. Put 4 of the eggs into a pan, cover with cold water and bring to the boil. Simmer for 6min exactly. Drain and cover with cold water, leave to cool, then peel.

2. Next cook the rice: toast the cumin, coriander and fennel seeds in a frying pan over medium hob heat for a few minutes until fragrant. Lightly crush using a pestle and mortar.

Hands-on time: 1hr, plus cooling, chilling and resting
Cooking time: about 1hr 30min
Serves 6

PER SERVING 983cals, 46g protein, 55g fat (27g saturates), 75g carbs (3g total sugars), 3g fibre

3. Melt the butter in the empty pan and gently cook the shallots, garlic, crushed toasted spices, star anise, cardamom, cinnamon and bay leaf for 10min until softened. Stir in the rice, turmeric (if using) and stock. Cover with a lid, bring to the boil and simmer for 20min. Turn off heat and set aside for 10min, until all the stock has been absorbed and the rice is fluffy and tender.

4. Spread on to a large plate or tray to cool quickly. When at room temperature, tip into a bowl (removing the whole spices and bay leaf). Using a fork, mix in the lemon zest and juice, parsley, flaked almonds and capers. Check the seasoning, cover and chill.

5. Lightly flour a work surface and roll out half the pastry to a rectangle a little larger than your fish, about 25 x 35cm. Transfer to a large sheet of baking parchment. Roll out the remaining pastry a little larger, about 30 x 35–40cm, and lay on another sheet of baking parchment. Stack in the fridge, covering with a final sheet of parchment. Chill for 30min (reserve the pastry trimmings).

6. Place the smaller pastry rectangle on a baking tray (still on its parchment). Spread over half the rice mixture, leaving a 4cm border all around. Top with the salmon. Halve the eggs lengthways and place cut-side down in a line down the centre of the salmon. Cover with the remaining rice mixture, pack it gently around the fish.

7. Preheat oven to 220°C (200°C fan) mark 7. Beat the remaining egg and brush it over the pastry border on the base. Lay on the larger pastry rectangle, pressing it gently into place and

sealing the edges. Trim the edges to neaten, then crimp using a fork. Brush all over with the egg. If you like, reroll the pastry trimmings and cut out decorations, lay them on top of your parcel and brush again with egg.

8. Cook for 15min, then reduce oven temperature to 190°C (170°C fan) mark 5 and cook for 40min more. Leave to rest for 10min, then transfer to a board to serve.

★ GET AHEAD
Prepare to the end of step 7 up to 1 day ahead, cover and chill. Complete the recipe to serve, cooking for an extra 5min if needed.

Smoked Salmon and Spinach Roulade

Make smoked salmon go further with this pretty main, served chilled or at room temperature, so there's no last-minute stress. You can leave out the prawns, if you like.

FOR THE ROULADE
400g frozen leaf spinach, defrosted
6 medium eggs, separated
40g plain flour
1 tsp baking powder
¼ tsp ground nutmeg
25g Parmesan

FOR THE FILLING
500g ricotta
Finely grated zest 1 lemon
2 tbsp finely chopped dill, plus extra to garnish
100g smoked salmon trimmings
100g cooked and peeled cold water prawns, defrosted if frozen

★ GET AHEAD
Assemble up to 1 day ahead, but don't garnish. Cover and chill. Complete the recipe to serve.

1. Preheat oven to 190°C (170°C fan) mark 5 and line a roughly 23 x 33cm swiss roll tin with baking parchment. For the roulade, lift handfuls of the defrosted spinach over the sink and squeeze out as much moisture as you can, then transfer to a food processor.

2. Add the egg yolks to the processor and whizz until the spinach is finely chopped. Scrape into a large bowl. Add the flour, baking powder, nutmeg, ½ tsp fine salt and plenty of freshly ground black pepper. Mix until combined.

3. In a separate large bowl and using a handheld electric whisk, beat the egg whites until they hold stiff peaks. Add a large spoon of the egg whites to the spinach bowl and mix in to loosen, then fold in the remaining whites, keeping in as much air as possible.

4. Scrape the mixture into the prepared tin and gently spread to level. Cook for 12–15min, or until firm to the touch and lightly golden. Meanwhile, lay a large sheet of baking parchment on a work surface and sprinkle over the Parmesan.

5. When cooked, invert the swiss roll tin on to the prepared baking parchment, remove the tin and allow the roulade to cool.

6. Meanwhile, make the filling. In a medium bowl, mix all the ingredients with some seasoning until combined.

7. Peel off the upper parchment from the roulade, then spread over the filling. With the help of the base parchment, roll up the roulade from a short edge. Transfer to a serving plate, seam down. Garnish with dill and serve.

Hands-on time: 30min, plus cooling
Cooking time: about 15min
Serves 6

PER SERVING 306cals, 26g protein, 19g fat (9g saturates), 8g carbs (3g total sugars), 2g fibre

Orange-roasted Zesty Salmon

A great-looking centrepiece that will serve a large group.

2 x 800g salmon fillets, skin on, small bones removed
3 tbsp extra virgin olive oil, plus extra for greasing
2 large oranges
300ml white wine
Finely grated zest and juice 1 lemon
40g hazelnuts, finely chopped and toasted
7 tbsp chopped mixed soft herbs, such as dill, parsley, chives, mint

FOR THE YOGURT DRESSING
200g Greek yogurt
3 tbsp good-quality mayonnaise
Zest of 1 orange
½ tbsp wholegrain mustard
1 tbsp finely chopped dill

★ GET AHEAD
Make the dressing as in step 1 up to 1 day ahead, but don't add the dill until ready to serve. Chill. Complete steps 2 and 3 up to 1 day ahead. Cool the salmon in the tin, then wrap and chill. To serve, bring to room temperature, then complete the recipe.

1. Mix together all the ingredients for the yogurt dressing, season and chill.

2. Preheat the oven to 200°C (180°C fan) mark 6. Line a roasting tin large enough to hold the salmon fillets snugly with foil. Lightly brush the foil with oil, then arrange the salmon fillets side by side in the tin, skin-side down.

3. Cut 1 orange into 10 wedges and nestle around the salmon. Pour over the wine and season to taste. Cover with foil, then roast for 15min or until the salmon is cooked through and flakes when pushed with a knife.

4. Meanwhile, finely zest and juice the remaining orange. Put into a bowl with the lemon zest and juice, hazelnuts, herbs and oil. Season and mix.

5. Serve the salmon warm or at room temperature topped with the herb mix and roasted orange wedges, with a bowl of yogurt dressing to dollop on the salmon.

Hands-on time: 20min
Cooking time: about 15min
Serves 10

PER SERVING 526cals, 36g protein, 35g fat (6g saturates), 5g carbs (5g total sugars), 1g fibre

Cured and Roasted Glazed Side of Salmon

As tasty as it is pretty, this beetroot-stained salmon can be cured for 8–24hr, depending on how much time you have.

1 skin-on side of salmon, boneless (about 850g)
300g raw beetroot
150g caster sugar
50g flaked sea salt
Finely grated zest 1 orange
Finely grated zest 1 lemon
Small handful dill, roughly chopped

FOR THE GLAZE
200ml cranberry juice
2 tbsp maple syrup
1 tsp wholegrain mustard
Finely grated zest ½ orange

TO SERVE
Small handful dill, roughly chopped

1. Put the salmon skin-side down in a large dish or tin (that will fit in the fridge). Wearing gloves, peel and coarsely grate the beetroot into a large bowl. Mix in the sugar, salt, orange and lemon zests and the dill. Press on to the salmon, then cover and chill for 8–24hr to lightly cure.

2. For the glaze, bubble the cranberry juice in a pan until reduced by half. Mix in the maple syrup, mustard and orange zest and bubble for 2min until slightly reduced and sticky. Set aside.

3. Preheat oven to 220°C (200°C fan) mark 7. Line a large baking tray with baking parchment. Rinse the beetroot mixture off the salmon under cold water and pat dry using kitchen paper. Transfer the salmon on to the lined tray, skin-side down. Brush over two-thirds

of the glaze (set the rest aside). Roast the salmon for 15–20min, until just cooked. To serve, brush over the remaining glaze and sprinkle with dill.

★ GET AHEAD
Make the glaze up to 1 day ahead. Cover and chill.

Hands-on time: 15min, plus (overnight) curing
Cooking time: about 30min
Serves 4

PER SERVING 516cals, 44g protein, 32g fat (6g saturates), 13g carbs (13g total sugars), 0g fibre

6

Vegetarian & Vegan Centrepieces

Root Vegetable and Lentil Terrine

This terrine is, unusually, served warm, which means it pairs perfectly with a vegetarian gravy.

50g butter, plus extra to grease
1 onion, finely chopped
300g sweet potatoes, peeled
300g parsnips, peeled and trimmed
2 garlic cloves, crushed
Small handful sage leaves, finely chopped
400g tin green lentils, drained and rinsed
100g cooked chestnuts, roughly chopped
50g dried cranberries
1 medium egg, beaten
2 tbsp Dijon mustard
75g pistachio kernels, roughly chopped
3 tbsp cranberry sauce

1. Grease a 900g loaf tin and line with a strip of baking parchment running along the length and up the short sides of the tin. Melt the butter in a large pan over medium heat. Cook the onion for 10min, until softened.

2. Slice the sweet potatoes and parsnips lengthways into 2mm slices – a mandoline is ideal for this.

3. Preheat oven to 190°C (170°C fan) mark 5. Stir the garlic and sage into the onion pan and cook for 2min until fragrant. Remove from the heat and leave to cool slightly before stirring in the lentils, chestnuts, cranberries, egg, mustard, most of the pistachios and plenty of seasoning.

4. Arrange a third of the potato slices in the tin, overlapping, with no gaps. Top with a third of the parsnips, then half the lentil mixture. Smooth to level. Repeat the layering, finishing with a layer of potatoes and parsnips. Cover the tin with foil.

5. Cook in the oven for 50min. Remove from the oven and invert on to a baking tray. Remove the tin and peel off the parchment. Return to the oven for 20min or until the sides and top are golden. Transfer to a warm serving plate or board, spoon over the cranberry sauce and sprinkle over the remaining pistachios. Serve in slices.

Hands-on time: 40min, plus cooling
Cooking time: about 1hr 25min
Serves 8

PER SERVING 245cals, 6g protein, 11g fat (4g saturates), 29g carbs (13g total sugars), 5g fibre

Nutty Apricot Filo Wreath

You can swap the nuts for whatever kind you fancy in this showstopper wreath. To make it vegan, omit the cheese or use a vegan alternative.

300g butternut squash, peeled, deseeded and cut into 1cm cubes
3 tbsp olive oil
250g baby spinach
150g halloumi, coarsely grated
50g pistachio kernels, roughly chopped
50g blanched hazelnuts, roughly chopped
50g dried apricots, roughly chopped
250g pack cooked mixed grains
7 large filo sheets, about 25 x 45cm each
75g fresh or frozen cranberries, defrosted if frozen
2 tsp sugar

TO DECORATE (optional)
1 tsp olive oil
Small handful large sage leaves

1. Preheat oven to 190°C (170°C fan) mark 5. On a baking tray mix the squash with ½ tsp olive oil and plenty of seasoning. Roast for 25min, turning halfway through, until tender. Leave to cool.

2. Put the spinach into a colander in the sink and pour over a full kettle of just-boiled water to wilt. When cool enough to handle, squeeze handfuls to release excess liquid. Roughly chop.

3. In a large bowl mix the halloumi, nuts, apricots, grains, spinach, squash and some seasoning.

Hands-on time: 30min, plus cooling
Cooking time: about 1hr 15min
Serves 8

PER SERVING 462cals, 9g protein, 18g fat
(7g saturates), 64g carbs (28g total sugars), 3g fibre

4. Put a large sheet of baking parchment in front of you, long side closest to you. Lay on a sheet of filo, long side closest to you, and brush with a little of the remaining oil. Lay a second filo sheet on top, with a short edge overlapping by 15cm (you should have a pastry rectangle about 25 x 75cm), and brush with oil. Repeat with 4 more filo sheet layers, putting them on top of the first 2 sheets and brushing with oil as before. Keep the rectangle as neat as possible.

5. Spoon the filling in a line along the bottom edge of the filo, leaving a 5cm border at either end. Fold the filo edges in over the filling. Starting at the bottom and using the parchment to help, roll up into a long sausage shape. Carefully bend into a ring, bringing the 2 edges together (don't worry if it tears). Transfer on the parchment to a baking tray; trim the parchment to fit.

6. Brush the remaining filo sheet with oil and slice into wide strips. Lay the strips over the filo ring, joining any cracks and tucking the ends under. Brush the remaining oil over the wreath.

7. Flatten the wreath a little with the palm of your hand. In a small bowl, mix the cranberries and sugar, then scatter on top of the wreath. Cook for 45–50min or until deep golden. Meanwhile, if decorating, heat the oil in a small pan over medium heat and fry the sage leaves for 2min or until crispy. Remove and drain on kitchen paper.

8. Carefully transfer the wreath to a serving plate or platter and top with the crispy sage, if made. Serve in slices.

⭐ GET AHEAD

Prepare the filling to the end of step 3 up to 1 day ahead. Cover and chill. Complete to the end of step 6 up to 2hr ahead. Wrap the tray tightly in clingfilm and chill. To serve, unwrap, brush with a little more oil and complete the recipe.

Cauliflower Cheese-topped Nut Roast

The topping adds a rich ooziness to this veggie centrepiece. Up the chilli flakes if you like things a little spicier.

FOR THE NUT ROAST
1 tbsp vegetable oil, plus extra to grease
1 onion, finely sliced
300g butternut squash (prepared weight), cut into
   1cm chunks
175g roasted red peppers from a jar, roughly chopped
50g mixed nuts, roughly chopped (we used pine nuts and
   blanched almonds)
2 medium eggs, beaten
100g cooked chestnuts, roughly chopped
100g fresh white breadcrumbs
75g Cheddar, grated
2 tsp dried mixed herbs
1 tsp dried chilli flakes

FOR THE CAULIFLOWER CHEESE
400g cauliflower florets
50g butter
50g plain flour
400ml milk
125g Cheddar, grated

★ GET AHEAD
Make and press the nut roast into the prepared tin up to 1 day ahead. Cover and chill. Make the cauliflower cheese up to 1 day ahead, then cool, cover and chill. Complete the recipe to serve, loosening the cauliflower mixture with a little milk, if needed.

Hands-on time: 40min, plus cooling
Cooking time: about 1hr 40min
Serves 8

PER SERVING 385cals, 16g protein, 23g fat
(11g saturates), 28g carbs (9g total sugars), 3g fibre

1. For the nut roast, heat the oil in a large frying pan over medium heat and cook the onion for 10min until softened. Add the squash and cook for 10min, stirring occasionally, until the squash is starting to soften. Tip into a large bowl and leave to cool slightly.

2. Preheat oven to 200°C (180°C fan) mark 6 and grease a 20.5cm round springform tin. Stir the remaining nut roast ingredients and plenty of seasoning into the squash bowl. Spoon into the prepared tin and press down to compact and level. Cook for 50min or until golden.

3. Meanwhile, make the cauliflower cheese. Cook the florets in a large pan of boiling water for 3–5min or until just tender. Drain well. Melt the butter in the empty pan over medium heat. Add the flour and cook, stirring, for 1min.

4. Remove the pan from heat and gradually stir in the milk to make a smooth sauce. Return the pan to the heat and cook, stirring, until bubbling. Remove from heat and stir in the Cheddar and some seasoning. Gently stir in the cauliflower.

5. Remove the nut roast from the oven and spoon the cauliflower cheese on top. Return to the oven for 30min, or until the topping is golden and bubbling. Leave to cool in the tin for 5min, then transfer to a cake stand or board. Serve in slices.

Spinach Roulade

An eye-catching offering that is served at room temperature, so no last-minute stress. Make sure you use cheese that is suitable for vegetarians.

400g baby spinach
6 medium eggs, separated
3 tbsp plain flour
1 tsp baking powder
¼ tsp grated nutmeg
40g vegetarian Italian-style hard cheese, plus extra to garnish

FOR THE FILLING
500g ricotta
3 tbsp chopped chives
1 red pepper, deseeded and finely chopped
25g chopped roasted hazelnuts, plus extra to garnish

1. Preheat oven to 190°C (170°C fan) mark 5 and line a rough 23 x 33cm Swiss roll tin with baking parchment. Empty the spinach into a large pan, add 50ml water and cook, stirring frequently, until the spinach wilts. Empty into a colander and cool under cold running water.

2. Lift out handfuls of the spinach and firmly squeeze out excess moisture. Put the spinach into a food processor with the egg yolks, flour, baking powder, nutmeg and some seasoning. Whizz until the spinach is finely chopped. Scrape into a large bowl.

3. In a separate large bowl, whisk the egg whites until they hold stiff peaks. Mix a third of the whites into the spinach bowl to loosen, then fold in the remaining whites, retaining as much air as possible.

4. Spread the mixture into the prepared tin and cook for 12–15min or until firm to the touch and lightly golden. Meanwhile, sprinkle the cheese over a large sheet of baking parchment on a work surface.

5. When cooked, invert the spinach tin on to the prepared baking parchment, remove the tin and allow the roulade to cool.

6. To make the filling, mix the ricotta, chives, red pepper, hazelnuts and plenty of seasoning.

7. Peel off the upper baking parchment from the roulade, then spread over the filling. With the help of the base parchment, roll up the roulade from one of the short edges. Transfer to a serving plate, seam-side down. Garnish with a sprinkle of cheese and hazelnuts. Serve.

Hands-on time: 40min
Cooking time: about 20min
Serves 8

PER SERVING 230cals, 15g protein, 15g fat
(7g saturates), 8g carbs (3g total sugars), 2g fibre

 GET AHEAD
Make up to 1 day ahead, but don't garnish. Cover and chill. To serve, allow to come up to room temperature, then complete the recipe.

Giant Savoury Mince Pie

We've taken inspiration from the sweet festive favourite for this veggie masterpiece. Swap the sage for fresh thyme, if you like.

FOR THE PASTRY
225g plain flour, plus extra to dust
115g unsalted butter, chilled and chopped
25g vegetarian Italian-style hard cheese, finely grated, plus extra, grated, to sprinkle

FOR THE FILLING
1 tbsp olive oil
2 onions, finely sliced
1 garlic clove, crushed
Small handful sage leaves, roughly chopped
250g chestnut mushrooms, finely sliced
180g pack cooked chestnuts, roughly chopped
50g dried cranberries
50g sultanas
50g pistachio kernels, chopped
2 medium eggs
75g full-fat cream cheese

1. First, make the pastry. Using a food processor, pulse the flour, butter, grated cheese and a pinch of salt until the mixture resembles fine breadcrumbs. Alternatively, rub the butter into the flour mixture using your fingers. Add 1 tbsp ice-cold water and pulse/mix until the pastry just comes together (add a little more water if mixture looks dry). Tip on to a work surface, shape into a disc, then wrap and chill for 30min.

2. Meanwhile, make the filling. Heat the oil in a large frying pan over medium heat and cook the onions for 10min, stirring occasionally, until softened. Add the garlic and sage and cook for 2min until fragrant. Turn up the heat to high, add the mushrooms and fry until golden and any liquid in the pan has evaporated (about 5min). Tip into a large bowl and allow to cool.

3. Lightly flour a work surface. Slice off two-thirds of the pastry (keep the rest wrapped and chilled). Roll out and use to line a 20.5cm round, 3.5cm-deep fluted tart tin. Trim excess pastry and prick the base all over with a fork. Chill for 10min.

4. Preheat oven to 190°C (170°C fan) mark 5. Add the chestnuts, dried fruit, pistachios, 1 egg, the cream cheese and plenty of seasoning to the onion bowl and mix to combine. Spoon into the chilled pastry case and level. On a lightly floured surface, roll out the remaining pastry to a rough 20.5cm circle. Using a small sharp knife, cut out a large star (see GH Tip). Using the base of a cake tin or a palette knife, lift the star and place it on top of the filling. Lightly beat the remaining egg and brush some over the star to glaze, then sprinkle over some extra grated cheese.

5. Cook for 35min or until the pastry is golden brown. Leave to cool in the tin for 10min before transferring to a serving plate. Serve in slices.

⭐ GET AHEAD
Prepare to the end of step 2 up to 1 day ahead. Cool, cover and chill the onion mixture. Complete the recipe to serve.

(V)

Hands-on time: 40min, plus chilling and cooling
Cooking time: about 55min
Serves 6

PER SERVING 503cals, 13g protein, 26g fat (13g saturates), 52g carbs (17g total sugars), 5g fibre

Whole Stuffed Celeriac

The earthiness of the mushrooms combined with the truffle oil makes this vegan dish mouthwatering. Meat eaters and vegetarians are sure to love it, too.

20g dried wild mushrooms
1 large celeriac (about 1kg; see GH Tip)
2 tbsp olive oil
1 echalion shallot, finely sliced
2 garlic cloves, crushed
100g chestnut mushrooms, sliced
150ml vegan white wine
2 tarragon stalks, leaves picked and roughly chopped
250ml dairy-free cream
100g baby spinach
1 tbsp truffle oil (optional)
25g cooked chestnuts, roughly chopped
15g pine nuts, toasted and roughly chopped
250g pouch cooked mixed grains
Pomegranate seeds, to garnish

1. Preheat oven to 200°C (180°C fan) mark 6. Put dried mushrooms in a heatproof bowl, cover with just-boiled water and soak for 20min.

2. Scrub the celeriac clean under cold running water, then pat dry with kitchen paper. Put in the centre of a large sheet of foil, rub all over with 1 tbsp oil and season. Wrap in the foil, place in a medium roasting tin and cook for 2hr or until tender, unwrapping the foil for the final 45min to allow the sides to become golden.

3. Meanwhile, make the filling. Heat the remaining oil in a large, deep frying pan over low heat and cook the shallot for 5min, stirring occasionally, until softened. Add the garlic and cook for 2min.

4. Increase heat to high, add the chestnut mushrooms and fry, stirring occasionally, until tender. Add the wine and bubble until reduced by half. Drain and roughly chop the soaked mushrooms, then add to pan with the tarragon, cream alternative, spinach (in batches if needed) and truffle oil, if using. Stir to wilt the spinach, then remove from heat and mix in the chestnuts, pine nuts, mixed grains and plenty of seasoning.

5. Remove the celeriac from the oven, transfer to a chopping board (discarding the foil) and leave to cool for 10min or until cool enough to handle. Cut off and discard the top 1–1.5cm of the celeriac, then use a spoon to scoop out the flesh, leaving a 1cm border and being careful not to break through the skin. Roughly chop the scooped-out celeriac and add to the mushroom mixture.

6. Return the hollowed-out celeriac to the roasting tin or a medium ovenproof serving dish. Fill with the mushroom mixture, spooning any extra around the sides. Cover the dish with foil and return to oven for 10–15min or until piping hot. Sprinkle over the pomegranate seeds to serve.

VN

Hands-on time: 30min, plus soaking and cooling
Cooking time: about 2hr 15min
Serves 6

PER SERVING 281cals, 7g protein, 14g fat (2g saturates), 22g carbs (6g total sugars), 11g fibre

★ GET AHEAD
Prepare to the end of step 2 up to 1 day ahead. Cool, wrap and chill. Complete the recipe to serve, allowing 40min in step 6.

⭐ GH TIP
If you can't find a large celeriac, use 2 smaller ones, roasting them until tender.

Chestnut and Artichoke En Croûte

Take the stress out of entertaining with this satisfying main course that can be made ahead.

100g spinach
50g butter
3 shallots, finely sliced
225g mixed mushrooms, roughly chopped (we used chestnut and shiitake)
3 garlic cloves, crushed
3 tbsp balsamic vinegar
100g cooked chestnuts, roughly chopped
4 thyme sprigs, leaves picked
150ml double cream
150g chargrilled artichoke hearts (drained weight), roughly chopped
Flour, to dust
500g block puff pastry
1 medium egg, beaten

1. Put the spinach into a colander. Slowly pour over a full kettle of freshly boiled water to wilt the leaves. When wilted, cool under cold running water. Lift out handfuls of the spinach and firmly squeeze out excess moisture. Roughly chop the spinach and set aside.

2. Melt the butter in a large deep frying pan over medium heat. Add the shallots and fry for 3min, stirring occasionally. Add the mushrooms and cook for another 3min, then stir in the garlic and balsamic vinegar and cook for 1min. Stir in the

Hands-on time: 35min, plus cooling and chilling
Cooking time: about 50min
Serves 6

PER SERVING 600cals, 9g protein, 43g fat
(27g saturates), 42g carbs (7g total sugars), 5g fibre

chopped chestnuts, thyme leaves and cream. Bring to the boil, then simmer for about 10min, or until there is barely any liquid in the pan.

3. Empty the mixture into a large bowl, stir through the spinach and artichokes and check the seasoning. Cool completely, then cover and chill for 1hr to firm up.

4. To assemble, dust a work surface with flour and roll out a third of the pastry to make a 14 x 30.5cm rectangle. Lay in the middle of a large baking sheet. Arrange the chilled filling on top in a large sausage – leaving a 2.5cm border of pastry all the way around. Brush the top of the visible pastry with some of the beaten egg.

5. Re-dust the work surface with flour and roll out the remaining pastry until large enough to cover the filling and base pastry. Lift into position, smoothing out any air bubbles and pressing the edges firmly to seal. Trim the edges to neaten (reserve the pastry trimmings), then crimp the edges or use the tines of a fork to press a seal between the layers.

6. Brush with more beaten egg. Thinly re-roll the trimmings and cut out festive shapes, if you like. Stick on to the pastry and brush again with egg. Chill for 30min.

7. Preheat oven to 200°C (180°C fan) mark 6. Cook for 25–30min until the pastry is deeply golden. Serve in slices.

GET AHEAD
Make to the end of step 6 up to 5hr ahead.
Complete the recipe to serve.

Luxury Vegan Wellington

Vegan food can often feel like an afterthought at Christmas, but not this recipe! There's so much flavour in this, and the pâté rivals any meat version.

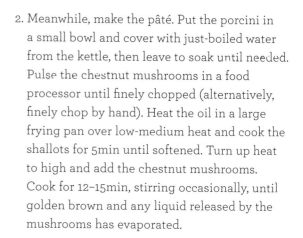

Neck end (1.1kg) of a large butternut squash (1.5kg), about 14cm long and 9cm in diameter
1 tbsp olive oil
2 x 320g sheets ready-rolled vegan puff pastry
Plain flour, to dust
Vegan cream or milk alternative, to glaze

FOR THE PÂTÉ
30g dried porcini mushrooms
800g chestnut mushrooms, roughly chopped
1 tbsp olive oil
2 echalion shallots, finely chopped
3 garlic cloves, crushed
½ x 25g pack thyme, leaves picked and chopped
50g dried cranberries
2 tbsp brandy (check the label to make sure it's vegan)
100g walnuts, roughly chopped
3 tbsp nutritional yeast flakes

1. Preheat oven to 200°C (180°C fan) mark 6 and line a baking sheet with baking parchment. Peel the squash neck and slice evenly in half lengthways. Lay cut-side down on a lined baking sheet and brush with oil. Season and roast for 40–50min or until just tender (you should be able to push a skewer through with just a slight resistance). Set aside to cool.

2. Meanwhile, make the pâté. Put the porcini in a small bowl and cover with just-boiled water from the kettle, then leave to soak until needed. Pulse the chestnut mushrooms in a food processor until finely chopped (alternatively, finely chop by hand). Heat the oil in a large frying pan over low-medium heat and cook the shallots for 5min until softened. Turn up heat to high and add the chestnut mushrooms. Cook for 12–15min, stirring occasionally, until golden brown and any liquid released by the mushrooms has evaporated.

3. Drain and finely chop the soaked porcini. Add to the mushroom pan with the garlic, thyme and cranberries, then cook for 2min. Add the brandy and bubble until there's no visible moisture in the pan. Remove from heat and stir in the walnuts, nutritional yeast and plenty of seasoning. Cool completely.

4. To assemble, unroll 1 pastry sheet on to lightly dusted baking parchment. Join the 2 butternut halves together again to make a single butternut 'fillet'. Spread half the mushroom pâté in the centre of the pastry in a rectangle just larger than the squash 'fillet', then sit the squash on top. Spread the remaining pâté evenly over the top and sides of the squash.

5. Brush the edges of the pastry with the cream/ milk alternative. Unroll the second sheet of pastry and lay over the filling, removing any air bubbles. Fold in the long edges of the pastry to join with the top sheet to create a sealed edge. Trim edges to 2.5cm, reserving the trimmings,

Hands-on time: 45min, plus cooling and chilling
Cooking time: about 1hr 40min
Serves 6

PER SERVING 731cals, 17g protein, 44g fat (15g saturates), 59g carbs (16g total sugars), 11g fibre

and crimp to seal. Brush lightly all over with the cream/milk alternative. If you wish to decorate the Wellington, re-roll the pastry trimmings very thinly, stamp or cut out the desired shapes and prick them all over with a fork. Stick on to the Wellington and brush with the cream/milk alternative. Chill for at least 30min (up to 24hr).

6. Reheat oven to 200°C (180°C fan) mark 6. Heat a sturdy baking tray on a low shelf of the oven for 10min. Brush the Wellington all over with

more cream/milk alternative and carefully slide on to preheated baking sheet (still on its parchment). Cook for 45–50min, or until the pastry is golden and crisp. Transfer to a serving board or plate and serve in slices.

⭐ GET AHEAD
Prepare to the end of step 5 up to 1 day ahead. Complete the recipe to serve.

Lentil and Sage Stuffed Aubergine

Tinned lentils and fresh veggies make for a thrifty yet delicious meat-free main.

1 large aubergine
1 tbsp vegetable oil
1 onion, finely chopped
2 garlic cloves, crushed
2 large tomatoes, roughly chopped
2 tsp dried sage
100g tinned green lentils, drained and rinsed
25g fresh white breadcrumbs

1. Preheat oven to 220°C (200°C fan) mark 7. Halve the aubergine lengthways and score the flesh in a criss-cross pattern with a small knife, taking care not to cut through the skin. Brush the cut sides with a little of the oil. Arrange cut-side up in a small roasting tin, cover with foil and cook for 20min or until the flesh has started to soften.

2. Meanwhile, heat ½ tbsp oil in a pan over medium heat and cook the onion for 5min until slightly softened. Add the garlic and cook for 2min. Stir in the tomatoes, sage and plenty of seasoning. Cook for 5min until the tomatoes have softened.

3. With a spoon, carefully scoop out the flesh from the aubergine (taking care not to tear the skin) and roughly chop. Stir into the tomato mixture together with lentils and spoon back into the empty aubergine skins.

4. Top with the breadcrumbs and some seasoning. Drizzle over the remaining oil and return to the oven for 25min or until breadcrumbs are golden.

⭐ GET AHEAD
Prepare to the end of step 3 up to 3hr ahead. Cover and chill. Complete the recipe to serve.

⭐ GH TIP
Add pine nuts or crumbled goat's cheese to the breadcrumbs for a change.

Hands-on time: 20min
Cooking time: about 45min
Serves 2

PER SERVING 204cals, 7g protein, 7g fat
(1g saturates), 24g carbs (11g total sugars), 10g fibre

Christmas Pie

The best Stilton matures at this time of year so it smells and tastes amazing in this stunning seasonal dish.

4 medium sweet potatoes, peeled and cut into
   2.5cm pieces
2 tbsp olive oil
5 rosemary sprigs
1 onion, finely chopped
Small bunch thyme, leaves picked
50g walnuts, roughly chopped
150g vegetarian Stilton, roughly crumbled
50g cranberries, fresh or frozen
Flour, to dust
500g block shortcrust pastry
1 medium egg, beaten

1. Preheat oven to 200°C (180°C fan) mark 6. Put the sweet potatoes in a roasting tin and drizzle over 1 tbsp oil. Add the rosemary and some seasoning. Roast for 20min or until just tender. Discard the rosemary sprigs and set the potatoes aside.

2. Meanwhile, heat the remaining 1 tbsp oil in a large pan and gently cook the onion and thyme for 5min to soften. Add the walnuts and cook for a couple more minutes. Take the pan off the heat and add the Stilton, cranberries and sweet potatoes. Check the seasoning and set aside.

3. Lightly flour a work surface, roll out two-thirds of the pastry and use to line a 20.5cm round springform cake tin. Fill with the sweet potato mixture and level the surface. Roll out the remaining pastry to make a lid. Brush the pastry border in the tin with the egg and cover with the lid, pressing gently to seal. Trim the edges to neaten and crimp. If you like, re-roll the trimmings and cut out shapes (we chose stars).

4. Brush the pastry lid with egg, stick on shapes (if using) and brush those with egg, too. Cut a small hole in the lid to allow steam to escape.

5. Cook in the oven for 40–50min until golden. Let stand for 5min, then carefully remove the pie from the tin and transfer to a stand to serve warm.

Hands-on time: 30min
Cooking time: about 1hr 15min
Serves 8

PER SERVING 524cals, 11g protein, 34g fat (13g saturates), 41g carbs (6g total sugars), 6g fibre

Pear and Blue Cheese Tart

Nut pastries can be tricky to handle, so this one is not rolled out but rather pressed into the tin. A small crack might appear after baking, but that's easily patched up and the flavour is worth the effort.

FOR THE PASTRY
50g walnut halves
200g plain flour, plus extra to dust
125g butter, chilled and cubed
1 medium egg

FOR THE FILLING
200ml double cream
200ml whole milk
4 medium eggs
150g vegetarian Stilton, crumbled
3 ripe pears

1. To make the pastry. Whizz the walnuts in a food processor until fine. Add the flour and butter and pulse until the mixture resembles fine breadcrumbs. Add the egg and pulse again until the mixture begins to clump together. Tip on to a work surface and bring together.

2. Press (don't roll) the pastry evenly into a 3.5cm deep, 23cm loose-bottomed fluted tart tin (keep a little pastry aside, wrapped, in case cracks appear in the pastry case on cooling). Chill for 30min.

3. Preheat oven to 190°C (170°C fan) mark 5. Line the pastry in the tin with a large sheet of greaseproof paper and fill with baking beans, pressing them gently into the flutes. Bake for 25min until the pastry sides are set and feel sandy. Carefully remove the paper and baking beans and set the tin aside while you make the filling. A couple of small cracks might appear in the pastry at this stage – just patch them up with the reserved raw pastry.

4. To make the filling. Lower oven temperature to 150°C (130°C fan) mark 2. In a jug, whisk the cream, milk, eggs and some seasoning. Scatter most of the Stilton into the base of the cooked pastry (still in the tin). Next, peel and halve the pears. Using a teaspoon, scoop out the cores. Place each half cut-side down on a board, and (leaving the tapered end of the pears intact), slice the fatter end into 5mm-wide strips.

5. To finish. Arrange the pear halves in the pastry on top of the Stilton. Press each gently to fan it out a little, then pour in the cream mixture. Scatter over the remaining Stilton. Crack over some black pepper and return the tart to the oven for about 50min or until the filling is set and golden. Allow to cool in tin for 10min before removing and serving in slices.

V

Hands-on time: 30min, plus chilling and cooling
Cooking time: about 1hr 15min
Serves 6

PER SERVING 719cals, 18g protein, 56g fat
(31g saturates), 34g carbs (10g total sugars), 4g fibre

⭐ GET AHEAD
Make to the end of step 3 up to 1 day ahead. Carefully wrap the cooled pastry (still in the tin) in foil. Complete the recipe up to 1hr ahead (to serve at room temperature).

Squash and Mushroom Lasagne

You can use 1 tsp dried sage instead of fresh, if you prefer. For added indulgence, sprinkle 75g torn mozzarella on top of the lasagne (making sure your cheese is vegetarian, if it needs to be) along with the hard cheese before cooking.

FOR THE FILLING
1 tbsp olive oil
1 onion, finely sliced
500g butternut squash (prepared weight), cut into rough 2cm chunks
200g chestnut mushrooms, roughly chopped
2 garlic cloves, crushed
Small handful sage, leaves picked and roughly chopped
½ tsp dried chilli flakes
400g tin chopped tomatoes
50g crème fraîche

FOR THE WHITE SAUCE
50g butter
50g plain flour
600ml milk
100g crème fraîche

TO ASSEMBLE
8 dried lasagne sheets
50g vegetarian Italian-style hard cheese, finely grated

★ GET AHEAD
Prepare to the end of step 4 up to 1 day ahead (no need to preheat oven). Cool, cover and chill. Complete the recipe to serve, cooking for 5min extra if needed.

Hands-on time: 30min
Cooking time: about 1hr 10min
Serves 6

1. For the filling, heat the oil in a large pan over medium heat and cook the onion for 10min until softened. Add the squash and mushrooms and cook for 10min, stirring occasionally, until the squash is starting to soften.

2. Meanwhile, make the white sauce. In a separate medium pan, melt the butter over medium heat. Add the flour and cook, stirring, for 1min. Remove the pan from heat and gradually stir in the milk and plenty of seasoning to make a smooth sauce. Return the pan to heat and cook, stirring, until thickened and bubbling. Remove from heat and stir in crème fraîche, then set aside.

3. Stir the garlic, sage and chilli flakes into the squash pan and cook for 2min until fragrant. Add the chopped tomatoes and plenty of seasoning. Remove from the heat and stir in the crème fraîche.

4. Preheat oven to 180°C (160°C fan) mark 4. Spoon half the tomato mixture into the base of a roughly 1.8 litre ovenproof serving dish and spread to level. Arrange 4 lasagne sheets on top and spread over half the white sauce. Repeat the layers once more, then sprinkle over the cheese.

5. Cook in the oven for 40–45min or until golden and bubbling. Serve.

PER SERVING 408cals, 11g protein, 23g fat (14g saturates), 38g carbs (10g total sugars), 5g fibre

Feta and Dolcelatte Cheesecake

Tangy, rich and exceedingly moreish, this savoury cheesecake is any cheese-lover's dream – and it's perfect for when you're hosting a crowd.

FOR THE BASE
75g unsalted butter, melted, plus extra to grease
150g digestive biscuits
100g walnuts
1 tsp thyme leaves

FOR THE FILLING
300g full-fat cream cheese
200g sheep's milk feta, crumbled (check it's vegetarian, if needed)
200g Dolcelatte
4 medium eggs, beaten
2 tbsp runny honey

FOR THE TOPPING
250g shallots, peeled and halved through the root
1 tbsp olive oil
250g red seedless grapes
6 thyme sprigs, plus extra to garnish
3 tbsp balsamic vinegar
2 tbsp runny honey

1. Lightly grease a 20.5cm round springform tin and line the base with baking parchment. For the base, whizz the biscuits, walnuts and thyme leaves in a food processor until crushed. Add butter and ½ tsp fine salt and whizz to combine. Press the mixture firmly into the base of the lined tin, levelling it with the back of a spoon. Chill while you make the filling.

2. Preheat oven to 140°C (120°C fan) mark 1. Wipe the food processor bowl clean. Add the cream cheese, feta and Dolcelatte and whizz until smooth. Add the eggs, honey, ¼ tsp fine salt and some freshly ground pepper and whizz again until combined. Pour into the tin and place on a baking sheet. Cover the tin with a foil.

3. Cook for 1hr 30min–1hr 45min, removing the foil for the final 15min, until golden with only a slight wobble in the centre when the tin is tapped. Leave the cheesecake to cool completely in the tin.

4. Meanwhile, make the topping. Turn up the oven to 200°C (180°C fan) mark 6. Toss the shallots and oil with some seasoning in a small roasting tin. Cover with foil and roast for 30min until just tender. Uncover, stir in the grapes and thyme sprigs and drizzle over the vinegar and honey. Return to the oven, uncovered, for 20min, until the grapes are starting to burst.

5. To serve, strain the juices from the roasted grapes and shallots into a small pan. Bubble vigorously over high hob heat until syrupy, about 5min, then mix with the shallots and grapes.

6. Transfer the cooled cheesecake to a cake stand or board. Top with the roasted grapes and shallots and drizzle over the warm reduced juices. Garnish with extra thyme sprigs and serve in slices.

Hands-on time: 30min, plus cooling
Cooking time: about 2hr 40min
Serves 12

PER SERVING 406cals, 12g protein, 31g fat (15g saturates), 18g carbs (13g total sugars), 2g fibre

⭐ GET AHEAD
Complete the recipe up to 1 day ahead.
Once cool, cover and chill the cheesecake
and topping separately. Allow both to come
to room temperature before serving.

White Nut Roast

You can also enjoy this as a wonderful stuffing for a vegetarian or turkey roast.

2 tbsp olive oil, plus extra to grease
200g pine nuts
100g blanched hazelnuts
2 onions, finely chopped
2 leeks, finely chopped
3 garlic cloves, crushed
250g fresh white breadcrumbs
Finely grated zest and juice 1 orange
3 tbsp chopped sage leaves
3 tbsp picked thyme leaves, plus extra sprigs to garnish (optional)
2 medium eggs, lightly beaten

1. Preheat the oven to 200°C (180°C fan) mark 6. Grease and line a 900g loaf tin with baking parchment. Next, pulse the nuts in a food processor until finely ground – don't overprocess, or they will become oily. Set aside.

2. Heat the oil in a deep frying pan and gently fry the onions and leeks for 10min until softened. Add the garlic and cook for 2min more. Empty into a large bowl and leave to cool.

3. Add the ground nuts, the remaining ingredients and some seasoning to the bowl. Mix well. Spoon the mixture into the prepared tin; press to level.

4. Cook in the oven for 1hr until golden and firm to the touch. Invert on to a serving plate, lift off the tin and peel off the baking parchment. Garnish with thyme sprigs, if you like, and serve in slices.

Hands-on time: 25min, plus cooling
Cooking time: about 1hr 15min
Serves 8

PER SERVING 423cals, 13g protein, 31g fat
(3g saturates), 21g carbs (6g total sugars), 4g fibre

Watercress Omelette Cake

This easily assembled veggie main can be served chilled or at room temperature – perfect for a Christmas buffet.

16 large eggs
5 tbsp chopped chives
2 tbsp vegetable oil
500g full-fat cream cheese
1 red pepper, deseeded and finely diced
50g watercress, chopped, plus extra to garnish

1. Beat the eggs in a large jug with 2 tbsp of the chives and plenty of seasoning. Heat ½ tbsp of the oil in a 20.5cm non-stick frying pan and pour in a quarter of the egg mixture. Swirl the pan to ensure the base is covered. Using a spatula, occasionally push the mixture in from the sides of the pan while it's cooking (but ensuring the base is always fully covered with egg). Cook for 2–3min until the underneath is golden, then flip the omelette and cook for a further 2–3min. Transfer to a plate to cool completely.

2. Repeat with the remaining oil and egg mixture to make 3 more omelettes (whisking the eggs before making each to redistribute the chives).

3. While the omelettes cool, mix the cream cheese, red pepper, watercress, remaining chives and some seasoning in a large bowl.

4. Line a 20.5cm cake tin with a double layer of clingfilm and place a cooled omelette in the base. Spread a third of the cream cheese mixture over the omelette (using the back of a spoon is easiest). Repeat the stacking and spreading twice more, then top with the remaining omelette. Cover with clingfilm and chill for at least 30min.

5. To serve, lift the omelette cake from the tin and peel off the clingfilm. Put on a serving plate or cake stand, garnish with watercress and serve in wedges.

⭐ GET AHEAD
Make to the end of step 4 up to 1 day ahead.
Complete the recipe to serve.

Hands-on time: 20min, plus cooling and chilling
Cooking time: about 25min
Serves 8

PER SERVING 455cals, 15g protein, 43g fat
(22g saturates), 1g carbs (1g total sugars), 1g fibre

Sprout, Fennel, Apple and Blue Cheese Tart

This impressive tart is full of sweet, salty, aromatic and bitter flavours, which balance perfectly. It's delicious served hot or cold.

50g butter
2 tbsp vegetable oil, plus extra to brush
200g Brussels sprouts, roughly sliced
1 garlic clove, crushed
2 thyme sprigs, leaves picked
1 fennel bulb, core removed, bulb chopped into 1.5cm slices (reserve the fennel fronds to garnish)
1 cooking apple, peeled, cored and finely chopped
3 large eggs
300ml double cream
6 sheets filo pastry
125g vegetarian Stilton, crumbled

FOR THE CARAMELISED WALNUTS
50g caster sugar
50g walnuts, roughly chopped

1. Preheat oven to 180°C (160°C fan) mark 4. Heat half the butter and half the oil in a large frying pan over low-medium heat. Cook the sprouts for 8–10min until soft. Stir through the garlic and thyme leaves, then cook for 1min more. Tip into a large bowl, return the pan to the heat and add the remaining butter and oil. Fry the fennel for 5min, then add the apple for a further 5min until turning golden. Add to the sprouts bowl.

2. Meanwhile, in a large jug, beat together the eggs, double cream and some seasoning.

3. Brush one side of each filo sheet with a little oil, then put oil-side down in a 20.5cm round fluted tin set on a baking sheet, overlapping the sheets and turning the tin to make sure the base and sides are covered (leave excess pastry hanging over the sides). Scrunch up the pastry edges into a ruffled crown. Spoon in the sprout mixture and sprinkle with Stilton. Pour in the cream mixture. Cook for 40–45min or until the filling is set.

4. Meanwhile, make the caramelised walnuts: in a small pan, gently heat the sugar with 50ml water. Once the sugar has melted, bring the liquid up to the boil, then simmer for 5min. Add the walnuts, bring back to the boil and bubble for 1min. Tip onto some baking parchment, discard excess syrup, and leave to cool.

5. Allow the tart to cool slightly, then remove from the tin. Serve warm or at room temperature, scattered with the caramelised walnuts and garnished with the fennel fronds.

Hands-on time: 20min, plus cooling
Cooking time: about 1hr 5min
Serves 6–8

PER SERVING (for 8) 501cals, 11g protein, 41g fat
(21g saturates), 21g carbs (10g total sugars), 4g fibre

Mushroom Wellingtons

Hearty lentil and mushroom fillings make these Wellingtons the perfect vegan or vegetarian main. Swap the green lentils for brown or Puy, if you like.

FOR THE WELLINGTONS
4 portobello mushrooms, stalks removed
1 tsp olive oil
Flour, to dust
2 x 500g blocks vegan puff pastry
Vegan milk alternative, to brush

FOR THE LENTIL FILLING
2 tsp olive oil
1 celery stick, finely chopped
1 echalion shallot, finely chopped
2 garlic cloves, crushed
2 tsp dried thyme or dried mixed herbs
1 tsp Dijon mustard
400g tinned green lentils, drained and rinsed
125ml vegan red wine

FOR THE SPINACH FILLING
1 tsp olive oil
1 echalion shallot, finely chopped
125g baby spinach

1. Preheat oven to 200°C (180°C fan) mark 6. For the Wellingtons, put the portobello mushrooms in a small roasting tin, gill-side up. Drizzle over the oil and season. Roast for 20min or until almost tender, then flip and roast for 5min more (this helps with evaporating some of the liquid). Set aside to cool completely.

Hands-on time: 45min, plus cooling and chilling
Cooking time: about 55min
Makes 4

PER WELLINGTON 595cals, 14g protein, 35g fat
(16g saturates), 47g carbs (2g total sugars), 7g fibre

2. For the lentil filling, heat the oil in a medium pan over medium heat and cook the celery and shallot for 10min, until softened. Stir in the garlic, dried herbs and mustard and cook for 2min. Stir through the lentils, wine and 100ml water. Increase the heat, bring to the boil and bubble hard for 10min until there's no liquid left in the pan. Check the seasoning, then set aside to cool.

3. Meanwhile, for the spinach filling, heat the oil in a medium frying pan and cook the shallot for 5min until softened. Add the spinach and some seasoning and fry, stirring, until wilted and any moisture has evaporated. Set aside to cool.

4. Lightly dust a work surface with flour and roll out the first pastry block until 3mm thick. Cut out 4 x 12.5cm rounds and place on a baking sheet lined with baking parchment.

5. Spoon 1 heaped tbsp of the lentil filling on to the centre of each round, leaving a 1.5cm border. Top with the mushrooms, gill-side down. (Trim the mushrooms if they don't fit within the filling circle.) Cover the mushrooms with the remaining lentil filling and top with the spinach.

6. Re-dust the work surface with flour and roll out the remaining pastry block as before and cut out 4 x 15cm rounds to make the lids (see GH Tip).

7. Brush the pastry borders on the bases with some vegan milk alternative, then lay the pastry lids on top to cover, working out any air pockets and pressing the edges to seal. Trim and crimp the edges with a fork, then chill for 20min.

★ GET AHEAD
Prepare to the end of step 7 up to
1 day ahead. Loosely cover and chill.
Complete the recipe to serve.

8. Preheat oven to 200°C (180°C fan) mark 6.
Brush the Wellingtons all over with vegan milk
alternative and cut a small steam hole into the
top of each. Cook for 25–30min or until golden
and puffed. Serve.

★ GH TIP
Re-roll the pastry trimmings, scatter over some
Cheddar or vegan cheese and paprika or caster
sugar and ground cinnamon. Roll up and slice into
pinwheels, then arrange on a lined baking sheet
and bake at 180°C (160°C fan) mark 4 until golden
and crisp. Serve warm or at room temperature.

Sweet Potato and Quinoa Crumble

The quinoa makes a delicious crunchy topping, while adding protein and keeping this dish gluten-free. Make sure to keep the sweet potato fairly chunky as this will give the crumble structure and texture.

900g sweet potatoes
3 tbsp oil
3 tsp ground cumin
2 tsp ground coriander
1 tsp ground cinnamon
500g leeks, trimmed and roughly sliced
1 red chilli, finely chopped, plus extra to serve
1 garlic clove, crushed
2 x 400g tins chopped tomatoes
Small bunch parsley, roughly chopped
Small bunch mint, roughly chopped
200g feta, chopped
75g pomegranate seeds

FOR THE CRUMBLE
300g cooked quinoa
75g butter, melted
100g unsalted pistachio kernels, roughly chopped
½ tsp ground cinnamon

⭐ GET AHEAD
Prepare to the end of step 2 up to 1 day ahead. Cool, cover and chill. Once ready to serve, preheat oven to 200°C (180°C fan) mark 6, bring the crumble up to room temperature and complete the recipe.

1. Preheat oven to 200°C (180°C) mark 6. Peel the sweet potatoes and chop into 2.5cm pieces. Put into a roasting tin, drizzle with 1 tbsp oil and sprinkle over 2 tsp cumin, the ground coriander and cinnamon. Toss to coat the potato, then roast for 25–30min until tender.

2. Meanwhile, in a medium pan, heat the remaining oil and fry the leeks for 10min until soft. Stir in the remaining cumin, the chilli and garlic and fry for 1min, then stir in the tomatoes. Simmer for 5min until thick. Stir in the sweet potatoes and most of the herbs. Transfer to a 2 litre baking dish and stir through the feta.

3. To make the crumble, mix the quinoa with the butter until the quinoa is nicely coated. Stir through 75g pistachios and the cinnamon. Scatter over the vegetables and cheese and bake in the oven for 25–30min until golden and hot. To serve, scatter over the remaining herbs and pistachios, the pomegranate seeds and extra chilli.

Hands-on time: 20min
Cooking time: about 1hr
Serves 6

PER SERVING 612cals, 17g protein, 34g fat
(14g saturates), 54g carbs (17g total sugars), 11g fibre

Pot Roast Cauliflower with Creamy Tomato Lentils

It's all too easy to overcook cauliflower, but slow cooking brings out its sweetness, which goes perfectly with the earthiness of Puy lentils. This makes a wonderful vegetarian alternative to a main course, but it also works well as a side dish to accompany a roast.

2 tbsp olive oil
2 large red onions, cut into thick wedges
5 garlic cloves
6 thyme sprigs, leaves picked
200ml vegetable stock
2 tsp fennel seeds
1 large cauliflower, leaves attached
500g cooked Puy lentils
100g sun-dried tomatoes in oil (drained weight),
    roughly chopped
3 tbsp 2%-fat Greek yogurt

⭐ GET AHEAD
Prepare to the end of step 2 a few hours ahead. Cover and keep at room temperature. Complete recipe to serve.

Hands-on time: 15min
Cooking time: about 1hr 40min
Serves 6

PER SERVING 285cals, 14g protein, 8g fat
(1g saturates), 34g carbs (13g total sugars), 10g fibre

1. Preheat oven to 180°C (160°C fan) mark 4. Heat 1 tbsp oil in a large casserole or deep ovenproof pan (that has a lid) and fry the onions for 8–10min until slightly softened. Slice 2 garlic cloves and add to the onions with the thyme leaves, then cook for a further minute. Season then stir in the stock.

2. Meanwhile, toast the fennel seeds in a dry pan over low-medium heat for 3–4min, until fragrant. Grind with a pestle and mortar. Crush the remaining garlic. Remove and discard any damaged or particularly tough outer leaves from the cauliflower. Rub the cauliflower with the remaining 1 tbsp oil, the ground fennel and crushed garlic, then season well and add to the pan on top of the onions.

3. Cover the pan with a lid and cook in the oven for 1hr 15min–1hr 30min, or until the cauliflower is tender when pierced in the middle with a knife.

4. Remove the cauliflower to a plate, cover with foil and keep warm. Stir the lentils and half the tomatoes into the pan and warm through over low hob heat for 5min.

5. Scoop out a ladleful of the lentils into a jug, add the remaining tomatoes and whizz with a stick blender until smooth. Stir back into the pan with the yogurt and warm through. Transfer to a serving dish and top with the cauliflower. Serve.

All the
Trimmings

CHOOSE YOUR VEG

Forked Roast Potatoes

Don't overcook the potatoes initially – you need them to soften just enough so you can mark them with a fork.

2.5kg floury potatoes, such as Maris Piper or King Edward
8 tbsp goose fat or olive oil
1 head of garlic, broken into cloves (still in skins)
3 bay leaves

1. Preheat oven to 190°C (170°C fan) mark 5. Peel the potatoes and cut into large, even-sized chunks (about 5cm). Put into a large pan, cover with cold water and bring to the boil over high heat. When the water boils, drain the potatoes into a colander and leave to steam dry until cool enough to handle.

2. Put the fat/oil into a roasting tin large enough to fit the potatoes in a single layer. Put into the oven to heat up for 10min.

3. Meanwhile, scrape the tines of a fork over each potato piece, marking them with stripes.

4. Carefully take the hot fat out of the oven. Add the potatoes, garlic, bay leaves and some seasoning. Turn the potatoes to coat in the fat. Roast for 1hr until golden, basting and turning occasionally. Transfer to a warm serving bowl.

★ GET AHEAD
Prepare to the end of step 3 up to 1 day ahead (no need to heat up the oil yet). Put the potatoes into a bowl, cover and chill. To serve, preheat oven and heat oil for 10min. Complete the recipe.

Hands-on time: 30min, plus cooling
Cooking time: about 1hr 10min
Serves 8

PER SERVING 345cals, 6g protein, 12g fat (4g saturates), 52g carbs (2g total sugars), 5g fibre

Squash and Kale Gratin

An unusual and comforting make-ahead side that works with any roast.

1 medium butternut squash
200g kale, shredded
100g butter, plus extra to grease
100g plain flour
200ml white wine
750ml milk
1½ tbsp English mustard
2–3 thyme sprigs, leaves picked

FOR THE CRUMB
50g fresh white or brown breadcrumbs
2 thyme sprigs, leaves picked
½ tbsp olive oil

1. Bring a large pan of salted water to the boil. Meanwhile, peel the squash and trim off ends. Slice off the neck of the squash just above the bulb. Slice this squash neck in half lengthways, then cut across each half to make 5mm-wide half moons. Next, slice the squash bulb in half lengthways. Scoop out and discard the seeds, then cut the flesh into similar slices to the neck. Set aside.

2. Cook the kale in the boiling water for 3–4min until just tender. Using a slotted spoon, lift out the kale into a colander set over a bowl. Set aside. Add the squash slices to the boiling water and cook for 4–5min until just tender. Drain.

3. Next, melt the butter in the empty pan, stir in the flour and cook, stirring, for 30sec. Take off the heat and gradually stir in the wine, followed by the milk. Return to the heat and cook, stirring, until thickened and smooth. Take the sauce off the heat, stir in the mustard, thyme and seasoning. In a small bowl, combine the crumb ingredients with seasoning. Set aside.

4. Preheat oven to 190°C (170°C fan) mark 5 and grease a large ovenproof serving dish. Squeeze out the excess moisture from the kale.

5. Spoon a third of the sauce into the base of the prepared dish, then top with half the squash pieces in an even layer. Scatter over half the kale. Repeat the layering again, topping with the remaining sauce. Scatter over the crumb mixture and cover the dish with foil.

6. Cook in oven for 45min, then remove the foil and cook for a further 20–30min until golden and piping hot. Serve.

V

Hands-on time: 40min
Cooking time: about 1hr 30min
Serves 8

PER SERVING 263cals, 7g protein, 14g fat (8g saturates), 23g carbs (7g total sugars), 3g fibre

★ GET AHEAD
Prepare to end of step 5 up to 1 day ahead, but keep breadcrumbs separate. Cover and chill separately. To serve, scatter the breadcrumbs over the gratin, re-cover with foil and complete the recipe.

Roasted Clementine Roots

A colourful side full of seasonal goodness.

4 carrots
4 parsnips
2 red onions, peeled
400g raw beetroot
2 tbsp olive oil
1 tbsp wholegrain mustard
3 clementines, unpeeled and quartered into wedges, or slice one orange into 8 wedges

1. Preheat oven to 190°C (170°C fan) mark 5. Peel the carrots and parsnips and cut into quarters or sixths lengthways, depending on size (trim to shorter lengths if you prefer). Put into a large roasting tin. Cut each onion through the root end into 6 wedges. Add to the tin.

2. Wearing gloves to prevent staining, peel the beetroot. Cut into similar-sized wedges to the onions. Add to the veg, toss in the oil, mustard, clementine/orange wedges and seasoning.

3. Roast for 1hr 15min, tossing occasionally, until the veg is tender and caramelised. Transfer to a large, warmed serving dish and serve.

★ GET AHEAD
Prepare to the end of step 2 up to 3hr ahead. Complete the recipe to serve.

Hands-on time: 15min
Cooking time: about 1hr 15min
Serves 8

PER SERVING 151cals, 3g protein, 4g fat (1g saturates), 21g carbs (15g total sugars), 9g fibre

Jewelled Sprouts

Pomegranate adds a fresh burst to rich Dolcelatte (suitable for vegetarians).

50g butter
2 shallots, finely sliced
500g sprouts
75–100g Dolcelatte, to taste
4 tbsp pomegranate seeds

1. Bring a medium pan of water to the boil. Meanwhile, heat the butter in a large deep frying pan and fry the shallots for 5min until tender.

2. Cook the sprouts in the boiling water for 3–5min until just tender. Drain well.

3. Turn up the heat under the shallot pan, add the sprouts and fry for 3–5min, turning, until the sprouts get some colour. Take the pan off the heat and mix through the Dolcelatte and some freshly ground black pepper. Empty into a warmed serving dish, sprinkle over the pomegranate and serve.

★ GET AHEAD
Prepare to the end of step 2 up to 1 day ahead, but cool the sprouts quickly under cold running water. Drain well. Transfer the cooled shallots and sprouts to a container, cover and chill. To serve, fry the mixture in large deep frying pan over medium-high heat until the sprouts get some golden colour. Complete the recipe.

Hands-on time: 15min
Cooking time: about 15min
Serves 8

PER SERVING 121cals, 4g protein, 9g fat (5g saturates), 4g carbs (3g total sugars), 4g fibre

Quick and Crispy Roast Potatoes

Once you realise the time you'll save by using tinned potatoes, you'll be converted! Swap the thyme for another herb, if you like.

---

4 tbsp olive oil
50g butter, chopped
900g tinned peeled potatoes (drained weight)
2–3 tbsp cornflour
4 thyme sprigs

1. Preheat oven to 190°C (170°C fan) mark 5. Once oven is hot, preheat oil and butter in a large roasting tin in the oven for 10min.

2. Meanwhile, rinse the potatoes in cold water, drain well, then pat dry with kitchen paper. In a large bowl, mix the potatoes, cornflour and plenty of seasoning, making sure the potatoes are evenly coated.

3. Carefully remove the roasting tin from the oven and add the potatoes and thyme to the hot oil and butter, turning to coat. Roast for 1hr, turning occasionally, until golden and crisp. Transfer to a serving dish and serve.

★ GET AHEAD
Roast the potatoes up to 4hr ahead. Once cool, cover and set aside at room temp. To serve, reheat in an oven preheated to 190°C (170°C fan) mark 5 for 10min, until piping hot.

Hands-on time: 15min
Cooking time: about 1hr 10min
Serves 6

PER SERVING 245cals, 2g protein, 14g fat (5g saturates), 26g carbs (1g total sugars), 2g fibre

Roasted Squash and Sprouts with Blue Cheese

We've left the skin on our squash as it adds a lovely texture, but feel free to peel it.

---

1 large butternut squash, around 900g
400g Brussels sprouts, halved
1½ tbsp olive oil
75g walnut halves
100g strong vegetarian blue cheese
100g pomegranate seeds

1. Preheat oven to 190°C (170°C fan) mark 5. Halve the squash lengthways and scoop out the seeds. Slice into a mixture of 2cm chunks and 1cm-wide wedges. Toss the squash, sprouts, oil and plenty of seasoning in a large roasting tin.

2. Roast for 30min or until starting to soften. Stir through the walnuts and return to the oven for 10min, until nuts smell toasty and vegetables are tender and starting to caramelise around the edges.

3. Transfer to a serving dish. Scatter over the blue cheese and pomegranate seeds. Serve.

★ GET AHEAD
Prepare to end of step 2 up to 4hr ahead, but don't add the walnuts. Cool, cover and set aside at room temperature. To serve, uncover, add walnuts and heat through in an oven preheated to 190°C (170°C fan) mark 5 for 10min. Complete the recipe.

Hands-on time: 20min
Cooking time: about 40min
Serves 6

PER SERVING 296cals, 10g protein, 19g fat (5g saturates), 18g carbs (11g total sugars), 8g fibre

Miso Butter Roast Potatoes

The miso adds umami depth and seasoning to these roasties. If you can't get hold of it, or for a cheaper alternative, use 2 tbsp Marmite instead.

2kg floury potatoes, such as Maris Piper
4 tbsp olive oil

FOR THE MISO BUTTER
3 tbsp olive oil
50g unsalted butter, softened
4 tbsp white miso paste

★ GET AHEAD
Complete steps 1 and 3 up to 1 day ahead. Cool, cover and chill. Complete the recipe to serve.

1. Preheat oven to 190°C (170°C fan) mark 5. Peel the potatoes and cut into large, even chunks. Put into a large pan (that has a lid) and cover with cold water. Cover and bring to the boil over high heat. Reduce the heat, uncover and simmer for 8–10min.

2. Meanwhile, pour the oil into a large roasting tin (or oven tray) that will hold the potatoes in a single layer. Heat in the oven for 15min.

3. Drain the potatoes well and leave to steam dry in a colander for 5min, then return to the empty pan. Shake to rough up their edges.

4. Carefully add the potatoes to the hot oil and turn to coat. Roast for 1hr, turning occasionally.

5. Meanwhile, mix all the ingredients for the miso butter in a small bowl until combined. Remove the potatoes from the oven, add the butter mixture and turn the potatoes to coat. Roast for 15min more, basting and turning once, until golden and crisp. Check the seasoning and empty into a warm dish. Serve.

Hands-on time: 20min, plus cooling
Cooking time: about 1hr 30min
Serves 8

PER SERVING 363cals, 6g protein, 15g fat (5g saturates), 48g carbs (3g total sugars), 5g fibre

Roasted Sprouts and Chantenay Carrots

An easy side that incorporates two Christmas classics. Swap the chorizo for bacon lardons, if you prefer.

500g Chantenay carrots, trimmed (see GH Tip)
2 tbsp olive oil
3 tbsp runny honey
1 tsp dried chilli flakes
500g Brussels sprouts, trimmed, large ones halved
125g chorizo, finely chopped

1. Preheat oven to 190°C (170°C fan) mark 5. On a large baking tray, toss the carrots, oil, honey, chilli flakes and some seasoning. Roast for 15min.

2. Add the sprouts and roast for 20min. Carefully remove the tray from the oven and stir through the chorizo. Roast for 10min more.

3. Check the seasoning and empty into a warm serving dish.

★ GET AHEAD
Trim the carrots up to 1 day ahead. Add to a bowl and mix in the oil, honey, chilli flakes and seasoning. Cover and chill. To serve, tip on to a large baking tray and complete the recipe.

★ GH TIP
Replace the Chantenay carrots with regular ones, if you prefer, scrubbed and cut into short lengths.

Hands-on time: 10min
Cooking time: about 45min
Serves 8

PER SERVING 165cals, 6g protein, 9g fat (3g saturates), 12g carbs (11g total sugars), 6g fibre

Baked Onions

If you can't get small onions, use 4 large ones instead (they will need a little longer in the oven) and halve to serve. Swap the wine for cider, if you prefer.

8 small red onions, peeled
50g butter
Small handful sage leaves, roughly chopped
50g dried breadcrumbs
1 tbsp plain flour
250ml vegetable stock
150ml white wine
3 tbsp double cream

★ MAKE IT VEGAN
Swap the butter and cream for dairy-free alternatives. Check that your wine and stock are vegan, too.

★ GET AHEAD
Prepare to the end of step 2 up to 1 day ahead (don't preheat oven). Cover and chill. Complete the recipe to serve.

1. Preheat oven to 190°C (170°C fan) mark 5. Slice the top and bottom off the onions, just so they sit flat. Using a teaspoon, scoop out the middle of each onion so you are left with a shell about 2 layers thick. Arrange the onion shells in an ovenproof dish and set aside. Roughly chop the scooped-out onion flesh.

2. Melt 25g butter in a medium pan over medium heat. Add the chopped onion and cook for 10min until softened. Stir in the sage and cook for 2min until fragrant. Remove from the heat and stir in the breadcrumbs and a little seasoning. Spoon the mixture into the onion shells, packing it down slightly to fit.

3. Return the pan to the heat and melt the remaining 25g butter. Stir in the flour and cook for 1min. Remove the pan from the heat and gradually mix in the stock, wine, cream and plenty of seasoning to make a smooth sauce. Return to the heat and cook, stirring constantly, until thickened. Check the seasoning, then pour the sauce around the onions.

4. Cover the dish with foil and cook in the oven for 1hr or until the onions are tender, removing the foil for the final 15min. Serve.

Hands-on time: 30min
Cooking time: about 1hr 20min
Serves 8

PER SERVING 155cals, 2g protein, 9g fat (5g saturates), 14g carbs (7g total sugars), 2g fibre

Spiced Carrots and Green Beans

Two side dishes in one. You could swap the carrots for parsnips, if you prefer.

125g unsalted butter, softened
Finely grated zest 1 orange
½ tsp ground cinnamon
¼ tsp ground cloves
¼ tsp freshly grated nutmeg
500g carrots
300g green beans, trimmed

1. Preheat oven to 190°C (170°C fan) mark 5. In a small bowl, mix the butter, orange zest, spices and plenty of seasoning.

2. Cut the carrots into quarters lengthways, then cut them in half to make shorter lengths. Put into a medium roasting tin with the beans and flavoured butter. Using your hands, mix to evenly coat the veg. Cover the tin with foil.

3. Roast for 30min, then remove the foil and stir gently. Re-cover with the foil and return to the oven for 30min until the veg are tender. Transfer to a warmed serving dish and serve.

★ MAKE IT VEGAN
Swap the butter for a dairy-free alternative.

★ GET AHEAD
Prepare to the end of step 2 up to 1 day ahead (do not preheat oven). Cover and chill. Complete the recipe to serve.

Hands-on time: 10min
Cooking time: about 1hr
Serves 8

PER SERVING 154cals, 1g protein, 13g fat (8g saturates), 6g carbs (5g total sugars), 4g fibre

Truffled Roast Potatoes

These potatoes have a savoury truffle note. If you prefer a stronger flavour, drizzle them with extra truffle oil when they're hot out of the oven (or replace the truffle oil with olive oil if you're not a fan).

2kg floury potatoes, such as Maris Piper
3 tbsp olive oil
6 tbsp truffle oil, plus optional extra to drizzle
2 tbsp polenta
4 bay leaves

1. Preheat oven to 190°C (170°C fan) mark 5. Peel the potatoes and cut in half or into 3 even-sized chunks if large. Put into a large pan and cover with cold salted water. Cover the pan, bring to the boil, then simmer for 8–10min.

2. Meanwhile, pour both oils into a large roasting tin and put into the oven to heat up. Drain the potatoes into a colander and leave to steam-dry for 2min. Shake the colander to roughen up the potato edges. Sprinkle over polenta and season.

3. Carefully put the potatoes into the hot oil with the bay leaves, turning to coat the potatoes in oil. Cook for 1hr 15min, turning occasionally, until golden and cooked through.

4. Toss through a little extra truffle oil, if you like, and serve.

Hands-on time: 15min
Cooking time: about 1hr 30min
Serves 8

PER SERVING 322cals, 5g protein, 13g fat (2g saturates), 44g carbs (1g total sugars), 4g fibre

Crumbed Roots

Cinnamon and pecans work wonderfully with the natural sweetness in carrots and parsnips – offset with bite from the mustard.

7 carrots
7 parsnips
1 tbsp olive oil
¾ tbsp wholegrain mustard

FOR THE CRUMB
2 tbsp olive oil
75g fresh white breadcrumbs
50g pecans, roughly chopped
½ tsp ground cinnamon

1. Preheat oven to 190°C (170°C fan) mark 5. Peel the veg and cut into quarters or sixths lengthways, depending on size. Put into a large tin and toss with oil, mustard and some seasoning.

2. Roast for 55min, tossing occasionally, until the veg is tender and lightly caramelised. Transfer to an ovenproof serving dish. In a medium bowl, mix the crumb ingredients with some seasoning.

3. Scatter crumb over the veg. Return to the oven for 15min until crumb is golden and crisp. Serve.

★ GET AHEAD
Prepare to the end of step 2 up to 3hr ahead. Cool, then cover the roots with foil. Cover crumb and keep both at room temperature. Complete the recipe to serve, cooking for 20–30min until golden and hot.

Hands-on time: 15min
Cooking time: about 1hr 15min
Serves 8

PER SERVING 222cals, 4g protein, 10g fat (1g saturates), 24g carbs (12g total sugars), 9g fibre

Maple Bacon Brussels

These gloriously glossy sprouts have a sweet and salty kick. If you like, add pecans instead of lardons if cooking for vegetarians, or simply for extra crunch.

900g Brussels sprouts, trimmed and tough outer leaves removed, if needed
½ tbsp oil
150g bacon lardons
25g butter
25ml maple syrup

1. Bring a large pan of water to the boil and blanch the sprouts in simmering water for 5min. Drain and plunge into cold water to cool. Drain well and dry on kitchen paper. Cut any large sprouts in half.

2. Meanwhile, heat the oil in a large, deep frying pan and fry the lardons for a few minutes until beginning to caramelise.

3. Add the sprouts to the bacon pan and fry until the sprouts are golden. Add the butter and maple syrup, fry for 3–5min, tossing occasionally. Check the seasoning and serve.

★ GET AHEAD
Complete step 1 up to 1 day ahead. Transfer the sprouts to a bowl, cover and chill. Complete the recipe to serve.

Hands-on time: 10min
Cooking time: about 15min
Serves 8

PER SERVING 144cals, 7g protein, 9g fat (4g saturates), 6g carbs (5g total sugars), 6g fibre

Nutty Butter Beans

This flavoured butter will keep for up to 2 weeks in your fridge – it's delightful on greens, or with fish and chicken.

750g fine green beans, trimmed

FOR THE BUTTER
50g unsalted butter, softened
Finely grated zest 1 lemon
40g chopped roasted hazelnuts
25g dried cranberries, finely chopped

1. Bring a large pan of water to the boil.

2. To make the butter, mix the butter ingredients with plenty of seasoning in a medium bowl. Set aside.

3. Cook the beans in boiling water for 4–5min until just tender. Drain well, then empty into a serving bowl. Mix through the flavoured butter and serve.

★ GET AHEAD
Make the flavoured butter up to 2 weeks ahead. Cover and chill. Allow to come up to room temperature before completing the recipe, or it will take the heat out of the cooked beans.

Hands-on time: 5min
Cooking time: about 10min
Serves 8

PER SERVING 120cals, 3g protein, 9g fat (4g saturates), 6g carbs (4g total sugars), 3g fibre

Clementine and Ginger Cabbage

Ginger and orange work wonderfully with red cabbage – an ideal accompaniment to ham or roast goose.

75g unsalted butter
2 red onions, sliced
3 clementines
10 whole cloves
2.5cm piece fresh root ginger, half finely grated and the rest left whole
1.4kg red cabbage, outer leaves removed, cored and shredded
3 tbsp muscovado sugar
5 tbsp red wine vinegar
300ml red wine
3 balls stem ginger, sliced (optional)

1. In a large casserole (that has a lid), melt 50g butter and gently fry onions for 5–8min until softened. Stud one of the clementines with cloves, then cut in half. Finely zest and juice remaining clementines (keep the zest and juice separate).

2. Stir the grated and whole piece of root ginger, the cabbage, sugar, vinegar, wine, clementine juice and clove-studded halves into the casserole. Bring the mixture to a simmer, turn down heat and cover. Cook gently for 2hr, stirring often.

3. Stir through the remaining butter, clementine zest and stem ginger, if using. Check the seasoning and serve.

★ GET AHEAD
Make to the end of step 2 up to 2 days ahead.
Cool, transfer to an airtight container and chill.
Alternatively, make up to 1 month ahead and freeze
in a suitable container. To serve, thaw overnight
in the fridge (if frozen), tip into a pan and reheat
gently with a splash of cold water until piping hot.
Complete the recipe.

Hands-on time: 20min
Cooking time: about 2hr 15min
Serves 8

PER SERVING 184cals, 3g protein, 8g fat (5g saturates),
15g carbs (14g total sugars), 7g fibre

Chicory and Clementine Salad

This zesty salad is a lovely palate cleanser.

FOR THE DRESSING
Finely grated zest 2 clementines
1 tbsp red wine vinegar
1 tsp caster sugar
2 tsp Dijon mustard
2 tbsp extra virgin olive oil

FOR THE SALAD
200g green beans, ends trimmed
3 clementines (use 2 zested from dressing)
4 red chicory
50g walnuts, roughly chopped
1 tbsp chopped chives (optional)

1. For the dressing, in a small bowl or jug whisk all the ingredients with some seasoning.

2. Bring a medium pan of water to the boil and prepare a bowl of iced water. Cook the beans for 4min or until just tender. Drain, then plunge into the iced water. Cool, then drain.

3. Peel the clementines (2 already zested) and slice across the segments into 1cm-thick rounds.

4. Trim the chicory and separate into leaves. Arrange on a platter and scatter over the beans, clementine slices and walnuts. Drizzle over the dressing and sprinkle with chives, if using. Serve.

Hands-on time: 15min, plus cooling
Cooking time: about 5min
Serves 8

PER SERVING 93cals, 2g protein, 7g fat (1g saturates), 4g carbs (2g total sugars), 2g fibre

Stir-fried Savoy Cabbage

This simple yet flavourful side requires very little effort.

1 medium savoy cabbage (roughly 700g)
50g butter
1 red chilli, deseeded and finely chopped
2–3 garlic cloves, thinly sliced, to taste
Pinch sugar
1 tbsp white wine vinegar

1. Halve the cabbage, then slice out and discard the core. Thinly shred the leaves. Melt the butter in a large, deep frying pan (that has a lid) over medium heat. Stir in the chilli and garlic, then cook for 1min until fragrant.

2. Turn up the heat to medium-high and add the cabbage. Cook, stirring occasionally, for 2min until the cabbage is charring slightly. Lower the heat, cover, and cook for 20min, stirring occasionally, until tender.

3. In a small bowl, whisk the sugar, vinegar and plenty of seasoning. Toss through the cabbage. Empty into a warm serving dish and serve.

★ GET AHEAD
Shred the cabbage up to 1 day ahead. Put into a bowl and cover with a damp tea towel. Chill. Complete the recipe to serve.

Hands-on time: 15min
Cooking time: about 25min
Serves 8

PER SERVING 76cals, 2g protein, 5g fat (3g saturates), 4g carbs (4g total sugars), 3g fibre

Caramelised Onion Cannellini Beans

A tasty, higher fibre alternative to potatoes. If you wish, turn this into a creamy mash by whizzing everything with a stick blender at the end.

1 tbsp olive oil
2 large onions, finely sliced
1 small garlic bulb, cloves separated, peeled and
  thickly sliced
2 thyme sprigs, leaves picked and finely chopped
1 rosemary sprig, leaves picked and finely chopped
3 x 400g tins cannellini beans, drained and rinsed
3 tbsp 2% fat Greek yogurt
Finely grated zest ½ lemon

1. Heat the oil in a large frying pan over medium-high heat and cook the onions, garlic, thyme and rosemary for 20–25min, stirring regularly, until the onions are golden and caramelised and the garlic is soft.

2. Stir in the cannellini beans and heat until just warmed through. Stir in the yogurt and lemon zest, season well and serve.

★ GET AHEAD
Complete the recipe up to 1 day ahead, then cool, cover and chill. Reheat in a covered pan over low heat with a splash of water, stirring regularly, until piping hot.

Hands-on time: 10min
Cooking time: about 30min
Serves 6

PER SERVING 190cals, 10g protein, 3g fat (1g saturates), 26g carbs (5g total sugars), 10g fibre

Braised Baby Carrots

Cooking carrots in vegetable stock and orange juice brings out their sweetness.

800g baby carrots, scrubbed
1 large onion, thickly sliced
4 thyme sprigs
Pared zest and juice 1 large orange
500ml hot vegetable stock
1 tbsp runny honey

1. Put the carrots and onion into a wide, deep frying pan or casserole dish. Scatter over the thyme, orange zest and some seasoning, then pour over the orange juice and stock.

2. Lay a piece of baking parchment, roughly the same size as the inside of the pan/dish, directly on top of the carrots (this will help steam the carrots, while allowing the liquid to reduce).

3. Bring to the boil over high heat, then reduce to medium and bubble gently for 30–40min, stirring occasionally, until the carrots are completely tender and the liquid has reduced.

4. Stir in the honey, transfer to a serving dish, season with extra black pepper and serve.

★ GET AHEAD
Prepare to end of step 3 up to 1 day ahead, cooking the carrots for 10min less so they still have a bit of resistance to them. Cool, cover and chill. Reheat on the hob before completing the recipe to serve.

Hands-on time: 10min
Cooking time: about 45min
Serves 6

PER SERVING 70cals, 1g protein, 0g fat (0g saturates), 13g carbs (12g total sugars), 4g fibre

CHOOSE YOUR STUFFING

Pork, Apricot and Hazelnut Stuffing

A new way with stuffing, and best presented and sliced at the table. Unless you're using it to stuff the turkey, keep the nuts chunky.

---

2 tsp oil, plus extra to grease
1 large onion, finely chopped
450g pork sausages, skinned
125g dried apricots, finely chopped
100g blanched hazelnuts, toasted and roughly chopped
   (see above)
75g fresh white breadcrumbs
1 medium egg
1 tsp dried sage or thyme
12 smoked streaky bacon rashers

★ GET AHEAD
Prepare to end of step 3 up to 2 days ahead and chill. Complete the recipe to serve.

1. Heat the oil in a medium pan and gently fry the onion for 10min, or until softened but not coloured. Empty into a large bowl and allow to cool. Preheat oven to 190°C (170°C fan) mark 5.

2. Add the sausage meat, apricots, hazelnuts, breadcrumbs, egg, sage or thyme and some seasoning to onion bowl; mix well.

3. Generously grease a large sheet of foil and place with a long edge closest to you. Stretch the bacon rashers out to lengthen them and arrange vertically side-by-side, edges slightly overlapping, to make a rough 30cm-long rectangle. Form the sausage mixture into an log and lay it horizontally across the bacon, leaving a 2cm border at bottom and sides. Using the foil to help and starting from a long edge, roll it up into a tight cylinder. Tuck in the bacon over the ends of stuffing at the sides, then roll the whole log up in the foil, twisting the ends to seal.

4. Transfer the foil-wrapped stuffing to a lipped baking tray or shallow roasting tin. Cook for 45min, then carefully unwrap and return to oven for 10–15min to crisp. Transfer to serving plate; serve in slices.

Hands-on time: 20min, plus cooling
Cooking time: about 1hr 10min
Serves 8

PER SERVING 422cals, 16g protein, 31g fat
(8g saturates), 18g carbs (10g total sugars), 5g fibre

Lentil and Nut Stuffing Balls

If you like a fruity twist, add some finely chopped dried cranberries.

2 tbsp olive oil
1 onion, finely chopped
2 garlic cloves, crushed
¾ tbsp dried mixed herbs
60g each pistachios and walnuts
2 x 400g tins green lentils, drained and rinsed
Large handful parsley, roughly chopped
1 tbsp wholegrain mustard
1 medium egg
40g fresh white breadcrumbs

1. Preheat oven to 190°C (170°C fan) mark 5. Heat the oil in a medium pan over low heat and fry the onion for 10min, until softened. Add the garlic and dried herbs and fry for 2min.

2. Meanwhile, pulse the pistachios in a food processor until finely chopped. Empty into a shallow bowl. Pulse the walnuts in the processor until finely chopped. Add the onion mixture when ready, then leave to cool. Line a large baking tray with baking parchment.

3. Tip the lentils into the food processor with the parsley and mustard. Pulse to a coarse but combined texture. Empty into a bowl, then mix in the egg, breadcrumbs and seasoning. Shape into golf ball-sized balls, dampening hands with water if mixture is sticking. Roll each in ground pistachios, then arrange on lined tray.

4. Cook the stuffing balls for 25–30min, until golden. Serve immediately.

★ GET AHEAD
Prepare to end of step 3 up to 1 day ahead, loosely cover with foil and chill. Complete recipe to serve.

Hands-on time: 20min
Cooking time: about 45min
Serves 8

PER SERVING 207cals, 8g protein, 13g fat (2g saturates), 12g carbs (2g total sugars), 4g fibre

Pork, Cranberry and Rosemary Stuffing Balls

A hint of warming spice adds seasonal character to these juicy stuffing balls.

FOR THE BALLS
½ tbsp olive oil
1 onion, finely chopped
2 celery sticks, finely chopped
2 rosemary sprigs, leaves picked and finely chopped
½ tsp mixed spice
¼ tsp ground nutmeg
2 tsp English mustard
40g dried cranberries, finely chopped
400g sausage meat
1 medium egg
75g fresh white breadcrumbs

TO WRAP
8 smoked streaky bacon rashers
16 small rosemary sprigs, optional

★ GET AHEAD
Prepare to end of step 4 up to 1 day ahead. Cover and chill. Complete the recipe to serve, cooking for 5min more, if needed.

1. For the balls, heat the oil in a medium pan over low-medium heat and fry the onion and celery for 10min, until softened. Add the rosemary, spices and mustard and fry for 1min. Tip into a large bowl and leave to cool.

2. Once cool, mix in the cranberries, sausage meat, egg, breadcrumbs and plenty of seasoning.

3. Preheat oven to 190°C (170°C fan) mark 5. To wrap, stretch the bacon rashers individually to lengthen slightly, then halve each to make shorter lengths. Divide the stuffing mixture into 16 portions and, with damp hands, roll into balls.

4. Wrap a bacon length around each stuffing ball, securing with a small rosemary sprig stripped of most of its leaves, if you like. Arrange the balls on a baking tray, with bacon seam down.

5. Cook for 30min, or until golden and cooked through. Transfer to a warm dish and serve.

Hands-on time: 20min, plus cooling
Cooking time: about 45min
Makes 16 balls

PER STUFFING BALL 135cals, 7g protein, 9g fat (3g saturates), 7g carbs (3g total sugars), 0g fibre

Caramelised Onion and Apple Stuffing

A simple stuffing that's rather moreish and loosely bound. If you prefer a firmer stuffing, mix a medium egg into the uncooked stuffing mixture. For vegans, leave out the Cheddar, or swap in a dairy-free alternative.

1 tbsp olive oil
2 red onions, finely sliced
1 tsp caster sugar
2 celery sticks, finely sliced
2 eating apples, cored and cut into 1cm pieces
½ tbsp dried sage
200g white or brown bread (stale is ideal), cut into roughly 1.5–2cm pieces
300ml strong vegetable stock
Large handful parsley, roughly chopped
75g mature Cheddar, coarsely grated

1. Heat ½ tbsp oil in a large frying pan over low heat. Add the onions and a large pinch of salt and cook for 15min, stirring occasionally, until completely softened. Turn up heat to medium, add the sugar and cook for 5min, stirring frequently, until caramelised. Empty into a medium bowl.

2. Preheat oven to 190°C (170°C fan) mark 5. Add the remaining ½ tbsp oil to the pan and lower the heat slightly. Cook the celery and apples for 5min, until slightly softened. Add to the onion bowl and mix in the sage, bread pieces, stock, plenty of seasoning and most of the parsley and cheese. Empty into an ovenproof serving dish.

3. Sprinkle over the remaining cheese and cook in the oven for 30min, or until golden and piping hot. Sprinkle over the remaining parsley. Serve.

★ GET AHEAD
Prepare to end of step 2 up to a day ahead. Cover and chill. Complete recipe to serve, cooking for 5min more, if needed.

Hands-on time: 20min, plus cooling
Cooking time: about 55min
Serves 8

PER SERVING 154cals, 5g protein, 5g fat (2g saturates), 20g carbs (8g total sugars), 2g fibre

CHOOSE YOUR SAUCES

Croissant Bread Sauce

Indulgent and fun to make, this sauce works best with day-old, stale croissants.

½ onion
6 whole cloves
800ml semi-skimmed milk
1 bay leaf
2 thyme sprigs, plus extra leaves to garnish
6 stale croissants (about 260g), roughly chopped

1. Stud the onion with cloves and put in a medium pan. Add the milk, bay leaf and thyme. Bring to the boil, then remove from heat and infuse for 30min.

2. Remove the onion and bay leaf (leave the thyme) and return the pan to low heat. Stir in the croissants and cook, stirring, until mushy. Remove thyme; whizz until smooth (if you like). Return to the pan and check the seasoning.

3. Reheat the sauce, if needed, then transfer to a warm bowl. Serve garnished with thyme.

★ GET AHEAD
Prepare to the end of step 2 up to 1 day ahead. Pour into a container, cover and chill. To serve, warm through in a pan, loosening with milk, if needed.

Hands-on time: 20min, plus infusing
Cooking time: about 15min
Serves 8

PER SERVING 176cals, 7g protein, 8g fat (4g saturates), 19g carbs (7g total sugars), 1g fibre

Mulled Cranberry Sauce

So easy to make and much more flavoursome than jarred varieties.

125ml port
500g cranberries, fresh or frozen
100–125g caster sugar, to taste
1 tsp ground cinnamon
¼ tsp each ground cloves and nutmeg
100ml apple juice, or use water

1. Bring the port to boil in medium pan, then simmer for 3min to reduce. Add the remaining ingredients (start with 100g sugar). Bubble for 10min, until most of the berries have burst. Taste and add remaining sugar, if needed.

2. Empty into a heatproof serving bowl and allow to cool – the sauce will thicken on cooling.

3. Chill until needed. Serve.

★ GET AHEAD
Make the sauce, cool, cover and chill up to 3 days ahead. Alternatively, freeze in a sealed container for up to 1 month. To serve, defrost in the fridge (if frozen).

Hands-on time: 5min, plus cooling
Cooking time: about 15min
Serves 8

PER SERVING 82cals, <1g protein, <1g fat (0g saturates), 17g carbs (17g total sugars), 3g fibre

Onion and Porcini Gravy

If not serving to vegetarians, you can replace some or all of the stock with roasting tin or resting juices from the cooked turkey. Simply scrape the base of the tin with a wooden spoon to loosen any sticky bits and strain into a jug.

25g dried porcini mushrooms
1 tbsp olive oil
2 large onions, finely sliced
2 tsp Dijon mustard
25g plain flour
300–500ml strong vegetable stock
200ml white wine
½ tsp instant coffee granules

1. Put the porcini in a small heatproof bowl, pour over 100ml freshly boiled water and soak for 20min.

2. Meanwhile, heat the oil in a large pan over low-medium heat. Add the onions and cook for 20min, stirring occasionally, until completely tender. Drain the porcini (reserving liquid), then finely chop and stir into the pan along with the mustard and flour. Cook for 1min. Remove the pan from the heat and gradually whisk in 300–500ml stock (depending on how thick you like your gravy), followed by the wine, coffee, reserved soaking liquid and seasoning. Return to the heat and bring to the boil, whisking regularly, then reduce heat and simmer for 10min, whisking occasionally, until thickened and slightly reduced.

3. Transfer to a gravy jug or boat and serve.

★ GET AHEAD
Make up to 1 day ahead, then cool, cover and chill. To serve, reheat on the hob until piping hot, thinning with stock or water, if you like.

Hands-on time: 30min, plus soaking
Cooking time: about 35min
Serves 8

PER SERVING 64cals, 2g protein, 2g fat (<1g saturates), 7g carbs (3g total sugars), 2g fibre

Brown Bread Sauce

No Christmas dinner would be complete without bread sauce, and this one's a real winner.

---

1 large onion
6 whole cloves
500ml full-fat milk
1 bay leaf
5 black peppercorns
150g fresh brown breadcrumbs
25g butter
75ml double cream
Freshly grated nutmeg, to sprinkle

1. Peel the onion, cut in half and stud with cloves. In a medium pan, heat the milk, onion halves, bay leaf and peppercorns until the mixture just begins to simmer. Remove from heat and leave to infuse for 30min.

2. Scoop out the onion halves, bay leaf and peppercorns from the milk. Return the pan to medium heat, add the breadcrumbs and cook until thickened.

3. Stir through the butter and cream. Season well and transfer to a serving bowl. Sprinkle over nutmeg to taste and serve.

★ GET AHEAD
Make to the end of step 2 up to 1 day ahead. Pour into a container and lay clingfilm on the surface to stop a skin from forming. Cover and chill.

Hands-on time: 15min, plus infusing
Cooking time: about 10min
Serves 8

PER SERVING 154cals, 4g protein, 10g fat (6g saturates), 10g carbs (3g total sugars), 1g fibre

Cranberry and Ginger Sauce

Any leftovers are wonderful stirred into vanilla ice cream or added to ham sandwiches.

500g cranberries, fresh or frozen
50g stem ginger, finely chopped
½ tsp ground ginger
125g light brown soft sugar

1. Put all the ingredients into a medium pan with 75ml water. Bring to the boil, then simmer, stirring occasionally, for 10–15min until most of the berries have burst and the liquid has thickened slightly. Empty into a heatproof serving bowl and cool completely – the sauce will thicken further on cooling.

2. Chill until needed. Serve.

★ GET AHEAD
Make, cover and chill the sauce up to 3 days ahead. Alternatively, freeze in a sealed container for up to 1 month. To serve, thaw the sauce in the fridge (if frozen).

Hands-on time: 5min, plus cooling
Cooking time: about 15min
Serves 8

PER SERVING 93cals, 0g protein, 0g fat (0g saturates), 22g carbs (21g total sugars), 3g fibre

Easiest Get-ahead Gravy

Gravy often adds last-minute stress, so make life easier and sort it in advance. For a vegetarian option, see GH Tip.

2 red onions, roughly chopped
2 carrots, roughly chopped
2 celery sticks, roughly chopped
3 smoked streaky bacon rashers, roughly chopped
3 thyme sprigs
3 garlic cloves, in their skins
1 tbsp olive oil
25g plain flour
125ml white wine
500ml store-bought fresh chicken stock

1. Preheat oven to 200°C (180°C fan) mark 6. Toss the veg, bacon, thyme, garlic, oil and a little seasoning in a sturdy roasting tin. Roast for 45–50min, turning halfway, until the veg is tender and lightly caramelised.

2. Carefully take out of the oven. If your roasting tin is not hob-proof, scrape the contents into a pan, otherwise continue in the tin. Add the flour to the tin/pan, and squash in using a potato masher, mashing the veg as much as possible.

3. Cook over low-medium heat for 2min, then stir in the wine, followed by the stock. Bring to the boil, stirring, then turn down the heat and simmer for 10min. Strain and check the seasoning. If not serving immediately, cool and chill. To serve, reheat in a pan until piping hot.

★ GET AHEAD
Make up to 3 days ahead. Cool, then chill in an airtight container. To serve, reheat until piping hot.

★ GH TIP
To make vegetarian gravy, omit the bacon and add 1 tsp Marmite with the flour at step 3. Use vegetable instead of chicken stock.

Hands-on time: 20min
Cooking time: about 1hr
Serves 8

PER 50ML 34cals, 1g protein, 1g fat (0g saturates), 2g carbs (1g total sugars), 0g fibre

CHOOSE YOUR EXTRAS

Pigs in Prosciutto with Cranberry Sweet Chilli Dip

A deliciously simple start to your meal, these would also be great served with the turkey. Replace the dip with sweet chilli sauce if you prefer.

6 Parma ham slices
18 raw cocktail sausages
2 tsp olive oil

FOR THE DIP
½ small red chilli, deseeded and finely chopped
3 tbsp smooth cranberry sauce (see GH Tip)
2 tbsp runny honey

★ GH TIP
If you can't find smooth cranberry sauce, you can mash or whizz a chunky variety. Replace the cocktail sausages with quartered figs for a fruity twist.

★ GET AHEAD
Complete steps 1 and 3 up to a day ahead (don't preheat oven). Cover the tray and dip, then chill. To serve, uncover and complete recipe.

1. Preheat oven to 190°C (170°C fan) mark 5 and line a baking tray with baking parchment. Cut each slice of Parma ham lengthways into 3 strips and wrap each sausage in a strip of ham (don't worry if the ham tears a bit). Place on the lined tray and brush wrapped sausages with the oil.

2. Cook for 20–25min, turning halfway, until cooked through and golden.

3. Meanwhile, whisk together the dip ingredients with a pinch of salt.

4. Transfer the cooked sausages to a warm bowl and serve with the dip.

Hands-on time: 15min
Cooking time: about 25min
Makes 18 canapés

PER CANAPÉ (with 1 tsp dip) 54cals, 3g protein, 3g fat (1g saturates), 3g carbs (2g total sugars), <1g fibre

Mini Mushroom Crackers

Cute, delicious and surprisingly simple to make! For speed, chop the mushrooms in a food processor.

50g butter, melted
250g chestnut mushrooms, finely chopped, see intro
2 garlic cloves, crushed
1 tsp finely chopped thyme leaves, plus extra small sprigs to garnish (optional)
40g dried cranberries, roughly chopped
40g walnuts, finely chopped
50g Stilton, crumbled
4 sheets filo pastry

YOU'LL ALSO NEED
Kitchen string

★ GET AHEAD
Prepare to end of step 4 up to 1 day ahead; chill. Once butter has set, loosely cover. Complete recipe to serve.

1. Heat 2 tsp of the butter in a large frying pan over medium-high heat and fry the mushrooms, stirring occasionally, for 10–12min, or until the pan is dry and the mushrooms are golden. Stir in the garlic and thyme and cook for 1min.

2. Set the mushrooms aside to cool completely, then stir in the cranberries, walnuts, Stilton and plenty of seasoning.

3. Line a large baking tray with baking parchment. Lay 1 filo sheet in front of you with a long edge closest to you. Cut vertically into 3 wide strips. Brush the borders of 1 strip lightly with some of the remaining melted butter. Put 1 heaped tbsp mushroom filling 4cm up from the short edge closest to you, then shape into a rough log, leaving a 2cm border on each side.

4. Roll up tightly from the bottom, then pinch the ends where the filling stops to form a cracker shape. Transfer to the lined tray, seam-down. Repeat the process to make 11 more crackers. Tie ends with string and brush the crackers all over with remaining butter. Chill for 30min.

5. Preheat oven to 190°C (170°C) mark 5. Lay a small thyme sprig on top of each cracker, if you like. Cook crackers for 18–20min, or until golden and crisp. Transfer to a warm plate and serve.

Hands-on time: 35min, plus cooling and chilling
Cooking time: about 35min
Makes 12 crackers

PER CRACKER 124cals, 3g protein, 8g fat (3g saturates), 10g carbs (3g total sugars), 1g fibre

Pigs in Blankets Yorkshire Puddings

Toad in the hole goes festive! Make your own pigs in blankets by wrapping 12 raw cocktail sausages in short strips of bacon, if you prefer.

2 tbsp vegetable oil
12 raw pigs in blankets
175g plain flour
1 tsp dried thyme
3 medium eggs
175ml semi-skimmed milk

1. Preheat oven to 190°C (170°C) mark 5. Divide the oil evenly among the holes of a 12-hole muffin tin and put a pig (wrapped sausage) into each. Roast for 15–20min, or until starting to brown on the underside.

2. Meanwhile, in a large jug or bowl, whisk the flour, thyme, eggs, half the milk and seasoning to make a thick paste. Gradually whisk in the remaining milk to make a smooth batter.

3. Carefully remove the tin from the oven. Turn the pigs, then quickly divide the batter among the holes. Cook for 30–35min more, or until golden and puffed. Transfer to a warm dish and serve.

★ GET AHEAD
Make batter up to 12hr ahead, cover and chill. To serve, whisk the batter to recombine and complete the recipe.

Hands-on time: 10min
Cooking time: about 55min
Makes 12 puddings

PER YORKSHIRE PUDDING 151cals, 7g protein, 7g fat (2g saturates), 14g carbs (1g total sugars), 1g fibre

8
Desserts

Black Forest Mess

An easy-to-assemble treat — just leave out the kirsch or brandy if serving to kids.

600ml double cream
1 tbsp kirsch or brandy (optional)
4 tbsp icing sugar
2 x 450g packs frozen Black Forest fruits, defrosted
125g chocolate brownies, crumbled into small pieces
16 mini meringues
20g pack giant milk and white chocolate stars (optional)

1. In a large bowl, whip the cream with the kirsch/brandy, if using, and 2 tbsp of icing sugar until it just holds its shape. Spread evenly into a 2-litre shallow serving dish and roughly level.

2. In a food processor, whizz half the defrosted fruits with the remaining 2 tbsp icing sugar to make a purée.

3. Drizzle the fruit purée over the cream layer. Dot the brownie pieces and 12 of the whole meringues over the fruit layer, then scatter over the remaining defrosted whole fruit.

4. Crumble over the remaining meringues and decorate with the chocolate stars, if using. Serve.

★ GET AHEAD
Prepare the recipe to end of step 2 up to 1 day ahead. Cover the serving dish with foil and chill. Keep the purée and whole fruit in separate covered containers. Complete the recipe to serve.

★ GH TIP
If you can't find mini meringues, break large ready-made meringues into bite-sized pieces.

Hands-on time: 10min
Serves 6

PER SERVING 777cals, 4g protein, 60g fat (36g saturates), 52g carbs, 49g total sugars, 5g fibre

Mulled Wine Jelly

A boozy jelly that's full of festive flavours and sure to be a popular choice. The poached pears hidden inside add a refreshing fruity hit.

2 small dessert pears
600ml medium-bodied red wine, such as Côtes du Rhône
450ml ruby port
175g caster sugar
3 tbsp brandy
Juice 2 lemons
1 cinnamon stick
25g pack leaf gelatine
Edible gold stars, to decorate

★ GET AHEAD
Make to end of step 6 up to 2 days ahead.
Complete the recipe to serve.

1. Peel, halve and core the pears, then cut into 5mm-wide slices.

2. Put the pears, wine and port into a large pan, then add the sugar, brandy, lemon juice, cinnamon stick and 300ml water. Heat, stirring carefully, to dissolve the sugar, then bring mixture to the boil. Turn down the heat and simmer for 5min to poach the pears. Take the pan off the heat.

3. Meanwhile, soak the gelatine in a bowl of cold water for 5min.

4. Using a slotted spoon, lift the pears out of the wine mixture and set aside. Lift the gelatine out of the cold water (squeeze out excess water) and stir into the hot wine mixture until dissolved. Strain the liquid through a fine sieve into a large jug. Discard the cinnamon stick.

5. Rinse a 1.4 litre jelly or bundt tin mould with cold water. Pour in three-quarters of the strained wine mixture, cool completely, then chill until set, about 3hr. Set aside the remaining wine mixture and pears at room temperature to use later.

6. When the jelly in the mould has set, cover with an even layer of the poached pears. Pour over the reserved unset jelly. Return to the fridge until completely set – preferably overnight.

7. To serve, quickly dip the moulded jelly into a sink of warm water (make sure no water comes in contact with the jelly), dry the outside of the mould, then invert on to a serving plate. If the jelly refuses to come out, give it a few firm shakes sideways (on the plate) or, if necessary, quickly dip the mould in warm water (and dry) again. Sprinkle over edible stars, if you like, and serve in all its trembling glory.

DF **GF**

Hands-on time: 25min, plus cooling, chilling and (overnight) setting
Cooking time: about 10min
Serves 10

PER SERVING 200cals, 3g protein, 0g fat (0g saturates), 24g carbs (24g total sugars), 0g fibre

Apple and Calvados Christmas Pudding

Calvados, or cider brandy, gives a lovely, fruity warmth to this pudding and balances the sweetness. You can replace it with extra apple juice if you prefer to keep it booze-free.

150g raisins
100g sultanas
100g soft dried apple, chopped
75ml cloudy apple juice
75ml Calvados
Butter, to grease
150g grated Bramley apple
125g dark brown soft sugar
75g fresh white breadcrumbs
50g plain flour
50g vegetarian suet
75g black treacle
1 large egg, beaten
1 tbsp mixed spice
1 tsp vanilla extract

1. Put the dried fruit, apple juice and Calvados into a large non-metallic bowl. Stir, cover and leave to soak overnight at room temperature.

2. Lightly grease a 1 litre pudding basin and line base with a disc of baking parchment. Put a 30cm square of foil on top of a square of baking parchment the same size. Fold a 4cm pleat across the centre and set aside.

3. Add the remaining ingredients to the soaked fruit and mix well. Spoon into the prepared basin, pressing down to level. Put the pleated foil and parchment square (foil-side up) on top of the basin and smooth down to cover. Using a long piece of string, tie securely under the lip of the basin. Loop over again and tie to make a handle.

4. To cook, put a heatproof saucer in the base of a large, deep pan that has a tight-fitting lid. Lower in the prepared pudding and pour in enough water to come halfway up sides of basin, taking care not to get any on top of the pudding. Cover the pan with the lid, bring to a boil, then simmer gently for 4hr 30min, checking the water level periodically and topping up as necessary. Carefully remove the pudding from the pan, then cool completely (see Get ahead).

5. When ready to reheat, remove the foil, clingfilm and lid. Re-cover with a new lid as per steps 2 and 3 then, following the method in step 4, reheat for 2hr until piping hot in the centre when pierced with a skewer. Remove from the pan and allow to sit for 5min. Carefully remove the lid and invert on to a lipped serving stand/plate. Peel off the baking parchment and serve with Boozy Butterscotch Custard (see right), if you like.

Hands-on time: 25min, plus (overnight) soaking, cooling and (optional) maturing
Cooking time: about 6hr 30min (including reheating)
Serves 8

PER SERVING 346cals, 4g protein, 6g fat (3g saturates), 61g carbs (52g total sugars), 3g fibre

★ GET AHEAD
To store the pudding, wrap the basin (still with its foil lid) tightly in clingfilm, followed by a further layer of foil. Store in a cool, dark place to mature for up to 2 months.

Boozy Butterscotch Custard

If you've made the Apple and Calvados Christmas Pudding, you should already have a bottle of apple brandy to hand, but regular brandy (or even an orange liqueur, such as Cointreau) would be delicious too.

2 tbsp cornflour
300ml milk
50g butter
125g dark brown muscovado sugar
1 tsp vanilla bean paste
75ml double cream
2–3 tbsp Calvados or brandy

1. Put the cornflour in a small bowl and whisk in 2 tbsp of the milk. Set aside.

2. Heat the butter and sugar in a medium pan over low heat, whisking occasionally, until smooth and bubbling. Gradually add the remaining milk (carefully – it will splutter), whisking until combined. Whisk in the cornflour mixture, then increase heat to medium and bring to the boil, whisking constantly, until the sauce thickens.

3. Remove from heat and stir in the vanilla, cream and Calvados or brandy to taste. Serve hot or warm with Christmas pudding.

★ GET AHEAD
Make up to 3 days ahead, then cool, cover and chill. To serve, reheat gently in a pan over low heat.

★ TO FLAME YOUR PUDDING Pour 50ml fresh brandy, rum or whisky into a large metal ladle. Warm carefully over a low gas hob. If you don't have a gas hob, heat in a small pan instead. Carefully light the alcohol using a gas lighter or long match and slowly pour over the pudding.

Hands-on time: 10min
Cooking time: about 10min
Serves 8

PER SERVING 193cals, 2g protein, 11g fat (7g saturates), 20g carbs (17g total sugars), 0g fibre

Brandysnap and Coffee Cups

This coffee parfait is a real winner – rich, thick and decadent, and no need to churn!

5 medium egg yolks
125g icing sugar, sifted
500g tub mascarpone cheese
2 tsp vanilla extract
3 tbsp cold strong coffee
1½ tbsp rum (optional)

FOR THE BRANDYSNAP CUPS
60g unsalted butter
2 tbsp golden syrup
60g caster sugar
60g plain flour
½ tsp ground ginger

TO DECORATE (optional)
Chocolate espresso beans
Cocoa powder, to dust

★ GET AHEAD
Make to end of step 1 up to 1 week ahead and leave the parfait in the freezer. Make the cups up to 1 day ahead. Store them in an airtight container at room temperature. Complete recipe to serve.

Hands-on time: 35min, plus cooling, freezing and softening
Cooking time: about 15min
Serves 8

PER SERVING 499cals, 6g protein, 37g fat (24g saturates), 33g carbs (28g total sugars), 0g fibre

1. Start by making the coffee parfait. Whisk the egg yolks and icing sugar in a medium bowl with a handheld electric whisk until moussey – about 5min. Beat in the mascarpone, vanilla, coffee and rum (if using). Transfer to a freezerproof container and freeze until solid – about 4hr.

2. Next make the brandysnap cups. Heat the butter, syrup and sugar in a medium pan until the mixture is melted and smooth. Set aside to cool to room temperature (about 20min).

3. Preheat oven to 190°C (170°C fan) mark 5 and line 2 large baking sheets with baking parchment. Sift the flour and ginger into the butter mixture and stir to make a thick paste.

4. Dollop 8 tbsp of the brandysnap mixture on to the lined baking sheets, spacing well apart (the brandysnaps spread a lot). Bake for 7–8min until deep golden and lacy.

5. Allow to cool for a few minutes on the trays until firmer but still pliable. Working quickly and one at time, lift off a brandysnap and gently press into a teacup/ramekin to make a bowl shape, then leave to set. Repeat with remaining brandysnaps (if they've hardened too much before shaping, return the tray to the oven for 1min to resoften). Once set, transfer the brandysnap cups to a wire rack to cool completely.

6. To serve, allow the parfait to soften at room temperature for 20min. Scoop into balls and serve in the brandysnap cups. Garnish with chocolate espresso beans and cocoa powder, if you like.

Dairy-Free Coconut 'Cheesecake'

You won't miss the dairy in this tropical bake. Add a splash of rum to your caramelised pineapple, if you like.

FOR THE BASE
2 tbsp coconut oil, melted, plus extra to grease
150g dairy-free digestive biscuits (we used Doves Farm)
40g desiccated coconut

FOR THE FILLING
250g cashews, soaked in just-boiled water for 1hr
100g caster sugar
400ml coconut cream
3 medium egg yolks
1 tsp vanilla bean paste

FOR THE TOPPING
150g pineapple (tinned or prepared), cut into 1cm chunks
50g caster sugar
½ tbsp coconut oil, melted
1 tbsp toasted coconut chips

1. Preheat oven to 150°C (130°C fan) mark 2. Lightly grease a 20.5cm round springform tin and line the base and sides with baking parchment. For the base, whizz the biscuits in a food processor until finely crushed (or bash them in a food bag with a rolling pin). Add the desiccated coconut and coconut oil and pulse/mix briefly to combine. Empty into the lined tin and press to level with the back of a spoon.

Hands-on time: 30min, plus soaking, cooling and (overnight) chilling
Cooking time: about 1hr 55min
Serves 10

PER SERVING 461cals, 8g protein, 33g fat (18g saturates), 33g carbs (21g total sugars), 3g fibre

Bake for 20min, then cool completely on a wire rack. Put a roasting tin filled with hot water in the bottom of the oven.

2. Drain the soaked cashews and empty into a high-speed blender. Whizz until smooth. Scrape into a large bowl and add the sugar, coconut cream, egg yolks and vanilla. Beat with a handheld electric whisk until smooth. Pour over the cooled biscuit base.

3. Bake the cheesecake on the shelf above the roasting tin for 1hr 15min, until set with a slight wobble in the centre when you gently tap the tin. Turn off the oven, then leave the cheesecake to cool inside for 1hr with the door ajar. Cool completely at room temperature, then chill for at least 4hr, or ideally overnight.

4. When you are almost ready to serve, make the topping. Pat the pineapple pieces dry with kitchen paper. Heat the sugar in a frying pan with 2 tbsp water over medium heat, stirring to dissolve the sugar. Turn up the heat and cook until a caramel colour (swirling the pan rather than stirring). Add the coconut oil and pineapple and cook, turning regularly, until the pineapple is golden all over, about 10min. Set aside to cool.

5. To serve, transfer the cheesecake to a cake stand or plate. Spoon on the caramelised pineapple and scatter over the toasted coconut chips. Serve.

Snowball Cocktail Tart

This old-school classic, with a nostalgic festive twist, is ideal for entertaining. The jelly layer on top adds texture and a citrus hit.

FOR THE PASTRY
200g plain flour, plus extra to dust
1 tbsp caster sugar
100g unsalted butter, chilled and cubed
1 medium egg, beaten

FOR THE CUSTARD FILLING
100ml double cream
175ml Advocaat liqueur
175ml milk
6 medium egg yolks
75g caster sugar

FOR THE TOPPING
3 sheets platinum-grade leaf gelatine
200g lemon curd

FOR THE TOPPING
Aerosol cream
12 maraschino/cocktail cherries

1. For the pastry, in a food processor pulse the flour, sugar and butter until they resemble fine breadcrumbs. Or rub the butter into the flour mixture using your fingertips. Add the egg and pulse/mix to combine. Tip on to a work surface, bring together and shape into a disc. Wrap and chill for 30min.

2. Dust a work surface with flour and roll out the pastry. Use to line a 23cm round, fluted, loose-bottomed tart tin that's at least 3.5cm deep. Trim the edges and prick the base all over with a fork. Chill for 30min.

3. Preheat oven to 180°C (160°C fan) mark 4. Line the pastry case with baking parchment and fill with baking beans. Put on a baking tray and bake for 20–25min, or until pastry sides are set. Remove the baking parchment and beans. Return the tin to the oven for 5–10min, or until the pastry is golden. Set aside to cool. Reduce oven to 140°C (120°C fan) mark 1.

4. For the filling, bring the cream, Advocaat and milk to a simmer over a low heat. Meanwhile, whisk together the egg yolks and sugar. Slowly pour the hot cream into the yolk bowl, whisking constantly. Strain through a fine sieve into the pastry case (still in the tin).

5. Bake for 35min, or until set with a slight wobble in the centre. Leave to cool completely in the tin.

6. For the topping, soak the gelatine in cold water for 5min. In a small pan, heat the lemon curd and 100ml water over low heat, stirring occasionally, until simmering. Remove from heat. Lift out the gelatine, squeeze out excess water and stir into the lemon mixture to dissolve. Set aside to cool to room temperature. Gently pour over the cooled tart filling. Chill for 1hr, or until set.

7. Transfer the tart to a cake plate or stand. Squirt 12 rosettes of aerosol cream, if using, in a ring around the edge of the tart and place a cherry, if using, on top of each rosette. Serve in slices.

Hands-on time: 40min, plus chilling and cooling
Cooking time: about 1hr 15min
Serves 12

PER SERVING 300cals, 5g protein, 16g fat (8g saturates), 32g carbs (21g total sugars), 1g fibre

Mincemeat tart

This easy, prepare-ahead pudding is great if you don't want any last-minute fuss!

375g pack ready-rolled puff pastry
300g shop-bought mincemeat or home-made mincemeat (p215)
Icing sugar, for icing
Brandy butter or cream, to serve (optional)

1. Preheat oven to 200°C (180°C fan) mark 6. Unroll the puff pastry on to a large baking sheet (remove plastic). Slice a strip off the rectangle from one of the short sides so you have a large square piece and a narrow rectangle. Use a knife to score a border 2cm in from the edge of the large square (cutting through half the depth of the pastry). Prick the pastry all over with a fork inside this border. Spread the mincemeat in an even layer inside the border.

2. Using a star cutter, cut out pastry stars from the rectangular strip. Arrange on top of the mincemeat, leaving spaces between them. Bake for 18–20min, until the pastry is crisp, golden and risen. Allow to cool slightly, then transfer to a serving board or plate.

3. Mix 4 tbsp icing sugar with a little water to make a runny icing, then drizzle over the tart and allow to set before serving. Alternatively, simply dust with icing sugar. Serve the tart warm with brandy butter or cream, if you like.

★ GH TIP
To help your tart really shine, brush the pastry borders and stars with a little beaten egg just before baking.

Hands-on time: 20min, plus cooling
Cooking time: about 20min
Serves 6

PER SERVING (without icing glaze) 380cals, 3g protein, 19g fat (9g saturates), 49g carbs (31g total sugars), 2g fibre

★ GET AHEAD
Bake the tart up to 3hr ahead, then leave to cool completely on a serving board/plate. To serve, dust with icing sugar or glaze and allow to set for a few min before serving.

Cheat's Soufflés

Yes, you can whip up a perfect soufflé with our clever recipe!

3 medium egg whites
75g caster sugar
225ml chilled fresh custard
Icing sugar, to dust

1. Heat the oven to 220°C (200°C fan) mark 7 and preheat a baking sheet (so you can cook the soufflés on it and take them out in one go).

2. Whisk the egg whites and caster sugar until stiff, then fold this mixture into the chilled custard. Spoon the mixture into 6 x 125ml ramekins and pop into the oven for 10–12min until well risen.

3. Dust with icing sugar and serve immediately (they'll sink quickly).

Hands-on time: 15min
Cooking time: about 15min
Makes 6 soufflés

PER SOUFFLÉ 105cals, 3g protein, 2g fat (2g saturates), 18g carbs (16g total sugars), 0g fibre

Vegan Chocolate Mousse Torte

We've topped this elegant dessert with raspberries, as they pair so well with chocolate, the tangy fruit cutting through the richness of the dairy-free mousse.

FOR THE BASE
40g dairy-free butter, plus extra to grease
100g blanched hazelnuts
2 tbsp caster sugar
2 tbsp cocoa

FOR THE CHOCOLATE MOUSSE
225g vegan dark chocolate, finely chopped, plus extra, grated, to decorate
150ml dairy-free whipping cream
125ml aquafaba
¼ tsp cream of tartar
3 tbsp caster sugar
200g raspberries, to decorate

1. Lightly grease a 20.5cm round springform tin and line the base and sides with baking parchment. Melt the butter alternative in a small pan, then remove from heat. Whizz the hazelnuts, sugar, cocoa and a pinch of salt in a food processor until finely ground. Add the melted butter and pulse until the mixture clumps together. Empty into the lined tin and press to level with the back of a spoon. Chill.

2. Make the chocolate mousse. Heat the chocolate and cream alternative in a large heatproof bowl set over a pan of barely simmering water, stirring occasionally, until melted and smooth. Set aside to cool to room temperature.

3. Meanwhile, put the aquafaba and cream of tartar in the bowl of a stand mixer fitted with a whisk attachment and beat on low speed for 1min. Increase the speed to medium and beat for 3–4min. Increase the speed to high and beat until the mixture holds stiff peaks, about 5min. Gradually beat in the sugar, 1 tbsp at a time, whisking constantly. Beat back up to thick, glossy peaks – it's vital the mixture is thick.

4. With a handheld electric whisk, briefly whisk the chocolate mixture until smooth and slightly aerated. Add a third of the aquafaba meringue to the chocolate mixture and fold in with a large metal spoon to loosen, then carefully fold in the remaining meringue (being careful not to knock out the air). Gently pour on to the set base then chill for at least 4hr, or until set firm.

5. To serve, remove from tin and carefully peel off baking parchment. Transfer to a cake stand or plate, top with raspberries and grated chocolate and serve in slices.

Hands-on time: 25min, plus cooling and chilling
Cooking time: about 10min
Serves 10

PER SERVING 305cals, 4g protein, 21g fat (9g saturates), 24g carbs (23g total sugars), 3g fibre

★ GET AHEAD
Prepare to the end of step 3 up to 2 days ahead. Once set, cover the tin with clingfilm and chill. Complete the recipe to serve.

White Chocolate and Cassis Crème Brûlées

These softly set, creamy brûlees with a tangy fruit filling are deliciously rich and indulgent. If you can't find frozen blackcurrants, you could use a forest fruit mix.

FOR THE CASSIS COMPOTE
300g frozen blackcurrants
75g caster sugar
3 tbsp cassis
2 tsp cornflour

FOR THE CUSTARD
100g caster sugar, plus 9 tsp to sprinkle
3 tbsp cornflour
300ml semi-skimmed milk
4 medium egg yolks
400ml single cream
150g good-quality white chocolate, finely chopped
1 tsp vanilla bean paste

★ GH TIPS
• If you don't have a blowtorch, make a caramel top instead. Gently heat the 9 tsp sugar in a small, heavy-based pan with 50ml water, stirring to dissolve. Turn up heat to high and bubble until the caramel turns golden, swirling the pan occasionally. Scrape on to a lined baking tray and leave to cool completely, then crush to fine crumbs. Sprinkle over the set pots and put under a hot grill briefly until melted. Chill before serving.
• To make this dessert even easier, mix 8 tbsp blackcurrant jam with the cassis and spoon into the bases of the ramekins instead of the compote.

Hands-on time: 20min, plus cooling and chilling
Cooking time: about 40min
Makes 6 brûlees

PER BRÛLÉE 546cals, 8g protein, 25g fat (14g saturates), 68g carbs (60g total sugars), 2g fibre

1. To make the compote, put the fruit, sugar and 1 tbsp cassis in a medium pan. Cook over medium heat, stirring occasionally, for about 10min until the fruit is very soft. Mix the remaining cassis with cornflour in a cup, then stir into the fruit. Bubble for 2min. Spoon the compote into 6 x 125–150ml ramekins, then set aside to cool.

2. Meanwhile, make the custard. In a medium bowl, use a balloon whisk to mix the sugar and cornflour with 4 tbsp of the milk to make a smooth paste. Whisk in the egg yolks until well combined. Pour the remaining milk and the cream into a large non-stick pan. Bring to the boil until the first few bubbles are rising, then take off heat.

3. Slowly pour hot milk into the egg mixture, whisking until combined. Transfer to a clean pan and cook over low heat, stirring with a wooden spoon for 10–15min until it's the consistency of yogurt. The temperature needs to be hot enough to cook and thicken the mixture but not so hot that the eggs scramble. If the eggs do begin to scramble, whisk until smooth.

4. Remove the custard from the heat and stir in the chocolate and vanilla until melted and smooth.

5. Spoon the custard into ramekins and cool for 15min, then chill, uncovered, for at least 1hr, until set. Sprinkle each with 1½ tsp sugar, then caramelise tops using a blowtorch (see GH Tips). Allow to cool for a few min afterwards, then chill again to set for 20min.

Free-from Christmas Pudding with Spiced Rum Cream

This traditional-style pudding is free from gluten, egg and nuts and suitable for vegans. If you'd prefer to make it alcohol-free, replace the rum with orange juice. Remember to check brands to make sure they are suitable for a gluten-free diet, if needed.

100g pitted dates, chopped
200g soft pitted prunes, chopped
250g mixed dried fruit
25g glacé cherries, halved
75ml dark rum
100g vegan butter alternative, chilled, plus extra to grease
100g dark muscovado sugar
75g gluten-free breadcrumbs
125g oat or soya yogurt alternative
Finely grated zest 1 orange
100g gluten-free plain flour
½ tsp baking powder
½ tsp bicarbonate of soda
2 tsp ground mixed spice

FOR THE RUM CREAM
270ml dairy-free cream
3 tbsp dark rum
3 tbsp icing sugar
⅛ tsp mixed spice

FOR THE DECORATION (optional)
Fresh holly leaves, washed and dried

Hands-on time: 40min, plus (overnight) soaking, cooling and maturing
Cooking time: about 7hr (including reheating)
Serves 8

PER SERVING 462cals, 4g protein, 12g fat (3g saturates), 73g carbs (56g total sugars), 4g fibre

1. Mix the dates, prunes, mixed dried fruit, cherries and rum in a large non-metallic bowl. Cover and leave to soak overnight at room temperature.

2. Generously grease a 1.2 litre pudding basin and line the base with a disc of baking parchment. Put a 30cm square of foil on top of a square of baking parchment the same size. Fold a 4cm pleat across the centre and set aside.

3. Coarsely grate the chilled butter alternative into the fruit mixture and add the sugar, breadcrumbs, yogurt alternative and orange zest. Mix well. Next add the flour, baking powder, bicarbonate of soda and mixed spice and stir to combine.

4. Spoon the mixture into the prepared basin, pressing down to level. Put the pleated foil and parchment square (foil-side up) on top of the basin and smooth down to cover. Tie a long piece of string securely under the lip of the basin and loop over top, then tie to make a handle.

5. To cook, put a heatproof saucer in the base of a large, deep pan that has a tight-fitting lid. Lower in the prepared pudding and pour in enough water to come halfway up sides of the basin, taking care not to get any on top of the pudding. Cover the pan with the lid, bring to a boil, then simmer gently for 5hr, checking the water level periodically and topping up as necessary.

6. Remove pudding from the pan; cool. Wrap the basin, still in its foil lid, in clingfilm, then foil. Store in a cool, dark place for up to 2 months.

7. To reheat, unwrap and remove the lid. Re-cover with a fresh parchment and foil lid as per step 4. Following the method in step 5, steam for 2hr, or until piping hot in the centre when pierced with a skewer. Remove from the pan and rest for 5min.

8. For the rum cream, using a handheld electric whisk, beat the cream alternative, rum, sugar and spice until until thick but pourable. Transfer to a jug. Remove the pudding lid and invert on to a serving plate. Peel off parchment and top with holly, if you like. Serve with the rum cream.

★ TO STORE

Keep in an airtight container in the fridge for up to 3 days. To serve, reheat portions for 1–2min in the microwave until piping hot. Freeze individual portions, well wrapped, for up to 3 months.

Brandy Butter Caramel Chocolate Fondants

With a seasonal twist on salted caramel, these fondants are a decadent treat to finish your meal.

FOR THE BRANDY BUTTER CARAMEL
100g caster sugar
50ml double cream
50g brandy butter
2 tbsp brandy
¼ tsp sea salt flakes
50g dark chocolate (70% cocoa solids), finely chopped

FOR THE FONDANTS
100g butter, plus extra, melted, to grease
Cocoa powder, to dust
225g dark chocolate (70% cocoa solids), chopped
½ tsp instant coffee granules
2 large eggs, plus 2 large egg yolks
100g caster sugar
50g plain flour
Vanilla ice cream, to serve (optional)

1. For the caramel, melt the sugar with 3 tbsp water in a medium heavy-based pan over medium heat, stirring to dissolve the sugar. Turn up heat and bubble to caramel colour (without stirring – swirl the pan instead). Remove from heat and mix in the cream (carefully, as it will splutter). Return to heat and stir until the sauce is smooth. Stir in the brandy butter, brandy and sea salt. Pour into a bowl, cool and chill to thicken (at least 4hr or up to 24hr).

Hands-on time: 35min, plus cooling and chilling
Cooking time: about 25min
Serves 4

PER SERVING (without ice cream and extra sauce)
762cals, 10g protein, 45g fat (26g saturates),
77g carbs (67g total sugars), 2g fibre

2. Preheat oven to 200°C (180°C fan) mark 6 and place a baking tray in the oven to heat up. Grease 4 dariole moulds well with melted butter, then add a generous spoonful of cocoa powder to each mould. Shake gently to coat completely, then tap out the excess. Chill until needed.

3. Melt the 225g chocolate, butter, coffee and ½ tsp fine sea salt in a heatproof bowl set over a pan of barely simmering water. Set aside to cool.

4. Using a handheld electric whisk, beat the eggs, yolks and sugar in a large bowl until pale and fluffy, about 5min. Fold in the cooled chocolate mixture and flour. Half fill the moulds with this mixture, then add 1 tbsp of the cooled caramel to each (it's crucial it doesn't touch the sides). Top with the remaining chocolate mixture.

5. Bake the fondants on the hot baking tray for 14–15min, until the tops are set and feel spongy.

6. Meanwhile, place the bowl with the remaining caramel over a pan of hot water; heat to warm. Remove from heat, add 50g chopped chocolate and leave until melted, stirring once.

7. Run a knife around the inside rim of each mould to release, then turn out on to a plate and serve straight away, with a scoop of ice cream, if you like, and the chocolate caramel sauce.

★ GET AHEAD
Prepare up to the end of step 4 up to 1 day ahead
(do not preheat oven). Cover and chill. To serve,
preheat oven and the baking tray, then complete
the recipe, adding 3–4min to the baking time.

Eggnog Panna Cotta with Boozy Mulled Figs

This elegant dessert is a great alternative if you're not a fan of Christmas pudding but still want something festive.

6 sheets leaf gelatine
800ml double cream
250ml whole milk
150ml golden rum
3 cinnamon sticks
1 vanilla pod, split lengthways
300g caster sugar
Whole nutmeg, to grate
250ml mulled wine
Pared zest 1 orange
4 figs, quartered
Gold leaf, to decorate (optional)

1. Soak the gelatine in cold water until soft. In a medium pan, heat the cream, milk, rum, cinnamon, vanilla pod and 225g sugar, stirring, until mixture comes to the boil. Remove from heat.

2. Lift the gelatine out of the water, squeeze out excess, and stir into the hot cream mixture to dissolve. Leave to cool and infuse.

3. Stir the cream mixture, then strain and divide among 8 glasses or ramekins and grate nutmeg generously over each. Chill for 4hr until set.

4. Meanwhile, heat the remaining 75g sugar, mulled wine and orange zest in a medium pan. Bring to the boil and reduce until syrupy. Add the figs in a single layer, poach gently for 2min, then leave to cool in the syrup.

5. Serve each panna cotta topped with figs, a drizzle of the syrup and a little gold leaf, if using.

★ GET AHEAD
Make the panna cottas up to 3 days ahead. Keep covered in the fridge. Poach the figs up to 3hr ahead. Cool and leave at room temperature. Complete the recipe to serve.

Hands-on time: 25min, plus cooling and chilling
Cooking time: 15min
Serves 8

PER SERVING 769cals, 5g protein, 55g fat (34g saturates), 47g carbs (47g total sugars), 0g fibre

Chai and Dark Chocolate Rice Pudding

Chocolate chips hold their shape better, but if you prefer you could use roughly chopped dark chocolate from a bar.

300ml oat or rice milk alternative
1 chai tea bag
1 cinnamon stick
1 tbsp vanilla bean paste
50g caster sugar, plus 1 tbsp for the oranges
2 large oranges
75g pudding rice
25g dark chocolate chips

1. Heat the milk alternative, tea bag, cinnamon, vanilla, 50g sugar and the zest of 1 orange with 400ml water in a pan over medium heat until steaming. Set aside to cool and infuse for 10min.

2. Preheat oven to 170°C (150°C fan) mark 3. Put the rice and chocolate chips into a 1 litre pie dish. Remove the tea bag from the milk mixture, pressing it to squeeze out as much flavour as possible, and discard it along with the cinnamon stick. Pour the milk mixture over the rice and chocolate chips, then bake for 1hr 45min, until the rice has cooked and most of the liquid absorbed.

3. Slice the tops and bottoms off the zested and remaining whole orange. Cut away the peel and pith, then cut the oranges into 5mm slices. Heat the remaining 1 tbsp sugar with ½ tbsp water in a pan over low heat, stirring until the sugar dissolves. Increase the heat, add the orange slices and bubble for 5min, turning halfway through, until caramelised. Set aside to cool. To serve, divide the pudding among 4 bowls and top with the orange slices.

★ GET AHEAD
The pudding is also delicious cold. Make the recipe to the end of step 3, then transfer the pudding and oranges to separate airtight containers and chill for up to 2 days. Complete the recipe to serve.

Hands-on time: 25min, plus cooling and infusing
Cooking time: about 1hr 50min
Serves 4

PER SERVING 235cals, 3g protein, 3g fat (1g saturates), 47g carbs (30g total sugars), 2g fibre

Christmas Pudding Cheesecake

A chilled, creamy dessert version of a favourite festive dessert – it's sure to become a year-round favourite.

FOR THE BASE
75g unsalted butter, melted, plus extra to grease
250g digestive biscuits
1 tsp mixed spice

FOR THE FILLING
550g full-fat cream cheese
150g soured cream
150g dark brown soft sugar
½ tbsp vanilla bean paste
Finely grated zest and juice 1 orange
2 tbsp brandy
½ tsp ground nutmeg
1 tsp ground cinnamon
3 large eggs, beaten
100g sultanas
100g chopped mixed candied peel

FOR THE GLAZE
50ml Cointreau
50ml brandy
Juice 1 orange
1 tbsp caster sugar

TO DECORATE
2 oranges, peeled and segmented

Hands-on time: 35min, plus cooling and (overnight) chilling
Cooking time: about 1hr 15min
Serves 12

PER SERVING 440cals, 6g protein, 25g fat (14g saturates), 41g carbs (30g total sugars), 1g fibre

1. Preheat oven to 150°C (130°C fan) mark 2. Lightly grease and line the base and sides of a 23cm round springform tin with baking parchment. Wrap the outside of the tin with a double layer of foil to make the tin completely watertight.

2. Whizz the biscuits in a food processor until crushed (or bash in a food bag with a rolling pin). Pulse/mix in the mixed spice and butter until combined. Empty into the tin and press with the back of a spoon to level. Chill for 20min.

3. Using a handheld electric whisk, beat the cream cheese, soured cream, sugar and a pinch of fine salt until smooth. Whisk in the vanilla, orange zest and juice, brandy and spices. Next, beat in the eggs, then fold in the sultanas and mixed peel with a large metal spoon. Scrape into the wrapped tin and smooth to level. Put the tin into a deep roasting tin and pour in just-boiled water to come halfway up the outside of the tin.

4. Bake for 1hr until set with a slight wobble in the centre when tin is gently tapped. Remove from oven and leave to cool in the roasting tin water for 1hr, then remove from the water and chill (still in tin) for at least 3hr, or ideally overnight.

5. To make the glaze, bring the ingredients to the boil in a small pan and bubble for 10min, until slightly reduced. Cool completely.

6. To serve, transfer to a cake stand or plate. Decorate with orange segments and spoon over glaze. Serve.

Tropical Baked Alaska

Not as tricky as you might think — just make sure the frozen yogurt is completely covered in meringue before baking to prevent it from melting.

2 x 500ml tubs coconut frozen yogurt
75g passion fruit curd or lemon curd
3 large egg whites
200g caster sugar
1 tsp cornflour
1 tbsp Malibu (optional)
1 medium sponge flan case, about 15cm diameter

1. Double-line a 1 litre pudding basin with clingfilm, leaving the excess hanging over the sides. Set aside. In a large mixing bowl, mash the frozen yogurt until softened slightly, then swirl through the curd as best you can. Spoon into the lined basin, pressing down to level, and freeze for 3hr or until solid again.

2. Preheat oven to 220°C (200°C fan) mark 7. In a large grease-free bowl, whisk the egg whites to soft peaks. Gradually add the sugar, whisking up to stiff peaks after each addition, until the meringue is stiff and glossy. Whisk in the cornflour and the Malibu, if using.

3. Put the flan case on an ovenproof serving plate. Invert the frozen yogurt into the central dip of the case, then remove the basin and clingfilm. Cover the frozen yogurt and case completely in meringue, swirling it into peaks with the back of a spoon. Ensure there are no gaps, and make sure the meringue goes right down to the plate.

4. Bake in preheated oven for 3–4min until golden. Let stand for 5–10min, to allow the frozen yogurt to soften slightly, then serve.

★ GET AHEAD
Prepare to the end of step 3 and freeze, uncovered, for up to 2 days. To serve, preheat oven to 220°C (200°C fan) mark 7 and bake on the plate for 6–7min until golden. Let stand for 5–10min (to allow the frozen yogurt to soften), then serve.

Hands-on time: 20min, plus freezing
Cooking time: about 5min
Serves 6

PER SERVING 503cals, 8g protein, 30g fat (26g saturates), 50g carbs (44g total sugars), 0g fibre

Clementine and Prosecco Trifle

The retro mix of almonds and sugar sprinkles gives a delicious crunch to the topping on this fruity yet rich pud, but you could use some pared orange zest instead.

FOR THE JELLY
7 leaves platinum-grade leaf gelatine
900ml fresh clementine or orange juice
100g caster sugar
100ml Prosecco
1 lemon swiss roll (about 230g)

FOR THE CUSTARD
8 clementines
300ml whole milk
300ml double cream
6 large egg yolks
75g caster sugar
1½ tbsp cornflour
2 tsp vanilla bean paste

TO FINISH
150ml double cream
250g mascarpone
100g icing sugar, sifted
75ml Prosecco
2 tbsp toasted flaked almonds
Orange sprinkles, to serve (optional)

★ GET AHEAD
Make the trifle to the end of step 6 up to 1 day ahead. Cover the trifle bowl with clingfilm and chill. Complete the recipe to serve.

Hands-on time: 1hr, plus cooling, chilling and infusing
Cooking time: about 30min
Serves 8–10

PER SERVING (for 10) 686cals, 8g protein, 43g fat (26g saturates), 63g carbs (56g total sugars), 2g fibre

1. For the jelly, soak the gelatine leaves in a bowl of cold water for 5min. Meanwhile, heat the clementine or orange juice and sugar in a medium pan, stirring until the sugar dissolves. Remove from heat, lift up the gelatine and squeeze out excess water. Stir into the hot liquid to dissolve. Pour into a jug, add the Prosecco and set aside to cool until lukewarm.

2. Cut the swiss roll into 1.5cm-thick slices and arrange in the base and slightly up the sides of a 2-litre trifle dish. Carefully spoon a third of the cooled (but still liquid) jelly mixture over the slices. Chill for 2hr, or until just set. Cover and chill the remaining jelly separately.

3. Meanwhile, make the custard. Finely grate the zest of the clementines and mix in a medium pan with the milk and double cream. Heat gently until just simmering. Remove from heat and leave to infuse for 10min, then strain into a jug, pressing to extract all the flavour from the zest. Discard the zest.

4. In a bowl, beat together the egg yolks, caster sugar, cornflour and vanilla until combined. Pour in the warm cream mixture, whisking constantly (reserve the jug). Return the mixture to the pan and cook over medium heat, stirring constantly, until thickened (don't let it boil). Pour back into the jug, lay clingfilm directly on the surface of the custard to prevent a skin from forming. Let cool, then chill for 1hr, until cold.

5. Peel and segment the zested clementines, removing as much pith as possible. Spoon half the custard over the sponge, then arrange half the clementine segments on top, starting with a ring around the edge of the bowl. Give the jelly a stir – it should be setting, but still soft. If it has set firm, put the jug in a bowl of hot water and stir to loosen. Spoon half the remaining jelly over the clementines, then chill the trifle for 30min– 1hr. Leave remaining jelly at room temperature.

6. Repeat the custard, clementine and jelly layers, then chill for another 30min–1hr.

7. To serve, whisk the cream, mascarpone and icing sugar to soft peaks. Add the Prosecco and whisk briefly, then spoon on to the trifle. Top with the toasted almonds and orange sprinkles, if using, and serve.

Chocolate Truffle Sauce

A delicious topping that will make any dessert extra special.

250ml single cream
2 tbsp sugar
100g dark chocolate, in small pieces
2 tbsp dark rum

1. Heat the cream and sugar in a pan, stirring until the sugar has dissolved. Bring the mixture just to the boil, removing from heat when steam rises from the surface.

2. Add the chocolate, set aside for 5min, then stir until smooth. Add the rum. Heat on low for 5min and serve in a warm jug, covering the surface in clingfilm to stop a skin from forming.

★ GET AHEAD
Make up to 4hr in advance. Reheat in a pan over a low heat, stirring often.

Rum Butter

For a twist on traditional brandy butter, try our warming rum butter with your Christmas pudding.

200g lightly salted butter, softened
100g icing sugar
4 tbsp dark rum

1. In a bowl, combine the butter and icing sugar, then beat until smooth. Beat in the rum. Keep at room temperature if serving within a couple of hours or cover and chill. Remove from the fridge 2hr before serving.

★ GET AHEAD
Make up to 1 week in advance. Cover and chill.

Hands-on time: 5min
Serves 8

PER 1 TBSP (25G) SERVING 144cals, 0g protein, 12g fat (7g saturates), 7g carbs (7g total sugars), 0g fibre

Hands-on time: 5min
Cooking time: about 5min
Serves 8

PER 1 TBSP (25G) SERVING 87cals, 1g protein, 7g fat (4g saturates), 5g carbs (5g total sugars), 0g fibre

PX and Pear Mincemeat

Rich, sweet Pedro Ximenez sherry, with its flavours of raisins, fig and caramel, is the perfect tipple to splash into your mincemeat, and matches so well with fragrant pear. Serve any leftover sherry alongside mince pies, Christmas pudding or cake.

200g raisins
200g golden sultanas
150g dried cranberries, halved
100g currants
50g crystallised stem ginger, finely chopped
100g mixed peel
2 firm but ripe pears (about 300g), peeled, cored and cut into 1cm cubes
50g blanched almonds, roughly chopped
1½ tsp each ground cinnamon and mixed spice
½ tsp freshly grated nutmeg
Pinch of ground cloves (optional)
Finely grated zest and juice 1 orange
150g vegetarian suet or unsalted butter
200g light muscovado sugar
3 tbsp brandy
250ml Pedro Ximenez sherry

1. Tip all the ingredients, except the sherry, into a large pan. Heat gently until the butter or suet has melted, then simmer gently for 10min, stirring occasionally.

2. Leave to cool for a few minutes, then stir through the sherry and spoon into sterilised jars (see tip on p10). Secure the lids tightly. Label and store in a cool place.

★ GET AHEAD
The mincemeat will keep for up to 6 months. Once opened, store in the fridge and use within 1 week.

Hands-on time: 5min, plus cooling
Cooking time: about 15min
Makes about 1.6kg

PER 1 TBSP SERVING 50cals, 0.3g protein, 2g fat (1g saturates), 8g carbs (7g total sugars), 0.3g fibre

9

Festive Baking

Easiest-ever Gingerbread

Nothing says Christmas quite like the scent of gingerbread filling your kitchen. These simple cookies not only taste delicious, but are also really easy to make.

75g unsalted butter
100g light brown soft sugar
100g golden syrup
225g plain flour, plus extra to dust
2 tsp ground ginger
1 tsp bicarbonate of soda
Coloured icing pens

YOU'LL ALSO NEED
8cm gingerbread man cutter

1. In a small pan, heat the butter, sugar and golden syrup over low heat, stirring until the sugar dissolves. Set aside to cool for 5min.

2. In a medium bowl, mix the flour, ground ginger and bicarbonate of soda. Make a well in the centre and pour in the butter mixture. Stir to combine. Using your hands, bring together to form a soft dough and knead briefly until smooth. Wrap and chill for 15min to firm up slightly.

3. Line 2 large baking sheets with baking parchment. On a lightly floured surface, roll out the dough to 3mm thick. Using the cutter, stamp out shapes, re-rolling trimmings as needed. Transfer to the baking sheets, spacing apart. You should have about 20 biscuits. Chill for 30min.

4. Preheat oven to 190°C (170°C fan) mark 5. Bake the biscuits for 10min, or until sandy to the touch. Leave to cool for 5min on the sheets, then transfer to a wire rack to cool completely. Use the icing pens to decorate. Serve.

★ TO STORE
Spare biscuits can keep in an airtight container at room temperature for up to 3 weeks. You can freeze unbaked dough, wrapped in clingfilm, for up to 1 month. Defrost overnight in the fridge, then complete the recipe.

Hands-on time: 10min, plus cooling and chilling
Cooking time: about 15min
Makes 20 biscuits

PER BISCUIT 96cals, 1g protein, 2g total fat (1g saturates), 18g carbs (9g total sugars), 0g fibre

Chocolate Candy Cane Cake

Wow your guests with our hidden-reveal chocolate cake. We used candy cane meringue kisses to decorate the top, but you could use shop-bought mini candy canes instead or leave the decoration off entirely.

FOR THE SPONGES

250g unsalted butter, softened, plus extra to grease
200g caster sugar
175g dark brown soft sugar
2 tbsp black treacle
3 medium eggs
350ml whole milk
300ml soured cream
2 tsp vanilla extract
350g plain flour
2 tsp bicarbonate of soda
125g cocoa powder

FOR THE PEPPERMINT BUTTERCREAM

300g white chocolate, roughly chopped
525g unsalted butter, chopped and softened
750g icing sugar
4 tsp peppermint extract
Purple food colouring gel or paste (optional)
Extra strong red food colouring paste

YOU'LL ALSO NEED

Peppermint candy canes, crushed (optional)
Meringue kisses, to decorate (optional)
3 large piping bags

★ GET AHEAD

Assemble and decorate the cake up to 1 day ahead. Chill until the buttercream is firm, then cover with clingfilm and chill. Keep any leftovers covered in the fridge for up to 3 days. Serve at room temperature.

Hands-on time: 2hr 15min, plus cooling and chilling
Cooking time: about 1hr
Makes 20 slices

PER SLICE (without meringue decoration) 734cals, 6g protein, 42g fat (26g saturates), 81g carbs (67g total sugars), 2g fibre

1. Preheat oven to 180°C (160°C fan) mark 4. Grease and line the base and sides of 2 x 20.5cm round, deep cake tins with baking parchment. Using a freestanding mixer or a handheld electric whisk and a large bowl, beat the butter, sugars and treacle until pale and fluffy (about 5min). Add the eggs 1 at a time, beating well after each addition.

2. In a jug, mix the milk, soured cream and vanilla. In a separate bowl, sift the flour, bicarbonate of soda and cocoa powder. With the motor running slowly, add a third of the flour mixture to the butter mixture. When almost incorporated, add a third of the milk mixture. Continue adding until all the dry and liquid ingredients have been mixed in (don't overwork it at this stage).

3. Divide between the prepared tins and smooth to level. Bake for 55min, or until a skewer inserted into the centre comes out clean. Cool in the tins.

4. Make the buttercream. Melt the white chocolate in a heatproof bowl set over a pan of barely simmering water. When melted and smooth, remove the bowl and set aside to cool for 15min. Using a freestanding mixer or a handheld electric whisk and a very large bowl (make in 2 batches if you don't have a very large bowl), beat the butter until very pale and fluffy. Sift in half the icing sugar and beat to combine (start on a low speed, to prevent a cloud of sugar). Sift in remaining icing sugar and add the peppermint extract and cooled chocolate. Using a cocktail stick, add a drop of purple food colouring, if using, and beat in – this will help neutralise the yellow colour of the buttercream. Beat until light and fluffy.

5. Spoon a quarter of the buttercream into a separate bowl and add enough red food colouring to dye it a rich red. Scrape into a piping bag. Divide the remaining white buttercream between 2 piping bags. Set aside (do not chill).

6. Slice each cake in half horizontally. Set aside 1 base and place the other 3 sponges in front of you. Snip 1.5cm off the end of the red and 1 white icing piping bags, and pipe concentric circles of alternating red and white buttercream on each of the 3 sponges, starting with white on the outside edge (see GH tips). Place 1 piped sponge on a cake board or flat plate, then carefully stack the remaining sponges on top, finishing with the undecorated base sponge, bottom-side up. Pipe and spread a thin layer of white buttercream over the top and sides of cake – this acts as a crumb coat – and chill for 30min.

7. Place the cake (on its board/plate) on a cake turntable, if you have one. Pipe and spread the remaining white buttercream over the top and sides of the cake, smoothing it carefully to get a flat, even finish (a large ruler or palette knife is useful for this, particularly for the sides). Chill briefly to firm up the icing.

8. To finish, gently press crushed candy canes, if using, on the bottom third of the cake. Top with meringues, if using, and serve.

★ GH TIPS
• It's important your outermost rings of buttercream filling are white, otherwise the red is likely to seep into the icing layer later on, making it pink.
• If you have fridge space, chill the piped sponges, uncovered, for 10min before stacking, to help keep the stripes neat.

Gin and Tea Christmas Cake

A celebration of two great British drinks.

1.2kg dried mixed fruit
75g dates (stoned), roughly chopped
6 tbsp loose leaf Earl Grey tea
100ml gin, to soak the fruit, plus extra to feed the cake
200g unsalted butter, softened
200g dark brown muscovado sugar
1 tbsp treacle
4 medium eggs, beaten
250g plain flour
1 tsp mixed spice
½ tsp ground allspice
75g walnut pieces

1. Put the dried fruit and dates into a large non-metallic bowl. Stir 2 tbsp tea leaves into 200ml hot water and pour over the fruit with the gin. Stir, then cover the bowl with clingfilm and leave to soak overnight at room temperature.

2. Preheat oven to 140°C (120°C fan) mark 1. Grease and line the base and sides of a deep, 20.5cm round cake tin with parchment, making sure it comes 2cm above the top. Wrap a double layer of parchment around the outside of the tin and secure with string.

3. Beat the butter, sugar and treacle with a handheld electric whisk until light and fluffy. Gradually beat in the eggs – if it looks like it might curdle, beat in 1 tbsp flour. With a metal spoon, mix in the flour, remaining tea, spices, soaked fruit with liquid, and walnuts. Scrape into the tin and level.

4. Bake for 3hr 15–3hr 30min, or until a skewer inserted into the centre comes out clean. Cool in the tin for 30min, then remove from tin (still in its parchment) and cool completely on a wire rack.

★ TO STORE AND FEED
Wrap the cooled cake (still in its parchment) in a couple of layers of clingfilm, then foil. Store in a cool place. After 2 weeks, unwrap, prick all over and pour over 1 tbsp gin. Rewrap and store, feeding every few weeks for a stronger flavour. Store for up to 3 months.

Hands-on time: 25min, plus (overnight) soaking, cooling and feeding
Cooking time: about 3hr 30min
Makes 16 slices

PER SLICE 489cals, 6g protein, 15g fat (7g saturates), 77g carbs (65g total sugars), 3g fibre

Gingerbread Liqueur Bundt

Gingerbread liqueur adds another level of flavour to this cake, but you can use whisky or spiced rum, if you prefer.

150g unsalted butter, chopped, plus extra to grease
200g dark brown soft sugar
75g black treacle
100ml vegetable oil
100ml gingerbread liqueur
300g plain flour
1 tbsp ground ginger
½ tsp ground allspice
2 tsp ground cinnamon
100ml whole milk
3 medium eggs

FOR THE DRIZZLE AND DECORATION
100g icing sugar, sifted
1½–2 tbsp non-creamy gingerbread liqueur
1 tbsp chopped dried cranberries
½ tbsp cranberry powder (optional; available online)

1. Grease a roughly 23cm bundt tin. In a medium pan over low heat, stir the butter, sugar and treacle until melted. Remove from the heat and stir in the oil and liqueur. Leave to cool slightly.

2. Preheat oven to 180°C (160°C fan) mark 4. In a bowl, mix the flour and spices and make a well in the centre. Whisk the milk and eggs into the butter mixture, pour into the dry ingredients and whisk well to make a smooth batter.

3. Pour into the tin and bake for 45min, or until a skewer inserted into the centre comes out clean. Leave to cool completely in the tin.

4. Invert the cake on to a stand and remove the tin. In a bowl, mix the icing sugar and 1½ tbsp gingerbread liqueur to make a thick drizzle. (Add up to ½ tbsp more liqueur, if needed.) Drizzle over the cake and scatter with dried and powdered cranberries, if using. Let the icing set, then serve.

★ TO STORE
Once the icing has set, keep in an airtight container at room temperature for up to 4 days.

Hands-on time: 25min, plus cooling and setting
Cooking time: about 50min
Serves 16

PER SERVING 313cals, 4g protein, 14g fat (6g saturates), 39g carbs (24g total sugars), 1g fibre

A Tree That Twinkles – Quick Christmas Cake Decoration

This easy, stylish decoration is quick to achieve, and you can adapt the sugarpaste colour and sprinkles to your taste. Once iced, the decorating takes just minutes.

FOR THE CAKE
2–3 tbsp smooth or sieved apricot jam
20.5cm fruit cake (see Gin and Tea Christmas Cake p220)
Icing sugar, to dust
500g natural or golden marzipan
500g navy sugarpaste (see GH Tip)
Brandy, gin, vodka or cooled boiled water, to brush

FOR THE DECORATION
80g royal icing sugar (see Firm royal icing tip, p11, to make your own)
Edible gold and/or silver balls
Festive sugar sprinkles, including gold stars
Edible silver glitter spray (optional)

YOU'LL ALSO NEED
Ribbon
3–4 mm plain or closed-star nozzle

★ GH TIP
Sugarpaste is also known as fondant or ready-to-roll icing. You can buy it readily online in many colours.

★ GET AHEAD
You can ice your cake up to a couple of weeks ahead. Store at room temperature.

1. A day before you want to decorate the cake, gently warm the apricot jam in a small pan to make it easier to brush. Put the cake on to a board and brush the top and sides with jam. Set aside.

2. Lightly dust a work surface with icing sugar and roll out the marzipan until large enough to cover the cake. Lift on to the cake, smooth into position and trim the excess. Leave overnight (ideally 24hr) at room temperature to harden slightly.

3. Dust a work surface with icing sugar and roll out the navy sugarpaste until large enough to cover the cake. Lightly brush the marzipan layer with alcohol/cooled boiled water to moisten. Lift the sugarpaste on to the cake and gently smooth it into position. Trim excess. Transfer to a cake stand or plate. Secure a ribbon around the base of the cake.

4. For the decoration, in a medium bowl, whisk the royal icing sugar with 10ml water to make a thick but pipeable paste. Transfer to a piping bag fitted with a 3–4mm plain or closed-star nozzle. Pipe a looping, descending pattern on top of the cake to resemble a tree. Pipe a triangle at the base to resemble a tree trunk. While still wet, decorate the royal icing with gold/silver balls and sprinkles.

5. If you like, pipe a cross at the top of the tree and load with gold star sprinkles. Spray with edible silver glitter, if using, and let set before serving.

Hands-on time: 20min, plus (overnight) hardening and setting
Makes 16 slices

Untangle the Lights – Christmas Cake Decoration

Have fun moulding these cute and cosy chilly-weather characters with their messy box of lights. You don't have to make all the elements – just pick your favourites and let the scene unfold.

FOR THE PENGUINS
Black, white, red, orange and white sugarpaste

FOR THE REINDEER AND BOX
Brown, white, black and red sugarpaste

FOR THE TREE
Green, brown and yellow sugarpaste

FOR THE LIGHTS
Your chosen colours of sugarpaste (we used blue, green, purple, red, orange and yellow)
Black liquorice laces or wheels (see GH Tips)

FOR THE CAKE
2–3 tbsp smooth or sieved apricot jam
20.5cm fruit cake (see Gin and Tea Christmas Cake p220)
Icing sugar, to dust
500g natural or golden marzipan
500g white sugarpaste
Brandy, gin, vodka or cooled boiled water, to brush
1 batch royal icing (see Firm royal icing tip, p11) or edible glue

YOU'LL ALSO NEED
2 cocktail sticks

1. A couple of days before you want to decorate the cake, make the figurines. For the penguins, use black sugarpaste to shape 2 ovals for the bodies and 2 balls for the heads. Lightly press the balls on to the ovals. With clean hands (as black sugarpaste can stain), shape a little white sugarpaste into a flat figure of 8, then press on to the body and head. Repeat for the other penguin.

2. Next, use black sugarpaste to shape 4 flippers and press to the sides of the bodies, arranging them as if hanging lights or holding a wire (use a little royal icing/edible glue/water, if needed, to stick). Using orange sugarpaste, shape 2 beaks and 4 feet (adding indentations to the feet, if you like, using a cocktail stick). Stick the beaks to the faces and the feet to the bodies of the penguins, either underneath the body or in front, depending on whether you want your penguins to sit or stand.

3. Using red sugarpaste, shape 2 cones, with indents in the bases to accommodate the heads. Gently press on to the penguin heads, then stick a white sugarpaste ball to the tips. Using a cocktail stick, press in some eyes. Place on a large baking sheet lined with baking parchment and leave at room temperature to harden (ideally for 48hr).

Hands-on time: 1hr 30min, plus 48hr hardening and setting
Makes 16 slices

Continues over the page...

★ GET AHEAD
You can ice your cake up
to 2 weeks ahead. Store
at room temperature.

4. Next, make the reindeer. Using brown sugarpaste, make an oval for the body and a head with a snout. Gently press the head on to the oval. Mix a little brown sugarpaste into some white sugarpaste to make a lighter brown. You'll need enough to shape the tummy, nose, antlers, the inside of the ears and the box.

5. Using some of the light brown sugarpaste, shape a rounded, flat triangle to fit on the reindeer tummy and snip the edges with scissors to resemble fur. Stick in place. Next, shape a flat oval and stick on to the end of the snout. Using a cocktail stick, press in some eyes.

6. Wrap a small amount of light brown sugarpaste around the top 2cm of a cocktail stick and shape the end into an antler. Repeat to make a second antler, then gently press both into the reindeer head. Using both light and darker brown sugarpaste, shape triangular ears and stick to the sides of the head.

7. Using the darker brown sugarpaste, shape 4 legs and stick a small black ball to the end of each. Add an indent to each ball using a cocktail stick to resemble a hoof. Stick the legs to the body of the reindeer and add a red sugarpaste ball for the nose. Put the reindeer on the lined sheet with the penguins to harden.

8. Use either light or darker brown sugarpaste to shape a box for the lights and add to the lined sheet to harden. To make the Christmas tree, shape green sugarpaste into a cone. To add some texture, snip into the cone using sharp pointed scissors. Set aside on the lined sheet to harden (on its side). Using brown sugarpaste, model a tree stump and then, using yellow sugarpaste, shape a star for the top of the tree. Set both aside to harden.

9. Finally, make the lights. Pinch off small pieces of sugarpaste in your chosen colours and shape into lightbulbs. Place on the lined sheet to harden.

10. A day before you want to decorate the cake, in a small pan, gently warm the apricot jam to make it easier to brush. Put the cake on to a board and brush the top and sides with jam. Set aside.

11. Lightly dust a work surface with icing sugar and roll out the marzipan until large enough to cover the cake. Lift on to the cake and gently smooth into position. Trim excess. Leave overnight (ideally 24hr) at room temperature to harden.

12. To finish icing the cake, dust a work surface with icing sugar and roll out the white sugarpaste until large enough to cover the cake. Lightly brush the marzipan layer with alcohol/cooled boiled water to moisten. Lift the sugarpaste on to the cake and gently smooth into position. Trim excess. Transfer to a cake stand or plate.

13. To assemble, using royal icing/edible glue, stick the tree cone to the stump and on to the cake, together with the animal figurines and box. Using the liquorice laces and royal icing/edible glue where needed, arrange a jumble of black 'cable' in the box and run lengths around the tree and among the animals. Remember, it doesn't all need to attach at all places, just visually from the front. Stick the laces in a looping line around the sides of the cake. Finally, stick your lights along the cable length and the star to the tree. Allow to set before serving in triumph.

★ GH TIPS
• If using liquorice wheels, unravel and, using scissors, snip in half along the length to make thinner strands.
• Add a cosy scarf for your animals by twizzling together thin strands of red and white sugarpaste.

Pumpkin Pie Brownies

If you don't tell people about the secret ingredient in these gluten-free brownies, we promise they'll never guess! These brownies are deep, rich and gooey.

200g unsalted butter, plus extra to grease
200g dark gluten-free chocolate (70% cocoa solids), roughly chopped
400g tin black beans, drained and rinsed
250g light muscovado sugar
50g cocoa powder
3 medium eggs
2 tsp vanilla extract
1½ tsp gluten-free baking powder

FOR THE PUMPKIN SWIRL
75g full-fat cream cheese
175g tinned pumpkin purée (100% pure)
75g caster sugar
1 medium egg
1 tsp mixed spice
1 tsp vanilla extract

1. Preheat oven to 180°C (160°C fan) mark 4. Grease and line a deep 20.5cm square tin with baking parchment. In a medium pan over low heat, melt the butter and chocolate until combined. Set aside to cool for 10min.

2. Whisk all the ingredients for the pumpkin swirl in a small bowl, until smooth. Set aside.

3. Put the black beans in a food processor, add the melted butter/chocolate mixture and whizz until smooth. Add the remaining brownie ingredients with a pinch of salt and whizz again, scraping down the sides with a spatula.

4. Scrape half the brownie batter into the prepared tin and spread to level. Spoon three-quarters of the pumpkin mixture on top, then finish with the remaining brownie batter, followed by the remaining pumpkin mix in dollops. Gently run a knife or skewer through layers to marble. Bake for 40–45min until the top feels set to the touch. Cool completely in the tin before cutting into squares.

Hands-on time: 20min, plus cooling
Cooking time: about 50min
Makes 16 brownies

PER BROWNIE 300cals, 5g protein, 17g fat (10g saturates), 30g carbs (28g total sugars), 3g fibre

Sugar Cookie Wreaths

Crisp and buttery, these will hold their shape during baking. Ideal for getting creative with icing.

150g unsalted butter, softened
150g golden caster sugar
1 tsp vanilla extract or vanilla bean paste
2 medium eggs
350g plain flour, plus extra to dust

FOR THE ROSE AND PISTACHIO ICING (optional)
200g icing sugar
75g slivered pistachios, roughly chopped (see GH Tip)
25g crystallised rose petal pieces

FOR THE FEATHERED ICING (optional)
300g icing sugar
Pink food colouring gel or paste

★ GH TIP
If you can't find slivered pistachios, use roughly chopped pistachio kernels instead.

★ TO STORE
Once set, keep in an airtight container at room temperature for up to 3 days. The biscuits will soften over time.

Hands-on time: 1hr, plus chilling, cooling and setting
Cooking time: about 15min
Makes about 36 cookies

PER COOKIE (Rose/pistachio) 123cals, 2g protein, 5g fat (2g saturates), 18g carbs (10g total sugars), 0g fibre

PER COOKIE (Feathered) 121cals, 1g protein, 4g fat (2g saturates), 20g carbs (13g total sugars), 0g fibre

1. For the cookies, in a large bowl using a handheld electric whisk, beat the butter, sugar and vanilla until pale and fluffy. Add the eggs 1 at a time, beating well after each addition. Add the flour and beat until just combined. Tip on to a work surface and shape into a disc. Wrap and chill for at least 1hr (or up to 24hr) to firm up.

2. Line 3 large baking sheets with baking parchment. Dust a work surface with flour, split the dough in half and roll out to 3mm thick. Stamp out circles using a 7cm round fluted cutter. Transfer the circles to the lined sheets, spacing slightly apart. Repeat the process with trimmings and the remaining dough.

3. Using a 2–2.5cm round fluted or plain cutter, stamp out the centres of the larger rounds. Re-roll trimmings as before and stamp out more cookies, if you like. You should have about 36. Chill again for 20min, to firm up.

4. Preheat oven to 180°C (160°C fan) mark 4. Bake the cookies for 12–14min, or until the edges are lightly golden. Cool completely on the sheets.

5. If making the rose and pistachio icing, sift the icing sugar into a medium bowl and mix in enough water to make a thick but pourable consistency (about 40ml). Working 1 cookie at a time, dip the top into the icing, gently shake off the excess, smooth with a palette knife and place on a wire rack (icing up). Sprinkle over some pistachios and crystallised rose petal pieces. Repeat with remaining cookies. Leave to set at room temperature before serving.

6. If making the feathered icing, sift 200g icing sugar into a medium bowl and mix in enough

water to make a thick, but pourable consistency (about 40ml) and enough food colouring to reach your desired shade of pink. In a medium bowl, sift the remaining 100g icing sugar and mix with enough water to make a drizzling consistency (about 25ml).

7. Working 1 cookie at a time, dip the top into the pink icing, gently shake off excess, smooth with a palette knife and place on a wire rack (icing up). Repeat with a few more cookies. Before the pink icing sets, using a tsp, drizzle horizontal lines of the white icing across the iced cookies. Using a cocktail stick, drag the white icing in vertical lines across the cookies to give a feathered effect.

8. Continue to ice the remaining cookies. Leave to set at room temperature before serving.

Marmalade and Chocolate Mince Pies

The orange zest in the pastry really brings out the flavour here. You'll have more mincemeat than you need, but it keeps well (see GH Tip)

FOR THE MARMALADE MINCEMEAT
150g mixed dried fruit
150g chopped mixed peel
Finely grated zest and juice 1 orange
3 tbsp fine-shred marmalade
100g light brown soft sugar
1 tsp ground mixed spice
50g vegetable suet
25ml orange liqueur

FOR THE PASTRY
350g plain flour, plus extra to dust
40g cocoa powder
100g icing sugar
275g unsalted butter, chilled and cubed
Finely grated zest 1 orange
2 medium eggs
Edible gold spray, to decorate (optional)

1. For the mincemeat, combine all the ingredients except the orange liqueur in a medium pan. Stir over low heat until the sugar dissolves, about 10min. Remove from the heat, stir in the liqueur and set aside to cool completely (it will thicken as it cools).

2. To make the pastry, pulse the flour, cocoa, icing sugar and a pinch of salt in a food processor to combine. Add the butter and orange zest and pulse until the mixture resembles fine breadcrumbs. Alternatively, mix the dry ingredients together in a large bowl, then rub in the butter and orange zest with your fingers.

3. Add 1 egg and pulse/mix until the pastry clumps together. Tip on to a work surface, bring together into a ball, then divide into 3 equal pieces and shape into flattish discs. Wrap each in clingfilm and chill for 1hr.

4. Lightly flour a work surface and, working with 1 portion of dough at a time (and keeping the others chilled), roll out the pastry to 3mm thick. Stamp out 12 circles using an 8cm cutter and use to line a 12-hole bun tin. Repeat with a second piece of dough and another tin.

5. Preheat oven to 190°C (170°C fan) mark 5. Put 1 heaped tsp mincemeat in each pastry case. Roll out the remaining pastry to 3mm thick and stamp out 24 stars with a 6cm cutter (re-roll trimmings as necessary). Top each mince pie with a star lid. Beat the remaining egg in a small bowl and use to glaze the pastry stars.

6. Bake for 20min, or until pastry is crisp and mincemeat bubbling. Leave to cool in the tins for 10min, then carefully transfer to a wire rack. Once cooled, decorate with gold spray (if using) and serve.

Hands-on time: 30min, plus cooling and chilling
Cooking time: about 30min
Makes 24 pies

PER MINCE PIE 247cals, 3g protein, 12g fat (7g saturates), 30g carbs (17g total sugars), 1g fibre

★ GET AHEAD
Make up to 3 days ahead, then store in an
airtight container at room temperature.
To serve warm, reheat in an oven preheated
to 170°C (150°C fan) mark 3 for 5min.

★ GH TIP
Store leftover mincemeat in an airtight container
in the fridge for up to 1 month. Use it to make
more mince pies, or try it rippled through
softened vanilla ice cream for an easy pud.

Chocolate Caramel Peanut Butter Cups

You can make these in paper cases, but the chocolate is more likely to stick, so leave the cups in the cases until just before serving.

300g milk, white or dark chocolate, finely chopped
2 tbsp coconut oil
200g crunchy peanut butter
25g icing sugar, sifted
1 tsp vanilla extract
12 tbsp Carnation caramel

YOU'LL ALSO NEED
12 silicone or foil-lined muffin cases

1. Line a 12-hole muffin tin with muffin cases.

2. Melt the chocolate and coconut oil together in a medium heatproof bowl set over a pan of barely simmering water. Remove from heat and set aside to cool for 10min, stirring occasionally.

3. Working one case at a time, spoon ½ tbsp chocolate into a muffin case, then use a small spoon or pastry brush to evenly spread it about two-thirds up the sides. Repeat until all 12 cases are coated (you will have leftover chocolate), then freeze for 15min to set. Repeat the coating and setting once more.

4. In a medium bowl with a handheld electric whisk, combine the peanut butter, icing sugar and vanilla.

5. Divide the peanut butter mixture among the chocolate cases and level. Spoon 1 tbsp caramel into each; spread evenly. Freeze for 30min until firm. If the remaining chocolate has set, melt it as before.

6. Top the cups with the remaining chocolate, spreading so it coats and seals the edges. Chill for 1hr until set, then peel off cases and serve.

★ TO STORE
Transfer the chocolate cups to an airtight container and store in the fridge or freezer for up to 2 weeks.

Hands-on time: 45min, plus cooling and chilling
Cooking time: about 10min
Makes 12 cups

PER CUP 317cals, 7g protein, 20g fat (9g saturates), 28g carbs (27g total sugars), 1g fibre

Double Chocolate and Chestnut Sandwich Biscuits

Chestnut purée adds a sweet nuttiness, but you could use a buttercream filling instead.

125g unsalted butter, chilled and cubed
60g golden caster sugar
150g plain flour, plus extra to dust
25g cocoa powder, plus extra to dust (optional)

FOR THE FILLING
100g white chocolate, melted and cooled
150g chestnut purée, drained (see GH Tip)
3 tbsp icing sugar, plus extra to dust (optional)

1. Line 2 large baking sheets with parchment. For the biscuits, in a food processor, whizz the butter, sugar, flour and cocoa powder until the mixture clumps together. Tip on to a lightly floured work surface and roll out to a rectangle roughly 18 x 34cm, about 3mm thick. Trim the edges to neaten.

2. Slice the rectangle into 24 rectangles, each roughly 3 x 8.5cm. Transfer to the baking sheets, spacing slightly apart. Chill for 30min.

3. Preheat oven to 180°C (160°C fan) mark 4. Bake the biscuits for 15min, or until the edges feel firm. Leave to cool on the sheets for 5min, then transfer to a wire rack to cool completely.

4. For the filling, whizz all the ingredients in the small bowl of a food processor until smooth. Chill to firm up a little, if needed.

5. Pipe or spread the filling over the bases of half the biscuits and sandwich together with the remaining biscuits. If you like, dust half of each with a little cocoa powder and icing sugar. Serve.

★ TO STORE
Keep in an airtight container at room temperature for up to 2 days.

★ GH TIP
Leftover chestnut purée is great for adding to soups, stews, pastas and creamy puddings.

Hands-on time: 30min, plus chilling and cooling
Cooking time: about 15min
Makes 12 sandwich biscuits

PER SANDWICH BISCUIT 226cals, 3g protein, 12g fat (7g saturates), 26g carbs (14g total sugars), 1g fibre

Aperol Spritz Upside-down Cake

The aromatic spritz isn't just for summer – when coupled with caramelised oranges and a light batter, it makes for a wonderful and warming pudding cake.

FOR THE CARAMELISED ORANGES
25g unsalted butter, plus extra to grease
3 oranges
25g caster sugar
1 tbsp Aperol

FOR THE CAKE
100g unsalted butter, softened
200g caster sugar
2 medium eggs, beaten
75ml Aperol
100g Greek-style yogurt
1 tsp vanilla extract
275g plain flour
2 tsp baking powder
100ml Prosecco

FOR THE SYRUP
75ml smooth orange juice
2 tbsp Aperol
1 tsp icing sugar

1. Preheat oven to 180°C (160°C fan) mark 4. Grease and line a 20.5cm round cake tin with a single large sheet of baking parchment, smoothing the base and edges as best you can. For the caramelised oranges, finely grate the zest of 2 oranges and set aside for the cake.

Hands-on time: 30min, plus cooling
Cooking time: about 1hr 20min
Serves 10

PER SERVING (without cream) 353cals, 6g protein, 12g fat (7g saturates), 52g carbs (31g total sugars), 2g fibre

Next, slice off the peel and white pith from all the oranges and cut the fruit into 1cm-thick slices.

2. Sprinkle the sugar into a large non-stick frying pan. Cook over low heat, swirling the pan rather than stirring, until golden and caramelised. Carefully add the butter and Aperol, stirring until smooth. Arrange the orange slices in the caramel and cook for 3–5min, until the bases are golden. Remove the pan from heat and transfer the orange slices only (caramelised side down) to the base of the tin in an even layer. Set the caramel pan aside for the syrup.

3. For the cake, in a large bowl using a handheld electric whisk, beat the butter, sugar and reserved orange zest until light and fluffy. Gradually beat in the eggs, then the Aperol, yogurt and vanilla, until combined. Using a large metal spoon, fold in the flour, baking powder and a pinch of fine salt. Finally, pour in the Prosecco and fold in.

4. Scrape the batter into the tin on top of the oranges and smooth to level. Bake for 1hr, or until a skewer inserted into the centre of the cake comes out clean. Leave to cool.

5. For the syrup, add all the ingredients to the reserved caramel pan. Bubble over high heat, whisking, for 5min, or until syrupy. Set aside.

6. To serve, invert the cake on to a stand or plate. Remove tin and parchment. Drizzle over the syrup and serve just warm or at room temperature.

★ TO STORE
Once cool, keep in an airtight container at room temperature for up to 2 days.

Spiced Chocolate Crinkle Cookies

These easy treats are somewhere between a cake and a biscuit in texture, with a grown-up aromatic spice twist from the cardamom and chilli.

75g salted butter
175g caster sugar
6 green cardamom pods, seeds finely ground and
    husks discarded
¼ tsp mild chilli powder
2 medium eggs
175g plain flour
75g cocoa powder
25g icing sugar

1. Melt the butter in a small pan, then pour into a bowl and set aside to cool for 5min. Stir in the caster sugar and spices, then the eggs, one at a time. Sift over the flour, cocoa, and a pinch of salt and stir to combine. Cover and chill for 1hr.

2. Preheat oven to 180°C (160°C fan) mark 4 and line 2 large baking sheets with baking parchment. Put the icing sugar into a small bowl. Divide the dough into 20 even pieces. If the dough is sticky, dust your hands with a little icing sugar as you work.

3. Roll the balls in the icing sugar, then arrange on the lined baking sheets, spacing apart. Flatten very slightly with the palm of your hand. Dust any remaining icing sugar over the cookies.

4. Bake for 20–25min, until cracked on top and fairly firm (they will continue to firm up as they cool). Allow to cool on sheets for 5min before transferring to a wire rack to cool completely.

★ TO STORE
Store in an airtight container at room temperature for up to 2 days.

Hands-on time: 15min, plus cooling and chilling
Cooking time: about 30min
Makes 20 cookies

PER COOKIE 122cals, 3g protein, 5g fat (3g saturates), 17g carbs (10g total sugars), 1g fibre

Nutella and Baileys Cheesecake Brownies

These delicious, fudgy squares store well – though you're unlikely to have leftovers.

FOR THE BROWNIES
150g butter, melted, plus extra to grease
300g chocolate hazelnut spread
150g light brown soft sugar
3 medium eggs
50ml Irish cream liqueur
1 tsp vanilla extract
50g cocoa powder
75g plain flour

FOR THE CHEESECAKE SWIRL
100g full-fat cream cheese
25g caster sugar
25g plain flour
1 medium egg yolk
50ml Irish cream liqueur

1. Preheat oven to 180°C (160°C fan) mark 4. Lightly grease and line a 20.5cm square tin with baking parchment. For the brownies, in a medium bowl using a handheld electric whisk, beat 250g chocolate hazelnut spread, the sugar, eggs, Irish cream liqueur and vanilla until smooth.

2. Sift in the cocoa and flour and add the butter. Beat until combined. Scrape into the lined tin.

3. For the cheesecake swirl, in a small bowl whisk all the ingredients until smooth. Dollop spoonfuls of the cheesecake mixture and remaining 50g chocolate hazelnut spread over the brownie mixture, then use a skewer to marble the dollops through the brownie mixture.

4. Bake for 35–40min, or until the top feels dry and there's no wobble when you shake the tin. Cool in the tin. Transfer to a board; cut into 16 squares.

★ TO STORE
Keep in an airtight container in the fridge for up to 5 days. Serve chilled or at room temperature.

Hands-on time: 15min, plus cooling
Cooking time: about 40min
Cuts into 16 brownies

PER BROWNIE 403cals, 6g protein, 24g fat
(12g saturates), 38g carbs (30g total sugars), 2g fibre

Black Forest Yule Log

This take on the Christmas classic features the flavours of another traditional favourite, with a fruity, boozy hit of cherries and kirsch.

FOR THE ROULADE
Butter, to grease
5 large eggs
100g caster sugar, plus 2 tsp to dust
1 tsp vanilla extract
60g plain flour
40g cocoa powder, plus 2 tsp to dust

FOR THE GANACHE
200g dark chocolate (70% cocoa)
200ml double cream
1 tbsp golden syrup

FOR THE FILLING
100ml double cream
75g white chocolate, melted and cooled
2 tbsp kirsch
5 tbsp cherry jam
125g black cherries in syrup (drained weight),
    roughly chopped

TO DECORATE (optional)
Cherries
Gold or silver leaf
White chocolate, melted

Hands-on time: 40min, plus cooling and chilling
Cooking time: about 20min
Serves 12

PER SERVING 378cals, 6g protein, 23g fat
(13g saturates), 35g carbs (31g total sugars), 1g fibre

1. Preheat oven to 180°C (160°C fan) mark 4. Grease and line a 23 x 33cm swiss roll tin with baking parchment. For the roulade, using a freestanding mixer or a handheld electric whisk and a large bowl, beat the eggs and sugar until thick, about 5min. Beat in the vanilla extract.

2. Sift over the flour and cocoa powder, and gently fold in using a large metal spoon. Scrape into the prepared tin and gently spread to level. Bake for 15min, or until the sponge is firm to the touch. Dust the top with the extra cocoa powder and caster sugar, lay a piece of baking parchment on top, then place a wire rack over the top. Invert the sponge on to the parchment and rack and gently peel away the top lining parchment. While warm, carefully roll up the sponge from a long edge, using the parchment to help. Cool on a wire rack (rolled).

3. To make the ganache, whizz the chocolate in a food processor until fine (or finely chop by hand), then tip into a heatproof bowl. Heat the cream and golden syrup in a small pan over medium heat until almost boiling. Pour over the chocolate, leave for 2min, then stir gently until melted and combined. Cover loosely and set aside while you make the filling.

4. Whisk the cream until it just holds its shape. Beat in the melted, cooled white chocolate until stiff. Gently unroll the sponge, then spread the cream mixture over the top. Mix the kirsch and jam and drizzle over the cream, then scatter over the chopped cherries. With the help of the parchment, roll up the sponge again. Using

a serrated knife, cut a short section diagonally from 1 end (this will become the 'branch').

5. Transfer the longer roulade to a serving plate or board, seam-side down, and place the cut section on 1 side to look like a 'branch'. Slowly pour or spoon the ganache over the roulade and spread with a small palette knife. Chill for at least 20min to set before serving.

★ GH TIP
For an extra luxe presentation, decorate with fresh cherries wrapped in gold or silver leaf, or dipped in white chocolate.

★ GET AHEAD
Make up to 1 day ahead, cover loosely and chill.

Chocolate and Orange Bundt

With a classic flavour combination, this easy-to-master cake is sure to become a new favourite.

225g unsalted butter, softened, plus extra to grease
225g caster sugar
2 tbsp apricot conserve
4 medium eggs, lightly beaten
175g self-raising flour
Finely grated zest and juice 1 orange, keep separate
1 tsp baking powder
50g cocoa powder
1 tsp vanilla extract

FOR THE GANACHE
200ml double cream
100g dark chocolate (70% cocoa solids), chopped
Chocolate stars, to decorate (optional)

★ TO STORE
Keep in an airtight container at room temperature for up to 3 days.

1. Preheat oven to 170°C (150°C fan) mark 3. Thoroughly grease a 23cm bundt tin (roughly 1.8 litre capacity).

2. Using a freestanding mixer, or with a handheld electric whisk, beat together the butter, sugar and apricot conserve until pale and fluffy (about 5min). Gradually add the eggs, beating well after each addition. If the mixture looks as if it might curdle, add 1 tbsp flour. Beat in the orange zest.

3. Sift in the remaining flour, baking powder and cocoa powder, then fold in with a large metal spoon. Next, fold in the vanilla extract and orange juice until combined.

4. Spoon the mixture into the tin and shake gently to level. Bake for 45–50min until risen and a skewer inserted into the centre of the cake comes out clean. Allow the cake to cool for 5min in the tin, then invert on to a wire rack, remove tin and leave to cool completely.

5. To make the ganache, heat the cream until warm in a heatproof bowl set over a pan of barely simmering water. Add the chocolate and stir until melted and smooth. Take the bowl off the heat and leave to cool for a few minutes – the texture should be loose enough to drizzle but thick enough to stay on the cake. If it is too thick, add a little more cream.

6. Transfer the cake to a cake stand or serving plate. Spoon the ganache over the cake and decorate with chocolate stars, if you like. Serve in slices.

Hands-on time: 25min, plus cooling
Cooking time: about 50min
Serves 8

PER SERVING 659cals, 8g protein, 44g fat (27g saturates), 57g carbs (39g total sugars), 2g fibre

Chestnut and Chocolate Macaroon

As beautiful as it is delicious – and the nuts add a wonderful chewiness to the meringue.

FOR THE MERINGUES
175g blanched hazelnuts
4 medium egg whites
275g icing sugar, sifted, plus extra to dust
½ tsp bicarbonate of soda

FOR THE DECORATION
50g plain chocolate, chopped
Gold sugared almonds (optional)

FOR THE FILLINGS
50g plain chocolate, chopped
125g chestnut purée
1 tbsp maple syrup
225g mascarpone cheese
200ml double cream

1. Heat oven to 130°C (110°C fan) mark ½. Line 3 large baking sheets with parchment. On each sheet of parchment, draw a 20.5cm circle, then flip over the sheets so the ink is on the bottom.

2. Whizz the hazelnuts in a food processor until coarsely ground (do not over-process the nuts or they will become oily). Set aside.

3. Put the egg whites into a large bowl and beat with a handheld electric whisk until they hold firm peaks. Add half the icing sugar and the bicarbonate of soda and (going slowly at first to prevent an icing-sugar cloud) beat until it forms stiff peaks again. Fold in the remaining icing sugar and ground nuts using a large metal spoon.

4. Divide the hazelnut mixture among the 3 circles on the prepared sheets and smooth into even rounds following the templates. Bake for 1hr 15min, then turn off the oven and leave the meringues inside to cool completely.

5. While baking the meringues, make the decoration. Melt the chocolate in a heatproof bowl set over a pan of barely simmering water. When the chocolate is melted and smooth, pour it on to a wooden board and spread to an even thickness of 3mm. Chill to firm up. When chilled, run a large sharp knife firmly across the firm chocolate to make long curls. Chill the curls until needed.

6. While the meringues are cooling, make the fillings. Melt the chocolate in a large heatproof bowl set over a pan of barely simmering water. When the chocolate is melted and smooth, take bowl off the pan and leave to cool completely.

7. In a separate bowl, mix the chestnut purée, maple syrup and 100g of the mascarpone until smooth. Set aside. In a final bowl, whip the cream until it just holds its shape. Fold half the cream into the chestnut filling. Beat the remaining cream and mascarpone into the cooled chocolate bowl.

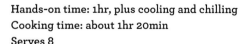

Hands-on time: 1hr, plus cooling and chilling
Cooking time: about 1hr 20min
Serves 8

PER SERVING 622cals, 8g protein, 44g fat (20g saturates), 48g carbs (45g total sugars), 2g fibre

8. To assemble, spread the chocolate filling over the top of one meringue and the chestnut filling over the top of another. Dollop a little chestnut filling on to a serving plate (to help the meringue stick in place) and lay on the chocolate-covered meringue. Top with the chestnut-covered meringue, then the final meringue disc.

9. Pile on the chocolate curls and scatter with gold sugared almonds, if using.

★ GET AHEAD
Make to end of step 8 up to 1 day ahead. Loosely cover with foil and chill. To serve, allow to come up to room temperature before completing the recipe.

Chocolate Gingerbread Cake with White Chocolate Buttercream

Festive spices meet chocolate in this rich and moist chocolate gingerbread cake – the perfect centrepiece for any gathering.

FOR THE SUGARED ROSEMARY TREES
1 egg white
5 rosemary sprigs, cut to varying lengths
Caster sugar, to dredge

FOR THE CAKE
175ml vegetable oil, plus extra to grease
300g plain flour, plus extra to dust
125g cocoa powder, sifted
400g granulated sugar
175g light brown soft sugar
1½ tbsp ground ginger
1 tbsp ground cinnamon
1 tsp ground allspice
½ tsp freshly grated nutmeg
2 tsp bicarbonate of soda
¾ tsp baking powder
½ tsp flaked sea salt
300ml whole milk
3 medium eggs
75g black treacle
1 tbsp vanilla extract

FOR THE BUTTERCREAM
125g white chocolate, chopped
175g unsalted butter, softened
225g full-fat cream cheese, at room temperature
175g icing sugar, sifted
175ml double cream

★ TO STORE
Keep covered in fridge for up to 4 days. Allow to come to room temperature before serving.

1. First make the sugared rosemary trees. Whisk the egg white until lightly frothy. Working with 1 rosemary sprig at a time, lightly brush with egg white, then dredge with caster sugar, gently shaking off excess. Lay on a baking tray lined with baking parchment. Repeat the process with the remaining rosemary sprigs. Leave to dry at room temperature for at least 3hr, until crisp.

2. For the cake, preheat oven to 180°C (160°C fan) mark 4. Lightly grease the base and sides of 3 x 20.5cm round cake tins and line the bases with baking parchment. Dust the inside of the tins with flour, tapping out excess.

3. In a large bowl, whisk the flour, cocoa powder, granulated and brown sugars, spices, bicarbonate of soda, baking powder and salt. In a large measuring jug or bowl, whisk the milk, oil, eggs, treacle and vanilla to combine. Add the wet ingredients to the flour bowl and mix thoroughly.

4. Add 250ml just-boiled water and mix well to combine (the batter will be thin). Divide evenly among the prepared tins and bake for 35–40min, or until a skewer inserted in the centre comes out clean. Cool in the tins for 10min, then transfer to a wire rack to cool completely.

5. To make the buttercream, melt the chocolate in a heatproof bowl set over a pan of simmering

water (don't let the bowl touch the water). Set aside to cool for 10min. Using a free-standing mixer or a handheld electric whisk, beat the butter and cream cheese until smooth. Add icing sugar and mix to combine (starting slowly), then mix in the cooled melted chocolate. Cover and chill for 30min to firm up.

6. To assemble, whip the double cream until it holds firm peaks. Stir 1 large spoonful of whipped cream into the cream cheese mixture to loosen, then carefully fold in the remaining cream with a large metal spoon.

7. Place 1 of the cooled cakes on a cake plate or stand and spread a layer of buttercream over the top. Top with another cake. Repeat with the buttercream and remaining sponge, then spread the remaining buttercream over the top and sides of the cake. Chill again for 30min, if needed, to firm up.

8. Decorate with the sugared rosemary trees just before serving.

Hands-on time: 50min, plus drying, cooling and chilling
Cooking time: about 45min
Serves 12

PER SERVING 806cals, 10g protein, 43g fat (20g saturates), 94g carbs (74g total sugars), 3g fibre

Love Your Leftovers

Turkey and Kale Salad with Tahini Dressing

This salad uses raw kale leaves, but feel free to blanch them if you prefer, or replace them with other leaves if you are not a fan.

300g mixed roasted vegetables (we used parsnips, butternut squash and carrots)
125g bag sliced kale, tough stalks removed
300g cooked turkey, shredded
100g feta cheese, crumbled
50g pumpkin seeds
50g pomegranate seeds

FOR THE DRESSING
2 tbsp extra virgin olive oil
2 tbsp tahini
½ tsp white wine vinegar
Juice ½ orange

1. Preheat oven to 190°C (170°C fan) mark 5. Scatter the roasted vegetables on a baking tray and reheat for 10min.

2. Meanwhile, in a small jug, mix the dressing ingredients and season to taste.

3. Put the kale into a large bowl with half the dressing and mix well. Set aside for 5–10min (this will help tenderise the leaves a little). Mix through the remaining salad ingredients, reserving some of the pomegranate seeds for garnish.

4. Toss through remaining dressing and garnish with the reserved pomegranate seeds. Serve.

★ GH TIP
Swap the orange juice for 2–3 tbsp clementine juice, if you have some left over.

Hands-on time: 15min
Cooking time: about 10min
Serves 4

PER SERVING 451cals, 35g protein, 28g fat (7g saturates), 12g carbs (7g total sugars), 6g fibre

Sprout Soup with Stilton Toasties

Use up your leftover sprouts in this nutritious soup. The toasties are perfect for dipping, and use whatever cheese you have to hand.

25g butter
2 leeks, finely sliced
2 garlic cloves, crushed
2 tsp thyme leaves
1 head of broccoli (about 300g), cut into florets
200g cooked Brussels sprouts
1.3 litres vegetable stock
Whole nutmeg, to grate

FOR THE TOASTIES
8 slices white bread (we used tiger bread)
50g butter, softened
100g Stilton

1. Melt the butter in a large pan and gently fry the leeks for 10–12min until softened. Add the garlic and thyme, cook for 1min, then add the broccoli, sprouts and stock. Bring to the boil and simmer for 15min, or until the veg is completely tender.

2. Whizz in a blender until smooth. Return to the pan; check the seasoning. Add grated nutmeg to taste.

3. For the toasties, butter the top of each slice of bread. Flip 4 slices butter-side down and top with Stilton. Sandwich with the remaining bread slices, butter-side up. Heat a heavy-based pan over medium heat and fry for 3min until the bases are golden, then flip and fry for 3min more. Serve with the soup, reheated if needed, and sprinkled with grated nutmeg and pepper.

Hands-on time: 25min
Cooking time: about 40min
Serves 4

PER SERVING 566cals, 22g protein, 29g fat (16g saturates), 49g carbs (12g total sugars), 12g fibre

Mushroom, Walnut and Chestnut Soup

Its earthy ingredients give this soup
a complex flavour, making it the perfect
winter warmer.

2 tbsp olive oil, plus extra to drizzle
1 large onion, roughly chopped
400g chestnut mushrooms, roughly chopped
2 garlic cloves, crushed
200g pack cooked chestnuts, chopped
50g walnuts
1.3 litres vegetable stock
4 tbsp crème fraîche
Large handful parsley, finely chopped (optional)

1. Heat the oil in a large pan and gently fry the
   onion for 10min or until softened. Turn up the
   heat, add the mushrooms and garlic and cook,
   stirring, for about 5min, or until any liquid
   given off by the mushrooms has evaporated.

2. Add the chestnuts, walnuts, stock and some
   seasoning. Bring to the boil and simmer for
   15min. Carefully whizz in a blender until
   completely smooth (do this in batches, if
   necessary), then return to the pan, stir in
   the crème fraîche and check the seasoning.

3. Reheat, if necessary, and divide among 4 bowls.
   Top each with a drizzle of oil and some parsley,
   if using. Serve immediately.

Hands-on time: 15min
Cooking time: about 30min
Serves 4

PER SERVING 312cals, 6g protein, 22g fat
(6g saturates), 24g carbs (8g total sugars), 4g fibre

Curried Bubble and Squeak Toasties

A tasty brunch option that's also delicious topped with a crispy fried egg. Wilted spinach, chard or cavolo nero would also work as the greens.

FOR THE BUBBLE AND SQUEAK
3 tsp olive oil
2 shallots, finely sliced
1 garlic clove, crushed
1 tsp mild curry powder
200g roast potatoes, finely chopped
50g cooked Brussels sprouts, finely sliced
50g cooked greens, finely sliced (we used kale)

FOR THE TOASTIES
40g butter, softened
4 slices white farmhouse bread
2 tbsp mango chutney
4 Cheddar cheese slices
Small handful coriander, roughly chopped

★ GET AHEAD
Prepare the recipe to the end of step 2 up to 1 day ahead. Store in an airtight container in the fridge. Complete the recipe to serve, making sure the patties are piping hot.

1. First, make the bubble and squeak. Heat 1 tsp oil in a medium-large frying pan (it will be used again later for the toasties) over low heat and fry the shallots for 5min, until tender. Stir in the garlic and curry powder and fry for 1min. Set aside to cool.

2. Put the potatoes, sprouts and cooked greens into a medium bowl and roughly mash before mixing in the curry shallots. Shape into 2 flattened patties.

3. Wipe out the shallot pan with kitchen paper and return to medium heat with 1 tsp oil. Fry the patties for 2min per side, until golden. Remove from the heat and set aside.

4. Butter the bread slices. Flip 2 of the slices butter-side down and spread mango chutney over them. Add a patty to each slice, followed by 2 Cheddar slices each and some coriander. Top with the remaining bread slices, butter-side up.

5. Heat the remaining oil in the pan over medium heat and fry the sandwiches for 3min per side, or until golden and crisp. Serve immediately.

Hands-on time: 15min
Cooking time: about 15min
Serves 2

PER SERVING 831cals, 25g protein, 47g fat
(23g saturates), 72g carbs (12g total sugars), 8g fibre

Boxing Day Pizza

This easy-to-adapt recipe is really enjoyable to put together and tastes a treat – just what you need to help you relax after Christmas Day.

FOR THE DOUGH
350g strong white flour, plus extra to dust
5g fast-action dried yeast
1 tsp caster sugar
2 tbsp extra virgin olive oil, plus extra to grease

FOR THE TOPPING
150g crème fraîche
50g Parmesan, finely grated
125g cooked turkey, shredded
125g Stilton, crumbled
50g walnuts, chopped
4 tbsp cranberry sauce
Handful parsley, roughly chopped

1. In a large bowl, mix the flour, yeast, sugar and 1 tsp fine salt. Add the oil and 200ml lukewarm water in one go and mix to combine. Tip on to a lightly floured surface and knead for 5min until smooth and elastic. Return to a clean bowl; cover with greased clingfilm (oil-side down). Leave to rise in a warm place for 30–45min.

2. Preheat oven to 240°C (220°C fan) mark 9, and put 2 large baking sheets in to heat up. Divide dough in half. Roll out each half on a lightly floured surface to a rough 33cm circle. Transfer each to a large sheet of baking parchment.

3. Mix the crème fraîche, Parmesan and some seasoning and spread on to the dough bases, leaving a 2.5cm border. Scatter over the turkey, Stilton and walnuts. Dollop on cranberry sauce.

4. Carefully remove a baking sheet from oven and slip the pizza on to it (still on its parchment). Repeat with the other pizza. Cook in the oven for 10–12min until golden and crisp. Scatter over the parsley and serve.

Hands-on time: 30min, plus rising
Cooking time: about 15min
Makes 2 pizzas, serves 4

PER ½ PIZZA 858cals, 36g protein, 45g fat (22g saturates), 74g carbs (8g total sugars), 4g fibre

Smoked Salmon, Courgette and Dill Frittata

If you don't have leftover roasties, cooked sweet potatoes or other roasted veg would work just as well.

1 tbsp olive oil
250g leftover roast potatoes, roughly chopped
8 medium eggs
100g full-fat cream cheese
1 tsp Dijon mustard
150g smoked salmon
Small handful dill, roughly chopped, plus extra to serve
1 small courgette, peeled into ribbons (discard the seedy centre)
Green salad, to serve

1. Preheat oven to 180°C (160°C fan) mark 4. Heat the oil in a rough 23cm ovenproof frying pan over medium heat and fry the potatoes for 5min, stirring occasionally, until crisping up.

2. Meanwhile, in a large jug, whisk the eggs, cream cheese, mustard and plenty of seasoning (don't worry if there are cream cheese lumps). Roughly chop 100g of the salmon and stir into the eggs along with the dill.

3. Pour the egg mixture on top of the potatoes and scatter over the courgette ribbons. Cook for 5min or until the base starts to set. Finish off in the oven for a further 20–25min, or until just set.

4. Garnish with the remaining salmon and extra dill. Serve with a green salad, if you like.

★ GH TIP
This frittata is also delicious served cold the next day. Simply leave to cool, cover and chill once cooked.

 GF

Hands-on time: 15min
Cooking time: about 35min
Serves 4

PER SERVING 401cals, 26g protein, 25g fat (8g saturates), 18g carbs (2g total sugars), 2g fibre

Parsnip and Pear Soup

Sweet and savoury pair beautifully here with the addition of warming spices.

2 tbsp olive oil
1 large onion, chopped
2 celery sticks, chopped
1 garlic clove, crushed
1 tsp curry powder
½ tsp ground cumin
2 pinches hot chilli powder
450g parsnips, roughly chopped
1 litre hot vegetable stock
3 pears
15g butter
1 tsp golden caster sugar
2 tbsp chopped flat-leaf parsley, to garnish

1. Heat the oil in a pan and add the onion, celery and garlic. Cover and cook gently for 10min until softened. Stir in the curry powder, cumin and chilli powder and cook for 1min.

2. Add the parsnips and stock, cover and simmer for 10min. Peel, core and chop 2 pears, then add to the pan. Simmer, covered, for 5min. Cool, then whizz in a processor until smooth. Rinse the pan.

3. Peel and core the remaining pear and slice thinly. Heat the butter in a pan and cook the pear for 3min until lightly golden, then sprinkle over the sugar. Cook for 3min, turning occasionally. Set aside.

4. Return the soup to the rinsed-out pan and reheat. Season to taste. Divide among 4 warmed bowls, garnish with caramelised pear slices and parsley, grind over some black pepper and serve.

★ GET AHEAD
Make the soup to the end of step 2 up to 2 days ahead. Cool, then pour into a lidded container and chill. To serve, complete the recipe.

Hands-on time: 25min
Cooking time: about 35min
Serves 4

PER SERVING 270cals, 4g protein, 11g fat (3g saturates), 33g carbs (25g total sugars), 11g fibre

Turkey Pad Thai

Get all your ingredients ready at the start so the dish comes together in minutes.

125g flat, folded dried rice noodles
4 tbsp fish sauce
2 tbsp tamarind paste
3 tbsp demerara sugar
1 tbsp soy sauce
3 tbsp vegetable oil
2 garlic cloves, finely chopped
1 red chilli, deseeded and sliced
2 medium eggs, beaten
125g cooked turkey, shredded
100g beansprouts
3 spring onions, finely sliced

TO GARNISH
2 tbsp unsalted roasted peanuts, roughly chopped
Small handful coriander, chopped
Lime wedges

1. Soak the noodles in cold water for 25min or until flexible. Drain. Meanwhile, mix the fish sauce, tamarind, sugar and soy with 2 tbsp water in a pan. Heat gently, stirring to dissolve, then set aside.

2. Heat the oil in a large frying pan or wok over high heat. Add the garlic and chilli, stir-fry for 30sec, then add the noodles and a splash of water and stir-fry for 2min more. Add the sauce and stir-fry for 1–2min until it is absorbed and the noodles are almost cooked through.

3. Push the noodles to one side, add the eggs to the empty part of the pan/wok and fry, stirring, until just set and scrambled. Stir through the turkey, beansprouts and spring onions to heat through. Scatter over the peanuts and coriander, and serve with lime wedges on the side.

Hands-on time: 15min, plus soaking
Cooking time: about 15min
Serves 2

PER SERVING 704cals, 41g protein, 32g fat (5g saturates), 62g carbs (10g total sugars), 3g fibre

Crispy Ham, Sprout and Garlic Spaghetti

Omit the ham and use a vegetarian hard cheese to make this veggie friendly.

350g spaghetti
3 tbsp olive oil
100g ham, finely shredded
40g fresh white or brown breadcrumbs
½ tsp dried chilli flakes
2 fat garlic cloves, finely chopped
200g raw or cooked Brussels sprouts, halved and shredded
Finely grated zest 1 lemon

1. Bring a large pan of salted water to the boil and cook the spaghetti according to pack instructions.

2. Meanwhile, heat 1 tbsp oil in a large, deep frying pan over medium heat, add the ham and fry until crisp. Remove to a plate with a slotted spoon.

3. Add the breadcrumbs to the empty pan with a pinch of the chilli flakes and some seasoning. Fry, stirring regularly, until deep golden brown. Add to the plate next to the ham. Wipe the pan clean with kitchen paper.

4. Return the frying pan to the heat and add the remaining oil. When hot, add the garlic, sprouts, remaining chilli and some seasoning and fry for 2–5min, until the sprouts are piping hot and tender (raw sprouts will take longer).

5. Drain the pasta when al dente, then add it to the frying pan with the sprouts. Add the lemon zest and half the ham and toss to mix. Divide among 4 bowls and top with the remaining crispy ham and breadcrumbs. Serve.

Hands-on time: 20min
Cooking time: about 20min
Serves 4

PER SERVING 469cals, 18g protein, 11g fat (2g saturates), 70g carbs (4g total sugars), 7g fibre

Bombay Vegetable Turnovers with Radish Raita

A cross between a samosa and a pasty, these vegetable parcels are flavoured with the spices of Bombay potatoes and served with a cooling yogurt sauce.

1 tbsp vegetable oil
1 small onion, finely sliced
2 garlic cloves, crushed
1 green finger chilli, finely chopped
2 tsp brown mustard seeds
2 tsp garam masala
1 tsp turmeric
75g frozen peas
250g mixed roasted vegetables (we used potatoes, parsnips and carrots), cut into 1cm pieces
Flour, to dust
500g block puff pastry
1 medium egg, beaten
1 tsp nigella seeds, to sprinkle

FOR THE RAITA
½ cucumber, peeled, halved lengthways and deseeded
200g Greek-style yogurt
4 fat radishes, cut into matchsticks
Small handful mint leaves, finely chopped
1 tbsp lemon juice

★ GET AHEAD
Prepare to the end of step 2 up to 1 day ahead. Put on a lined baking tray, cover and chill. Make the raita up to 1hr ahead. Complete the recipe to serve.

Hands-on time: 40min, plus cooling and chilling
Cooking time: about 30min
Serves 4

PER SERVING 518cals, 12g protein, 31g fat (17g saturates), 45g carbs (8g total sugars), 4g fibre

1. Heat the oil in a large frying pan over medium heat, add the onion with a pinch of salt and fry for 7–8min, until softened. Add the garlic and chilli, fry for 2min, then add the spices and stir for 1min. Add the peas and cook for 2min until tender, then remove from heat. Stir in the roasted vegetables and season. Cool.

2. Preheat oven to 220°C (200°C fan) mark 7 and line a large baking tray with baking parchment. Lightly flour a surface and roll out the pastry to a 33cm square, about 3mm thick. Trim any wonky edges, then cut into 4 even squares. Put a quarter of the vegetable mixture on one diagonal half of each rectangle (leaving a border), then brush around the edges with egg. Fold the empty half of the pastry over the vegetables and press the edges to seal.

3. Transfer the turnovers to the prepared tray and brush with egg. Cut a few slashes into top of each parcel and scatter over the nigella seeds. Cook for 12–15min until dark golden and crisp.

4. Meanwhile, make the raita. Coarsely grate the cucumber, then squeeze the flesh in your hands over a sink to remove excess juice. Mix in a bowl with the remaining ingredients and some seasoning. Serve with the turnovers.

Sprout, Salmon and Brie Gratin

Just what's needed on a chilly night. If you have leftover raw sprouts, you can use these too – just roast them for a little longer. Any roasted roots to make up the roast potato amount would work well, too.

500g Brussels sprouts, cooked or raw
2 tbsp oil
50g butter
50g plain flour
2 tsp English mustard powder
600ml milk
175g Brie or Camembert, cut into 1cm pieces
350g roast potatoes, roughly chopped
100g smoked or hot smoked salmon, roughly chopped
100g sourdough bread, cut or torn into 1cm pieces

1. Preheat oven to 200°C (180°C fan) mark 6. Tip the sprouts into a roasting tin, toss through 1 tbsp oil and season. Roast for 20–30min (pre-cooked ones will need less time than raw), shaking midway through, until tender and beginning to char.

2. Meanwhile, melt the butter in a large pan, add the flour and mustard powder and cook, stirring, for 1min. Remove the pan from the heat and gradually mix in the milk. Return to the heat and cook, stirring, until thickened. Simmer for 2min. Stir in 125g of the cheese and some seasoning. Remove from heat and set aside.

3. Tip the sprouts into a 2-litre ovenproof serving dish and mix through the potatoes and salmon. Pour on the sauce. Mix the bread, remaining oil and cheese in a bowl, then scatter on top.

4. Cook in the oven for 35min until bubbling and crisp on top. Serve with a green salad, if you like.

Hands-on time: 25min
Cooking time: about 1hr 5min
Serves 4

PER SERVING 703cals, 29g protein, 38g fat
(17g saturates), 55g carbs (12g total sugars), 10g fibre

★ GET AHEAD
Prepare to the end of step 3 up to a day ahead, then cover and chill. To serve, complete the recipe, adding more cooking time if needed.

Hands-on time: 25min
Cooking time: about 30min
Makes 4 pasties

PER PASTY 1003cals, 23g protein, 70g fat (25g saturates), 66g carbs (12g total sugars), 9g fibre

Speedy Pasties

These get-ahead pasties are great for using up leftover veggies. Add some chopped ham or turkey, if you like, in place of the sausage meat.

450g pork sausage meat
150g leftover roast vegetables, roughly chopped (we used parsnips and carrots)
4 tbsp cranberry sauce
Small handful parsley, finely chopped
500g block shortcrust pastry
Flour, to dust
1 large egg, beaten

1. Preheat oven to 200°C (180°C fan) mark 6. In a large bowl, mix the sausage meat, roast veg, cranberry sauce, parsley and some seasoning.

2. Line a large baking tray with parchment. Cut the pastry into quarters. Lightly flour a work surface and roll out each quarter to a rough 20cm circle.

3. Working one at a time, spoon a quarter of the pork mixture on to one side of a pastry circle, leaving a 2.5cm border. Brush the edges of the pastry with some beaten egg and fold the empty half over the filling to make a semi-circle. Press the edges firmly to seal, then crimp. Place on the lined baking tray. Repeat with the remaining pastry circles and filling.

4. Brush the pasties with more egg and cook for 25–30min, or until deeply golden and piping hot throughout. Serve hot, warm or at room temperature with a green salad.

Kale, Sprout and Tofu Salad

Fancy a break from rich, festive food? This seasonal salad will hit the spot and leave room for more treats later!

396g block firm tofu
250g Brussels sprouts, finely sliced
100g kale, finely shredded, woody stalks removed
200g pack cooked chestnuts, halved
250g pouch cooked mixed grains
40g vegetarian Italian-style hard cheese, grated
6 tbsp cornflour
3 tbsp rapeseed oil

FOR THE DRESSING
2 tbsp rapeseed oil
2 tbsp white wine vinegar
1 garlic clove, crushed
2 tsp Dijon mustard
Finely grated zest and juice 1 lemon

1. Press the tofu over a sink to drain excess moisture. Line a baking tray with kitchen paper and put the tofu on top. Cover with kitchen paper, then top with a plate or baking tray, weighted with some tins. Leave to drain for 30min, then cut into 2cm cubes.

2. To make the salad, in a large bowl mix the sprouts, kale, chestnuts, grains and grated cheese. In a small jug, whisk together all the dressing ingredients. Mix into the salad and set aside for the flavours to develop.

3. In a bowl, mix the cornflour with some seasoning. Toss the tofu cubes in the cornflour mixture. Heat the oil in a large frying pan over medium heat. Fry tofu (in batches, if needed) for 5–8min, turning, until all sides are golden. Toss through the salad and serve.

Hands-on time: 20min, plus draining
Cooking time: about 10min
Serves 4

PER SERVING 553cals, 26g protein, 26g fat (4g saturates), 50g carbs (6g total sugars), 9g fibre

Turkey Peanut Curry

A creamy curry with satay flavours, this simple midweek supper would be great served with basmati rice or even boiled new potatoes.

2 tsp vegetable oil
3 ripe tomatoes, roughly chopped
4cm piece fresh root ginger, peeled and finely grated
1 red chilli, halved, deseeded and sliced
Large handful coriander (about 25g), leaves and stems separated
3 tbsp Thai red curry paste
100g crunchy peanut butter
400ml full-fat coconut milk
100ml hot chicken stock
300g cooked turkey, in chunks or strips
1 red pepper, deseeded and sliced
200g fresh or frozen edamame beans
Finely grated zest and juice 1 lime

1. Heat the oil in a large pan over medium heat and cook the tomatoes, ginger and chilli for 4min, stirring occasionally. Finely chop the coriander stems and add to the pan with the curry paste. Cook for 1min. Stir in the peanut butter until melted, then stir in the coconut milk and stock.

2. Bring to a simmer, add the turkey and bubble gently for 15min, stirring occasionally, until the turkey is piping hot and the sauce has reduced slightly.

3. Add the pepper strips and edamame and cook for a further 5min until cooked through. Remove from heat, stir in the lime zest and juice and most of the coriander. Check the seasoning and serve sprinkled with the remaining coriander.

Hands-on time: 15min
Cooking time: about 30min
Serves 4

PER SERVING 582cals, 40g protein, 40g fat (19g saturates), 13g carbs (7g total sugars), 7g fibre

Creamy Smoked Salmon Cobbler

Use smoked salmon leftovers to make this inventive twist on fish pie.

50g butter
2 leeks, thickly sliced
40g plain flour
400ml semi-skimmed milk
Finely grated zest and juice 1 lemon
350g frozen white fish fillets, defrosted and drained (if needed)

FOR THE COBBLER
175g self-raising flour
½ tbsp baking powder
2 tsp dried chives
75g full-fat cream cheese
75ml milk, plus extra to brush
1 medium egg
½ tbsp vegetable oil
50g smoked salmon trimmings
Seasonal greens, to serve (optional)

1. Preheat oven to 200°C (180°C fan) mark 6. Melt the butter in a medium pan and gently fry the leeks over medium heat for 10min until softened. Stir in the flour. Gradually add the milk, stirring until smooth. Bring to the boil, stirring, then turn down heat and simmer until thickened, giving an occasional stir. Stir in the lemon zest and juice and some seasoning. Set aside.

2. For the cobbler, mix the flour, baking powder and chives with some seasoning in a bowl. In a jug, whisk together the cream cheese, milk, egg and oil. Add the liquid to the dry ingredients and stir until evenly mixed. Stir in the smoked salmon.

3. Cut the fish fillets into large chunks and put in an ovenproof serving dish. Mix through leek sauce. Spoon the cobbler mix on top in 6 evenly spaced dollops.

4. Brush with milk and cook for 25min until piping hot and golden.

Hands-on time: 25min
Cooking time: about 40min
Serves 6

PER SERVING 349cals, 20g protein, 15g fat (8g saturates), 32g carbs (5g total sugars), 1g fibre

Ham and Cauliflower Stew

Cooked chicken or turkey would work equally well in this Moroccan-inspired dish.

1 tbsp oil
1 red onion, finely chopped
1 small cauliflower, roughly chopped
1 tbsp paprika
1 tsp cumin
2 x 400g tins chopped tomatoes
300ml hot chicken or vegetable stock
125g ham hock or cooked ham
400g tin chickpeas, drained
Large handful coriander, roughly chopped
Crusty bread, to serve

1. Heat the oil in a large pan over medium heat and fry the onion until softened, about 10min. Add the cauliflower and fry for 5min before adding the paprika and cumin.

2. Stir in the tomatoes, stock, ham and chickpeas, turn up the heat and bring to the boil. Simmer for 5–10min until the mixture is piping hot and the cauliflower is cooked through.

3. Stir through most of the coriander and season to taste. Garnish with the remaining coriander and serve with crusty bread.

Hands-on time: 15min
Cooking time: about 25min
Serves 4

PER SERVING 147cals, 16g protein, 3g fat (1g saturates), 12g carbs (10g total sugars), 5g fibre

Brie and Cranberry Turkey Burgers

Leftover cooked turkey makes great burgers, and bacon adds extra juiciness.

40g fresh breadcrumbs
3 tbsp milk
350g cooked skinless turkey, roughly chopped
100g smoked streaky bacon, roughly chopped
1 tbsp wholegrain mustard
1 garlic clove, crushed
1 tbsp runny honey
1 medium egg, beaten
1 tbsp vegetable oil
4 thick slices Brie (about 50g total)
4 brioche buns, split
2 tbsp light mayonnaise
4 soft round lettuce leaves
3 tbsp cranberry sauce

1. Mix the breadcrumbs and milk in a large bowl and set aside to soak. Pulse the turkey and bacon in a food processor until it resembles mince. Add to the breadcrumbs and mix in the mustard, garlic, honey and egg; season.

2. Shape into 4 patties about 1.5cm thick. Put on a plate, then cover and chill for 30min to firm up.

3. Preheat oven to 200°C (180°C fan) mark 6. Heat the oil in a large frying pan over medium heat and brown the burgers for 5min, turning halfway. Transfer to a baking tray and cook in oven for a further 8–10min, or until cooked through. Remove the tray from oven and preheat grill.

4. Top the burgers with Brie. Add the buns to the tray, cut-side up, and grill for 1–2min until the cheese is melting (grill buns separately if the tray is too crowded). Spread mayo on the bottom buns, then top with a lettuce leaf, the burgers, some cranberry sauce and the top bun. Serve.

★ GET AHEAD
Prepare to the end of step 2 up to 1 day ahead and keep chilled. Complete the recipe to serve.

Hands-on time: 20min, plus chilling
Cooking time: about 20min
Serves 4

PER SERVING 549cals, 44g protein, 24g fat (8g saturates), 40g carbs (17g total sugars), 1g fibre

Gammon and Piccalilli Pies

Making your own pastry works out cheaper than shop-bought, but if you don't have a food processor, you may find it easier to buy a couple of blocks of ready-made shortcrust pastry.

FOR THE FILLING
600g leftover smoked gammon
3 tbsp parsley, roughly chopped
50–75ml ham stock
125g piccalilli
1 large egg, to glaze

FOR THE PASTRY
600g plain flour, plus extra to dust
300g cold butter, cut into cubes
3 large egg yolks

1. For the pastry, put the flour and butter into a food processor and pulse until the mixture resembles fine breadcrumbs. In a small bowl, stir together the egg yolks and 75ml ice-cold water. Add the liquid to the food processor and pulse until the mixture just comes together. Tip the dough on to a work surface, bring together with your hands and shape into a flat disc. Wrap in clingfilm and chill until needed. If you don't have a food processor, rub the butter into the flour using your fingers, then mix in the yolks/water with a blunt-ended cutlery knife. Bring the dough together into a flat disc and chill.

2. Shred the gammon using 2 forks or your fingers (discarding any skin and fat). Tip the meat into a bowl, stir through the parsley and add enough stock to give it a little juiciness. Set aside.

3. Preheat oven to 220°C (200°C fan) mark 7. Lightly dust a work surface with flour and roll out two-thirds of the pastry until 3mm thick. Stamp out 12 x 10cm circles and press them into the 12 holes of a deep muffin tin, working the pastry so that it comes just above the edges of the holes. Set the trimmings aside. Divide the gammon mixture among the pastry cases, pressing down gently to pack the meat in. Spoon the piccalilli over the meat in an even layer.

4. Roll out the remaining pastry and trimmings as before and stamp out 12 x 7cm circles (keep the trimmings). Lightly beat the remaining egg. Brush the edges of the filled pies with some of the beaten egg, then press on the lids, sealing the edges firmly. If you like, re-roll any trimmings and stamp out letters or shapes and use to decorate the pies. Brush the top of pies with egg.

5. Cook the pies for 30–35min or until deep golden brown. Cool for 5min in the tin, then carefully run the tip of a knife around the edge to loosen and remove the pies from the tin. Cool for 10min, then serve warm or at room temperature.

Hands-on time: 45min, plus chilling and cooling
Cooking time: about 35min
Makes 12 pies

PER PIE 416cals, 18g protein, 23g fat (13g saturates), 34g carbs (2g sugars), 2g fibre

★ GET AHEAD
Cook and cool the pies up to 1 day ahead. Store
in an airtight container in the fridge. To serve,
warm the pies through on a baking sheet in
a 170°C (150°C fan) mark 3 oven for 15–20min
(or serve them at room temperature).

Roast Potato, Rosemary and Cheeseboard Loaf

Perfect for dunking into a steaming bowl of soup, this bread also makes cracking good toast.

400g strong white flour

7g sachet fast-action dried yeast

2 tbsp rosemary, finely chopped, plus 1 tsp extra
    for topping

1 tbsp olive oil, plus extra to grease

200g mix of soft and hard cheeses (we used Cheddar,
    vegetarian Camembert and vegetarian Brie), cut
    into small chunks

200g roast potatoes, finely chopped

2 tbsp runny honey

★ TO STORE
Keep in clingfilm in a cool, dark place for up
to 2 days.

Hands-on time: 30min, plus rising and cooling
Cooking time: about 30min
Makes 1 loaf (10 slices)

PER SLICE 271cals, 10g protein, 9g fat (4g saturates),
38g carbs (3g total sugars), 2g fibre

1. Put the flour, yeast, 2 tbsp rosemary, oil, cheese and 1 tsp salt into a large bowl (or into a mixer fitted with a dough hook) and mix to combine. Add 300ml cold water and mix until it forms a sticky dough. Knead by hand on a lightly greased surface for 10min, or for 8min in the mixer, until smooth and elastic. Return it to the bowl, cover with clingfilm and leave to rise in a warm place for 1hr, or until doubled in size.

2. Grease a 900g loaf tin with oil. Punch down the dough in the bowl and tip it on to a greased surface. Knead it a couple of times to knock out the air, then pat it into a rough 18 x 25.5cm rectangle. Scatter over the potatoes and press them firmly into the dough. Roll up the dough from a short end to make a long, fat rectangle. Tuck the ends under and transfer it to the prepared tin, seam-side down. Cover loosely with greased clingfilm (oil-side down) and leave to rise for 30min–1hr, or until noticeably puffed up and risen just over the top of the tin. Preheat the oven to 220°C (200°C fan) mark 7.

3. Using a sharp knife, cut a few slashes into the top of the loaf and bake for 30min, or until deep golden brown. Carefully remove from the tin and leave to cool completely on a wire rack.

4. When cool, gently heat the honey and 1 tsp chopped rosemary in a small pan until loose. Brush over the loaf and serve.

Black Forest Panettone Queen of Puddings

A wonderful new way to use up leftover panettone, which will transform into a spectacular dessert even if it's stale.

40g unsalted butter, plus extra to grease
500ml semi-skimmed milk
200g panettone, crumbled or chopped into small cubes
100g dark chocolate, chopped
4 medium eggs, separated
225g caster sugar
450g frozen cherries
1 tbsp cornflour
3 tbsp kirsch
Cream, to serve (optional)

Hands-on time: 25min, plus soaking
Cooking time: about 1hr 10min
Serves 8

PER SERVING (without cream) 400cals, 8g protein, 14g fat (8g saturates), 60g carbs (50g total sugars), 2g fibre

1. Preheat oven to 180°C (160°C fan) mark 4 and lightly butter a round baking dish, roughly 1 litre. Heat the milk and butter in a pan until just boiling. Put the panettone and chocolate in a large bowl, pour over the hot milk mixture and leave to soak for 5min, then stir until the chocolate has melted and is mixed in.

2. In a separate bowl, whisk the egg yolks and 50g sugar until pale and foamy. Whisk into the panettone mixture until evenly mixed, then pour into the buttered baking dish and bake for 30min or until just set with a slight wobble.

3. Meanwhile, bring the cherries, cornflour and kirsch to the boil in a pan, stirring occasionally. Simmer until it thickens, then set aside to cool.

4. When the base has cooked, make the meringue topping. In a clean bowl, whisk the egg whites to stiff peaks with a handheld electric whisk. Gradually whisk in the remaining 175g sugar, beating well after each addition until you have a smooth, stiff and glossy meringue.

5. Spoon the cherries and syrup over the chocolate base, then spoon or pipe on the meringue in an even layer. Bake for 30min until the meringue is firm and pale golden. Leave to cool for 10min before serving with cold cream, if you like.

Baked Mince Pie Apples

Using eating apples for baking helps these indulgent desserts keep their shape, as well as giving them a little bit of crunch. And it's a novel way to use up leftover mince pies!

4 eating apples (we used Braeburn)
4 mince pies
15g flaked almonds
Brandy butter, to serve

1. Preheat oven to 200°C (180°C fan) mark 6. Halve the apples and scoop out the cores. Put on a baking sheet and roast for 10min.

2. Carefully remove the apples from the oven and press half a mince pie into each apple half. Sprinkle over a few almond slivers and return to the oven for 15min, or until the top is golden and the apple is soft. Serve immediately with the brandy butter.

Hands-on time: 10min
Cooking time: about 25min
Serves 4

PER SERVING 357cals, 4g protein, 15g fat (8g saturates), 48g carbs (33g total sugars), 4g fibre

Use up mince pies

Mince Pie and Cranberry Brownies

Easy to make and dangerously moreish.

175g unsalted butter, chopped, plus extra to grease
175g dark chocolate (70% cocoa solids), chopped
250g caster sugar
3 medium eggs
50g cocoa powder
75g plain flour
4 mince pies, about 225g, roughly chopped
4 tbsp cranberry sauce

1. Preheat oven to 180°C (160°C fan) mark 4 and grease and line a 20.5cm square tin with baking parchment. In a large pan over low heat, melt butter and chocolate until combined. Set aside to cool for 10min.

2. Stir in the sugar, followed by the eggs. Sift in the cocoa powder and flour and mix to combine. Stir through most of the chopped mince pies. Scrape into the prepared tin, smooth, then scatter over the remaining mince pies. Using a teaspoon, dollop on the cranberry sauce.

3. Bake for 35-40min until firm to the touch. Cool completely in the tin. To serve, transfer to a board and slice into 16 squares.

★ TO STORE
Cool, then wrap in foil and store at room temperature for up to 5 days.

Hands-on time: 15min, plus cooling
Cooking time: about 45min
Cuts into 16 squares

PER BROWNIE 302cals, 4g protein, 16g fat
(9g saturates), 36g carbs (28g total sugars), 1g fibre

11

Edible Gifts & Decorations

Kendal Mint Cake Bars

We've turned the Cumbrian confection into dark chocolate-dipped gifts, but milk or white work well, too.

Butter, to grease
600g granulated sugar
3 tbsp liquid glucose
¾ tsp peppermint extract
200g dark chocolate, chopped
1 candy cane, crushed, to decorate (optional)

YOU'LL ALSO NEED
A sugar thermometer

1. Grease and line a 20cm square tin with baking parchment. Mix the sugar, glucose and 250ml water in a large pan. Stir over a low heat until the sugar dissolves. Turn up the heat to medium and bubble, swirling the pan occasionally rather than stirring.

2. As soon as the mixture reaches 120°C on a sugar thermometer, remove the pan from the heat. Add the peppermint extract and a pinch of salt and stir well with a wooden spoon for about 3min – this will give the mint cake its signature cloudy appearance. The mixture should be gloopy and opaque. Carefully scrape into the lined tin and leave to set at room temperature (about 30min).

3. Once set, line a large tray with baking parchment. Melt the chocolate in a heatproof bowl set over a pan of barely simmering water. Turn the mint cake out on to a board and slice into 12 rectangles. Dip half of each rectangle lengthways into the melted chocolate and put on the lined tray. Sprinkle crushed candy cane, if using, over the chocolate and leave to set before serving.

★ TO STORE
Once set, keep in an airtight container in the fridge, layers separated with baking parchment, for up to 2 weeks.

Hands-on-time: 30min, plus cooling and setting
Cooking time: about 25min
Makes 12 bars

PER BAR 278cals, 1g protein, 4g fat (2g saturates), 61g carbs (59g total sugars), 0g fibre

Christmas Brownie Bites

These are great fun to bake with children (minus the brandy!). They look fantastic, taste divine and are really easy to make.

175g butter
125g dark chocolate, roughly chopped
1½ tbsp brandy (optional)
250g light brown soft sugar
2 medium eggs
100g plain flour
1 tsp ground cinnamon
1 tsp mixed spice
100g sultanas

TO DECORATE
White chocolate, melted
Sprinkles or edible stars

1. Preheat oven to 180°C (160°C fan) mark 4. Line a 20.5cm square tin with baking parchment.

2. In a large pan, gently heat the butter, chocolate and brandy, if using, until melted. Take pan off the heat and mix in the sugar, followed by the eggs (the mixture will become smooth and glossy as you mix it). Sift over the flour and spices, then add the sultanas and stir everything together. Scrape the mixture into the tin and bake for 30min, until a crust forms. Cool completely in the tin.

3. Lift the brownie out of the tin and cut into 24 squares. Arrange the bites on a wire rack set over a baking tray or board, drizzle with melted white chocolate, then decorate with sprinkles or stars. Leave to set before serving or putting in gift boxes.

Hands-on time: 25min
Cooking time: about 35min
Makes 24 bites

PER BITE 156cals, 1g protein, 8g fat (5g saturates), 19g carbs (16g total sugars), 1g fibre

Cranberry and Orange Shortbread

We've rolled these biscuits in demerara sugar for extra crunch and prettiness. Replace the orange with lemon, if you like.

FOR THE SHORTBREAD
200g unsalted butter, softened
40g icing sugar, sifted
50g rice flour
250g plain flour
1 tsp vanilla extract
40g dried cranberries, finely chopped
Finely grated zest 2 oranges, plus 1 tbsp orange juice

TO FINISH
50g demerara sugar

1. For the shortbread, in a medium bowl using a handheld electric whisk, beat all the ingredients until combined. Scrape on to a work surface and roll into a log about 24cm long and 6cm wide, with flat ends. Wrap and chill for at least 1hr 30min (or up to 24hr), until the dough is firm.

2. Preheat oven to 180°C (160°C fan) mark 4 and line 2 baking sheets with baking parchment. Sprinkle the demerara sugar on to a small baking tray or large plate.

3. Unwrap the shortbread and roll the outside firmly in the demerara sugar to coat. Slice the log into 5–7.5mm rounds. Transfer to the lined sheets, spacing slightly apart, and bake for 25min, or until lightly golden.

4. Allow to cool on sheets for 5min, then transfer to a wire rack to cool completely before serving.

★ TO STORE
Once cool, keep in an airtight container at room temperature for up to 4 days.

Hands-on time: 15min, plus chilling and cooling
Cooking time: about 25min
Makes about 18

PER BISCUIT 166cals, 2g protein, 9g fat (6g saturates), 18g carbs (5g total sugars), 1g fibre

Hot Chocolate Stirrers

These stirrers make adorable gifts for chocolate lovers – simply stir 1 or 2 into a mug of warm milk and enjoy.

Sunflower oil, to grease

FOR WHITE AND MILK CHOCOLATE STIRRERS
100g white chocolate, chopped
10g freeze-dried raspberry pieces
200g milk chocolate, chopped
30g mint chocolate biscuits, broken into small pieces
2 tbsp strong espresso, cooled
15 mini marshmallows

FOR DARK CHOCOLATE STIRRERS
140g dark chocolate, chopped
30g salted caramel sauce
½ tsp flaked sea salt
25g mini fudge pieces
30g smooth peanut butter
25g mini honeycomb pieces

YOU'LL ALSO NEED
Wooden lolly sticks and/or candy canes

1. Lightly grease 2 silicone ice-cube trays with sunflower oil.

2. For the white chocolate stirrers, melt the white chocolate in a medium heatproof bowl over a pan of barely simmering water. Remove from the heat and gently stir until smooth. Stir in most of the raspberry pieces, saving some to decorate.

3. Divide equally among 5 ice-cube tray holes. Sprinkle over the reserved raspberries. Chill for 30min, until starting to set, then insert a lolly stick into the middle of each and return to the fridge until completely set (about 3hr 30min).

4. For the milk chocolate stirrers, repeat steps 2 and 3 with 100g milk chocolate, stirring in most of the mint chocolate biscuits when melted (use the remainder to decorate) and using candy canes in place of the lolly sticks, if you like.

5. Repeat steps 2 and 3 with the remaining 100g milk chocolate and the espresso, melting them together, then decorating with a few mini marshmallows.

6. For the dark chocolate stirrers, repeat steps 2 and 3 with 70g dark chocolate, stirring in all the caramel sauce and sea salt and most of the fudge pieces when melted (use the remainder to decorate).

7. Repeat steps 2 and 3 with the remaining 70g dark chocolate, stirring in all the peanut butter and most of the honeycomb pieces (use the remainder to decorate).

8. Once all the stirrers are set, carefully remove from the tray. Stir into hot milk to serve.

Hands-on time: 45min, plus chilling
Cooking time: about 15min
Makes 25 stirrers

PER STIRRER 127cals, 2g protein, 7g fat (4g saturates), 15g carbs (14g total sugars), 1g fibre

★ TO STORE
Keep the stirrers in an airtight container at cool room temperature, or in the fridge for up to 1 week. To gift, pack into cellophane bags and tie with a festive ribbon and tag.

Christmas Tree Linzer Cookies

These melt-in-the-mouth biscuits are a cross between the iconic Jammie Dodger and a traditional Austrian Christmas bake – Linzer cookies. You can flavour them with either cinnamon or vanilla, both are delicious.

200g plain flour, plus extra to dust
125g icing sugar, plus extra to dust
100g ground almonds
1 tsp ground cinnamon or vanilla extract
200g butter, chilled and cubed
2 medium egg yolks
8 tbsp smooth strawberry or raspberry jam

YOU'LL ALSO NEED
6cm round cutter, fluted or plain
2–3cm mini cutter (see GH tip)

★ GH TIP
Use any shape cutter you like for the centre holes: a tree, star, heart etc. Look for cutters intended for fondant or crafting to find designs that are small enough. Alternatively, use a round piping nozzle to make the holes.

★ TO STORE
Keep for up to 5 days in an airtight container. To give as a gift, pack into boxes lined with tissue or baking paper.

1. Put the flour, sugar, ground almonds, cinnamon or vanilla, butter and ¼ tsp salt in a food processor and pulse until the mixture resembles breadcrumbs. Add the egg yolks and pulse again until the mixture clumps together. Add a drop of ice-cold water, if needed, to help it come together. Tip out on to a work surface and bring together with your hands. Divide dough into 2, then shape each piece into a disc, wrap in clingfilm and chill for 1hr.

2. Lightly flour a work surface and line 2 large baking sheets with baking parchment. Roll out one of the pieces of dough to 3mm thick. Stamp out 6cm rounds and transfer to one of the lined trays, re-rolling trimmings as necessary, until you have 24 rounds. Repeat with the remaining dough and stamp out a further small shape in the centre of each round. Make sure you have the same number of plain and stamped circles.

3. Chill for 20min. Meanwhile, preheat oven to 180°C (160°C fan) mark 4.

4. Bake for 12–15min or until very pale gold, then carefully remove the tray and spoon 1 tsp jam on to the middle of each solid base, spreading it out slightly. Dust the tops of the hole-stamped rounds thickly with icing sugar, then carefully place the dusted tops on top of the jammy ones and press down lightly. Return the stacks (hole-side up) to one of the baking trays and bake for 5min more. Transfer to a wire rack and leave to cool completely.

Hands-on time: 35min, plus chilling and cooling
Cooking time: about 20min
Makes 24 cookies

PER SANDWICH COOKIE 136cals, 2g protein, 8g fat (4g saturates), 13g carbs (7g total sugars), 0g fibre

Christmas Tree Meringues

Kids will love creating these trees – and it's easy to double the recipe for gifting.

3 medium egg whites
150g caster sugar
⅛ tsp cream of tartar
Green food colouring paste or gel

TO DECORATE
Sugar sprinkles, including gold stars
Edible glitter

1. Preheat oven to 110°C (90°C fan) mark ¼. Line 2 baking trays with baking parchment.

2. Using a mixer or handheld electric whisk, beat the egg whites to stiff peaks. Gradually beat in the sugar until the meringue is thick and glossy. Beat in the cream of tartar and enough food colouring for a festive green.

3. Transfer the meringue to a piping bag fitted with a 5mm nozzle. Pipe tree-shaped mounds on to the lined trays (about 4cm wide at the base and 4cm tall), spacing them apart. Decorate each with sprinkles, edible glitter, and a gold star.

4. Bake for 1hr 20min–1hr 30min, or until the trees easily peel off the parchment. Cool completely in the oven with the door ajar. Serve.

Hands-on time: 20min, plus cooling
Cooking time: about 1hr 30min
Makes about 26 meringues

PER MERINGUE 25cals, 0.5g protein, 0g fat (0g saturates), 6g carbs (6g total sugars), 0g fibre

Choc and Nut Biscotti

Use up whatever nuts and chocolate you have in these versatile biscuits.

225g plain flour, plus extra to dust
1 tsp baking powder
175g caster sugar
2 medium eggs, beaten
75g each whole hazelnuts and pistachios
75g milk chocolate, chopped into small chunks

1. Preheat oven to 180°C (160°C fan) mark 4. Line a large baking sheet with baking parchment. Mix the flour, baking powder and sugar in a large bowl. Add the eggs, stir until clumps form, then bring together with your hands, kneading until smooth. Add the nuts and chocolate and knead until evenly distributed (the dough will be stiff and a bit sticky).

2. On a lightly floured surface, divide the dough in half and roll into 2 sausage shapes roughly 33cm long. Put on the baking sheet, spaced apart.

3. Bake for 20–25min until the dough is lightly golden and has spread, then cool for 10min on a wire rack. Turn oven down to 140°C (120°C fan) mark 1.

4. With a bread knife, cut the rolls diagonally into 1cm-thick slices and lay flat on the baking sheet. Bake for 15min until lightly golden – they'll harden on cooling – then cool completely on a wire rack.

★ TO STORE
Keep in an airtight tin for up to 2 weeks.

Hands-on time: 20min, plus cooling
Cooking time: about 40min
Makes about 40 biscotti

PER BISCOTTI 76cals, 2g protein, 3g fat (1g saturates), 10g carbs (6g total sugars), 1g fibre

Rocky Road

Our version uses white chocolate and coconut for a moreish treat.

400g white chocolate, chopped
25g mini marshmallows
50g desiccated coconut, plus extra to decorate
50g dried cranberries
40g pistachios
50g ginger nut biscuits, roughly chopped
Silver balls, to decorate (optional)

1. Line a rectangular tin about 15 x 20.5cm with clingfilm. Put the chocolate into a microwave-safe bowl. Microwave on full power for 1min. Stir, then return to the microwave for 10sec bursts until the chocolate is melted and smooth. (Don't be tempted to give it longer blasts – white chocolate burns easily.)

2. Stir in the remaining ingredients (apart from the silver balls, if using), then empty into the prepared tin and level the surface.

3. Scatter over extra coconut and silver balls, if using, then freeze for 15min until solid. Cut into squares and serve.

Hands-on time: 5min, plus freezing
Cooking time: about 5min
Cuts into 20 squares

PER SQUARE 159cals, 2g protein, 9g fat (5g saturates), 16g carbs (15g total sugars), 1g fibre

Tropical Vegan Coconut Ice

This fruity (and dairy-free) twist on a sweet shop favourite is best a few days after you make it.

400g vegan coconut condensed milk alternative
375g icing sugar, sifted
375g desiccated coconut
3 tbsp mango purée
50g dried mango, finely chopped
Orange food colouring gel (optional)

1. Line the base and sides of a 20.5cm square tin with baking parchment.

2. In a large bowl, mix together the condensed milk alternative and 325g icing sugar, then stir in 350g of the coconut. Spoon half the mixture into the tin and press with damp hands to level.

3. To the remaining mixture, add the mango purée, chopped mango, remaining 50g icing sugar and a few drops orange food colouring (if using). Mix well. Spoon into the tin and press on top of the white mixture, smoothing to level. Sprinkle over the remaining 25g coconut; press gently to stick.

4. Wrap the tin in clingfilm or foil and leave to set overnight, then cut into squares.

★ TO STORE
Keep squares or the whole uncut slab in an airtight container at room temperature for up to 2 weeks.

Hands-on time: 20min plus (overnight) setting
Makes 40 pieces

PER PIECE 134cals, 1g protein, 7g fat (5g saturates), 16g carbs (16g total sugars), 2g fibre

Mix and Match Chocolate Lollipops

Let your imagination run riot using different chocolates, flavourings and toppings to make these fun sweets.

100g dark, milk or white chocolate, chopped

FLAVOUR SUGGESTIONS
Peppermint extract or rose water
½ tsp finely grated orange, lemon or lime zest
Large pinch cayenne pepper, rock salt or freshly ground black pepper

TOPPING SUGGESTIONS
Fudge chunks, chopped nuts, poppy seeds, chopped dried fruit, chilli flakes, crystallised rose petals, crystallised ginger, sugar sprinkles or silver balls

YOU'LL ALSO NEED
Lollipop sticks

1. Line 2 baking sheets with baking parchment. Melt your chosen chocolate in a heatproof bowl over a pan of simmering water, making sure the bowl doesn't touch the water. Stir in your choice of flavouring.

2. Spoon 1 tbsp of the chocolate mixture on to a lined sheet and spread into a circle. Lay on a lollipop stick and add a little more chocolate to cover. Repeat with the remaining chocolate.

3. While chocolate is wet, sprinkle over your chosen toppings and leave to set.

Hands-on time: 20min, plus setting
Cooking time: about 5min
Makes 4 lollipops

PER LOLLIPOP (average) 130cals, 2g protein, 8g fat (5g saturates), 14g carbs (14g total sugars), 0g fibre

Spiced Pineapple Liqueur

This is delicious sipped by itself, shaken into a piña colada, or mixed with ice-cold cola. Tinned pineapple provides the sweetest, ripest fruit possible, and saves on prep time.

435g tin crushed pineapple in juice
150g golden caster sugar
1 vanilla pod, split vertically
2 star anise
1 cinnamon stick
20 black peppercorns
350ml white rum or vodka

1. In a pan (with a lid) stir the pineapple, juice and sugar over medium heat, until the sugar dissolves and the mixture is bubbling. Add the spices, remove from heat, then cover and infuse for 10min.

2. Scrape the mixture into a 1 litre Kilner jar and pour over the rum or vodka. Cover with the lid and shake gently to mix. Infuse for at least 2 weeks (up to 2 months) in a cool, dark place. Give the jar a gentle shake every couple of days.

3. Line a colander or sieve with muslin or a clean j-cloth and set over a jug. Strain the pineapple mixture, pressing down on the pulp to extract as much liquid as possible. Discard pulp. Decant into sterilised bottles (see p10).

★ TO STORE
Keep for up to 6 months in a cool, dark place.

Hands-on time: 10min, plus (at least 2 weeks) infusing
Cooking time: about 10min
Makes 700ml

PER 25ML SERVING 57cals, 0g protein, 0g fat (0g saturates), 7g carbs (7g total sugars), 0g fibre

Mulled Pomegranate Gin

Infusing your own gin is easy and delicious – and makes for a wonderfully seasonal G&T.

40g caster sugar
1 cinnamon stick
4 cloves
½ tsp allspice berries
3cm piece fresh root ginger, peeled and roughly chopped
2 pomegranates, halved
700ml dry gin

1. Heat 100ml water with the sugar, spices and ginger in a small pan over a low heat until the sugar dissolves. Turn up the heat and boil for 5min.

2. Meanwhile, working over a bowl, scoop the seeds from the pomegranates, catching any juices in the bowl. Discard any white pith and transfer to a large jug or Kilner jar with the spiced syrup and gin. Cover and leave to infuse in the fridge for 2 weeks.

3. Strain through a fine sieve and decant into sterilised bottles (see p10).

★ TO STORE
Keep the bottled gin in a cool, dry place for up to 3 months (it will darken in colour).

Hands-on time: 10min, plus (2 weeks) infusing
Cooking time: about 10min
Makes about 800ml

PER 25ML SERVING 54cals, 0g protein, 0g fat (0g saturates), 2g carbs (2g total sugars), 0g fibre

Marinated Olives and Goat's Cheese

A gift that's easy to make but looks impressive – and it will be a hit with any food lovers.

Pared zest 1 unwaxed lemon
1 sprig each fresh thyme, rosemary and oregano
1 bay leaf
1 small red chilli, deseeded and finely sliced
1 garlic clove, quartered
300g mixed black and green olives
100g soft goat's cheese, roughly crumbled
450ml extra virgin olive oil, plus extra to cover
½ tbsp peppercorns

1. Prepare a small bowl of iced water. Bring a small pan of water to the boil and cook the lemon zest, herbs, chilli and garlic for 1min. Lift out using a slotted spoon and plunge into the iced water. Drain and dry on kitchen paper.

2. In a large bowl, mix together the blanched ingredients, olives, goat's cheese, oil and peppercorns. Spoon into 2 x 500ml sterilised jars (see p10), making sure everything is covered with oil (top up with extra if needed). Cover and chill. Use within 1 to 2 weeks.

Hands-on time: 10min, plus marinating
Cooking time: about 5min
Makes 2 x 500ml jars

PER 50G SERVING 181cals, 1g protein, 19g fat (4g saturates), 0g carbs (0g total sugars), 1g fibre

Candy Cane Macarons

These bite-sized treats are a bit fiddly to make, but well worth it in terms of wow factor and flavour. Measure the ingredients exactly and don't substitute anything. When beating the egg white mixture, set a timer. This is one recipe you can't take shortcuts on!

FOR THE MACARONS
200g ground almonds
225g icing sugar
150g egg whites (from roughly 4 large eggs)
70g granulated sugar
Red food colouring paste, optional

FOR THE FILLING
150g unsalted butter, softened
250g icing sugar, sifted
1 tsp vanilla extract
2 tsp peppermint extract
2–3 peppermint candy canes, roughly crushed

★ TO STORE
The macarons will keep in an airtight container at room temperature for up to 4 days.

1. Preheat oven to 170°C (do not use fan) mark 3. Line 2 large baking sheets with baking parchment. Draw 3cm circles on the parchment, spacing about 2.5cm apart. Flip so the ink is underneath. Shake/tap the ground almonds through a fine sieve until you have 115g (save the excess for another recipe) – have patience, as you might need to do this a couple of times. Sift the icing sugar and a pinch of salt into the sieved almonds. Set aside until needed.

Hands-on time: 45min, plus cooling
Cooking time: about 25min
Makes about 30 macarons

PER MACARON 140cals, 2g protein, 6g fat (3g saturates), 19g carbs (19g total sugars), 0g fibre

2. Using a freestanding mixer, beat the egg whites and granulated sugar at medium speed for 3min. Increase to medium-high speed for 3min, then turn up to maximum speed for 3min. If dyeing your macarons red, add a smear of food colouring paste and beat in. Add the almond mixture in one go and use a silicone spatula to fold together, counting the folds. Initially it will look like it won't come together, but after about 40 folds, the mixture should be well combined and move like lava. Don't be gentle here – the aim is to knock the air out of the whites.

3. Transfer half the mixture to a piping bag fitted with a 1cm plain nozzle and pipe inside the drawn circles. Repeat with remaining mixture. Drop the baking trays down hard against your counter a few times to burst any air bubbles in the mixture (see GH Tip). Bake for 20–25min (if dyed red, they may take a few minutes more) or until you can peel the macarons from the parchment (cook for 1min more if not ready and test again). Cool completely on trays.

4. For the filling, beat the butter, icing sugar, vanilla and peppermint extracts until combined. Use to sandwich the macarons together, piping for a neater finish, then roll the edges of the macarons in crushed candy canes. Serve.

★ GH TIP
Macarons can crack if there are air bubbles in the mixture, so don't be afraid to drop the trays hard to ensure a smooth finish.

Candied Fruit and Nut Chocolate Bark

Gold sprinkles add a touch of festive glam, but leave them out for a pared-back look.

75g mixed nuts (we used hazelnuts, pecans and almonds)
2 tbsp mixed candied peel
200g dark chocolate, finely chopped
100g milk chocolate, finely chopped
100g white chocolate, finely chopped
2 tbsp dried sour cherries, chopped
Edible gold stars or pearls (optional)

1. Preheat oven to 160°C (140°C fan) mark 3. Spread the nuts on a large baking tray and cook in oven for 10min, until toasted. Remove to a chopping board, roughly chop and leave to cool. Line baking tray with baking parchment.

2. Meanwhile, put the candied peel in a small sieve and rinse to remove any sticky residue. Shake off excess water; dry thoroughly with kitchen paper.

3. Put each chocolate type into a separate, heatproof bowl; set over a pan of simmering water to melt. Remove from the heat and stir until smooth.

4. Thinly spread two-thirds of the dark chocolate on to the prepared tray in a large rectangle or oval, then spoon the milk, white and remaining dark chocolate on top in alternate dollops. Tap the tray on the work surface a couple of times so the chocolate forms an even layer, then swirl it gently with a skewer to create a marbled pattern.

5. Scatter over the chopped nuts, candied peel, cherries and gold sprinkles (if using). Leave to set in a cool place (not the fridge unless your house is warm) for at least 2hr. When set, package up in a slab or break into irregular shards.

⭐ TO STORE
Keep in an airtight container in the fridge for up to 2 weeks. To gift, pack into a large, shallow box lined with baking parchment or tissue paper. Or break into shards, pack into cellophane bags and tie with ribbon.

Hands-on time: 20min, plus cooling and setting
Cooking time: about 15min
Makes 1 large sheet (serves 16)

PER SERVING 136cals, 2g protein, 8g fat (4g saturates), 13g carbs (7g total sugars), 0g fibre

Gingerbread Cream Liqueur

Enjoy this liqueur as a smooth after-dinner tipple or add a dash to coffee or hot chocolate for some boozy indulgence.

75g light muscovado sugar
30g fresh root ginger, peeled and finely sliced
3 cinnamon sticks
350ml whisky or vodka
397g tin condensed milk
300ml single cream

1. In a small pan (that has a lid) over low heat, stir the sugar and 200ml water until the sugar dissolves. Add the ginger and cinnamon, turn up the heat and bring to the boil. Cover, turn down the heat and simmer gently for 10min.

2. Remove the pan from heat, stir in the whisky or vodka and re-cover. Set aside to infuse at room temperature for at least 6hr, or ideally overnight.

3. Empty the condensed milk into a large jug, then gradually whisk in the single cream until smooth. Strain in the infused alcohol through a fine sieve (discard the spices), add a large pinch of salt and whisk to combine.

4. Decant into sterilised bottles (see p10), using a clean funnel if needed. Chill well before serving.

★ TO STORE

Keep chilled for up to 1 month. To serve, shake well to recombine – the cream naturally rises to the top but will mix back in.

Hands-on time: 15min, plus (overnight) infusing
Cooking time: about 15min
Makes 1.1 litres

PER 25ML SERVING 55cals, 1g protein, 1g fat (0.5g saturates), 7g carbs (7g total sugars), 0g fibre

Gingerbread Biscuits

This recipe makes lots of biscuits, but they keep well and make tasty homemade gifts for friends and family.

225g unsalted butter, chopped
150ml golden syrup
175g light brown muscovado sugar
500g plain flour, plus extra to dust
2 tsp ground ginger
2 tsp ground cinnamon
1 tsp ground cloves
1 tsp baking powder
1 medium egg, beaten, to decorate
250g icing sugar, sifted
Edible silver balls

★ FREEZE AHEAD
At the end of step 2, freeze the unbaked dough, wrapped, for up to 1 month. Defrost overnight in the fridge and complete the recipe.

★ TO STORE
The biscuits will keep in an airtight container at room temperature for up to 3 weeks. Store the spare icing, covered, for up to 2 days in the fridge.

1. In a medium pan over a low heat, melt the butter, syrup and brown sugar, stirring until the sugar dissolves. Set aside to cool. Meanwhile, in a large bowl, mix the flour, spices, baking powder and ½ tsp salt.

2. Beat the egg into the cooled syrup mixture, then add the wet mixture to the dry ingredients and stir to combine. Divide the mixture in half and wrap each portion in clingfilm. Chill for at least 4hr or overnight – or follow the freezing instructions below.

3. Preheat oven to 190°C (170°C fan) mark 5. Line 3 large baking sheets with baking parchment. On a lightly floured surface, roll out one dough portion to 5mm thickness. Use festive cookie cutters to stamp out biscuits, then space 2cm apart on the prepared baking sheets. Bake for 8–10min until golden. Cool for 5min on the sheets before transferring to a wire rack to cool completely. Repeat with the remaining portion of dough to make a second batch.

4. Mix the icing sugar with 2 tbsp hot water to make a thick icing. Scrape into a piping bag with a small plain nozzle (or snip off the end of a disposable piping bag). Pipe patterns on to the biscuits; decorate with silver balls. Leave to set.

Hands-on time: about 1hr, plus chilling, cooling and setting
Cooking time: about 20min
Makes about 50 biscuits

PER BISCUIT 95cals, 1g protein, 4g fat (2g saturates), 13g carbs (6g total sugars), 0.4g fibre

Best-ever Nougat

This favourite treat — whether enjoyed with the family or given as an edible gift — is all the nicer when it's homemade.

Few sheets rice paper
250g granulated sugar
150g clear honey
1 tbsp liquid glucose
2 large egg whites
1 tsp vanilla extract
175g blanched almonds, toasted
125g unsalted pistachio kernels, toasted
50g candied peel

YOU'LL ALSO NEED
Sugar thermometer

1. Line a 20.5cm square tin with clingfilm, overlapping the sides of the tin. Cover the base with rice paper.

2. Put the sugar, honey, glucose and 125ml cold water into a medium-sized heavy-based pan over a low heat. Stir to dissolve. Bring to the boil, then cook until the mixture reaches 143°C on the sugar thermometer. Remove from the heat at once.

3. Just before the syrup reaches the right temperature, beat the egg whites in a mixer until stiff. Keeping the motor running, carefully add the syrup in a thin stream. Add the vanilla, then quickly fold in the nuts and peel – the mixture should still be stiff.

4. Spoon the mixture into the tin, then cover with more rice paper. Put another baking tin on top and weigh it down. Leave in a cool place overnight or store for up to 2 weeks in the fridge. To wrap, turn out on to a board and remove clingfilm. Cut into pieces and pack into boxes lined with waxed paper. Keeps for up to 2 weeks.

Hands-on time: 40min, plus (overnight) standing
Cooking time: about 15min
Makes 64 pieces

PER PIECE 55cals, 1g protein, 3g fat (<1g saturates), 7g carbs (6g total sugars), <1g fibre

Snowball Truffles

Presented in a box, these will look like
they have come from a master chocolatier.

175g plain chocolate
150ml extra-thick double cream
25g unsalted butter
2 tbsp Grand Marnier or brandy
1 tbsp crème fraîche
40g icing sugar

YOU'LL ALSO NEED
Petit four paper cases

1. Break the chocolate into pieces and put in
   a food processor. Whizz for about 30sec, or
   until the chocolate is very finely chopped.

2. Put the cream, butter and liqueur into a small
   pan and bring to the boil.

3. Switch on the processor and, with the motor
   still running, add the hot cream mixture to the
   chopped chocolate. Blend until evenly mixed.

4. Spoon the chocolate mixture into a large bowl
   and stir in the crème fraîche. Leave to cool,
   cover with clingfilm and put in the fridge
   overnight to thicken.

5. Arrange the petit four cases on a tray. Sieve the
   icing sugar on to a baking sheet lined with foil
   or baking parchment. Drop teaspoonfuls of the
   chocolate mixture on to the icing sugar and roll
   to cover. Use 2 forks to lift the truffles and drop
   them carefully into the paper cases.

6. Put the truffles into a shallow gift box. Tie a
   ribbon around the lid, then label with storage
   instructions and an eat-by date (see To store).

★ TO STORE
Keep the truffles in an airtight container in the
fridge for up to 1 week.

Hands-on time: 20min, plus chilling
Cooking time: about 5min
Makes 25 balls

PER BALL 86cals, 1g protein, 6g fat (4g saturates), 6g
carbs (6g total sugars), <1g fibre

Ricciarelli Mince Pies

Chewy almond biscuits make a different and moreish mince-pie topping.

FOR THE PASTRY
125g plain flour, plus extra to dust
50g icing sugar
50g butter, chilled and cubed
1 medium egg yolk, the white reserved for later
1 tsp vanilla extract

FOR THE FILLING
300g mincemeat (see PX and Pear Mincemeat, p215)

FOR THE RICCIARELLI TOPPING
100g blanched almonds, toasted
75g icing sugar, plus extra to dust
Finely grated zest 1 lemon
½ tsp almond extract
1 medium egg white (from earlier)
2 tbsp flaked almonds

★ GH TIP
If you don't have a food processor, use ground almonds and mix with the ingredients rather than whizzing.

★ TO STORE
Keep the mince pies in an airtight container at room temperature for up to 5 days. To serve warm, reheat in an oven preheated to 170°C (150°C fan) mark 3 for 5min.

Hands-on time: 30min, plus chilling and cooling
Cooking time: about 30min
Makes 12 pies

PER PIE 253cals, 4g protein, 11g fat (3g saturates), 34g carbs (26g total sugars), 2g fibre

1. To make the pastry, pulse the flour, icing sugar and butter in a food processor until the mixture resembles fine breadcrumbs. If you don't have a food processor, rub the butter into the flour and icing sugar with your fingers. Add the egg yolk, vanilla extract and 1 tbsp cold water and pulse/mix until the pastry just comes together. Tip on to a surface, shape into a disc, wrap in clingfilm and chill for 30min.

2. Lightly flour a work surface and roll out the pastry to 3mm thick. Stamp out 12 rounds using an 8cm cutter (re-roll the trimmings as necessary). Use the rounds to line a 12-hole cupcake tin and fill with the mincemeat. Chill while you make the ricciarelli topping.

3. Preheat oven to 170°C (150°C fan) mark 3. Whizz the toasted almonds, icing sugar, lemon zest and almond extract in a food processor until very fine (see GH Tip). In a separate bowl, whisk the egg white to stiff peaks, then carefully fold in the almond mixture with a large metal spoon.

4. Using slightly damp hands, mould the mixture into 12 long almond shapes and sit one on top of each mince pie. Sprinkle with flaked almonds and dust liberally with icing sugar. Bake for 25–30min, until golden. Cool in the tin for 10min, then transfer to a wire rack to cool completely.

Espresso Martini Fudge

This rich, flavoursome fudge looks super-chic, yet is simple to make.

15g instant coffee granules or espresso powder
1½ tbsp coffee liqueur
4 tbsp vodka
397g tin condensed milk
350g dark chocolate (70% cocoa solids), chopped
225g white chocolate, chopped
36 whole or chocolate-covered coffee beans and/or a little
  ground coffee, to decorate (optional)

1. Line a 20.5cm square tin with baking parchment.
   In a large heatproof bowl, stir together the
   instant coffee, coffee liqueur and 2 tbsp vodka,
   until dissolved. Stir in 250g condensed milk,
   then the dark chocolate.

2. Set the bowl over a pan of barely simmering
   water and heat gently, stirring frequently, until
   melted and smooth. Scrape into the prepared
   tin, smooth to level and chill until needed.

3. Clean the heatproof bowl and set back over the
   pan of simmering water. Add white chocolate
   and the remaining vodka and condensed milk.
   Heat gently, stirring, until melted and smooth.

4. Scrape on to the dark chocolate layer and
   spread to level. If decorating, working quickly
   before the fudge starts to set, arrange 36 coffee
   beans in 6 evenly spaced rows of 6 and/or
   sprinkle over a light dusting of ground coffee.
   Chill for at least 4hr, or ideally overnight.

5. Lift the fudge on to a board and cut into
   36 squares, cleaning the knife between
   slices for the neatest finish. Serve.

★ TO STORE
Keep in airtight container at room temperature
for up to 1 week, or in the fridge for up to 1 month.

Hands-on time: 20min, plus (overnight) chilling
Cooking time: about 15min
Cuts into 36 pieces

PER PIECE 124cals, 2g protein, 6g fat (3g saturates),
15g carbs (15g total sugars), <1g fibre

Hot Chocolate Mix with Chocolate Spoons

This easy-to-make, long-lasting gift is jazzed up with a set of pretty, decorated spoons. Feel free to add chocolate chips instead of marshmallows to your hot chocolate mix.

75g cocoa powder
25g powdered milk
100g finely grated dark chocolate
150g icing sugar
1 tbsp cornflour
50g mini marshmallows (or chocolate chips)

FOR THE CHOCOLATE SPOONS
100g each dark, milk and white chocolate, chopped and
   kept separate
Wooden spoons
Your choice of toppings – contrasting/coloured chocolate,
   fudge chunks, mini marshmallows, chopped chocolate
   sweets, chopped nuts, crushed sweets, chilli flakes,
   chopped crystallised ginger, sugar sprinkles, silver balls

1. In a large bowl, mix together the cocoa, powdered milk, chocolate, icing sugar and cornflour. Put into a large, sterilised 1 litre Kilner jar (see p10), or divide among smaller jars, and top with marshmallows (or chocolate chips).

2. For the chocolate spoons (we made 10), melt your chosen chocolate in a heatproof bowl set over a pan of barely simmering water. Dip the wooden spoons into the chocolate up to the handle, then lay on a baking sheet lined with baking parchment. While the chocolate is still melted, sprinkle over your chosen toppings and leave to set. When the spoons are hard, remove them from the paper and wrap in a cellophane bag to seal.

3. To make up a single serving of hot chocolate, add 2 tbsp hot chocolate mix and 350ml milk to a pan. Gently warm over a medium heat until combined and piping hot. Serve immediately with extra mini marshmallows, chocolate spoons to dip and whipped cream, if you like.

Hands-on time: 10min, plus setting
Cooking time: about 10min
Makes 400g (enough for about 6 servings)

PER SERVING (2 tbsp mix, 350ml semi-skimmed milk, without a chocolate spoon) 286cals, 14g protein, 9g fat (6g saturates), 36g carbs (34g total sugars), 1g fibre

Gingerbread Advent Mobile

Great fun to do with kids, this delicious project helps build festive anticipation! These biscuits also make great tree decorations or a tasty afternoon nibble.

125g unsalted butter, chopped
50g golden syrup
125g dark brown soft sugar
275g plain flour, plus extra to dust
1 tsp ground cinnamon
½ tsp ground nutmeg
1 tsp ground ginger
¼ tsp ground cloves
½ tsp baking powder
1 medium egg white

FOR THE ICING AND DECORATION
1 medium egg white
250g icing sugar, sifted
Sugar sprinkles (optional)
Thin ribbon and string, to hang (optional)
3 coated-metal rings around 15cm, 20cm and 25cm for the mobile (optional)

1. In a medium pan over low heat, melt the butter, syrup and sugar, stirring until the sugar dissolves. Leave to cool. Meanwhile, in a large bowl, mix the flour, spices, baking powder and ½ tsp fine salt.

2. Beat the egg white into the cooled syrup mixture, then mix the liquid into the flour bowl and stir to combine. Bring together, wrap in clingfilm and chill for at least 3hr or overnight.

Hands-on time: 1hr 30min, plus chilling and cooling
Cooking time: about 20min
Makes 24 biscuits

PER BISCUIT 150cals, 2g protein, 4g fat (3g saturates), 26g carbs (17g total sugars), 1g fibre

3. Preheat oven to 190°C (170°C fan) mark 5. Line 3 baking sheets with baking parchment. Lightly flour a work surface and roll out the dough to 3-5mm thick. Stamp out festive shapes, re-rolling trimmings as needed (you'll need at least 24). Transfer to lined trays, spacing apart. If you intend to hang the biscuits, use a skewer to make a hole in the top of each.

4. Bake for 10-12min until golden. Allow to cool for 5min on trays, re-opening the ribbon holes if needed. Transfer to wire racks to cool completely.

5. For the icing, beat the egg white in a bowl with a handheld electric whisk to stiff peaks. Beat in the icing sugar. Add a couple of drops of water if needed to make into a stiff, pipeable consistency. Spoon into a piping bag with a small plain or star nozzle. Ice the biscuits and add sugar sprinkles, if you like, adding the numbers 1-24 if needed. Leave to dry fully.

6. Tie 3 long strings to each mobile ring, spacing evenly and feeding the strings from the smaller two rings up through the centre of the larger one (leave your chosen distance between them). Tie all the strings together at the top, ensuring the rings hang horizontally and evenly. Trim excess string; tie on a string loop to hang the mobile.

7. Loop ribbons on to each biscuit and tie them evenly to the rings, allowing them to slide so their weight can be redistributed after the biscuits are removed (we hung numbers 1-6 on the smallest ring, 7-15 on the middle ring and 16-24 on the largest ring, so the calendar is eaten from lower tier up). Stand back and admire your handiwork!

Sticky Tomato Jam

The perfect accompaniment to any cheeseboard. Try spreading on a cheese toastie or stirring into sauces and stews. Adjust the amount of chilli to suit your heat tolerance.

2kg ripe tomatoes, roughly chopped
350g jam sugar
125ml white wine vinegar
Juice 2 lemons
50g fresh root ginger, peeled and finely grated
4 tbsp sweet smoked paprika
½–1 tbsp dried chilli flakes

1. Put all the ingredients, plus 1 tbsp salt and 2 tsp freshly ground black pepper, into a large pan. Stir over low heat until the sugar dissolves.

2. Turn up heat to medium and bubble, stirring occasionally, until thick with a jam-like consistency (about 50min). Remove from heat and leave to cool completely before dividing among sterilised jars (see p10). Seal and cool before serving or storing.

★ TO STORE
Keep in a cool, dry place for up to 2 months. Chill after opening and use within 2 weeks.

Hands-on time: 25min, plus cooling
Cooking time: about 1hr
Makes 4 x 250ml jars

PER 1 TBSP SERVING 27cals, 0g protein, 0g fat (0g saturates), 6g carbs (6g total sugars), 0g fibre

Mango and Scotch Bonnet Hot Sauce

This fiery, fruity hot sauce has the perfect blend of heat and sweetness.

1 tbsp oil
1 red onion, roughly chopped
4 garlic cloves, crushed
4 pitted dates
2 tbsp tomato purée
2 tsp ground cumin
2 tsp ground coriander
1 tsp ground turmeric
10 cherry tomatoes, roughly chopped
5 Scotch bonnet chillies, about 100g, deseeded and
    roughly chopped
2 ripe mangoes, destoned and roughly chopped
100ml white wine vinegar
50ml lemon juice

1. Heat the oil in a large pan over medium heat.
   Add the onion and fry for 5min until beginning
   to brown. Add the garlic, dates, tomato purée
   and spices and cook for 1min.

2. Stir in the tomatoes, chillies and mangoes, then
   cook until beginning to break down, about 5min.
   Add the vinegar, lemon juice, 1 tsp salt, plenty
   of freshly ground black pepper and 100ml water.
   Bring to the boil, then reduce heat and simmer,
   stirring occasionally, for 10min.

3. Leave to cool for 10min, then transfer to a
   blender. Whizz until smooth, adding a little
   just-boiled water if needed to thin to a drizzling
   consistency. Leave to cool completely before
   dividing among sterilised bottles (see p10).
   Serve.

★ TO STORE
Keep in a cool dry place for up to 3 months. Chill
after opening and use within 3 weeks.

Hands-on time: 20min, plus cooling
Cooking time: about 25min
Makes 650ml

PER 1 TSP SERVING 6cals, 0g protein, 0g fat
(0g saturates), 1g carbs (1g total sugars), 0g fibre

Deluxe Mango Chutney

Packed with aromatics, this gorgeously sticky chutney is an ideal gift for spice lovers. Wonderful with a curry or served alongside a cheese board. Gold leaf adds a luxurious sparkle to the finished chutney, but is optional.

2 cardamom pods
1½ tsp cumin seeds
10 black peppercorns
2 whole cloves
1 tsp nigella seeds
900g diced fresh mango chunks
300ml distilled malt vinegar
350g granulated sugar
½ tsp garam masala
2 garlic cloves, finely chopped
2.5cm piece fresh root ginger, peeled and finely chopped
2–3 sheets edible gold leaf (optional)

★ TO STORE
Keep unopened in a cool, dark place for up to 6 months. Once opened, store in the fridge and use within 1 month.

1. Using a pestle and mortar, bash the cardamom pods to break open the husks. Pick out the seeds (discard the husks) and roughly crush along with the cumin, peppercorns and cloves.

2. Empty the spices into a large pan or preserving pan and add the nigella seeds. Heat over medium heat for 1min, or until aromatic. Add a pinch of salt and all the remaining ingredients apart from the gold leaf. Turn the heat down to low and stir to dissolve the sugar.

3. Bring to the boil, then simmer for 50min–1hr, stirring frequently, until thickened. The chutney is ready when you can scrape a wooden spoon across the base of the pan and the chutney doesn't immediately flow back into the gap.

4. Remove from heat and leave to stand for 5min. Add the gold leaf, if using, and stir until evenly distributed in small flakes.

5. Carefully ladle into hot sterilised jars (see p10), then seal and leave to cool completely. You can eat the chutney straight away, but it's best left for at least 2 weeks to mellow and mature.

Hands-on time: 15min, plus cooling and (optional) maturing
Cooking time: about 1hr
Makes about 750g

PER 1 TBSP SERVING 40cals, <1g protein, 0g fat (0g saturates), 9g carbs (9g total sugars), 1g fibre

Chunky Cranberry and Orange Marmalade

Try to use unwaxed or organic lemons and oranges if you can find them. The marmalade will keep unopened in a cool, dark place for up to 6 months. Once opened, store in the fridge for up to 1 month.

1 lemon
450g navel oranges (about 2)
2 small cinnamon sticks
2 whole cloves
2.5cm piece fresh root ginger, peeled and chopped
900g granulated sugar
250g fresh or frozen cranberries
2 tbsp whisky or brandy (optional)

YOU'LL ALSO NEED
Small square of muslin or white cotton

1. Lay out a small sheet of muslin or cotton. Halve and juice the lemon into a large pan, then put the squeezed halves and any pips into the centre of the cloth.

2. Cut each orange into 8 wedges, then thinly slice each wedge widthways to make small triangles about 3mm–5mm thick. Add any pips to the squeezed lemon cloth. Alternatively, you can remove the pips from the wedges, then pulse the wedges in a food processor until chopped to your liking (you won't get neat shreds, but it is much faster). Add the chopped orange (and any juice) to the pan.

Hands-on time: 25min, plus cooling and setting
Cooking time: about 1hr 30min
Makes about 1.6kg

PER 1 TBSP SERVING 37cals, <1g protein, 0g fat (0g saturates), 9g carbs (9g total sugars), <1g fibre

3. Add the cinnamon sticks, cloves and ginger to the cloth, then bring up the sides of the cloth and tie tightly with string to make a bag. Add to the pan, then pour in 1.1 litres just-boiled water.

4. Bring the mixture to the boil, making sure the bag is submerged, then turn down the heat and simmer for 1hr–1hr 15min, stirring occasionally, or until the peel has completely softened. Remove the pan from the heat.

5. Lift out the bag and set aside until cool enough to handle. Meanwhile, stir the sugar into the pan. Squeeze the cooled bag into the pan to extract as much thick and sticky liquid from the lemon halves as you can.

6. Add the cranberries to the pan, then stir over gentle heat to dissolve any remaining sugar crystals. Turn up the heat, bring back to the boil and bubble for 15min or until the marmalade reaches setting point (see p10), stirring occasionally and crushing some of the cranberries to release their juice.

7. Remove the pan from heat, stir in the whisky or brandy, if using. Leave to cool for 10min, then stir once more to re-distribute the fruit. Ladle into hot sterilised jars (see p10). Seal and allow the marmalade to cool and set before using (setting can take 1–2 days, depending on the size of the jar).

Gluten-free Seeded Crackers

These go wonderfully with cheese and pickles, or can simply be enjoyed as a snack by themselves.

225g gluten-free plain/white flour blend, plus extra to dust
2tsp caster sugar
½ tsp xanthan gum
½ tsp bicarbonate of soda
50g unsalted butter, chilled and cubed
1 tsp each fennel and caraway seeds
125ml buttermilk, plus extra to brush
6 tbsp mixed seeds

★ TO STORE
Once cool, keep in an airtight container at room temperature for up to 3 weeks.

1. Preheat oven to 180°C (160°C fan) mark 4. Put the flour, sugar, xanthan gum, bicarbonate of soda and ½ tsp salt into a food processor and pulse to combine. Add the butter, fennel and caraway seeds and pulse until the mixture resembles fine breadcrumbs (alternatively, rub butter into the mixture using your fingertips).

2. Add the buttermilk and pulse until the pastry comes together. Tip on to a work surface, bring together, then cut in half. Wrap the first half and set aside at room temperature.

3. Generously flour a large piece of baking parchment and roll out the other pastry half as thinly as possible (about 1mm), to a rough 32 x 24cm rectangle. Brush the top all over with buttermilk, sprinkle generously with half the mixed seeds and pat down gently with the palm of your hand to help them stick. Score into 9 rectangles. Slide the pastry (still on its parchment) on to a baking sheet.

4. Repeat step 3 with the remaining pastry and slide on to a separate baking sheet. Bake for 30–35min, swapping the baking sheets after 20min, until crisp and golden. Remove to a wire rack to cool. Snap into individual rectangles and serve.

Hands-on time 25min, plus cooling
Cooking time about 35min
Makes 18 crackers

PER CRACKER 88cals, 2g protein, 4g fat (2g saturates), 12g carbs (1g total sugars), 0.5g fibre

12
Round the World

Spanish Polvorones

Traditionally, these Spanish shortbread Christmas cookies are made with pork fat, but we've given the option here to use butter for a vegetarian version instead.

150g plain flour
50g ground almonds
100g lard or unsalted butter, softened
75g icing sugar, sifted, plus extra to dust
½ tsp ground cinnamon
Finely grated zest 1 lemon

1. Preheat oven to 180°C (160°C fan) mark 4. Scatter the flour on to a baking tray and cook in the oven for 30min, mixing in the ground almonds for the final 15min. Leave to cool completely (don't worry if the mixture looks clumpy, it will be sieved).

2. In a large bowl, using a wooden spoon, mix the lard or butter and icing sugar until combined. Sift over the flour mixture and cinnamon (adding the remnants from the sieve into the bowl, too). Add the lemon zest and 1 tbsp cold water and mix until just combined. Bring the dough together, shaping into a rough 18cm-long sausage shape. Wrap and chill for 30min.

3. Reheat oven to 180°C (160°C fan) mark 4 and line a large baking sheet with baking parchment. Cut the log into 1cm-thick rounds (you should have 18) and arrange on the lined sheet, spacing them apart.

4. Bake for 20–25min, or until golden brown. Leave to cool completely on the sheet. Dust with icing sugar and serve.

★ TO STORE
Keep in an airtight container at room temperature for up to 3 days.

Hands-on time: 20min, plus cooling and chilling
Cooking time: about 55min
Makes 18 cookies

PER COOKIE 114cals, 2g protein, 7g fat (2g saturates), 11g carbs (4g total sugars), 0g fibre

Swedish Gravadlax

Gravadlax means 'buried salmon' and refers to the medieval practice of salting fish then burying it in sand to preserve it. Raw salmon is cured in salt, sugar and herbs to make this classic Swedish starter. We've added citrus and juniper for extra zing.

60g flaked sea salt
75g caster sugar
20 juniper berries
2 tsp freshly ground black pepper, plus extra to serve
60g dill, roughly chopped, plus extra to serve
Finely grated zest 1 lemon
Finely grated zest 1 orange
2 x 500g pieces thick skin-on salmon fillet (see GH tip)

FOR THE DILL AND MUSTARD SAUCE
2 tbsp Dijon mustard
2 tbsp runny honey
2 tbsp sunflower oil
1½ tbsp cider vinegar
20g dill, stalks discarded, fronds finely chopped

★ GH TIP
Try to find thick pieces of salmon that are an even size all over (so they cure evenly). Be sure to buy the freshest fish available for this – if you wish to be extra cautious you can freeze the fish for 1 day before curing (to kill off any bacteria).

★ GET AHEAD
Cure the salmon 2 days in advance and make the sauce up to 1 day in advance, cover and chill.

1. Put the salt, sugar, juniper berries, pepper, dill and lemon and orange zests in a small food processor and pulse until combined.

2. Check the salmon for bones (pull any out with tweezers and discard). Pat dry with kitchen paper, then put 1 fillet skin-side down on a large piece of clingfilm. Sprinkle evenly with the salt mix, then put the second piece of salmon on top, skin-side up.

3. Wrap the fillets together tightly with clingfilm and place in a snug-fitting dish. Place a baking tray or chopping board directly on top of the salmon and weigh it down with a couple of tins. Chill for 48hr, turning the fish parcel every 8hr or so, re-covering and weighting each time.

4. To serve, mix all the sauce ingredients together in a small bowl. Remove the salmon from the clingfilm and brush off the cure with kitchen paper. Remove the skin, sprinkle with a little extra dill and freshly ground black pepper and serve with the dill and mustard sauce and some rye or pumpernickel bread on the side.

Hands-on time: 15min, plus (2 days) curing
Serves 8 as a starter

PER SERVING 274cals, 28g protein, 16g fat
(3g saturates), 5g carbs (5g total sugars), 0g fibre

German Crispy Roast Pork with Dark Beer Gravy

Known in Germany as krustenbraten, this roast pork shoulder has crisp crackling and a gravy made with dark wheat beer. It's traditionally served with potato dumplings, but mashed or roast potatoes also go well, as does cabbage or other greens.

1.8–2kg boneless skin-on pork shoulder joint
2 tsp caraway seeds
2 tsp cumin seeds
2 tsp smoked paprika
3 medium carrots, peeled and roughly chopped
3 celery stalks, roughly chopped
2 leeks, trimmed and roughly chopped
250ml vegetable stock
400ml dark beer (we used Leffe Brune)
2 tbsp cornflour
Runny honey, to taste (optional)

1. One hour before cooking, remove the pork from the fridge to come up to room temperature. If the skin of the pork isn't already scored, do so with a sharp knife or scalpel in a diamond pattern (or ask your butcher to do this). Pat dry thoroughly with kitchen paper, then season all over, working it into the scores in the skin. Set aside (uncovered).

2. Preheat oven to 240°C (220°C fan) mark 9. Toast the caraway and cumin seeds in a small frying pan over medium-high heat until fragrant, then grind to a powder with a pestle and mortar. Mix in the paprika, then rub the spice mix all over the meat, avoiding the skin. Put in a medium roasting tin skin-side up. Roast for 30min until the skin starts to crackle.

3. Remove the pork from the oven and reduce the temperature to 180°C (160°C fan), mark 4. Add the vegetables to the roasting tin and lift the pork so it's sitting on top of them. Pour the stock and beer into the tin and return it to the oven for 1hr 30min until pork is cooked and tender.

4. If the crackling isn't crisp, turn the oven back up to 240°C (220°C fan) mark 9 and return the pork to the oven for 15min to crisp up. Alternatively, crisp under a medium-high grill, keeping a careful eye on it to make sure it doesn't burn. Once crisp, transfer the pork to a plate, loosely cover with foil and leave to rest in a warm place for 20min.

5. Meanwhile, tip the vegetables and all the cooking juices from the roasting tin into a large sieve set over a medium pan, press to extract as much liquid as possible. Discard the vegetables, then spoon off the excess fat from the gravy.

6. In a small bowl, mix the cornflour and 2 tbsp cold water to a smooth paste. Add to the gravy pan and cook, whisking, until the gravy thickens (it will need to boil). Check the seasoning, adding a little honey, if needed, to balance the bitterness of the beer. Transfer to a jug. Serve the pork in chunky slices with the crackling and gravy alongside.

Hands-on time: 25min, plus resting
Cooking time: about 2hr 15min
Serves 6

PER SERVING 500cals, 75g protein, 15g fat
(5g saturates), 11g carbs (6g total sugars), 4g fibre

Austrian and Hungarian Roast Goose with Bread Dumplings

Stuffed goose was at one time eaten at the Feast of St Martin (11 November), traditionally the last big meal before Christmas. Nowadays it's a popular choice for Christmas dining in Austria, as well as in Hungary, Germany and neighbouring countries. Browning the dumplings in goose fat after poaching isn't traditional, but adds a lovely flavour.

5–6kg goose, giblets removed (see GH tips)
2 tbsp plain flour
150ml red wine
350ml hot chicken stock

FOR THE STUFFING
350g floury potatoes, peeled
1 large onion, finely sliced
2 Granny Smith apples, peeled, cored and chopped
100ml apple juice
Finely grated zest 1 lemon

FOR THE BREAD DUMPLINGS
250g fresh white breadcrumbs
100ml milk
4 smoked streaky bacon rashers, finely chopped
1 onion, finely chopped
2 tbsp each finely chopped chives and flat-leaf parsley
1 egg, beaten
½ tsp freshly grated nutmeg

★ GET AHEAD
Prepare the dumplings to the end of step 6 up to 1 day ahead. Chill. Bring to room temperature for 10min before cooking.

Hands-on time: 50min, plus cooling and resting
Cooking time: about 4hr 15min
Serves 6, with leftovers

PER SERVING 716cals, 45g protein, 31g fat (7g saturates), 58g carbs (14g total sugars), 3g fibre

1. Remove any wrappings or trussing from the goose and pat dry with kitchen paper inside and out. Remove and set aside the excess solid fat from the cavity (see GH tips). Prick the skin all over with a fork, particularly on the legs and the underside of the breast (this will help release the fat). Put on a large plate and return to the fridge (uncovered) while you prepare the stuffing.

2. For the stuffing, cut the potatoes into even chunks. Put into a medium pan, cover with cold water and bring to the boil. Simmer for 8–10min until just tender, then drain and leave to steam dry and cool slightly in a colander.

3. Meanwhile, melt 1 tbsp reserved goose fat in a frying pan and cook the onion on low-medium heat for 10min, until softened. Add the apples and apple juice, increase the heat to high and bubble for 5min until the apples are tender but still holding their shape. Add the potatoes, lemon zest and plenty of seasoning and mix well, breaking up the potatoes slightly. Set aside to cool.

4. Preheat oven to 220°C (200°C fan) mark 7. Remove the goose from the fridge and rub the outside all over with salt and freshly ground black pepper, then spoon the potato mix loosely into the cavity. Weigh the stuffed goose and calculate the cooking time, allowing 13–15min per 500g.

Continues over the page…

Put the goose on a rack in a deep roasting tin, breast-side up, and loosely cover tin with foil.

5. Roast for calculated cooking time, turning oven down to 200°C (180°C fan) mark 6 after 30min. Baste the goose twice during cooking, carefully spooning/pouring off the excess fat into a bowl (reserving to use later, if you like, see GH tips). Remove the foil for the final hr of cooking.

6. While the goose is cooking, make the dumplings. Put the breadcrumbs in a large bowl, pour over the milk, stir and set aside to soak. Melt 1 tbsp reserved goose fat in a frying pan over low-medium heat, add the bacon and onion (and liver – if using – see GH tips) and cook for 10min until pale golden. Stir into the bowl with the soaked bread. Add the remaining dumpling ingredients, ½ tsp salt and plenty of freshly ground black pepper. Mix well with a wooden spoon until the mixture clumps together then, with slightly wet hands, roll the mixture into 18 golf ball-sized dumplings. Arrange on a plate, loosely cover and chill until needed.

7. Start checking the goose 30min before the end of the cooking time. To check it's cooked, insert a fork into thickest part of the breast and check that the juices run golden and clear. If not, return to the oven and keep checking every 10min. Alternatively, use a meat thermometer – the temperature needs to be at least 72°C when inserted into thickest part of the breast. Transfer to a large serving platter, cover with foil and leave to rest in a warm place for at least 30min. Spoon off as much fat as possible from the roasting tin, reserving any meaty juices and other roasting remains.

8. For the gravy, melt ½ tbsp reserved goose fat in a medium pan over medium hob heat and whisk in the flour. Cook, whisking, for 1min. Whisk in the red wine and bubble for a few min. then whisk in the stock, roasting remains from the tin and any juices from the resting goose and bubble, whisking occasionally, for a couple of minutes until thickened. Strain into a warmed gravy jug or clean pan (to reheat when needed). Check the seasoning.

9. Shortly before serving, bring a large pan of salted water to the boil, add the dumplings and simmer for 10min. Remove with a slotted spoon to a plate lined with kitchen paper. Melt 1 tbsp reserved goose fat in a (clean) frying pan, add the dumplings and fry until golden, about 7–8min. Remove to a plate, cover with foil and keep warm.

10. To serve, scoop the stuffing from the goose cavity and place in a warm dish. Unwrap the goose and arrange the dumplings around the platter. Serve with the gravy and stuffing.

★ GH TIPS
• There should be plenty of excess fat from the goose for the stuffing and dumplings, but you could use vegetable oil (or shop-bought goose fat).
• If your goose comes with giblets, use the liver in the dumplings. Pat dry, cut into small pieces and cook with the onions at step 6. The other giblets (including the neck) will give a big flavour boost to the gravy, simmered with the chicken stock and an equal quantity of water in a partially covered pan for 1hr (strain before using).
• Reserve the rendered goose fat from cooking and strain through a fine sieve into a jar. Use for roast potatoes or chill/freeze for use at a later date.

Filipino Bibingka

A coconut rice cake from the Philippines, traditionally cooked in a banana leaf, which imparts aroma and a subtle sweetness. This recipe is naturally gluten free but check your baking powder and rice flour as brands vary.

50g unsalted butter, melted, plus extra to grease
300g rice flour
1½ tbsp gluten-free baking powder
225g granulated sugar
3 medium eggs, beaten
400ml tin coconut milk
2 tsp vanilla extract
2 tbsp desiccated coconut (optional)

YOU'LL ALSO NEED
½ banana leaf, washed and dried (available online, or use baking parchment)

1. Preheat oven to 190°C (170°C fan) mark 5. Lightly grease a 20.5cm round tin. Hold the banana leaf over hob heat (gas or induction) until it turns bright green and glossy, moving it around to treat it all. Cut into pieces as needed to line the greased tin, overlapping the sections so there are no gaps.

2. In a large bowl, whisk the rice flour, baking powder, sugar and a large pinch of salt. In a large jug, whisk the eggs, coconut milk, melted butter and vanilla until combined. Whisk the wet ingredients into the dry until combined and smooth. Scrape into the lined tin. If you like, scatter over desiccated coconut.

3. Bake for 55min–1hr, covering with foil after 30min, or until a skewer inserted into the centre of the cake comes out clean. Leave to cool in the tin for 10min, then transfer to a wire rack to cool completely. Serve in slices.

★ TO STORE
Once cool, keep in an airtight container at room temperature for up to 5 days.

Hands-on time: 15min, plus cooling
Cooking time: about 1hr
Serves 14

PER SERVING 250cals, 4g protein, 10g fat (8g saturates), 34g carbs (17g total sugars), 1g fibre

Norwegian Julekaka

This intensely cardamom-scented Christmas bread is popular in Norway. It's best served warm and spread with butter, but can also be toasted the next day and makes very good French toast.

275ml whole milk
75g caster sugar
7g sachet fast-action dried yeast
50g unsalted butter, chopped
500g strong white flour, plus extra to dust
1 tsp ground cardamom (the seeds from about 20 pods)
Vegetable oil, to grease
100g raisins
100g chopped mixed peel
1 egg, beaten
2 tsp pearled sugar

1. Heat the milk in a small pan over medium heat until just steaming. Spoon 3 tbsp of the milk into a small bowl and mix in 1 tbsp of the sugar and all the yeast. Set aside for 5–10min until bubbling. Add the butter to the milk pan and set aside to melt.

2. Meanwhile, in a large bowl, mix the flour, remaining sugar, ground cardamom and 1 tsp fine salt with a wooden spoon. Make a well in the centre and pour in the warm milk and yeast mixture. Mix to combine, then bring together with your hands to form a soft, cohesive dough. Tip on to a work surface and knead for 8–10min until smooth and elastic, lightly flouring your hands if the dough is sticky or adding a splash more milk if the dough feels dry.

Hands-on time: 40min, plus proving and cooling
Cooking time: about 45min
Cuts into 10 slices

PER SLICE 337cals, 7g protein, 7g fat (4g saturates), 61g carbs (21g total sugars), 3g fibre

3. Return the dough to a clean, oiled bowl and cover with a tea towel. Leave the dough to rise in a warm place for 1hr–1hr 30min, or until doubled in size.

4. Line a large baking tray with baking parchment. Tip the dough out on to a lightly floured work surface and sprinkle with the raisins and mixed peel. Knead until evenly distributed. Shape the dough into a smooth, roughly 18cm-diameter even round. Place in the middle of the lined baking tray and gently pat the top to flatten slightly. Loosely cover and leave to rise again until puffed and almost doubled in size, about 45min–1hr.

5. Preheat oven to 180°C (160°C fan), mark 4. Uncover the dough and brush all over with beaten egg. Scatter over the pearled sugar and bake for 40min or until golden brown and risen.

6. Transfer to a cooling rack and leave to cool for at least 1hr. Slice and serve with salted butter.

★ GET AHEAD
Prepare the dough up to end of step 2, then place in a large, lightly oiled food bag and chill overnight. In the morning, bring to room temperature for 1hr before continuing with the recipe.

★ TO STORE
Keep in an airtight container at room temperature for up to 2 days.

French and Belgian Chocolate, Chestnut and Almond Bûche de Noël

Better known here as a yule log, bûche de Noël is a popular festive dessert in France and Belgium. This version combines chocolate, chestnut and almond liqueur for a deliciously heady way to top off a meal.

Vegetable oil, to grease
60g plain flour
3 tbsp ground almonds
1 tsp baking powder
6 medium eggs, separated
75g caster sugar, plus 2 tbsp extra to dust
¼ tsp almond extract
Edible gold stars, to decorate (optional)

FOR THE CHESTNUT AMARETTI GANACHE
200g chestnut purée
50g dark chocolate, finely chopped
150ml double cream
1 tbsp Amaretto almond liqueur
5 amaretti biscuits, plus extra to serve (optional)

FOR THE AMARETTO CHOCOLATE BUTTERCREAM
100g dark chocolate
100g unsalted butter, softened
100g icing sugar
1 tbsp cocoa powder
2 tbsp Amaretto almond liqueur

★ GET AHEAD
Assemble and decorate up to 1 day ahead, then loosely cover and chill.

Hands-on time: 40min, plus cooling and chilling
Cooking time: about 15min
Serves 12

PER SERVING 414cals, 8g protein, 24g fat (12g saturates), 39g carbs (27g total sugars), 1g fibre

1. Preheat oven to 180°C (160°C fan) mark 4. Lightly grease and line a 23 x 33cm Swiss roll tin with baking parchment. Combine the flour, almonds and baking powder in a small bowl and set aside.

2. Using a handheld electric whisk, beat egg whites in a large bowl to stiff peaks, then set aside.

3. In a separate bowl, whisk the egg yolks with the sugar and almond extract until pale and thick, about 5min. Using a large metal spoon, stir a third of the egg whites into the yolk mixture to loosen, then gently fold in the remaining egg whites in 2 additions. Sift in the dry ingredients and gently fold in until just combined. Scrape into the prepared tin and gently spread to level. Bake for 12–14min until golden, risen and a toothpick inserted into the centre comes out clean.

4. Dust the sponge with the extra 2 tbsp caster sugar, lay a piece of baking parchment on top, then place a wire rack over the tin. Invert the sponge on to the parchment and rack and gently peel away the top lining parchment. While warm, carefully roll up the sponge from a short edge, using the parchment to help. Cool on a wire rack (rolled) for about 1hr.

5. Meanwhile, make the chestnut ganache. Whizz the chestnut purée, chocolate and cream in a small food processor until fairly smooth. Scrape

into a small pan and heat gently, stirring, until the chocolate melts. Stir in the almond liqueur, leave to cool, then cover and chill until firm.

6. Beat the chestnut ganache briefly with a handheld electric whisk to a stiff but spreadable consistency. Roughly crush the amaretti and stir into the ganache. Gently unroll the sponge, then evenly spread the ganache over the top. Using the parchment to help, roll up the sponge again and place seam-side down on a board. Chill.

7. For the buttercream, melt the chocolate in a bowl set over a pan of gently simmering water, then set aside to cool for 5min. In a large bowl, beat the butter and icing sugar with a handheld electric whisk until smooth. Beat in the cocoa powder and a pinch of salt, followed by the cooled melted chocolate and almond liqueur.

8. Using a serrated knife, cut a short section diagonally from one end of the cake. Transfer to a serving platter or board, and use a little of the buttercream to attach the cut section to one side of the longer log to look like a stump.

9. Spread the buttercream over the top and sides of the cake, then drag the tip of a cutlery knife through the surface to create a bark-like texture. Sprinkle with gold stars (if using) and serve.

German Lebkuchen

The mixed peel and hazelnuts are traditional, but you can leave them out to make delightful, soft-baked gingerbread cookies instead.

FOR THE BISCUITS
100g mixed peel
100g blanched hazelnuts
125g runny honey
125g dark muscovado sugar
40g butter
2 tbsp ground ginger
1 tbsp ground cinnamon
1 tsp mixed spice
225g plain flour, plus extra to dust
1 tsp baking powder
¼ tsp bicarbonate of soda
1 medium egg, beaten
50g ground almonds

FOR THE GLAZE
300g icing sugar

1. For the biscuits, pulse the mixed peel and hazelnuts in a food processor to coarse crumbs. Set aside.

2. Heat the honey, muscovado sugar, butter, spices and a large pinch of freshly ground black pepper in a large pan over low heat, stirring until melted and just combined. Remove from the heat and stir in the flour, baking powder, bicarbonate of soda, egg and ground almonds to make a smooth, soft dough. Add the mixed peel mixture and stir

(V)

Hands-on time: 30min, plus (overnight) chilling, cooling and setting
Cooking time: about 35min
Makes about 28 biscuits

PER BISCUIT 162cals, 2g protein, 5g fat (1g saturates), 27g carbs (20g total sugars), 1g fibre

again until evenly distributed. Tip the dough on to a large sheet of baking parchment, wrap and chill for at least 4hr, or overnight.

3. Preheat oven to 180°C (160°C fan) mark 4 and line 2 large baking trays with baking parchment. Allow the dough to soften a little, if needed, then roll out on a lightly floured surface to 1cm thick. Stamp out shapes using 6–8cm festive cutters, re-rolling the trimmings. Alternatively, roll the dough into walnut-sized balls. Arrange the shapes or balls on the lined trays, spacing apart. Flatten any balls slightly.

4. Working 1 batch at a time, bake the first biscuit tray for 12–15min, until risen and the tops feel dry. Meanwhile, make the glaze. Sift the icing sugar into a bowl and mix in 3 tbsp water to make a thick but spreadable icing. When the biscuits are ready, leave to cool for a few minutes. Then put in the second tray of biscuits to bake.

5. Working quickly while they are still hot, brush the glaze over the top and sides of the baked biscuits (see GH Tips). Leave to cool and set on the tray. Repeat with the second tray of baked biscuits.

6. The biscuits will be a little crisp at first, but store in an airtight container overnight so they soften slightly before serving, if you like (see GH Tips).

★ TO STORE
The biscuits will keep in an airtight container at room temperature for up to 2 weeks. The glaze will stay crisp, but will become less white over time – the biscuits will still taste great.

★ GH TIPS

• For the neatest finish, as soon as you are able, hold the top and bottom of a biscuit between your thumb and forefinger. Brush the sides of the biscuit first, then return to the lined tray and brush the top. Try not to brush back over where you've glazed if partially set, as this will give an uneven finish. If the biscuits begin to cool before you've glazed them, you can warm them back up in the oven briefly.
• If the glaze feels too thick to brush, stir in a few more drops of water.

• If you would like the biscuits even softer, store overnight in an airtight container with a strip of orange peel, then remove the peel for the rest of the storage time.

Italian Cranberry, Pistachio and White Chocolate Panettone

A labour of love, but well worth it. If you can't get hold of a panettone case, bake in an 18cm round, deep tin that's been greased and lined with baking parchment.

FOR THE FRUIT
150g dried cranberries
Finely grated zest 1 orange
75g mixed peel, finely chopped
2½ tbsp dark rum

FOR THE STARTER
75g strong white flour
1 tsp fast-action dried yeast
75ml whole milk

FOR THE DOUGH
500g strong white flour, plus extra to dust
10g fast-action dried yeast
4 large eggs
1 tsp orange blossom water
1 tbsp vanilla bean paste
150g unsalted butter, softened
100g white chocolate chips
50g pistachio kernels, roughly chopped
Icing sugar, to dust

YOU'LL ALSO NEED
1 large 750g panettone case

Hands-on time: 30min, plus (overnight) rising and chilling
Cooking time: about 1hr 10min
Serves 12

PER SERVING 434cals, 10g protein, 18g fat
(9g saturates), 55g carbs (16g total sugars), 3g fibre

1. The day before you want to bake, soak the fruit. In a non-metallic bowl, mix the cranberries, orange zest, mixed peel and rum. Cover and set aside for 4hr. Next, make the starter. In the bowl of a freestanding mixer fitted with a dough hook, mix the flour, yeast and milk until combined. Cover, then leave to rest at room temperature for 4hr until risen and bubbly.

2. For the dough, to the starter bowl, add the 500g flour, yeast, eggs, orange blossom water, vanilla, 1 tsp salt and 2 tbsp cold water. Mix and knead for 10min, until the dough is smooth and elastic.

3. Gradually mix in the butter. Add the soaked fruit, white chocolate and pistachios and mix briefly to combine. Cover and leave to rise in the fridge for at least 6hr, ideally overnight (the slow rise helps to give the panettone more flavour).

4. Scrape the dough on to a lightly floured surface and shape into a ball. Place seam-side down into the panettone mould or prepared tin. Cover and leave to rise for 4hr or until well risen.

5. Preheat oven to 180°C (160°C fan) mark 4. Put the panettone on a baking tray (still in its case/tin) and bake for 1hr 10min, or until well browned, covering with foil after 45min if it's looking a little dark. Lift the mould/tin on to a wire rack and leave to cool completely. Serve dusted with icing sugar.

★ TO STORE
Once cool, wrap well in clingfilm and keep at room temperature for up to 1 week.

Danish Risalamande

Laced with whipped cream and chopped almonds and topped with cherry sauce, this rice pudding is a classic Danish dessert. Traditionally, a large bowl is made on 23 December and eaten across the holiday.

FOR THE RICE PUDDING
100g short grain pudding rice
25g caster sugar
450ml whole milk

FOR THE CHERRY SAUCE
425g tin pitted black cherries in light syrup
1 tbsp caster sugar
1 tbsp lemon juice
2 tsp cornflour

TO FINISH
70g whole blanched almonds
150ml whipping cream
1 tsp vanilla bean paste
1 tbsp icing sugar
¼ tsp almond extract

★ GET AHEAD
Prepare the rice pudding up to end of step 1 and the cherry sauce to the end of step 2 up to 1 day ahead. Cool, cover and chill separately. Reheat the sauce gently until warm, then complete the recipe to serve. At Christmas, a whole almond is hidden inside the pudding as a gift for whoever finds it.

1. Make the rice pudding. Put the rice, sugar, milk, 250ml water and a pinch of salt in a large pan. Bring to the boil, stirring occasionally, then reduce to a gentle simmer and cook for about 30–40min, stirring regularly, until the rice is tender and coated in a creamy sauce (add a splash more water or milk if it's looking dry). Scrape into a large bowl and leave to cool. Cover and chill for at least 2hr, or ideally overnight.

2. Meanwhile, make the cherry sauce. Put the cherries and their syrup in a pan with the sugar and lemon juice and set over medium heat. In a small bowl, mix the cornflour with 2 tsp cold water until smooth, then stir into the cherries. Bring to the boil, then bubble gently for 8–10min until the cherries are coated in a fairly thick syrup. Remove from heat and set aside.

3. To serve, set aside 1 whole almond and roughly chop the rest. Stir both whole and chopped almonds through the chilled rice pudding. In a separate bowl, whisk the cream, vanilla, icing sugar and almond extract to soft peaks. Fold the cream mixture through the rice pudding, then divide among 6 bowls. Spoon the warm cherry sauce on top and serve immediately.

Hands-on time: 30min, plus cooling and (overnight) chilling
Cooking time: about 50min
Serves 6

PER SERVING 370cals, 7g protein, 19g fat (9g saturates), 40g carbs (25g total sugars), 1g fibre

Mini Bûches de Noël

Think of these as fancy festive mini rolls. For an alcohol-free version, swap the Cointreau for extra zest, and use standard plain flour if you don't need the recipe to be gluten free.

Butter, to grease
5 large eggs
100g caster sugar
1 tsp vanilla bean paste
60g gluten-free plain flour
40g cocoa powder

FOR THE GANACHE
150g dark chocolate, chopped
150g milk chocolate, chopped
300ml double cream

FOR THE FILLING
150ml double cream
½ tbsp Cointreau
1 tbsp icing sugar
Finely grated zest ½ orange

TO DECORATE (optional)
8 chocolate orange segments
Pared orange zest

1. Preheat oven to 180°C (160°C fan) mark 4. Grease and line a 23 x 33cm Swiss roll tin with baking parchment. Using a freestanding mixer or a large bowl and a handheld electric whisk, beat the eggs and caster sugar until extremely thick, about 5min. Beat in the vanilla.

2. Sift over the flour and cocoa powder, then gently fold in using a large metal spoon. Scrape into the prepared tin and gently spread to level. Bake for 15min, or until the sponge is firm to the touch.

3. Lay a piece of baking parchment on a wire rack and carefully invert the sponge on to it. Remove the tin and gently peel away the top lining parchment. Using kitchen scissors, slice the sponge and base parchment in half lengthways. Using the base parchment to help and starting from a long edge, tightly roll up the sponge halves separately, leaving them seam-down to cool completely on the wire rack (rolled).

4. Meanwhile, make the ganache. Put both chocolates into a heatproof bowl. Heat the cream in a small pan until almost boiling. Pour into the chocolate bowl, leave for 2min, then stir until melted and smooth. Set aside to cool and firm up to a spreadable consistency.

5. Make the filling. Whisk the cream, Cointreau and icing sugar to firm peaks. Fold in the orange zest. Chill until needed.

6. Once cool, gently unroll both sponges and spread half the filling over each. Re-roll and cut each into quarters, to make 8 mini roulades. Transfer to a board and spread ganache over each with a palette knife. Gently pull a fork or cocktail stick through the ganache to resemble bark. Decorate with orange segments, if using. Chill for 30min.

7. Serve scattered with pared orange zest, if you like.

Hands-on time: 1hr, plus cooling and chilling
Cooking time: about 20min
Makes 8 rolls

PER ROLL 639cals, 11g protein, 46g fat (27g saturates), 43g carbs (37g total sugars), 2g fibre

★ GET AHEAD
Make up to end of step 6 up to 1 day ahead.
Store in an airtight container in the fridge.
Complete the recipe.

American White Velvet Cake

A fluffy American cake that uses the reverse creaming method to help it rise, and only incorporates egg whites to keep the cake pale in colour. We've made a Swiss meringue buttercream here instead of the classical ermine frosting.

FOR THE CAKES
225g unsalted butter, cubed and just softened, plus
    extra to grease
300g plain flour
1 tsp baking powder
½ tsp bicarbonate of soda
300g caster sugar
250g Greek-style yogurt
1 tbsp vanilla bean paste
6 medium egg whites

FOR THE SHARDS
300g white chocolate, chopped

FOR THE MERINGUE BUTTERCREAM
100g white chocolate, roughly chopped
6 medium egg whites
250g caster sugar
300g unsalted butter, cubed and just softened
Lindt Lindor White Chocolate Truffles, to decorate
    (optional)

★ TO STORE
Remove any shards on top, then loosely cover and chill for up to 2 days (the cake will firm up slightly). Allow to come to room temperature before serving.

Hands-on time: 1hr 30min, plus cooling and chilling
Cooking time: about 50min
Serves 20

PER SERVING (without shards or balls) 413cals,
5g protein, 25g fat (16g saturates), 43g carbs
(31g total sugars), 1g fibre

1. Preheat oven to 190°C (170°C fan) mark 5. Grease 2 x 20.5cm round springform tins and line with baking parchment.

2. For the cakes, using a freestanding mixer with a paddle attachment, mix the flour, baking powder, bicarbonate of soda, 200g of the caster sugar and ¾ tsp fine sea salt. With the motor on low speed, add the butter piece by piece, followed by half the yogurt, until combined. Add the remaining yogurt and the vanilla. Increase the speed to high and mix for 4min, until silky and fluffy.

3. In a separate bowl, using a handheld whisk, beat the egg whites until they hold stiff peaks. Gradually beat in the remaining 100g caster sugar, beating back up to stiff peaks after each addition. Using a large metal spoon, fold the egg whites into the cake batter in 3 additions, being careful to keep in as much air as possible.

4. Divide the batter evenly between the lined tins. Bake for 35–40min or until risen and golden on top. Leave to cool in tins for 10min, then transfer to a wire rack to cool completely.

5. For the shards, line a rough 20.5cm square tin with baking parchment. Melt the chocolate in a heatproof bowl set over a pan of barely simmering water. Once melted, pour into the lined tin, tilting to spread to an even layer. Chill to set.

6. For the meringue buttercream, melt the white chocolate as above. Set aside to cool. In a

separate large heatproof bowl set over the pan of barely simmering water, using a handheld electric whisk, beat the egg whites and sugar until the mixture is warm to the touch and the sugar has dissolved, about 5min.

7. Scrape the egg white mixture into the bowl of a freestanding mixer with a whisk attachment, or continue with the bowl off the heat and the handheld electric whisk. Beat on high speed for 10min, or until the meringue is thick and the outside of the bowl is completely cool. Gradually add the butter, 1 piece at a time, beating well after each addition (it might look curdled but keep beating and it will come together). Once all the butter has been added, beat on medium-high speed for 4min. Add the cooled white chocolate and beat again until smooth.

8. To assemble, slice the cakes in half horizontally. Sandwich the halves and cakes back together with generous layers of buttercream. Scantly cover the top and sides of the cake with some of the remaining buttercream, smoothing with a palette knife to finish. Chill for 30min to firm up.

9. Once firm, use most of the remaining buttercream to generously ice the top and sides as smoothly as possible. Chill again for 30min.

10. To decorate, slice the set white chocolate into shards and arrange on the sides or top of the cake, along with the Lindor balls, if using. Serve in slices.

Swedish Saffron Buns

These buns are enjoyed in Sweden on Saint Lucia's Day, 13 December, and throughout the festive period.

100g caster sugar
½ tsp saffron
1 tbsp rum or vodka, or use milk
250ml milk
625g plain flour, plus extra to dust
7g sachet fast-action dried yeast
2 medium eggs
75g quark cheese or soured cream
75g unsalted butter, softened, plus extra to grease

TO GLAZE AND DECORATE
1 medium egg, beaten
24 raisins

★ GET AHEAD
Once cool, freeze the buns in a container for up to 3 months. To serve, defrost at room temperature.

1. Using a pestle and mortar, grind 1 tbsp of the sugar and the saffron to a powder (or as fine as you can get it). Add the rum or vodka (or milk) and set aside for 20min. In a small pan, heat the milk until just steaming, then set aside to cool until just warm.

2. In the bowl of a freestanding mixer fitted with a dough hook, mix the flour, remaining sugar, yeast and 1 tsp fine salt. Crack in the eggs and add the quark or soured cream, the butter, saffron mixture and cooled milk.

3. Mix and knead for 10min, or until the dough is springy and elastic (it will be slightly sticky). Cover and leave to rise in a warm place for 1hr, until visibly risen.

4. Line 2 large baking sheets with baking parchment. Punch down the dough in the bowl and tip on to a lightly floured work surface. Divide into 12 equal pieces (weigh for best results). Working one piece at a time, roll into a 30cm long sausage. Shape into a tight S-shape, curling the ends into the centre from opposite sides. Place on the lined sheets, spacing apart. Repeat with the remaining dough pieces.

5. Cover with greased clingfilm, butter-side down, and leave to rise again in a warm place for 30min, until puffed.

6. Preheat oven to 200°C (180°C fan) mark 6. Brush the buns with beaten egg to glaze, then press a raisin into the centre of each swirl. Bake for 12–13min until lightly golden. Remove from the oven, cover with a clean tea towel (to keep the buns soft) and leave to cool completely. Serve.

Hands-on time: 25min, plus infusing, rising and cooling
Cooking time: about 15min
Makes 12 buns

PER BUN 318cals, 9g protein, 8g fat (4g saturates), 51g carbs (11g total sugars), 2g fibre

Mexican Buñuelos

These flat fritters are popular in the Oaxaca region of Mexico. Different areas specialise in different shapes, such as balls, twists and stars.

FOR THE DOUGH
375g plain flour, plus extra to dust
1 tsp baking powder
50g caster sugar
1 medium egg
125ml fresh orange juice, about 2 oranges
50g butter, softened
1 litre vegetable oil, to fry

FOR THE CINNAMON SUGAR
150g caster sugar
1 tbsp ground cinnamon

1. For the dough, using a freestanding mixer fitted with a dough hook, mix the flour, baking powder, sugar and a pinch of salt. Add the egg and orange juice and briefly mix on low speed. Add the butter and mix on low speed for 5min, until the dough is smooth and elastic.

2. Scrape on to a work surface. Divide and roll into 15 balls, cover with a clean, slightly damp tea towel and leave to rest for 30min.

3. Meanwhile, in a large, wide bowl, mix the cinnamon sugar ingredients. Set aside.

4. Heat the oil in a large, high-sided pan over medium heat to 180°C. On a lightly floured surface, working one at a time, roll the balls into 15cm circles, stacking them as you go (making sure they are lightly dusted with flour first).

5. Fry a dough circle for 30–45sec per side or until golden brown. Remove with a slotted spoon to a tray lined with kitchen paper to drain, then toss in the cinnamon sugar to coat. Repeat the frying, draining and coating process with the remaining dough circles, monitoring the oil temperature as you go. Serve.

Hands-on time: 40min, plus resting and cooling
Cooking time: about 15min
Makes 15 fritters

PER FRITTER 192cals, 3g protein, 6g fat (2g saturates), 30g carbs (11g total sugars), 1g fibre

German Spiced Chocolate Stollen

Although not traditional, chocolate lovers will rejoice its addition to this seasonal spiced German bread. This makes one triumphant, large stollen.

FOR THE STOLLEN
125g mixed dried fruit
50g mixed peel, finely chopped
75g glacé cherries, quartered
Finely grated zest and juice 1 small orange
30ml rum
200ml milk
60g caster sugar
125g unsalted butter, plus extra to grease
1 medium egg
400g strong white flour, plus extra to dust
25g cocoa powder
1½ tsp mixed spice
½ tsp freshly grated nutmeg
7g sachet fast-action dried yeast
50g flaked almonds

FOR THE MARZIPAN
150g ground almonds
40g caster sugar
50g icing sugar, sifted
1 medium egg and 1 medium yolk

FOR THE GLAZE
20g unsalted butter, melted
Icing sugar, to dust

★ GH TIP
Slices of stollen are also wonderful toasted under the grill until golden.

Hands-on time: 35min, plus (overnight) soaking, rising and cooling
Cooking time: about 40min
Makes 1 large stollen, cuts into 16 slices

PER SLICE 360cals, 8g protein, 17g fat (7g saturates), 42g carbs (18g total sugars), 2g fibre

1. For the stollen, in a non-metallic bowl, mix the dried fruit, mixed peel, cherries, orange zest and juice and the rum. Cover and set aside to soak for at least 2hr, ideally overnight.

2. For the marzipan, mix all the ingredients in a medium bowl, cover and set aside (up to 4hr).

3. For the stollen, in a small pan heat the milk, sugar and butter over low heat, stirring until the sugar dissolves and the butter melts. Set aside until just warm. Whisk in the egg.

4. In the bowl of a freestanding mixer, or a large bowl, mix the flour, cocoa powder, spices, yeast and ½ tsp fine salt. Add the warm milk mixture, then mix and knead for 5–10min until springy and elastic (the dough will be a little sticky at first but will come together with kneading). Cover and leave to rise in a warm place for 1hr, until visibly risen.

5. Line a large baking sheet with baking parchment. Punch down the dough in the bowl and tip on to a lightly floured work surface. Add the soaked fruit (strain out any liquid in the bowl) and flaked almonds. Knead briefly to combine.

6. Press or roll out to a large oval about 25.5 x 35cm. Roll the marzipan into a sausage and lay centrally down the length of the oval. Fold the left side of the dough over to cover the marzipan, then fold in the right side to just cover the left (the edge should be just past the centre). Pinch and tuck under the top and bottom of the stollen to seal in the marzipan.

7. Transfer to the lined sheet. Using the side of your hand, press down the length of the top seal to create the classic stollen shape. Cover with greased clingfilm (butter-side down) and leave to rise again in a warm place for 45min, until puffed.

8. Preheat oven to 180°C (160°C fan) mark 4. Remove the clingfilm and bake the stollen for 25–35min, until risen and lightly golden. Brush immediately with the melted 20g butter to glaze, then dust generously with icing sugar to coat. Leave to cool completely before serving.

★ TO STORE
Best eaten on the day, but will keep well-wrapped in foil for up to 3 days. Alternatively, wrap well and freeze for up to 1 month. To serve, allow to defrost at room temperature.

13

Buffet & Boxing Day

Fondue Bread Bowl

This Swiss classic is sure to please your guests. If you can't find a large bread boule, serve the fondue straight from the pan.

750g baby new potatoes
3 tbsp olive oil
Few rosemary sprigs
1 large round bread loaf, about 400g

FOR THE FONDUE
3 tbsp cornflour
325ml white wine
2 garlic cloves, crushed
200ml double cream
300g Gruyère cheese, grated
300g strong Cheddar, grated
1 rosemary sprig, leaves picked and finely chopped

TO SERVE
Charcuterie
Cornichons

1. Preheat oven to 200°C (180°C fan) mark 6. In a large roasting tray, toss the potatoes with 1 tbsp oil and the rosemary sprigs. Season generously. Roast for 40–45min until golden.

2. Meanwhile, slice the top quarter off the loaf (reserve for later). Scoop out the soft bread inside, leaving a crusty shell. Roughly tear the pulled-out bread into bite-sized croutons. Place the bread bowl and torn croutons on a large baking tray. Brush the inside of the bread bowl with 1 tbsp oil and drizzle 1 tbsp oil over croutons. Bake for 10–12min until starting to crisp. Remove both from the oven and allow to cool slightly.

3. Meanwhile, put all the fondue ingredients into a medium pan. Bring to a simmer, whisking often, and bubble until thick – about 10min. Transfer to the bread bowl. If it won't all fit, keep in the pan and top up as needed) and top with the bread lid.

4. Serve the fondue bowl with the roast potatoes, croutons, charcuterie and cornichons for dipping.

Hands-on time: 25min
Cooking time: about 45min
Serves about 12

PER SERVING (without potatoes, croutons or charcuterie) 319cals, 13g protein, 26g fat (16g saturates), 4g carbs (0g total sugars), 0g fibre

Beetroot Terrine

This striking vegetarian terrine adds real wow factor to any table.

FOR THE TERRINE
900g medium beetroot (see GH tip)
2 large garlic cloves (unpeeled)
Oil, to grease
300g soft rindless goat's cheese
150g full-fat cream cheese
15g dill, stems discarded, fronds roughly chopped
Finely grated zest 1 lemon

FOR THE SALAD
2 tbsp pistachio kernels, roughly chopped
3 clementines
Large handful watercress
1 tsp extra virgin olive oil

1. Preheat oven to 180°C (160°C fan) mark 4. Put the beetroot and garlic cloves, whole and unpeeled, in a small roasting tin, cover with foil, and roast for 1hr–1hr 30min, or until the beetroot is tender. Set aside to cool completely.

2. Meanwhile, lightly oil a 900g loaf tin and line with a couple of layers of clingfilm, making sure there is plenty hanging over the sides (to make removal easier).

3. Squeeze the roasted garlic from the skins into a large bowl. Add the goat's cheese and mash together thoroughly, then mix in the cream cheese until smooth and combined. Add the dill, lemon zest, ½ tsp freshly ground black pepper and salt to taste. Mix together.

**Hands-on time: 55min, plus cooling and (overnight) chilling
Cooking time: about 1hr 30min
Serves 8**

PER SERVING 243cals, 12g protein, 16g fat (10g saturates), 11g carbs (10g total sugars), 3g fibre

4. Wearing gloves to prevent staining, peel the beetroot, then cut into even 2mm slices (a mandoline is useful). If you are using golden beetroot (see GH tip), peel and slice these first to prevent staining, and keep separate.

5. Put a thin layer of purple beetroot over the base and up the sides of the lined loaf tin, slightly overlapping the slices. Spread a quarter of the goat's cheese mixture over the beetroot, then top with another layer of beetroot, trimming the slices so they sit flush with the edges of the tin. Continue layering until you have used all the ingredients, finishing with a layer of beetroot. If you are using golden beetroot, put these in the middle of the terrine. Fold over the beetroot at the sides, followed by the overhanging clingfilm. Cover with a piece of card just large enough to sit inside the tin. Lay 3 tins of tomatoes (or similar) on top of the terrine and chill for 8hr, or overnight.

6. Shortly before serving, toast the pistachios in a dry pan until aromatic; set aside to cool. Slice the top and bottom off each clementine, then cut away the peel and white pith. Working 1 at a time, hold a clementine over a bowl (to catch the juice) and carefully cut between the membranes to separate the segments. Add these to the bowl with any remaining juice. Repeat with remaining clementines. Add the watercress, olive oil, toasted pistachios and some seasoning and toss to mix.

7. To serve, remove the terrine from the fridge and remove the tins and cardboard. Unwrap and invert on to a serving platter or board. Top with some of the watercress salad and serve with the rest in a bowl alongside. Use a sharp serrated knife to cut the terrine into neat slices.

★ GH TIP
For a striking colour contrast, use a mix
of purple and golden beetroot, layering the
golden beetroot in the centre of the terrine.

Prawn Cocktail Quiche

Inspired by arguably the finest retro seafood dish – prawn cocktail – this lovely quiche is great warm or cold.

FOR THE PASTRY
200g plain flour, plus extra to dust
100g butter, chilled and chopped
1 medium egg yolk
2 tbsp sundried tomato paste

FOR THE FILLING
3 medium eggs
1 tbsp sundried tomato paste
300ml double cream
200g crème fraîche
1 tbsp Worcestershire sauce
¼ tsp Tabasco
Finely grated zest 1 lemon
½ tsp ground mace
200g Atlantic (cold water) cooked peeled prawns
100g semi-dried/sundried tomatoes in oil, drained

TO SERVE
45g rocket leaves
2 tbsp Marie Rose/seafood sauce

1. First make the pastry. Using a food processor, pulse the flour and butter until the mixture resembles fine breadcrumbs. Alternatively, rub butter into the flour using your fingers. Pulse/ mix in the egg yolk, tomato paste and a large pinch of fine salt until the pastry just comes together (add 1–2 tsp ice cold water, if needed, to bring it together). Tip on to a work surface, shape into a disc, wrap and chill for 30min.

2. Lightly flour a work surface and roll out the pastry. Use it to line a 20.5cm round, 3.5cm deep fluted tart tin, leaving excess pastry hanging over the sides. Prick the base all over with a fork. Chill for 30min.

3. Preheat oven to 190°C (170°C fan) mark 5. Put the tart tin on a baking sheet, line the pastry in the tin with a large sheet of baking parchment and fill with baking beans. Cook for 20min, until pastry sides are set. Carefully remove the parchment and baking beans. Return the tin to the oven for 12–15min, until the pastry feels sandy to the touch. Remove from oven and turn oven temperature down to 170°C (150°C fan) mark 3.

4. Meanwhile, make the filling. In a large jug, whisk the eggs, tomato paste, cream, crème fraîche, Worcestershire sauce, Tabasco, lemon zest, mace and some seasoning. Pat the prawns and drained tomatoes dry with kitchen paper.

5. Trim the overhanging pastry with a sharp serrated knife. Pour the cream mixture into the tart case and scatter over half the prawns and tomatoes (they will sink). Cook for 25min, then carefully remove from the oven and scatter over the remaining prawns and tomatoes. Return to the oven for 20–25min, or until the filling is golden and just set. Cool in the tin for at least 30min before transferring to a serving plate or board. Top with the rocket and serve warm, at room temperature or cold, with the sauce on the side.

Hands-on time: 40min, plus chilling and cooling
Cooking time: about 1hr 25min
Serves 8

PER SERVING 590cals, 12g protein, 49g fat (28g saturates), 24g carbs (3g total sugars), 2g fibre

★ GET AHEAD
Store covered in fridge for up to 3 days.

Wild Mushroom, Cranberry and Hazelnut Sausage Plait

A delicious vegetarian centrepiece that everyone will enjoy. It's easy to make this vegan too – just use a dairy-free puff pastry and brush with vegan mayo rather than egg. To make this meaty, swap the veggie sausages for good-quality pork ones.

30g dried wild mushrooms
600g vegetarian sausages
100g dried cranberries
1 tbsp thyme leaves, finely chopped
75g chopped roasted hazelnuts
Flour, to dust
500g block puff pastry
1 egg, beaten
1 tbsp mixed seeds

★ GET AHEAD
Prepare to end of step 4 up to 1 day ahead.
Complete the recipe to serve.

Hands-on time: 20min, plus soaking and chilling
Cooking time: about 40min
Serves 8

PER SERVING 475cals, 15g protein, 24g fat (8g saturates), 45g carbs (12g total sugars), 8g fibre

1. Put the mushrooms in a small heatproof bowl, cover with boiling water and set aside to soften for 15min, then drain and roughly chop.

2. In a large bowl, mix together the sausage meat (discarding skins, if necessary), dried cranberries, thyme, hazelnuts, chopped mushrooms and plenty of seasoning. Set aside.

3. On a lightly floured surface, roll out the pastry to a neat rectangle (about 26 x 36cm) and transfer it to a large sheet of baking parchment. Brush beaten egg all over the pastry. Shape the sausage meat into a neat log (about 8cm wide) and position it lengthways down the middle of the pastry. With a sharp knife, cut 2cm-wide slits in the pastry, running 1cm away from the sausage meat to the edges of the pastry, slanting the slits towards you.

4. Starting at the end furthest from you, fold the pastry strips over the sausage meat, alternating sides, to give a plait effect. Trim the short ends to neaten so the pastry is flush with the sausage meat at both ends. Brush the pastry all over with beaten egg, then sprinkle the mixed seeds on top. Transfer to a large baking tray (still on baking parchment) and chill for 30min.

5. Preheat oven to 200°C (180°C fan) mark 6. Cook the plait in the oven for 35–40min until deep golden. Serve warm or at room temperature.

Christmas Pie with Jewelled Cranberry Topping

All the flavours of Christmas in a delicious, meaty pie that's crowned with a fruity, tangy, cranberry and shallot topping.

FOR THE PASTRY
300g plain flour, plus extra to dust
1 tsp English mustard powder
1 medium egg, beaten
50g lard, cubed
50g butter, cubed

FOR THE FILLING
2 tsp vegetable oil
1 large onion, chopped
600g piece skinless ham (cooked)
700g skinless chicken or turkey breasts
100g streaky bacon, roughly chopped
Large handful (30g) mixed herbs, leaves picked and
    finely chopped (we used sage, thyme and parsley)
175g cooked chestnuts

FOR THE TOPPING
1 tbsp vegetable oil
200g shallots, thinly sliced into rounds
100ml port
1 tbsp balsamic vinegar
125g caster sugar
300g cranberries (fresh or frozen)

Hands-on time: 55min, plus chilling and cooling
Cooking time: about 1hr 45min
Serves 8

PER SERVING 593cals, 41g protein, 21g fat
(8g saturates), 55g carbs (23g total sugars), 5g fibre

1. To make the pastry, put the flour, mustard, egg and ½ tsp salt into a food processor and pulse briefly to combine. Melt the lard, butter and 100ml water in a small pan over low heat, then increase heat to high and bring just to the boil. With the motor running, add the hot liquid to the processor and whizz until the pastry just comes together. Tip on to a work surface, bring together with your hands and knead until smooth. Wrap well and chill for 1hr to firm up.

2. Meanwhile, start the filling. Heat the oil in a medium frying pan over low-medium heat and cook the onion with a pinch of salt for 10–12min until softened and turning golden. Scrape into a large bowl and set aside to cool slightly.

3. On a lightly floured work surface, roll out the pastry to a large circle and use to line the base and sides of a 20.5cm springform tin, leaving excess pastry hanging over the edge. Loosely cover and chill while you prepare the filling.

4. Slice the cooked ham and raw chicken or turkey into 3–4mm thick slices. In the food processor, whizz the bacon with 200g each ham and chicken/turkey (see GH Tip), until coarsely minced. Tip into the cooled onion bowl. Add the chopped herbs, chestnuts, 1 tsp each salt and freshly ground black pepper, and mix well.

★ GH TIP

Save the best, largest slices of meat for the pie, and use the smaller pieces and offcuts for mincing. This pie is meant to be served hot or warm, but leftovers are also delicious cold, as part of a buffet.

★ GET AHEAD

Prepare to the end of step 5 up to a day ahead and keep chilled. Complete the recipe to serve. The cooked and topped pie can also be kept, cooled, covered and chilled, for 2–3 days. Serve cold.

5. Arrange half the sliced ham in an even layer in the base of the pastry case, followed by half the sliced chicken/turkey. Top with half the mince mixture, then repeat the layering once more, pressing down firmly so everything's tightly packed with no air pockets. Trim the pastry with a small, sharp knife so it sits flush with the top of the tin. Chill for 30min.

6. Preheat oven to 200°C (180°C fan) mark 6 and put in a baking sheet to preheat. Cover the tin loosely with foil, slide on to the baking sheet and cook for 1hr 25min. Remove the foil, carefully unclip and remove the outside of the tin and return the pie to the oven for 10min to set and brown the sides and finish cooking through.

7. Meanwhile, make the topping. Heat the oil in a medium frying pan over low-medium heat and cook the shallots for 8–10min until softened. Add the port, vinegar and sugar and bring to the boil, stirring, until the sugar dissolves. Stir in the cranberries and bubble gently until they soften and start to split. Using a slotted spoon, lift the cranberries and shallots into a bowl. Turn up the heat under the pan to high and bubble until reduced and sticky. Return the cranberries and shallots to the pan and stir very gently to combine. Set aside until needed.

8. Let the pie cool on its base for 15min, then transfer to a serving plate or board. Spoon the cranberry topping on top and serve hot or warm, in slices.

Winter Panzanella

This traditional Italian salad was originally devised to use up stale bread, but this version works just as well with fresh bread.

1 medium butternut squash, peeled, deseeded and cut into 2.5cm chunks (about 800g prepared weight)
2 large red onions, each cut into 8 wedges through the root
8 tsp olive oil
400g vine tomatoes, roughly chopped
1 garlic clove, crushed
3 tbsp sherry vinegar
1 tsp sugar
300g ciabatta or sourdough, torn into large pieces
100g blanched hazelnuts
100g large green olives, pitted and roughly chopped
25g flat-leaf parsley, leaves picked
25g basil, leaves picked and roughly torn

1. Preheat oven to 190°C (170°C fan) mark 5. Toss the squash, onions, 2 tsp oil and some seasoning in a large roasting tin. Roast for 40–45min, stirring, until tender, then set aside to cool.

2. Meanwhile, in a large bowl, mix the tomatoes, garlic, sherry vinegar, sugar, 2 tsp oil and some seasoning, set aside to macerate.

3. In a second roasting tin, toss the bread, hazelnuts and remaining 4 tsp oil. Spread out in a single layer and roast alongside the veg for 10–15min until toasted and golden. Set aside to cool.

4. Add the cooled squash, onions, bread, hazelnuts, olives and herbs to the tomato bowl and mix everything gently. Tip on to a serving platter and serve.

★ GH TIP
If you're not wanting to keep this vegan, some crumbled feta on top would be delicious.

★ GET AHEAD
Prepare the salad up to 4hr ahead but do not add the bread, hazelnuts or herbs. Cover and keep at room temperature. Stir the remaining ingredients through shortly before serving.

Hands-on time: 25min, plus cooling
Cooking time: about 45min
Serves 8

PER SERVING 300cals, 8g protein, 15g fat
(2g saturates), 30g carbs (9g total sugars), 6g fibre

Turkey Biryani

It wouldn't be Christmas without leftover turkey, and while a cold cut sandwich is great, this dish transforms your bird into something warming and deliciously different.

500g basmati rice
2 tbsp vegetable oil
3 large onions, finely sliced
6 garlic cloves, crushed
6.5cm piece fresh root ginger, finely grated
1–2 green chillies, deseeded and finely chopped
1 cinnamon stick
12 cardamom pods
2 tsp garam masala
1 tsp turmeric
4 tomatoes, roughly chopped
250g natural yogurt
400g cooked turkey, shredded to assemble
Pinch saffron
100g butter, melted
½ tsp rose water (optional)
20g flaked almonds, toasted
Small handful coriander, chopped

FOR THE RAITA
½ cucumber, halved and deseeded
250g natural yogurt

1. Soak the rice in cold water for 15min. Meanwhile, heat the oil in a large, deep pan and cook the onions with a large pinch of salt over low-medium heat for 30min, stirring, until soft and golden brown. Transfer to a plate lined with kitchen paper.

2. Add the garlic, ginger, chillies and cinnamon to the pan with half the cardamom pods. Cook for 3min, add the ground spices and cook, stirring, for 2min. Add the tomatoes with a splash of water; cook over high heat for 7–8min until starting to break down. Stir in the yogurt, remove from the heat and season. Stir in the turkey; set aside.

3. Put the saffron in a bowl and pour over 100ml hot water. Set aside until needed.

4. Bring a large pan of salted water to the boil. Drain the rice and boil for 4–5min with the remaining cardamom pods, until the rice is just tender but still firm in the middle. Drain well.

5. To assemble, pour half the melted butter and 100ml water into a deep casserole dish (with a tight-fitting lid); spoon in a third of the rice. Stir the rose water into the saffron water and spoon a third evenly over the rice. Add half the turkey mixture and a third of the onions. Add further layers of rice, saffron water, turkey and onions. Top with the final layer of rice and saffron water (you should have some onions left; set these aside). Drizzle over the remaining butter.

6. Cover with the lid and put over medium-high heat until you can see steam, then turn down to a low heat and cook for 30min without lifting the lid.

7. Meanwhile, coarsely grate the cucumber and squeeze out excess water. Mix into the yogurt with some seasoning. Cover and chill.

8. Once the biryani is cooked, leave it off the heat with the lid on for 10min. Remove the lid, scatter over the remaining onions, the flaked almonds and coriander. Serve with the raita.

Hands-on time: 45min, plus soaking and standing
Cooking time: about 1hr 30min
Serves 8

PER SERVING 509cals, 26g protein, 18g fat (8g saturates), 60g carbs (9g total sugars), 3g fibre

Pomegranate, Turkey and Wild Rice Salad

This salad is a great way to use up leftover roast turkey. If you haven't got turkey, use roast chicken breast.

200g white basmati and wild rice mix
400g tin chickpeas, drained and rinsed
300g cooked turkey or chicken, shredded
3 spring onions, finely sliced
2 carrots, peeled and coarsely grated
1 cucumber, peeled into ribbons
150g pomegranate seeds
Large handful mint, leaves picked and torn

FOR THE DRESSING
1 garlic clove, crushed
1 tsp sugar
4 tbsp lime juice
3 tbsp rice vinegar
1 tbsp fish sauce
2 tbsp vegetable oil

1. Cook the rice in a pan of boiling water according to pack instructions, then drain and rinse briefly with cold water to stop the cooking. Drain well.

2. In a small bowl or jug, whisk together the dressing ingredients with some seasoning.

3. Tip the drained rice and chickpeas into a large bowl, pour over half the dressing and toss gently. Add the shredded meat, spring onions, carrot and cucumber, the remaining dressing and most of the pomegranate and mint (reserving some for a garnish). Toss (with your hands is easiest).

4. Tip the salad on to a large serving plate, piling the cucumber on top, sprinkle over the reserved pomegranate seeds and mint and serve.

★ GET AHEAD
Assemble the salad, without the pomegranate and mint, up to 2hr before serving. Cover and chill. Add the pomegranate and mint just before serving.

Hands-on time: 20min
Cooking time: about 25min
Serves 8

PER SERVING 231cals, 16g protein, 5g fat (1g saturates), 29g carbs (5g total sugars), 3g fibre

Sausage and Marmalade Plait

Once cooked, this crowd-pleaser will keep for a couple of days in the fridge (serve chilled or at room temperature).

½ tbsp olive oil
1 red onion, finely sliced
600g sausage meat
1 tbsp wholegrain mustard
1 tsp dried mixed herbs
320g sheet ready-rolled puff pastry, roughly 23 x 36cm
1 large egg, beaten
75g marmalade
1 tsp nigella seeds (optional)

1. Heat the oil in a medium pan over medium heat and cook the onion for 10min, until softened. Tip into a large bowl to cool completely. Add the sausage meat, mustard, dried herbs and plenty of seasoning and mix well.

2. Unroll the pastry, keeping it on its baking parchment. Slide on to a baking sheet and arrange so the pastry is lengthways in front of you, with a short edge closest to you. Brush the top of the pastry with beaten egg.

3. Spread marmalade lengthways down the centre of the pastry, in a roughly 7cm-wide rectangle. Shape the sausage meat mix into a neat log, about 7cm wide, and lay it on top of the marmalade.

4. With a sharp knife, cut 2cm-wide slits in the pastry on either side of the log, slanting them slightly towards you. Starting at the end furthest from you, fold the pastry strips over the filling, alternating sides for a plait effect. Trim ends to neaten.

5. Brush the pastry all over with beaten egg, then sprinkle the nigella seeds on top, if using. Chill

for 30min (don't worry if a little liquid leaks out during chilling).

6. Preheat oven to 200°C (180°C fan) mark 6. Cook the plait for 50min, or until the pastry is deep golden. Serve warm, or at room temperature, in slices.

Hands-on time: 25min, plus cooling and chilling
Cooking time: about 1hr
Serves 8

PER SERVING 390cals, 14g protein, 27g fat (11g saturates), 22g carbs (9g total sugars), 2g fibre

Marmalade and Bourbon Glazed Ham

It wouldn't be Christmas without a ham, and this simple citrus and bourbon infused one is a real delight. Poaching the clementines with the ham cooks them gently, so the peel is tender enough to eat once you've decorated the ham with them.

3kg whole boneless smoked or unsmoked gammon
Pared zest and juice 2 oranges
2 clementines, scrubbed
1 onion, thickly sliced
2 bay leaves
20 black peppercorns
40–50 whole cloves

FOR THE GLAZE
4 tbsp fine-shred marmalade
100ml bourbon
1½ tsp English mustard powder
1 tbsp demerara sugar

1. Weigh the gammon and calculate the cooking time, allowing 25min per 450g. Put the gammon into a large deep pan, then add the orange zest and juice. Top up with cold water to cover, then add the whole clementines, sliced onion, bay and peppercorns. Bring to the boil over medium-high heat, then reduce heat to low, cover and simmer gently for the calculated time, skimming off surface scum occasionally and topping up with water if needed to cover. After 1hr, remove the clementines and set aside to cool.

2. Remove the ham from cooking liquid to a board and leave to cool for 15min. Meanwhile, make the glaze. In a small pan, bubble the marmalade and bourbon for 8–10min until sticky and slightly reduced. Remove from heat and whisk in the mustard powder. Thinly slice the clementines (leaving the peel on).

3. Preheat oven to 220°C (200°C fan) mark 7. Untie the ham, then use a knife to remove the skin, leaving a thin layer of fat on the meat. Roughly score a diamond pattern into the fat, spacing the cuts about 1cm apart (not cutting into the meat). Brush half the glaze over the fat and arrange the clementine slices on top, securing each in place with several cloves. Brush with a little more glaze (reserving some for finishing) and sprinkle with the demerara sugar.

4. Line a roasting tin that will just fit the ham with a double layer of foil. Add the ham, fat-side up. Roast for 25–30min, until deeply caramelised. Brush with reserved glaze (if it is too thick, reheat briefly over low heat) and serve warm or at room temperature in slices.

★ GET AHEAD
Complete the recipe up to 2 days ahead. Cool, then loosely wrap in foil and chill. Any leftovers will keep well in the fridge for up to 4 days.

Hands-on time: 25min, plus cooling
Cooking time: about 3hr 45min
Serves 8, with leftovers

PER SERVING 373cals, 39g protein, 21g fat (7g saturates), 4g carbs (4g total sugars), 0g fibre

Coq au Vin

Chicken legs are much cheaper than other portions, and we think tastier too, especially when slow cooked in a hearty stew like this.

1 tbsp olive oil
4 chicken legs
150g smoked bacon lardons
12 small shallots, larger ones halved
200g baby chestnut mushrooms
2 large garlic cloves, crushed
2 tbsp plain flour
250ml chicken stock
350ml French red wine (we used Pinot Noir, see GH Tip)
2 bay leaves
Small handful thyme sprigs, plus extra to garnish
Pared zest ½ orange

★ GH TIP
As the wine you use is key to this recipe, opt for a variety that you like to drink.

★ GET AHEAD
Complete the recipe up to 2 days ahead, then cool, cover and chill. To serve, cover and gently reheat until boiling. Alternatively, cool and transfer to a freezer-safe container and freeze for up to 1 month. To serve, defrost in the fridge overnight and reheat as above.

1. Heat the oil in a large, shallow casserole dish (that has a lid) that can hold the legs in a single layer. Fry the chicken over medium-high heat for 8-10min or until golden all over. Transfer to a plate and set aside.

2. Add the bacon lardons and shallots to the casserole and fry over medium heat for 5min, or until the shallots are beginning to soften and turn golden. Stir in the mushrooms and garlic and fry for 3-4min, until golden.

3. Stir in the flour and cook for 1min. Gradually stir in the stock, followed by the wine, herbs, orange zest and some seasoning. Return the chicken (and any juices from the plate) to the casserole, nestling the legs down so they are mostly covered by liquid.

4. Bring to the boil, reduce heat to low, cover and bubble gently for 45min, or until the chicken is cooked through and tender.

5. Remove the chicken to a plate, cover and keep warm. Bubble the sauce over a high heat (uncovered) for 8-10min, or until slightly reduced and thickened. Return the chicken to the casserole, check the seasoning and serve with buttery mash or a crusty baguette, if you like.

Hands-on time: 30min
Cooking time: about 1hr 20min
Serves 4

PER SERVING 467cals, 38g protein, 22g fat (7g saturates), 10g carbs (5g total sugars), 3g fibre

Luxury Fish Pie

Using tinned bisque is a wonderfully affordable way to ramp up flavour. If you can't find any, swap the quantity for fish stock or milk.

FOR THE FILLING
50g butter
2 leeks, finely chopped
1 fennel bulb, finely chopped (discard central core)
2 tsp Dijon mustard
50g plain flour
400g tin lobster bisque (we used Baxters)
300ml milk
400g skinless fish fillets, cut into 2cm chunks (we used smoked haddock and cod)
250g cooked crayfish tails (see GH Tip)

FOR THE TOPPING
1kg floury potatoes, peeled and roughly chopped
50g butter
180g cream cheese
25g Gruyère, grated (optional)

★ GH TIP
To make this even more affordable, swap the crayfish tails for cooked and peeled king prawns or North Atlantic prawns, both available in the freezer aisle.

★ GET AHEAD
Prepare to the end of step 4 up to 1 day ahead, allowing the bisque sauce to cool completely before adding the fish and crayfish. Loosely cover and chill. To serve, uncover and complete the recipe.

1. For the filling, melt the butter in a large pan over medium heat and cook the leeks and fennel for 10min, until softened. Stir in the mustard and flour and cook for 1min. Remove from the heat and gradually stir in the lobster bisque and milk. Return to the heat and cook, stirring, until thickened. Set aside.

2. Meanwhile, make the topping. Put the potatoes into a separate large pan (that has a lid) and cover with cold water. Cover with the lid and bring to the boil over high heat. Reduce heat and simmer, uncovered, for 10–15min, or until the potatoes are tender. Drain and allow to steam dry in the colander for 5min.

3. Preheat oven to 200°C (180°C fan) mark 6. Return the potatoes to the empty pan and mash until smooth. Beat in the butter, cream cheese and plenty of seasoning. If you want to pipe the mash, transfer to a piping bag fitted with a large plain or fluted nozzle (alternatively, you can cut a roughly 2.5cm hole into a disposable piping bag). Set aside.

4. Stir the fish, crayfish tails and plenty of seasoning into the bisque sauce, then empty into a shallow ovenproof serving dish. Pipe/spoon the mash on to the filling. Sprinkle over the Gruyère, if using.

5. Cook in the oven for 30–40min, or until bubbling and golden. Serve.

Hands-on time: 30min, plus cooling
Cooking time: about 1hr
Serves 6

PER SERVING 553cals, 29g protein, 26g fat (16g saturates), 48g carbs (8g total sugars), 7g fibre

Tempeh, Pistachio and Apricot Pastilla

This pastilla – a filo pastry pie – is made with tempeh, a soya bean product that's firmer and chewier than tofu, and also higher in protein.

Pinch of saffron
200ml vegetable stock
2 tbsp olive oil
400g tempeh, cut into 1cm pieces
2 red onions, finely chopped
3 garlic cloves, crushed
3cm piece fresh root ginger, peeled and finely chopped
2 tbsp ras el hanout spice blend
½ tsp ground cinnamon
½ tsp ground cumin
100g dried apricots, roughly chopped
3 medium eggs, beaten
100g pistachio kernels, roughly chopped
1 tsp finely grated orange zest
Small handful parsley, roughly chopped
75g butter, melted
6 sheets filo pastry

1. Add the saffron to the hot vegetable stock and leave to infuse. Heat 1 tbsp oil in a large frying pan over high heat. Fry the tempeh pieces until beginning to caramelise (you may need to do this in batches). Empty into a bowl. Lower the heat under the pan to medium, add the remaining oil and cook the onions and a pinch of salt until softened, about 10min.

2. Add the garlic, ginger and spices and cook for a further 2min. Pour in the infused stock and add the apricots and some seasoning. Bubble for a few minutes.

3. Add the eggs to the pan sauce and cook over low heat, stirring, until they resemble lightly scrambled eggs, about 4–5min. Return the tempeh to the pan and stir through the pistachios, orange zest and parsley. Remove from the heat and set aside to cool.

4. Preheat the oven to 200°C (180°C fan) mark 6. Lightly brush a 20.5cm round cake tin (either springform or loose-bottomed) with some of the melted butter. Brush the top of a filo sheet with butter and press into the tin. Repeat with a further 3 sheets, rotating them so the base and sides of the tin are completely covered. Leave the excess hanging over the top of the tin.

5. Spoon in the tempeh filling and smooth it until level. Cut the remaining 2 filo sheets into rough circles just larger than 20.5cm – use the base of your tin as a guide. Brush the top of each with butter, then layer them up. Put on top of the filling (butter-side up), then scrunch in the overhanging filo and brush with the remaining butter. Put the tin on a baking tray to catch any escaping butter.

6. Cook for about 45min until golden, covering the top with foil if it's browning too much. Leave to cool in the tin for 10min, remove and serve.

Hands-on time: 30min, plus cooling
Cooking time: about 1hr 15min
Serves 6

PER SERVING 513cals, 24g protein, 31g fat (9g saturates), 31g carbs (12g total sugars), 9g fibre

★ GET AHEAD
Prepare to the end of step 3 up to 1 day ahead.
Cover and chill. Complete the recipe to serve.

Guinea Fowl, Leek and Pancetta Pie

A flavour-packed, impressive dish that's well worth the effort. Use any pastry trimmings to decorate the top of your pie.

8 shallots, unpeeled
1.4kg guinea fowl
1 lemon, halved
Handful thyme sprigs
200g diced pancetta
2 leeks, sliced
2 carrots, chopped
25g butter
25g plain flour, plus extra to dust
250ml whole milk
150ml white wine
2 tbsp full-fat cream cheese
1 tsp Dijon mustard
Large handful flat-leaf parsley, roughly chopped
500g block puff pastry
1 medium egg, beaten

★ GH TIP
You can use a similar-sized chicken instead of a guinea fowl. Or use leftover shredded turkey – you'll need about 750g meat – and chicken stock for the sauce.

★ GET AHEAD
The filling or the whole pie (to the end of step 6) can be prepared a day ahead. Complete the recipe to serve, allowing an extra 5min if needed.

Hands-on time: 1hr, plus cooling and resting
Cooking time: about 2hr 15min
Serves 6

PER SERVING 739cals, 42g protein, 45g fat (23g saturates), 35g carbs (7g total sugars), 4g fibre

1. Preheat oven to 200°C (180°C fan) mark 6. Put the shallots and 2 tbsp water in a medium roasting tin that will fit the guinea fowl snugly. Remove any string or trussing from the guinea fowl, season all over and put half the lemon and the thyme in the cavity. Sit the bird breast side-down in the tin on top of the shallots and roast for 30min, then turn and roast breast-up for 30min.

2. Remove from oven (turn off oven) and lift the bird on to a board, letting any juices from the cavity run back into the roasting tin. Scrape up any sticky bits from the base of the tin with a wooden spoon, adding 2–3tbsp water to help if it's looking a bit dry. Pass the liquid through a sieve into a jug, pressing the shallots to extract any juices. You should have about 150ml juices – top up with water or stock if needed. Discard the shallots and set the bird and roasting juices aside to cool.

3. Fry the pancetta in a large, deep frying pan over medium heat for 8min until golden. Remove to a bowl with a slotted spoon. Add the leeks and carrots to the pan with a pinch of salt, cover with a lid and fry gently for 8min, stirring occasionally, until softened. Add to the pancetta bowl.

4. Add the butter to the pan and, once foaming, stir in the flour. Cook for 2–3min, stirring regularly. Off the heat, gradually stir in the milk, followed by the wine to make a smooth sauce. Stir in the cream cheese, mustard, 1–2 tsp lemon juice (from the remaining half lemon) and the reserved strained juices. Return to the heat and simmer for 2–3min, stirring occasionally, then set aside.

5. Roughly shred the meat and discard the bones (finely chop any crispy skin, if you like, or discard). Stir the guinea fowl, pancetta mixture and parsley through the sauce and check the seasoning. Transfer to a 1.6–2 litre ovenproof pie dish.

6. Preheat oven to 200°C (180°C fan) mark 6. Lightly flour a work surface and roll out the pastry so it's large enough to cover the pie dish with plenty of overhang. Brush the rim of the dish with beaten egg. Lay the pastry on to the dish and cut a small hole in the centre to let steam escape. Trim and crimp the edges on to the dish and brush the pastry with beaten egg. Cut out some festive shapes, letters or decoration from the trimmings, if you like, and stick on to the pastry lid. Reglaze with egg.

7. Cook for 40-45min until deep golden and puffed. Leave to rest for 10min before serving.

Christmas Cake Trifle

A great way to serve leftover fruitcake, this dessert is ready in just 10 minutes!

200g iced fruitcake loaf (or leftover Christmas cake), cut into slices
150g fresh cranberry sauce
Icing sugar, to sweeten
Brandy or rum, to taste
500g tub good-quality fresh vanilla custard
250ml can squirty cream (aerosol UHT)
Silver sugar balls, to decorate

1. Arrange the cake slices in the bottom of a large glass bowl. Put the cranberry sauce into a small bowl, then stir in enough icing sugar to sweeten (to taste). Spoon over the cake layer. Stir a splash of brandy or rum into the tub of custard (to taste) and pour over the cranberry layer.

2. Squirt over enough whipped cream to cover the top of the trifle and decorate with silver balls. Serve immediately (the cream deflates quickly).

★ GET AHEAD
Make up to end of step 1 up to 4hr ahead and chill. To serve, top with the squirty cream, decorate with the balls and serve immediately.

Hands-on time: 10min
Serves 6-8

PER SERVING (for 8) 331cals, 4g protein, 20g fat (11g saturates), 34g carbs (32g total sugars), 0.3g fibre

Mulled Clementine Meringue Wreath

This impressive dessert is easy to assemble.

4 medium egg whites
200g caster sugar
1 tsp cornflour

FOR THE SYRUP AND TOPPING
75g caster sugar
100ml white wine
2 clementines, zest pared, then peeled and sliced
   into 8 rounds
100g fresh or frozen cranberries
2 cinnamon sticks
2 star anise
4 cloves
300ml double cream
3 tbsp icing sugar, sifted
1 tsp vanilla extract

1. Preheat oven to 140°C (120°C fan) mark 1. Using a pencil, draw a 25.5cm circle on baking parchment and put, pencil-side down, on a large baking sheet.

2. Using a handheld electric whisk, beat the egg whites to stiff peaks. Gradually add the sugar, whisking, until thick and glossy. Beat in the cornflour.

3. Secure the parchment to the baking sheet with a few small smears of meringue. Spoon 8 equal mounds of meringue around the circle you drew, touching slightly, to make a wreath shape. Flatten the middle of each mound slightly with the back of a spoon. Bake for 1hr 30min, then cool completely in the oven, ideally overnight.

4. Meanwhile, heat the sugar, wine and 100ml water in a large frying pan over medium heat, stirring to dissolve the sugar. Add the zest, cranberries and spices. Turn up heat; bubble for 15min or until reduced and syrupy. Strain into a jug; set aside.

5. Carefully transfer the meringue to serving plate. Whip the cream, icing sugar and vanilla to soft peaks, then spoon on to mounds. Top with clementine slices, drizzle with syrup and serve.

Hands-on time: 40min, plus (overnight) cooling
Cooking time: about 1hr 30min
Serves 8

PER SERVING 377cals, 2g protein, 20g fat (13g saturates), 44g carbs (43g total sugars), 1g fibre

Mulled Berry Trifle

Nothing says winter quite like the warming aromas of mulling spices. You can buy mulled wine spice mixes in shops or make your own – see GH tip. For an added boozy hit, swap some or all of the cordial for sloe gin.

FOR THE COMPOTE
500g frozen mixed berries
2 tbsp icing sugar
4 bags mulling spice (see GH tip)
3 tbsp Mulled Winter Cordial (we used Belvoir)

FOR THE PRALINE
50g caster sugar
40g pistachio kernels, roughly chopped

FOR THE TRIFLE
375g raspberry or strawberry jam Swiss roll(s)
300g mixed fresh berries (we used raspberries and blackberries)
500ml fresh vanilla custard
300ml double cream
2 tbsp icing sugar
150g crème fraîche
5 tbsp Mulled Winter Cordial (we used Belvoir)

★ GH TIP
Mulled spice bags are generally a mix of ground cinnamon, cardamom, allspice and cloves and sometimes citrus zest. You could use ground spices instead, adding them to the berries to taste.

★ GET AHEAD
Make the trifle to the end of step 3 up to 1 day ahead. Cover and chill. Cover and chill reserved berry compote. Store praline in an airtight container at room temperature. Complete recipe to serve.

Hands-on time: 40min, plus cooling and chilling
Cooking time: about 15min
Serves 8

PER SERVING 610cals, 8g protein, 34g fat (19g saturates), 66g carbs (58g total sugars), 3g fibre

1. First, make the compote. In a medium pan, heat the frozen berries, icing sugar, mulling spice and cordial over medium heat for 5–8min until the berries soften. Set aside to cool and infuse for 1hr, then remove the mulling spice bags, lightly squeeze and discard.

2. Meanwhile, make the praline. Line a baking tray with baking parchment. In a small, heavy-based pan, gently heat the caster sugar and 3 tbsp water, stirring to dissolve. Turn up heat to high and bubble until the caramel turns golden – do not stir, but swirl the pan instead. Take the pan off the heat and add the pistachios. Scrape on to the prepared baking tray and leave to cool.

3. Cut the Swiss roll(s) into 1cm-thick slices and arrange in the base and slightly up the sides of a 2-litre trifle dish or serving bowl. Spoon a third of the compote over the slices and top with half the fresh berries. Spoon the custard on top and chill for 1hr.

4. To serve, whip the cream and icing sugar until it just holds its shape. Add the crème fraîche and 4 tbsp cordial and whisk again briefly to combine. Spoon the remaining berry compote over the custard, then spoon the cream on top. Toss the remaining berries with the remaining 1 tbsp cordial, then arrange on top of the cream. Crumble over the praline and serve.

Trifle Layer Loaf

An impressive new way to serve this classic pud: worthy of a dinner party!

Vegetable oil, to grease

FOR CREAM LAYER
2 sheets platinum-grade leaf gelatine
200ml double cream
100g cream cheese
50g icing sugar

FOR CUSTARD LAYER
2 sheets platinum-grade leaf gelatine
40ml sweet/cream sherry
300ml custard, fresh chilled or tinned

FOR JELLY LAYER
2 sheets platinum-grade leaf gelatine
200g frozen raspberries

FOR SPONGE LAYER
275g bought Madeira sponge

TO DECORATE (optional)
Fresh raspberries
Toasted flaked almonds
Sugar sprinkles

1. Lightly grease a 900g loaf tin and line with a layer of clingfilm. Next, place a strip of foil lengthways (shiny side down) along the base and ends so it comes up at least 2.5cm over top of tin. Repeat with foil widthways, smoothing it out as much as you can. Lightly grease the foil.

2. For the cream layer, cover the gelatine with cold water and soak for 5min. Heat the cream in a pan until warm. Take off the heat, lift the gelatine out of the water, squeeze out excess water and stir into the cream to dissolve. Whisk in the cream cheese and icing sugar until smooth. Pour into the lined tin, then bang the tin down on the work surface a few times to burst any bubbles in the mixture. Cool and chill until set – about 1hr.

3. Meanwhile, make the custard layer. Cover the gelatine with cold water and soak for 5min. Gently heat the sherry in a pan until warm. Take off the heat, lift the gelatine out of the water, squeeze out the excess water and stir into sherry to dissolve. Stir in the custard and set aside at room temperature.

4. When the cream layer has set, pour on the custard layer, then chill until set (about 1hr).

5. Meanwhile, make the jelly layer. Cover the gelatine with cold water and let soak for 5min. Heat the raspberries and 100ml water in a small pan until the raspberries are mushy. Lift the gelatine out of the water, squeeze out excess water and stir into the raspberries to dissolve. Work well through a fine sieve into a jug (discard the seeds). Set aside at room temperature.

6. When the custard has set, pour on the jelly. Chill until just set (about 40min). Cut the brown edges off the Madeira sponge and slice into 1cm slices. Press on to the jelly layer to stick, trimming the slices to fit to make an even layer. Wrap the tin in clingfilm and chill for at least 4hr (or up to 24hr).

7. To serve, unwrap and invert on to a serving plate and gently peel off the foil and clingfilm. Decorate with fresh raspberries, almonds and sugar sprinkles, if you like. Serve in slices.

Hands-on time: 40min, plus cooling and chilling
Cooking time: about 10min
Serves 8

PER SERVING 347cals, 6g protein, 23g fat (14g saturates), 28g carbs (21g total sugars), 1g fibre

★ GET AHEAD
Prepare to the end of step 6 up
to 1 day ahead and chill. Complete
the recipe to serve.

★ GH TIP
We used tinned custard for
a more vibrant colour.

Irish Cream Crème Brûlée Cheesecake

Spoons at the ready to crack the caramel on top of this creamy baked cheesecake.

125g butter, melted, plus extra to grease
250g digestive biscuits
550g full-fat cream cheese
200g caster sugar
200ml double cream
100ml Irish cream liqueur
½ tbsp vanilla bean paste
3 large eggs, beaten

★ GH TIP
The crisp caramel adds great crunch, but if you don't have a blowtorch, skip this step rather than trying to grill the sugar.

★ GET AHEAD
Caramelise the sugar up to 1hr ahead. Keep the cheesecake at room temperature before serving.

Hands-on time: 25min, plus cooling and
  (overnight) chilling
Cooking time: about 1hr 15min
Serves 12

PER SERVING 487cals, 6g protein, 36g fat
(21g saturates), 33g carbs (24g total sugars), 1g fibre

1. Preheat oven to 170°C (150°C fan) mark 3. Lightly grease a 23cm round springform tin and line with baking parchment. Whizz the biscuits in a food processor until finely crushed (or bash them in a food bag with a rolling pin). Add the melted butter and pulse/mix until combined. Tip into prepared tin, level and press firmly with the back of a spoon. Bake for 15min, remove and leave to cool slightly.

2. Reduce oven temperature to 160°C (140°C fan) mark 3. In a large bowl, whisk the cream cheese and 150g of the sugar until smooth. Add double cream, liqueur and vanilla and whisk to combine. Finally, whisk in the eggs until combined. Pour the mixture over the biscuit base.

3. Put an ovenproof dish half-filled with hot water on the bottom shelf of the oven. Bake the cheesecake on the shelf above the water for 45min–1hr, until just set with a slight wobble. Turn off oven and leave to cool completely with the door ajar. Once cool, chill overnight to set.

4. To serve, peel off the baking parchment and transfer the cheesecake to a cake stand or plate. Sprinkle the remaining 50g caster sugar evenly over the top and use a blowtorch to gently caramelise the sugar (see GH Tip). Serve.

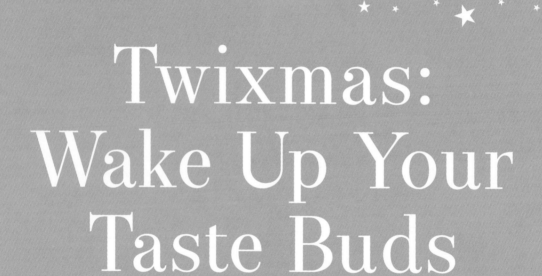

14

Twixmas: Wake Up Your Taste Buds

Spicy Chicken Peanut Noodles

On the table in minutes and packed with flavour, this will be a recipe you turn to time and time again.

1 tbsp vegetable oil
300g chicken thigh fillets, cut into finger-sized strips
200g egg noodles
125g green beans, trimmed and cut into shorter lengths
3cm piece fresh root ginger, peeled and finely grated
1 red chilli, finely sliced
3 spring onions, finely sliced
25g roasted salted peanuts

FOR THE PEANUT SAUCE
75g peanut butter, crunchy or smooth
2 tbsp soy sauce
1 tbsp rice vinegar
1 tbsp sriracha

1. Bring a large pan of water to the boil. Meanwhile, heat the oil in a large, deep frying pan or wok over medium-high heat. Fry the chicken for 5min until golden and cooked through.

2. Cook the noodles and beans in the boiling water for 5min or until tender. Drain. In a jug, whisk the sauce ingredients with 125ml just-boiled water until combined.

3. Add the ginger to the chicken pan and fry for 1min. Add the sauce and heat through until melted and combined. Add the drained noodles and beans and toss to heat through and coat.

4. Garnish with chilli, spring onions and peanuts and serve immediately.

★ GH TIP
If you prefer, you can use dried chilli flakes instead of whole chillies.

Hands-on time: 15min
Cooking time: about 15min
Serves 4

PER SERVING 464cals, 30g protein, 19g fat (4g saturates), 30g carbs (4g total sugars), 6g fibre

Roasted Squash with Porcini Mushroom and Dolcelatte Risotto

The sweetness of roasted squash is a great foil to an earthy and rich mushroom risotto laced with nuggets of mild blue cheese. Pistachio gremolata adds a lovely finish of colour, crunch and zest.

30g dried porcini mushrooms
3 small butternut squash (each about 600g/15cm long)
4 tbsp olive oil
1 litre vegetable stock
25g unsalted butter
1 large onion, finely chopped
1 celery stalk, finely chopped
2 garlic cloves, crushed
400g arborio risotto rice
1 tbsp thyme leaves
200ml white wine
150g Dolcelatte, cut into 1cm pieces

FOR THE PISTACHIO GREMOLATA
15g flat-leaf parsley, leaves picked and finely chopped
Finely grated zest 1 lemon
30g pistachio kernels, roughly chopped
1 small garlic clove, crushed

★ GET AHEAD
Roast the squash up to 1 day ahead, then cool, cover and chill. Reheat briefly in the oven while you are making the risotto and complete the recipe to serve.

Hands-on time: 40min, plus soaking
Cooking time: about 55min
Serves 6

PER SERVING 630cals, 15g protein, 23g fat (9g saturates), 80g carbs (15g total sugars), 9g fibre

1. Preheat oven to 200°C (180°C fan) mark 6 and line a baking tray with baking parchment. Put the porcini in a heatproof bowl, pour over 500ml just-boiled water and soak for 20min.

2. Meanwhile, halve the squash and scoop out the seeds. Score the flesh with a sharp knife in a criss-cross pattern, being careful not to cut through the skins. Sprinkle the flesh of the squash with a little water, then arrange cut-side down on the prepared baking tray. Roast for 20min, then remove from oven. Turn them cut-side up and brush the insides with 1 tbsp oil, season and return to the oven for a final 20–35min until the flesh is completely tender (cooking times will vary, pierce the squash flesh with a fork to check it's completely tender).

3. While the squash are cooking, make the risotto. Strain the soaked porcini through a fine sieve into a medium pan. Add the vegetable stock to the soaking liquid, then set over low-medium heat to keep warm. Roughly chop the porcini.

4. In a large pan, heat the butter and remaining 3 tbsp oil over medium-high heat. Add the onion, celery, garlic, chopped porcini and a pinch of salt. Cook, stirring occasionally, for about 15min until softened. Add the rice and thyme leaves to the pan and stir to coat. Add the wine and bubble for a couple of minutes until the liquid has been almost completely absorbed.

5. Gradually add the hot stock, 1–2 ladlefuls at a time, adding more only when the previous liquid has been absorbed. Stir well after each addition. Continue until the rice is tender – about 30–35min (adding more or less stock as needed). When cooked, the rice should be tender but still have a little bite, and the risotto should be quite loose.

6. Meanwhile, mix all the ingredients for the pistachio gremolata in a small bowl. Set aside.

7. When the risotto is ready, remove from the heat and let stand for a couple of minutes. Arrange the squash on plates. Fold three-quarters of the Dolcelatte through the risotto, then divide the risotto among the squash. Top with the remaining cheese, scatter with the pistachio gremolata and serve.

★ GH TIP
You don't need to stir the rice constantly while making a risotto, but you should stir regularly, ensuring it doesn't stick to the bottom of the pan, to release the starch from the rice and create a lovely, creamy texture.

Chicory, Pea Shoot and Orange Salad

A refreshing, crunchy salad that pairs well with rich and creamy dishes.

---

2 medium oranges
2 tbsp toasted walnut or hazelnut oil
6 small or 4 large mixed colour chicory heads,
   leaves separated
75g pea shoots
2 tbsp balsamic glaze

1. Slice the top and bottom off each orange and sit on a board. Cut away the peel and white pith. Working 1 at a time, hold an orange over a large bowl (to catch the juice) and carefully cut between the membranes to separate the segments. Squeeze any remaining juice into the bowl and set the segments aside. Repeat with the remaining orange.

2. Add the nut oil and plenty of seasoning to the juice bowl and whisk to combine. Add the chicory leaves, pea shoots and orange segments and toss gently to coat.

3. Arrange the salad on a large platter and drizzle with the balsamic glaze. Serve.

★ GET AHEAD
Complete step 1 up to 1 day ahead, then cover and chill the juice and segments separately. Complete the recipe to serve.

Hands-on time: 10min
Serves 6

PER SERVING 82cals, 1g protein, 4g fat (0g saturates), 9g carbs (7g total sugars), 2g fibre

Kimchi and Tofu Cabbage Stew

Gochujang is a Korean hot red pepper paste, and is now available in most large supermarkets. If you can't find it, substitute with sriracha to taste.

---

1 tbsp sunflower oil
250g firm tofu, cut into 1cm-thick slices
1 onion, finely sliced
1 garlic clove, crushed
½–1 tbsp gluten-free gochujang paste
400g kimchi
150g shiitake mushrooms, sliced if large
1 litre gluten-free vegetable stock
1 tbsp tamari (gluten-free soy sauce)
2 spring onions, finely sliced

1. Heat half the oil in a large frying pan (that has a lid) over medium heat and fry the tofu (in batches if needed) until golden (about 5min per side). Set aside on a plate.

2. Add the remaining oil to the pan and fry the onion for 5min until softened. Stir in the garlic and gochujang, fry for 1min, then add the kimchi, mushrooms, stock and tamari. Bring to the boil, then reduce the heat and simmer for 10min or until mushrooms are tender.

3. Return the tofu to the pan to heat through, then check the seasoning. Garnish with the spring onions and serve with noodles or rice, if you like.

Hands-on time: 15min
Cooking time: about 30min
Serves 4

PER SERVING 188cals, 12g protein, 9g fat (1g saturates), 13g carbs (9g total sugars), 6g fibre

Tofu Gong Bao

We've used whole dried chillies to give this dish its authentic look and fiery flavour, but don't eat them unless you're a real chilli fan!

1 tbsp cornflour
2 tbsp soy sauce
3 tbsp Shaoxing wine or dry sherry
450g firm tofu, cut into 2cm pieces
1 tbsp vegetable oil
3 garlic cloves, crushed
5cm piece root ginger, peeled and finely chopped
1 tbsp small dried bird's eye chillies
6 spring onions, chopped
2 tsp sugar
Small handful skin-on peanuts
Cooked rice, to serve

1. In a bowl, mix the cornflour, soy sauce and Shaoxing wine/sherry until smooth. Add the tofu and turn to coat. Leave to marinate for 20min, if you have time.

2. Heat the oil in a large wok or frying pan over high heat. Reserving the marinade, use a slotted spoon to lift the tofu into the wok/frying pan. Cook for 8-10min, turning carefully, until crisp. Add the garlic, ginger, chillies and most of the spring onions, then fry for 2min until fragrant.

3. Stir 3 tbsp water into the reserved marinade. Add to the wok/pan along with the sugar and peanuts. Bubble for 30sec. Garnish with the remaining spring onions and serve with the rice.

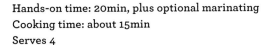

Hands-on time: 20min, plus optional marinating
Cooking time: about 15min
Serves 4

PER SERVING 206cals, 15g protein, 12g fat
(2g saturates), 9g carbs (5g total sugars), 1g fibre

Fish Finger Tacos

These speedy tacos give the humble fish finger a makeover. For a more substantial meal, serve with rice.

16 breaded cod fish fingers
25g butter
200g frozen peas
½–1 tsp dried chilli flakes
Finely grated zest 1 lemon
150g mayonnaise
1 tbsp gochujang
8 small tortilla wraps
½ iceberg lettuce, thickly shredded
75g Cheddar, coarsely grated

1. Preheat oven to 220°C (200°C fan) mark 7. Put the fish fingers on a baking tray lined with baking parchment and cook for 12–15min or until golden and cooked through (or according to pack instructions).

2. Meanwhile, in a medium pan over low heat, cook the butter, peas, chilli flakes and plenty of seasoning until the peas are piping hot. Remove from heat, lightly mash with a fork and stir in the lemon zest. In a small bowl, mix the mayonnaise, gochujang and plenty of seasoning.

3. Spread the mayonnaise mixture over the tortillas and top with the shredded lettuce, fish fingers, crushed peas and cheese. Serve.

Hands-on time: 20min
Cooking time: about 15min
Serves 4

PER SERVING 743cals, 25g protein, 58g fat
(13g saturates), 27g carbs (3g total sugars), 4g fibre

Grated Halloumi Quesadillas

Mix and match the filling ingredients – shredded cooked chicken, refried beans and Cheddar all make great additions.

2–3 tbsp olive oil
2 tbsp fajita seasoning mix
4 large tomatoes, roughly chopped
150g fresh guacamole, plus extra to serve (optional)
8 large flour tortillas
250g halloumi, grated

1. Heat 1 tbsp oil in a large non-stick frying pan over a medium heat and fry the fajita mix for 1min until fragrant. Stir in the tomatoes and cook for 5min, until starting to break down. Remove from heat.

2. Spread the guacamole evenly over 4 tortillas, then top with the tomato mixture and grated halloumi. Lay on the remaining 4 tortillas to cover.

3. Wipe the frying pan clean, add a little oil and return to medium-high heat. Add a quesadilla and cook for 2min until the base is golden. Carefully flip with a spatula and cook for 2min more, again until the base is golden. Slide on to a board and cover to keep warm.

4. Repeat the frying to make 4 quesadillas, adding a little more oil between each batch. Serve in quarters with extra guacamole, if you like.

Hands-on time: 25min
Cooking time: about 25min
Serves 4

PER SERVING 595cals, 23g protein, 32g fat (15g saturates), 51g carbs (10g total sugars), 6g fibre

Risotto Carbonara

This makes a comforting main or an easy starter for six.

200g bacon lardons
15g butter
1 small onion, finely chopped
2 garlic cloves, crushed
400g risotto rice
200ml white wine
1 litre chicken or vegetable stock
2 medium egg yolks
2 tbsp double cream
50g Parmesan, finely grated, plus extra to garnish
Small handful parsley, finely chopped

1. Heat a large frying pan over high heat and fry the lardons until golden, about 5min. Using a slotted spoon, lift out on to a plate. Turn down the heat to low-medium, add the butter to the pan and fry the onion for 5min until softened.

2. Stir in the garlic and fry for 1min, then stir in the rice and cook, stirring, for 1min. Add the wine and bubble until absorbed. Gradually add the stock 1 ladleful at a time, stirring constantly, only adding the next ladleful when the previous one has been absorbed – this should take about 20min. Remove from heat, cover and set aside to rest for 5min.

3. Meanwhile, in a small bowl whisk the egg yolks and cream to combine. Mix into the rested rice along with the bacon and Parmesan. Check the seasoning. Divide among 4 bowls and garnish with parsley, black pepper and Parmesan. Serve.

Hands-on time: 30min
Cooking time: about 30min
Serves 4

PER SERVING 723cals, 26g protein, 27g fat (13g saturates), 84g carbs (2g total sugars), 3g fibre

Paneer Jalfrezi

Not a fan of chickpeas? Simply double the quantity of paneer.

---

2 tbsp vegetable oil
225g block paneer, cut into 2cm cubes
2 onions, roughly chopped
1 each red and green pepper, deseeded and sliced
1 red chilli, deseeded and finely chopped
2 garlic cloves, crushed
1 tbsp ground cumin
1 tbsp garam masala
1 tsp ground coriander
1 tsp ground turmeric
6 tomatoes, roughly chopped
400g tin chickpeas, drained and rinsed
Juice 1 lemon

1. Heat 1 tbsp oil in large pan over medium heat. Fry the paneer for 5min, turning regularly, until browned all over. Remove to a plate.

2. Add the remaining oil to the pan, lower the heat and fry the onions for 20min, stirring occasionally, until completely softened, adding the peppers for the final 5min. Add the chilli, garlic and spices to the pan and fry for 2min, until fragrant. Stir through three-quarters of the tomatoes, 200ml water and 1½ tsp fine salt. Bring to the boil, then simmer, stirring occasionally, for 10min, until the tomatoes have broken down.

3. Return the paneer to the pan with the remaining tomatoes and chickpeas; simmer for 2min. Stir through the lemon juice and check the seasoning.

Hands-on time: 20min
Cooking time: about 45min
Serves 4

PER SERVING 381cals, 21g protein, 21g fat (9g saturates), 22g carbs (12g total sugars), 8g fibre

Stir-fried Broccoli with Garlic and Chilli

A simple but aromatic side dish, with a tangy miso and lemon dressing.

600g Tenderstem broccoli
1 tbsp olive oil
2 garlic cloves, thinly sliced
1 red chilli, deseeded and finely chopped

FOR THE DRESSING
2 tsp white miso paste
2 tsp runny honey
Juice 1 lemon

1. Trim the broccoli and cut any thick stalks in half lengthways. Put into a large frying pan (with a lid) over medium heat, pour in 150ml just-boiled water, then cover with the lid and steam for 10–12min until the water has mostly evaporated and the broccoli is just tender.

2. Meanwhile, whisk the dressing ingredients together in a small bowl.

3. Remove the broccoli to a plate with tongs. Add the oil, garlic and chilli to the pan and fry for 2–3min. Remove half the aromatics to a small bowl or plate, then return the broccoli to the pan with the dressing. Cook for 2min to warm through, tossing gently to coat.

4. Transfer the broccoli to a warm serving dish, sprinkle with the reserved garlic and chilli; serve.

Hands-on time: 25min
Cooking time: about 20min
Serves 6

PER SERVING 70cals, 5g protein, 3g fat (0g saturates), 5g carbs (4g total sugars), 4g fibre

Jacket Potato Soup

This comforting soup is an ideal winter warmer. If you're entertaining, let people add their own toppings or get creative with leftovers from the cheeseboard, shredded ham or turkey. If you want to make it extra special, add a drizzle of truffle oil.

3-4 baking potatoes (about 600g)
4 unsmoked bacon rashers, roughly chopped
50g butter
50g plain flour
600ml milk
500ml vegetable stock
150ml soured cream, plus extra to serve (optional)
50g Cheddar, coarsely grated
1 tbsp chopped chives

1. Preheat oven to 180°C (160°C fan) mark 4. Wash the potatoes and prick all over with a fork. Put into a roasting tin (or directly on the oven rack) and cook for 45min–1hr, or until tender and you can easily pierce them with a knife. Set aside until cool enough to handle.

2. Meanwhile, heat a large pan over high heat and fry the bacon until crisp, about 5min. Empty into a bowl. Return the pan to heat and melt the butter. Whisk in the flour and cook, whisking, for 2min. Remove from heat and gradually whisk in the milk and stock until smooth. Return to heat and cook, whisking, until slightly thickened. Set aside.

3. Roughly chop the cooled potatoes, add to the pan, then blend the soup until smooth (in batches, if needed). Return to the pan, if needed, and stir through the soured cream. Check the seasoning. Warm through, if needed.

4. Ladle into 6 bowls and top with bacon, cheese, chives and a dollop of soured cream, if you like.

Hands-on time: 20min, plus cooling
Cooking time: about 1hr 5min
Serves 6

PER SERVING 360cals, 12g protein, 20g fat (12g saturates), 32g carbs (7g total sugars), 3g fibre

Slow-roast Harissa Salmon

Wild salmon, like sockeye, cooks faster than its farmed cousin. Check wild salmon at 20min to see whether it's cooked.

FOR THE HARISSA SALMON
500g salmon fillet, checked for bones
1½ tbsp harissa paste
½ tbsp olive oil
2 lemons
1 garlic clove, crushed
Small bunch dill, roughly chopped

FOR THE QUINOA SALAD
1.2 litres gluten-free vegetable stock
200g quinoa
400g tin chickpeas, drained and rinsed
50g sultanas or dried cranberries
50g pistachio kernels, roughly chopped
2 spring onions, finely chopped
Small bunch mint, leaves picked and finely chopped
1½ tbsp olive oil

TO FINISH
½ tbsp harissa
100g Greek-style yogurt

1. Preheat oven to 120°C (100°C fan) mark ½ and line a large baking tray with baking parchment. Lay the salmon on the lined tray. Mix the harissa, oil, the finely grated zest of 1 lemon and the garlic to combine. Spread over the salmon. Thinly slice half the unzested lemon and lay it on the fish. Cook for 35min.

2. Meanwhile, make the quinoa salad. Bring the stock to the boil in a large pan over high heat. Add the quinoa and reduce to simmer. Cook for 20min, stirring occasionally, until tender. Drain well and empty into a serving bowl. Fork though the chickpeas, dried fruit, pistachios, spring onions and mint.

3. Whisk together 1½ tbsp oil and the juice of the zested lemon; season. Stir into the quinoa.

4. Squeeze the remaining ½ lemon over the cooked salmon and scatter with dill. Swirl the harissa into the yogurt and serve with the salmon and quinoa.

Hands-on time: 30min
Cooking time: about 35min
Serves 4

PER SERVING 712cals, 45g protein, 34g fat (7g saturates), 52g carbs (18g total sugars), 10g fibre

Cauliflower 'Meatballs' in Masala Sauce

The homemade masala curry paste makes double what you need in this recipe. The extra paste can be kept covered in the fridge for up to a week or frozen in an airtight container for up to a month.

FOR THE CAULIFLOWER BALLS
4 tbsp ground flaxseed
250g cauliflower florets
25g fresh/dried breadcrumbs
350g cooked brown rice
1 tsp garlic granules
1 tsp ground cumin
1 tsp paprika
1 tbsp vegetable oil

FOR THE MASALA SAUCE
1 onion, roughly chopped
3 garlic cloves, crushed
1½ tbsp garam masala
1–1½ tsp cayenne pepper, to taste
½ tbsp ground turmeric
½ tbsp ground cumin
¼ tsp ground cloves
Small handful coriander, leaves and stalks separated
Juice 1 lemon
½ tbsp vegetable oil
400g passata
400ml tin coconut milk

1. For the cauliflower balls, mix the ground flaxseed with 5 tbsp cold water and set aside for 15min. Next, start the masala sauce: in the small bowl of a food processor, whizz the onion, garlic, spices, coriander stalks (reserve the leaves to use in the cauliflower balls), lemon juice, 50ml water and some seasoning until smooth.

2. Heat the oil in a large frying pan over medium heat and fry half the masala paste (see intro) until fragrant, about 3–5min. Stir in the passata and 125ml water, turn up the heat and bubble for 5–10min. Add the coconut milk, then turn down the heat again and simmer for 20min until thickened. Set aside.

3. Meanwhile, make the cauliflower balls. Bring a medium pan of water to the boil and cook the cauliflower florets until tender (about 5min). Drain well, then empty into a food processor and leave to cool slightly.

4. To the processor, add the soaked flaxseed, breadcrumbs, cooked rice, most of the coriander leaves, the garlic granules, spices and seasoning. Pulse to a coarse paste. With damp hands, shape the mixture into 28 walnut-sized balls.

5. Heat the oil in a large, non-stick frying pan over medium heat and fry the cauliflower balls, in batches if needed, until crispy all over and piping hot, about 10min.

6. Reheat the sauce, if needed. Add the cauliflower balls and toss gently to coat. Garnish with the remaining coriander and serve with naan breads and a crisp green salad, if you like.

Hands-on time: 30min, plus soaking
Cooking time: about 45min
Serves 4

PER SERVING 486cals, 12g protein, 29g fat
(16g saturates), 41g carbs (11g total sugars), 9g fibre

Harissa Chicken Tagine Traybake

Although not a traditional tagine ingredient, rose harissa adds sweet, smoky heat and a great depth of flavour – for minimal effort!

2 tbsp olive oil
1 onion, finely sliced
8 skin-on chicken thighs
4 large tomatoes, roughly chopped
1 tsp ground ginger
½ tbsp ground cumin
5 tbsp rose harissa paste
75g pitted green olives
2 preserved lemons, deseeded and finely chopped
175g couscous
Pinch saffron
200ml hot chicken stock
Small handful mint leaves, roughly chopped

1. Preheat oven to 200°C (180°C fan) mark 6. In a large roasting tin, toss the oil, onion, chicken, tomatoes, ginger, cumin, harissa and plenty of seasoning. Arrange the chicken on top, skin-side up, and roast for 25min or until the chicken is starting to crisp up.

2. Carefully remove the tin from the oven. Transfer the chicken to a plate. Add the olives, preserved lemons and couscous to the tin and stir to combine. Mix the saffron into the stock and pour into the tin.

3. Return the chicken to the tin, skin-side up. Return to the oven for 10–15min or until the chicken is cooked through and the couscous has absorbed the liquid and is tender.

4. Fluff up the couscous using a fork, if needed. Scatter over the mint leaves and serve.

Hands-on time: 15min
Cooking time: about 40min
Serves 4

PER SERVING 508cals, 41g protein, 19g fat (4g saturates), 41g carbs (8g total sugars), 5g fibre

Hearty Veg Tartiflette

An indulgent main or luxurious side.
Sliced cooked ham or turkey would make
a tasty addition instead of the bacon.

1.2kg mixture of hearty vegetables, eg swede, celeriac,
 potato, sweet potato, butternut squash
250g bacon lardons
2 shallots, thinly sliced
1 garlic clove, crushed
100ml white wine
200ml double cream
300g Reblochon cheese, thinly sliced (see GH Tip)

1. Bring a large pan of salted water to the boil.
   Meanwhile, peel and finely slice the vegetables
   – a mandoline is ideal for this. Boil the veg, in
   batches if needed, until just tender, about 2min.
   Drain and set aside.

2. Heat a medium frying pan over a high heat and
   fry the lardons for 10min until golden and crispy.
   Transfer to a plate lined with kitchen paper.

3. Add the shallots to the pan, turn down the heat
   to low and fry for 8min until softened. Stir in
   the garlic and cook for 1min. Add the wine and
   simmer until most has evaporated. Stir in the
   bacon and some seasoning. Remove from the heat.

4. Preheat oven to 200°C (180°C fan) mark 6.
   Arrange a third of the vegetables in the base of
   a 2 litre ovenproof dish. Sprinkle over a third of
   the bacon mixture and some seasoning. Repeat
   the layers twice more. Pour over the cream, then
   top with a layer of Reblochon slices.

5. Cook in the oven for 30min, or until piping hot
   and the cheese is golden and bubbling. Serve
   with a crisp green salad, if you like.

★ GH TIP
Reblochon, a soft, full-flavoured, washed-rind cheese
from France, is traditionally used in tartiflette, but if
you can't find it you could use a mixture of Gruyère
and Taleggio

Hands-on time: 30min
Cooking time: about 1hr
Serves 4 as a main or 6 as a side

PER SERVING (if serving 4) 863cals, 29g protein, 63g fat
(35g saturates), 35g carbs (12g total sugars), 9g fibre

Malaysian Chicken Satay Skewers

You can make a delicious easy version of satay with peanut butter and red curry paste, but the real thing is so much more complex and exciting that it's well worth doing for special occasions. The sauce keeps well and only deepens in flavour, so all the work can be done a few days ahead.

FOR THE SKEWERS
2 lemongrass stalks, trimmed and roughly chopped
3 garlic cloves
1 tbsp demerara or granulated sugar
2 tbsp vegetable oil
1 tbsp ground turmeric
1 tbsp ground cumin
1½ tsp ground coriander
600g chicken thigh fillets

FOR THE SAUCE
100g unsalted roasted peanuts, plus extra
    chopped to sprinkle
1 lemongrass stalk, trimmed and roughly chopped
3cm piece fresh root ginger, peeled and roughly chopped
2 garlic cloves
1 red chilli, deseeded, plus extra, sliced, to serve
2 tsp vegetable oil
1 tbsp demerara or granulated sugar
1½ tbsp tamarind paste
1 tbsp kicap manis (sweet soy sauce)
100ml full-fat coconut milk

TO SERVE
Cooked sticky rice
Cucumber slices

YOU'LL ALSO NEED
12 metal or soaked wooden skewers

Hands-on time: 35min, plus (overnight) marinating
Cooking time: about 30min
Makes 12 skewers

PER SKEWER (without sauce) 183cals, 11g protein,
13g fat (4g saturates), 5g carbs (4g total sugars), 1g fibre

1. For the skewers, using a pestle and mortar, grind the lemongrass, garlic, sugar and a big pinch of salt to a fairly smooth paste. Alternatively, whizz in the small bowl of a food processor with the oil. Scrape into a large, non-metallic bowl and mix in the oil (if not whizzed), the ground spices and 1 tbsp water.

2. Trim and discard excess fat from the chicken and slice each fillet into 2cm-wide strips. Add to the marinade and mix well to coat the chicken thoroughly (see GH Tip). Cover and chill for 4hr or ideally overnight.

3. Meanwhile, make the sauce. Whizz the peanuts in a food processor until finely chopped (or do this by hand). Using a pestle and mortar or in the small bowl of the processor, grind the lemongrass, ginger, garlic and chilli until smooth. (If using a processor, you may need to add a splash of water.)

4. Heat the oil in a medium, heavy-based pan over medium heat. Add the lemongrass paste and fry for 2–3min, stirring, until fragrant. Add the peanuts, sugar, tamarind, kicap manis, coconut milk, 75ml water and a generous pinch of salt. Bring to a simmer, then reduce heat to low and simmer, stirring frequently, for 15min, until thickened and the oil from the coconut milk has separated out (it will look split). If you prefer a smoother finish, blend the sauce with a stick blender.

5. Preheat the grill to high. Thread the chicken onto the skewers and arrange on a large baking tray. Grill for 7–8min, turning halfway, or until cooked through. Sprinkle over some chopped peanuts and sliced chillies. Serve with the sauce in a bowl for dipping or spooning over, with rice and cucumber on the side.

★ GH TIP
Use disposable gloves when mixing the chicken and skewering, to prevent the turmeric from staining your hands.

★ GET AHEAD
Make the sauce up to 5 days ahead, then cool, cover and chill. Reheat gently to serve, adding a splash of water if needed to loosen.

Tomato, Egg and Lentil Curry

Make this as hot or mild as you like using a chilli powder to suit you.

2 tbsp ghee or vegetable oil
6 garlic cloves, crushed
5cm piece fresh root ginger, peeled and grated
1 tbsp cumin seeds
1 tbsp brown/black mustard seeds
2 tsp mild or hot chilli powder
Handful dried curry leaves
175g dried red lentils, rinsed
2 x 400g tins chopped tomatoes
6 medium eggs
2 tsp sugar
Handful coriander leaves
Natural yogurt, to serve

1. Heat the ghee or oil in a wide, high-sided pan (that has a lid) over low heat and fry the garlic, ginger, spices and curry leaves for 2min, stirring, until aromatic. Add the lentils, tomatoes and 200ml water, then turn up the heat and bring to the boil.

2. Turn down the heat to low, partially cover with a lid and simmer gently for 20min, stirring frequently, or until the lentils are tender and the liquid has reduced.

3. Meanwhile, cook the eggs in a medium pan of simmering water for 7min. Drain, then transfer to a bowl of cold water to stop the cooking. Leave to cool slightly before peeling.

4. Once the lentils are cooked, stir in the sugar and a generous pinch of salt. Halve the eggs and add to the pan, yolks up. Simmer for 2min to warm through, then sprinkle over the coriander. Serve with the yogurt drizzled over.

Hands-on time: 10min
Cooking time: about 25min
Serves 4

PER SERVING 365cals, 22g protein, 15g fat (6g saturates), 33g carbs (11g total sugars), 5g fibre

Quick Thai Drunken Noodles

This delicious recipe is a great example of how a simple blend of sauces can infuse noodles with complex flavours. The noodles don't actually contain alcohol, rather the name is believed to come from the fact that they're best served late at night with an ice cold beer.

300g flat, folded dried rice noodles
4 tbsp light soy sauce
2 tsp dark soy sauce
5 tbsp oyster sauce
2 tbsp fish sauce
1 tsp palm sugar
1 tbsp vegetable oil
1 onion, finely chopped
2 garlic cloves, finely chopped
1 tsp dried chilli flakes
400g pork loin medallions, cut into finger-sized strips
200g Swiss chard, stems cut into 3cm slices, leaves roughly chopped
Small handful Thai basil leaves
1 red chilli, sliced
Lime wedges, to serve

1. Put rice noodles in a large bowl and cover with water from a freshly boiled kettle. Leave to soak for 5min or until flexible. Drain and rinse under cold water.

2. Mix the soy, oyster and fish sauces and palm sugar in a bowl until the sugar dissolves. Set aside.

3. Heat the oil in a large, deep frying pan or wok over high heat. Add the onion and fry for 1min, then add the garlic and chilli flakes and fry for 30sec or until fragrant.

4. Add the pork loin and stir-fry for 3min or until cooked through and opaque. Add the chard stems and continue to fry for 1min until starting to soften, then add the chard leaves, drained noodles and sauce. Stir-fry for 3min until the sauce is absorbed and the noodles are cooked through.

5. Remove the pan or wok from heat and stir through the basil leaves. Serve garnished with chilli and with lime wedges on the side.

Hands-on time: 15min
Cooking time: about 15min
Serves 4

PER SERVING 506cals, 35g protein, 7g fat (2g saturates), 74g carbs (7g total sugars), 2g fibre

Spicy Thai Beef Salad

Thai basil has an aromatic, slight aniseed flavour that pairs well with mint and mango, but you could swap it for coriander if you prefer. Toasted ground rice is a traditional choice to add crunch and flavour.

FOR THE DRESSING
5 tbsp lime juice (about 3 limes)
2 tbsp fish sauce
2 tsp sugar
2–3 bird's eye chillies, deseeded and sliced
4 fresh kaffir lime leaves (2 doubles), deveined and finely shredded (see GH Tip)
1 echalion shallot, thinly sliced into rings

FOR THE SALAD
1½ tbsp Thai sticky rice or other short grain rice
2 tsp vegetable oil
2 x 200g beef fillet steaks, trimmed
½ cucumber, sliced into half moons
1 mango, peeled, de-stoned and shredded/julienned
100g mizuna or wild rocket
25g bunch mint, leaves picked
25g bunch Thai basil, leaves picked
40g salted peanuts, roughly chopped

⭐ GH TIP
If you can't find fresh kaffir lime leaves you can finely crumble in dried leaves or use the grated zest of 1 lime. It won't have quite the same aroma, but will be close.

1. For the dressing, in a small bowl, mix the lime juice, fish sauce and sugar until the sugar dissolves. Stir in the chillies, shredded lime leaves and shallot rings and set aside.

2. For the salad, toast the rice in a frying pan over medium-high heat, shaking frequently, until it is deep golden-brown (about 5–10min). Tip on to a plate, leave to cool completely, then grind to a coarse powder with a pinch of salt using a pestle and mortar.

3. Return the pan to high heat and add the oil. Pat the steaks dry using kitchen paper and fry for 4–6min, turning halfway, until well browned on the outside but still rare in the middle. Remove to a plate and leave to rest for 5min while you assemble the rest of the salad.

4. In a large bowl, toss half the dressing, the cucumber, mango, salad leaves, herbs and most of the peanuts. Tip on to a large platter (or divide among 4 plates). Thinly slice the steaks and arrange on top. Spoon over the remaining dressing and scatter over the remaining peanuts and the ground toasted rice. Serve.

Hands-on time: 30min, plus cooling
Cooking time: about 15min
Serves 4

PER SERVING 297cals, 27g protein, 13g fat
(4g saturates), 15g carbs (9g total sugars), 3g fibre

Pissaladière

Anchovies give a salty punch to this pizza-style tart, balanced beautifully by the sweetness of the meltingly soft onions and crisp pastry.

2 tbsp olive oil
1kg onions, finely sliced
1 tbsp thyme leaves, roughly chopped
320g sheet ready-rolled puff pastry
95–100g jar anchovy fillets in oil, drained
About 15 pitted black olives
6–8 cherry tomatoes, halved

1. Heat the oil in a large pan (that has a lid) over low heat. Cook the onions, covered and stirring occasionally, until completely tender, about 15min. Remove the lid, turn up the heat to medium and cook for 10min, stirring frequently to prevent catching, until pale golden.

2. Remove from the heat and stir in the thyme and some freshly ground black pepper. Set aside to cool completely.

3. Preheat oven to 200°C (180°C fan) mark 6. Unroll the pastry on to a large baking sheet (leaving it on its baking parchment). Score a border about 1.5cm in from the edge (making sure not to cut all the way through the pastry). Prick inside the border all over with a fork.

4. Spread the onions inside the border in an even layer. Use the anchovy fillets to make a lattice pattern on top of the onions, halving any fillets lengthways if needed to complete the lattice. Place alternating olives and cherry tomatoes (cut-side up) in the lattice diamonds.

5. Cook for 25min or until golden. Serve with a crisp, green salad, if you like.

Hands-on time: 25min, plus cooling
Cooking time: about 50min
Serves 4

PER SERVING 520cals, 13g protein, 30g fat (11g saturates), 46g carbs (16g total sugars), 8g fibre

'Nduja and Mussel Spaghetti

A Calabrian speciality, 'nduja is a spreadable pork salami with chilli pepper.

500g mussels
1 tbsp olive oil
2 garlic cloves, crushed
200g cherry tomatoes, halved
40g 'nduja (see GH Tip)
300g spaghetti
Small handful parsley, roughly chopped

1. Put the mussels into a colander and rinse under cold running water. Scrape off any barnacles with a cutlery knife and pull off and discard any stringy beards. Throw away any mussels that don't close when tapped firmly (it's okay if they open again).

2. Heat the oil in a large deep pan (that has a lid) over low heat. Add the garlic and cook for 1min until fragrant. Stir in the tomatoes and cook for 8min, crushing with the back of the spoon to help break them down. Stir in the 'nduja and cook for 2min, until melted and combined.

3. Cook the pasta in a large pan of salted boiling water according to the pack instructions. Drain, reserving 250ml of the cooking water.

4. Add 100ml of the reserved pasta water to the tomato sauce. Bring to a simmer, stir in the mussels, cover with a lid and cook for 3–4min, shaking the pan occasionally, or until the mussel shells are fully open. Discard any shellfish that remain closed.

5. Add the drained pasta and the remaining pasta water to the seafood pan and toss to combine Mix in the parsley and season to taste. Serve.

★ GH TIP
You can buy 'nduja in either a block or as a paste in a jar. Both versions are fine to use here.

Hands-on time: 30min
Cooking time: about 20min
Serves 4

PER SERVING 395cals, 18g protein, 10g fat (3g saturates), 56g carbs (3g total sugars), 4g fibre

Za'atar Chicken on Chickpeas

Za'atar is a Middle Eastern herb and spice mix that typically includes thyme, oregano, sumac and sesame seeds. Both harissa and za'atar are usually gluten free, but do check the labels to be sure.

3 tbsp olive oil
1 tsp harissa
Finely grated zest and juice 2 lemons, keep separate, plus 4 lemon slices
3 tbsp za'atar
4 large garlic cloves, crushed
4 skin-on chicken breasts
3 x 400g tins chickpeas
200g spinach
100g pomegranate seeds
Small bunch fresh parsley, roughly chopped

1. Preheat oven to 200°C (180°C fan) mark 6. In a large bowl, mix the olive oil, harissa, half the lemon juice, 2 tbsp za'atar, three-quarters of the crushed garlic and some seasoning. Add the chicken and turn to coat. Put the chicken, skin-side up, and the marinade into a roasting tin and top each breast with a lemon slice. Roast for 25min or until cooked through.

2. Meanwhile, drain 1 chickpea tin. Add to a large pan with the other 2 tins of chickpeas and their water, the lemon zest, remaining lemon juice, za'atar and garlic, and the spinach. Season, bring to the boil, then reduce to a simmer for 5min. Stir in the pomegranate seeds and adjust the seasoning to taste.

3. Divide the chickpea mixture among 4 bowls and serve topped with a chicken breast and any roasting juices, and a scattering of parsley.

Hands-on time: 15min
Cooking time: about 25min
Serves 4

PER SERVING 608cals, 47g protein, 28g fat (6g saturates), 35g carbs (6g total sugars), 13g fibre

Thakkali Meen Kari Spicy Tomato Fish Curry

This fish stew is commonly eaten with plain rice. Ask your fishmonger for bone-in steaks or use thick, skinless fillets and slightly lower the cooking time.

1 tbsp mild chilli powder
1 tbsp ground coriander
1 tsp ground turmeric
3 tbsp vegetable oil
2 tsp black mustard seeds
1 small onion, finely sliced
8–10 fresh or dried curry leaves
4 garlic cloves, chopped
2.5cm piece fresh root ginger, peeled and chopped
4 tomatoes, chopped
1 tsp tomato purée
700g chunky bone-in sea bass or sea bream steaks, skinned (see GH Tip)
Juice 1 lime
Pinch of sugar

1. In a small bowl, mix the dried spices and 4 tbsp water (to ensure the spices don't burn while cooking) to make a paste, then set aside.

2. Heat the oil in a large, heavy-based pan (with a lid) over medium heat. Add the mustard seeds and, once they crackle, add the onion. Fry for 6–7min or until softening. Add the curry leaves, garlic and ginger, fry for 1min; stir in the tomatoes and tomato purée. Fry for 6min, stirring frequently, or until the tomatoes have softened.

3. Add the spice paste, fry for 1min, then add 500ml water. Season. Bring to the boil, then turn down heat to low. Add the fish, cover and simmer for 6min or until the fish is nearly cooked, swirling rather than stirring so the fish stays intact.

4. Remove the pan from the heat and gently swirl through the lime juice and sugar. Re-cover and leave to rest for a few minutes, until the fish is cooked through. Serve with plain rice or appams.

Hands-on time: 15min, plus resting
Cooking time: about 25min
Serves 4

PER SERVING 392cals, 36g protein, 26g fat (4g saturates), 4g carbs (1g total sugars), 1g fibre

Teriyaki Tofu Traybake

Store-bought teriyaki sauce is the secret to this fuss-free dinner. Using extra-firm tofu is important here to stop it from breaking apart.

3 tbsp toasted sesame oil
2 x 280g packs extra firm tofu
4 tbsp cornflour
300g Tenderstem broccoli, roughly chopped
4 spring onions, finely sliced
1 red chilli, deseeded and finely sliced
125g vegan teriyaki sauce
2 x 250g pouches microwave basmati rice
1 tbsp black sesame seeds

1. Preheat oven to 200°C (180°C fan) mark 6. Pour the oil into a large roasting tin and heat in the oven for 10min.

2. Pat the tofu dry with kitchen paper and cut each block into 3 thick slices. Pat dry again with kitchen paper. Next cut each slice diagonally into 2 triangles.

3. Measure the cornflour on to a lipped plate or into a shallow bowl and mix in plenty of seasoning. Working a couple of tofu triangles at a time, toss in the seasoned cornflour to coat, gently shaking off any excess.

4. Carefully remove the tin from the oven. Add the tofu and turn to coat in the oil. Return to the oven for 10min or until starting to crisp up.

5. Remove the tin from the oven and add the broccoli, most of the spring onions and the chilli. In a small jug, mix the teriyaki sauce with 3 tbsp just-boiled water and pour into the tin. Toss gently to combine. Return to the oven for 15min or until the broccoli is tender.

6. Remove the tin from the oven and push the tofu mixture to one side so about a third of the tin is empty. Add the rice to the empty part of the tin and break up any clumps with a fork. Drizzle 2 tbsp water over the rice.

7. Return to the oven for 5-10min or until the rice is piping hot. Scatter over the remaining spring onions and the sesame seeds and serve.

Hands-on time: 30min
Cooking time: about 50min
Serves 4

PER SERVING 604cals, 26g protein, 22g fat (3g saturates), 72g carbs (19g total sugars), 5g fibre

Speedy
Midweek
Suppers

Tandoori Salmon Kebabs with Tomato Coconut Salad

The fresh, zingy flavours of this tomato coconut salad pair wonderfully with these simple but tasty kebabs.

75g coconut yogurt, plus extra to serve (optional)
4 tbsp tandoori paste
4 skinless salmon fillets, cut into 2.5cm chunks
1 red onion, cut into large chunks
75g fresh coconut
300g cherry tomatoes, quartered
Handful coriander leaves
1 lime, plus wedges to serve
4 pitta breads, toasted

YOU'LL ALSO NEED
4 skewers, soaked in cold water for 15min if wooden or bamboo

1. Preheat grill to high. In a large bowl, mix the yogurt and tandoori paste. Add the salmon and stir to coat.

2. Thread the salmon and onion on to 4 skewers and arrange on a sturdy baking sheet. Grill for 8–10min, turning carefully halfway through, until the salmon is cooked.

3. Meanwhile, make the salad. Finely grate the coconut flesh, discarding the brown skin. Mix gently in a bowl with the tomatoes, coriander leaves and the finely grated zest and the juice of the lime, to taste.

4. Serve the skewers with the toasted pitta and salad, with lime wedges and extra yogurt on the side, if you like.

Hands-on time: 20min
Cooking time: about 10min
Serves 4

PER SERVING 504cals, 31g protein, 23g fat (11g saturates), 41g carbs (9g total sugars), 6g fibre

King Prawn and Pineapple Fried Rice

Swap the prawns for 300g cooked chicken, if you prefer.

1 tbsp vegetable oil
1 red onion, finely sliced
200g mangetout, sliced lengthways
2 peppers, deseeded and finely sliced (we used red and orange)
½–1 tsp dried chilli flakes
2 x 250g pouches microwave rice
300g cooked king prawns
227g can pineapple in juice, drained and cut into chunks
3 tbsp light soy sauce
½ tsp fish sauce
Large handful coriander leaves, to garnish
Lime wedges, to serve

1. Heat the oil in a large frying pan or wok over medium heat and fry the onion for 8min until softened. Add the mangetout and peppers, and fry for another 6min, until nearly cooked through.

2. Stir in the chilli flakes (to taste), the rice, prawns, pineapple chunks, soy sauce and fish sauce, then heat through thoroughly. Garnish with coriander and serve with lime wedges.

DF

Hands-on time: 10min
Cooking time: about 20min
Serves 4

PER SERVING 318cals, 24g protein, 2g fat (0g saturates), 50g carbs (13g total sugars), 5g fibre

Tofu con Molé

This is a lovely simplified version of a Mexican dish that is similar in flavour to a chilli con carne.

250g basmati rice
1 tbsp sunflower oil
450g firm tofu, cut into 2cm pieces
1 onion, finely chopped
¾–1 tbsp ancho or chipotle chilli paste, to taste
1 tsp ground cumin
½ tsp ground cinnamon
400g tin chopped tomatoes
2 x 400g tins kidney beans, drained and rinsed
25g dark chocolate (at least 70% cocoa solids), chopped

1. Cook the basmati rice according to the pack instructions. Drain.

2. Meanwhile, heat the oil in a large, deep frying pan over medium heat and fry the tofu until golden and crisp all over (about 15min). Transfer to a plate. Turn down the heat under the pan, then add the onion and cook for 5min until softened.

3. Stir in the chilli paste and spices, cook for 1min, then add the tomatoes and kidney beans. Bring to the boil, then simmer for 5min to thicken. Return the tofu to the pan, add the dark chocolate and warm through. Check the seasoning and serve with rice and a green salad, if you like.

★ GH TIP
If you don't like tofu, you could use jackfruit instead.

Hands-on time: 15min
Cooking time: about 30min
Serves 4

PER SERVING 572cals, 29g protein, 12g fat (3g saturates), 80g carbs (12g total sugars), 14g fibre

Speedy Coq au Vin

This French-style chicken is rich and delicious with a red wine kick.

1 tbsp plain flour
3 chicken breasts, cut into bite-sized pieces
2 tbsp sunflower oil
1 onion, finely sliced
125g smoked streaky bacon, roughly chopped
125g small button mushrooms, left whole
1 garlic clove, crushed
1 tbsp brandy
150ml each red wine and hot chicken stock
1 bay leaf
1 tbsp curly parsley, freshly chopped

1. Put the flour in a plastic bag with salt and freshly ground black pepper. Shake to combine, then add the chicken and toss well. Heat half the oil in a large pan and fry the coated chicken over a high heat until browned. Set aside.

2. In the same pan, heat the remaining oil and gently fry the onion and bacon for 5min. Add the mushrooms and cook for 3–4min until lightly golden. Add the garlic and cook for 1min.

3. Return the chicken to the pan and sprinkle over the brandy. Carefully light with a match, then let the flames die down. Pour in the wine, simmer for 2min, then add the stock and bay leaf. Simmer for 10–15min until the chicken is cooked through and the sauce is lightly syrupy. Serve with freshly cooked pasta, such as pappardelle, or boiled rice, with a sprinkling of parsley on top.

Hands-on time: 15min
Cooking time: about 30min
Serves 4

PER SERVING (without pasta) 329cals, 35g protein, 14g fat (4g saturates), 6g carbs (3g total sugars), 1g fibre

Fragrant Chicken and Rice Soup

This simple soup has so much flavour. Add lime juice before serving for extra zing.

100g Thai green curry paste
400ml tin coconut milk
4 small skinless chicken breasts, about 500g
150g basmati rice, rinsed
100g coriander, leaves picked and very roughly chopped

1. Heat a large pan over medium heat. Add the curry paste and fry for 1min until fragrant. Add the coconut milk, chicken, rice, some seasoning and 1 litre water.

2. Bring to the boil, then simmer gently for 15min or until chicken is cooked through and rice is tender. Remove the chicken to a board and shred with 2 forks. Return to the pan and stir through the coriander. Check the seasoning. Divide among 4 bowls and serve.

Hands-on time: 10min
Cooking time: about 20min
Serves 4

PER SERVING 469cals, 33g protein, 21g fat (16g saturates), 35g carbs (3g total sugars), 3g fibre

Quick Chicken Korma

Adding water to the chicken as it cooks helps to keep the meat tender.

2 tbsp sunflower oil
1 large onion, finely sliced
4 tbsp korma paste
4 skinless chicken breasts, cut into bite-sized pieces
160ml tin coconut cream
40g ground almonds
75g coconut flakes or desiccated coconut, toasted
Steamed rice, lime wedges and coriander sprigs, to serve

1. In a large frying pan, heat the oil and fry the onion over a medium heat for 10min until beginning to soften. Add the korma paste to the pan, cooking for 3min until fragrant and adding 4 tbsp of water to protect the spices from burning. Add the chicken pieces with 150ml water and simmer gently for 10–15min until the chicken is cooked through.

2. Pour the coconut cream into the curry and cook for 2min. Remove from heat and stir through the ground almonds. Scatter the chicken korma with coconut flakes and serve with rice, lime wedges and coriander sprigs, if you like.

Hands-on time: 10min
Cooking time: about 30min
Serves 4

PER SERVING 564cals, 37g protein, 42g fat (23g saturates), 8g carbs (6g total sugars), 4g fibre

Sea Bass with Chorizo and Potatoes

This sea bass recipe is complemented with slices of tasty chorizo and golden potatoes.

700g new potatoes, thickly sliced
1 tbsp olive oil
4 x 125g sea bass fillets, skin on
150g chorizo, sliced
150ml dry white wine
Zest 1 lemon plus 1 lemon, quartered, to serve
1 tbsp flat-leaf parsley, chopped

1. Cook the potatoes in a pan of lightly salted boiling water for 8–10min until tender. Drain in a colander and leave to steam dry for 2min.

2. Heat the oil in a large pan over medium heat. Fry the fish skin-side down for 3min until golden, then turn and cook for 30sec. Transfer to a warm plate, cover loosely with foil and keep warm.

3. Fry the chorizo in the pan for 2min until golden. Remove with a slotted spoon. Add the potatoes and fry over a high heat, turning often, for 3min until golden. Return the chorizo to the pan with the wine and lemon zest. Bubble until slightly syrupy. Divide the potatoes and chorizo among 4 plates, top with the fish and drizzle with juices. Garnish with parsley and serve with a lemon quarter to squeeze over.

Hands-on time: 15min
Cooking time: about 20min
Serves 4

PER SERVING 515cals, 37g protein, 24g fat (7g saturates), 3g carbs (3g total sugars), 3g fibre

Thai-style Mussels

Serve up a steaming plate of fragrant mussels with a Southeast Asian flavour.

2kg fresh mussels
2 tbsp olive oil
3 shallots, finely chopped
1 stalk lemongrass, finely chopped
1 red chilli, sliced into rings
150ml dry white wine
165ml tin coconut milk
20g pack fresh coriander, roughly chopped
1 lime, quartered, to serve

1. Scrub the mussels in cold water, removing any beards or barnacles. Discard any with damaged shells or that stay open when lightly tapped.

2. Heat the oil in a large pan deep enough to hold the mussels. Add the shallots, lemongrass and chilli and fry gently for 3min.

3. Add the white wine to the pan and simmer for 1min, then add the coconut milk. Simmer for a further 5min, then add the mussels. Cover the pan tightly with a lid and cook for 5min until the mussels are opened. Discard any that remain closed.

4. Stir in the coriander and divide the mussels among 4 warmed bowls. Pour over the sauce and serve with a quarter of lime for squeezing over and crusty bread to mop up the juices.

Hands-on time: 20min
Cooking time: about 15min
Serves 4

PER SERVING 476cals, 61g protein, 22g fat (9g saturates), 2g carbs (2g total sugars), 1g fibre

Speedy Chilli Soup

If you can't find kidney beans in chilli sauce or tomatoes with added chilli, use unflavoured ones and add 1–2 deseeded and finely chopped red chillies instead. Serve with rice, if you prefer.

---

1 tbsp oil
500g pack beef mince (we used 5% fat)
2 x 400g tins (or 2 x 390g cartons) chopped tomatoes with chilli
400g tin kidney beans in chilli sauce
4 tbsp soured cream
Nachos, to serve (optional)

1. Heat the oil in a large pan over medium-high heat and fry the mince until browned.

2. Add the tomatoes, plenty of seasoning and 200ml water. Bring to the boil, then turn down the heat and simmer for 15min to tenderise the beef.

3. Stir through the contents of the kidney bean tin (don't drain), heat through and check seasoning.

4. Serve in bowls topped with a dollop of soured cream and nachos on the side, if you like.

Hands-on time: 10min
Cooking time: about 25min
Serves 4

PER SERVING 383cals, 34g protein, 18g fat (8g saturates), 17g carbs (8g total sugars), 7g fibre

Pork Stroganoff

We've used pork fillet, which is quick to cook, with cider for a variation on the classic beef recipe.

2 tbsp sunflower oil
500g pork fillet, sinew removed, cut into 1cm slices
25g unsalted butter
1 onion, sliced
2 garlic cloves, crushed
1 tsp paprika
300g button mushrooms, sliced
1 green pepper, sliced
150ml dry cider
300ml sour cream
2 tbsp Dijon mustard
Small bunch parsley, finely chopped
Tagliatelle, to serve (optional)

1. Heat 1 tbsp oil in a large frying pan over a high heat. Fry the pork for 2min each side, in batches if necessary, draining any liquid so the meat browns more readily. Remove from the pan. Add the butter to the pan and gently fry the onion until soft, about 8min. Add the garlic and paprika to the pan and continue to cook for 1min, then remove from the pan.

2. Heat the remaining 1 tbsp oil and fry the mushroom slices for 5min before adding the pepper and frying for about 2min until cooked through. Put the pork, onions and garlic back into the pan.

3. Pour in the cider and reduce for 3min before stirring through the sour cream. Bubble everything for 5min until the sauce is reduced, and season well. Stir though the mustard and chopped parsley. Serve with fresh tagliatelle.

Hands-on time: 15min
Cooking time: about 25min
Serves 4

PER SERVING 496cals, 36g protein, 35g fat
(16g saturates), 6g carbs (5g total sugars), 3g fibre

Lamb and Oregano Meatball Traybake

If you can find it, use finely chopped
fresh oregano rather than dried. You
can also use beef mince instead of lamb,
if you prefer.

FOR THE SAUCE
1 red onion, finely chopped
150g jarred red peppers, drained and roughly chopped
2 x 400g tins chopped tomatoes
½ tbsp dried oregano
400g tin haricot beans, drained and rinsed
150g feta, crumbled

FOR THE MEATBALLS
500g lamb mince
75g fresh white breadcrumbs
1 medium egg, beaten
1 tsp dried oregano
½ tbsp olive oil

1. Preheat oven to 220°C (200°C fan) mark 7.
   In a large roasting tin or ovenproof serving dish,
   mix all the sauce ingredients, apart from the
   feta, with plenty of seasoning.

2. For the meatballs, in a medium bowl, mix all
   the ingredients, except for the oil, with plenty
   of seasoning. Shape into 20 small balls and
   drop into the sauce, pushing them down a little.
   Brush the tops of the meatballs with the oil.

3. Cook for 15min, then sprinkle over the feta and
   return to the oven for 5–10min, or until the feta
   is lightly golden and the meatballs are cooked
   through. Serve with a green salad and crusty
   bread, if you like.

★ GH TIP
For an even speedier supper, use shop-bought
meatballs and drop them into the sauce, then
brush with the oil before cooking.

Hands-on time: 10min
Cooking time: about 25min
Serves 4

PER SERVING 570cals, 41g protein, 28g fat
(14g saturates), 35g carbs (12g total sugars), 7g fibre

Chicken Yakisoba

Yakisoba is a popular dish made both at home and on the streets in Japan. You could make this dish with fresh egg noodles, if you prefer. You can also use a mix of pork, prawns and squid for an extra-savoury combination.

250g dried ramen noodles
1 tbsp vegetable oil
500g skinless chicken breasts, cut into finger-sized strips
1 onion, finely sliced
300g green cabbage, cored and thickly shredded
4 tbsp Worcestershire sauce
1 tbsp ketchup
1 tbsp oyster sauce
2 tsp light soy sauce
1 tsp mirin
2 tsp caster sugar
1 large carrot, peeled and julienned
Sushi ginger, shredded nori and sesame seeds,
    to garnish (optional)

1. Bring a large pan of water to the boil. Add the noodles and cook according to pack instructions. Drain and rinse under cold water to cool. Set aside.

2. Heat ½ tbsp oil in a wok or large frying pan over high heat. Add the chicken and fry, stirring occasionally, for 4–5min, until pale golden and opaque. Remove to a plate, cover and keep warm.

3. Heat the remaining ½ tbsp oil in the wok or pan. Stir-fry the onion and cabbage for 3min. Meanwhile, stir the Worcestershire sauce, ketchup, oyster sauce, soy, mirin and sugar together in a small bowl.

4. Return the chicken to the wok or pan along with the carrot, noodles and sauce mixture. Stir-fry for 1–2min, until the sauce is absorbed by the noodles. Garnish with sushi ginger, nori and sesame seeds, if using. Serve.

DF

Hands-on time: 20min
Cooking time: about 15min
Serves 4

PER SERVING (without sushi ginger, nori and sesame seeds) 447cals, 32g protein, 5g fat (1g saturates), 65g carbs (16g total sugars), 6g fibre

Greek Salad Feta Traybake

Bring a taste of holiday sunshine to your kitchen with this traybake inspired by the flavours of a Greek salad. Unlike most cheeses, feta doesn't go gooey when baked, instead it becomes tender, yielding and delicately caramelised at the edges.

1 small red onion, cut into 12 wedges
200g mixed colour cherry tomatoes, larger ones halved
150g mixed colour baby peppers, halved and deseeded
1 large bread roll, torn into chunks (we used ciabatta)
1 garlic clove, crushed
Large handful basil leaves, torn, plus extra to garnish
3 tbsp extra virgin olive oil, plus extra to drizzle
200g block sheep's milk feta
1½ tbsp balsamic vinegar
1 tbsp runny honey
Handful Kalamata olives, pitted

1. Preheat oven to 200°C (180°C fan) mark 6. Put the onion, tomatoes, peppers and bread into a medium ovenproof dish or shallow roasting tin. Add the crushed garlic, basil and some seasoning, then drizzle with the olive oil and toss gently to coat.

2. Push everything to the edges of the dish or tin and put the feta in the middle. Drizzle with the balsamic vinegar and honey and sprinkle over the olives.

3. Cook in the oven for 20min, until the tomatoes and peppers are tender and the feta has softened slightly to the touch. Finish with more basil leaves and an extra drizzle of olive oil and serve.

Hands-on time: 10min
Cooking time: about 20min
Serves 2

PER SERVING 633cals, 22g protein, 42g fat (17g saturates), 40g carbs (22g total sugars), 6g fibre

Loaded Chilli Potatoes

A dash of cocoa powder adds a richness and depth of flavour to the chilli mixture. Make it veggie by using vegetarian mince and adding Henderson's Relish instead of Worcestershire sauce.

4 large baking potatoes
1 tbsp olive oil
1 onion, finely chopped
1 garlic clove, crushed
½ tbsp chilli powder
400g mince (we used beef)
2 x 400g tins chopped tomatoes
400g tin kidney beans, drained and rinsed
1 tbsp tomato purée
½ tsp cocoa powder
Worcestershire sauce, to taste
Large handful coriander, chopped
Soured cream or Greek yogurt, to serve
Grated Cheddar, to serve

1. Preheat oven to 200°C (180°C fan) mark 6. Pierce the potatoes all over with a fork and put on a heatproof plate. Microwave on high for 15min, or until beginning to soften. Transfer to the oven to crisp up for 10min.

2. Meanwhile, heat the oil in a large pan over medium heat and fry the onion until softened (about 8min). Stir in the garlic, chilli powder and mince and brown all over (about 5min). Stir through the tomatoes, kidney beans, tomato purée, cocoa powder and Worcestershire sauce. Bring to the boil, then simmer for 10min to reduce slightly. Stir in most of the coriander and season to taste.

3. To serve, cut a cross into each potato. Top with a quarter of the chilli mixture, the soured cream or yogurt, cheese and the remaining coriander.

Hands-on time: 10min
Cooking time: about 25min
Serves 4

PER SERVING 537cals, 31g protein, 20g fat (8g saturates), 53g carbs (11g total sugars), 11g fibre

Prawn and Chorizo Pasta

This Spanish-influenced pasta recipe is packed full of flavour and quick and easy to make. If you're including the sherry, use a dry one, such as Amontillado, Oloroso or Manzanilla.

290g roasted red peppers (from a jar), drained
1 tbsp tomato purée
½ tsp caster sugar
350g conchiglie pasta
150g chorizo ring, sliced
150g raw king prawns
1 garlic clove, finely chopped
¼ tsp chilli flakes
2 tbsp sherry (optional)
200g spinach
Small handful parsley, chopped

1. Slice about a third of the drained roasted peppers into short strips. Set aside. Add the remaining peppers to a food processor and whizz with tomato purée, sugar and some seasoning until smooth. Set aside.

2. Bring a large pan of salted water to the boil and cook the pasta according to pack instructions until al dente. Drain well, reserving a cupful of the cooking water.

3. Meanwhile, heat a large, deep frying pan over medium heat. Add the sliced chorizo and fry until golden and some of the oil has been released into the pan (about 5min). Add the prawns, garlic and chilli, and cook until the prawns are just pink. Add the sherry, if using, and bubble for 30sec, then stir in the reserved sliced peppers and the blended pepper mixture. Bring to a simmer.

4. Add the spinach and drained pasta to the frying pan. Stir, then cook until the spinach has wilted, adding a splash of the reserved cooking water if the pan is looking a little dry. Check the seasoning, then sprinkle over chopped parsley and serve.

Hands-on time: 20min
Cooking time: about 15min
Serves 4

PER SERVING 519cals, 27g protein, 13g fat (4g saturates), 68g carbs (6g total sugars), 6g fibre

Mozzarella Stuffed Meatballs

Instead of couscous, you could serve these meatballs in pitta bread with chopped lettuce, tomatoes and sliced onions for a tasty kebab-style dinner.

450g mince (we used beef mince)
125g ball mozzarella, finely chopped
50g sun-dried tomatoes in oil, drained and finely chopped
50g fresh breadcrumbs
1 medium egg
1 tbsp chopped basil leaves, plus extra to garnish
1 tbsp vegetable oil
5 tbsp natural yogurt
4 tbsp houmous

1. Preheat oven to 200°C (180°C fan) mark 6. In a large mixing bowl, mix together the mince, mozzarella, sun-dried tomatoes, breadcrumbs, egg, chopped basil and some seasoning. Roll the mixture into 20 balls, each about the size of a walnut.

2. Heat the oil in a large ovenproof frying pan over medium heat and fry the meatballs until golden all over. Transfer to the oven for 10–15min to cook through.

3. In a bowl, stir the yogurt and houmous together. Drizzle over the cooked meatballs, garnish with extra basil and serve with couscous and seasonal veg, if you like.

Hands-on time: 15min
Cooking time: about 20min
Serves 4

PER SERVING 493cals, 35g protein, 31g fat (13g saturates), 17g carbs (5g total sugars), 3g fibre

Sausage Stew

We used a pouch of ready-to-eat Puy lentils, but you could use a 400g tin cooked brown lentils instead, if you like.

---

8 sausages (we used Toulouse)
2 tbsp oil
2 red onions, sliced
2 garlic cloves, chopped
3 thyme sprigs, leaves picked
2 x 250g packs ready-to-eat Puy lentils
300ml chicken stock
3 tbsp balsamic vinegar
150g kale, torn

1. In a large frying pan over high heat, brown the sausages in 1 tbsp oil for 3min. Remove to a plate.

2. Add the remaining 1 tbsp oil to the pan with the onions and fry, covered, over low heat for 10min, until softened and lightly browned. Add the garlic and thyme leaves, stirring for 1min.

3. Return the sausages to the pan, add the lentils, stock and balsamic vinegar. Cover and simmer for 10min. Stir in the kale to wilt for 1min; serve.

Hands-on time: 5min
Cooking time: about 25min
Serves 4

PER SERVING 632cals, 44g protein, 32g fat (10g saturates), 41g carbs (10g total sugars), 4g fibre

Pozole

This Mexican soup or stew is traditionally made with hominy (corn kernels that have been soaked in a mineral lime solution) but we've used chickpeas instead.

---

1 tbsp vegetable oil
2 garlic cloves, crushed
2 tsp ground cumin
1½ tbsp fresh oregano, chopped (or use 1 tsp dried)
1–2 green chillies, to taste, deseeded and finely chopped
1 litre strong vegetable stock
2 plum tomatoes, chopped
2 x 400g tins chickpeas, drained and rinsed
About 300g vegetarian or vegan chicken-style pieces

TO SERVE
½ iceberg lettuce, shredded
Lime wedges
6 radishes, finely sliced
½ red onion, finely sliced
1 avocado, stoned and sliced
Large handful coriander, roughly chopped

1. Heat the oil in a large, deep frying pan over medium-high heat. Stir in the garlic, cumin, oregano and chillies and fry for 1min.

2. Pour in the stock and bring to the boil. Add the tomatoes and chickpeas; simmer for 5min until the tomatoes break down. Add the chicken-style pieces and heat through. Check the seasoning.

3. Ladle into 4 bowls, bring to the table with the garnishes and let people tuck in.

Hands-on time: 20min
Cooking time: about 10min
Serves 4

PER SERVING 472cals, 32g protein, 22g fat (3g saturates), 29g carbs (7g total sugars), 15g fibre

'Chicken' Noodle Soup

This restorative bowl of goodness couldn't be simpler to prepare, and can easily be made vegan – just check that your chicken-style strips and stock are suitable.

---

1 tbsp olive oil
2 carrots, cut into fine matchsticks
2 litres strong vegetable stock
150g rice vermicelli noodles
Small bunch spring onions, finely sliced
2 x 195g tins sweetcorn, drained
150g frozen peas
300g vegetarian or vegan chicken-style strips, frozen or chilled
Small bunch parsley, chopped

1. Heat the oil in a large pan and fry the carrots for a few minutes until beginning to soften. Add the stock and bring up to the boil.

2. Add the noodles, and simmer just until tender (about 4min), then stir in the spring onions, sweetcorn, peas and chicken-stye strips. Reheat to piping hot and check the seasoning.

3. Divide among 4 bowls, garnish with parsley and serve.

Hands-on time: 15min
Cooking time: about 10min
Serves 4

PER SERVING 500cals, 31g protein, 14g fat (2g saturates), 55g carbs (18g total sugars), 14g fibre

Frying Pan Pizza alla Putanesca

The base and toppings can be easily
doubled to make two pizzas. Make sure
your pan and grill are really hot for that
tasty pizzeria experience.

175g self-raising flour, plus extra to dust
1 tbsp olive oil
3 tbsp tomato purée
50g passata
½ tsp dried chilli flakes
1 garlic clove, crushed
3 anchovy fillets in oil, drained
1 tsp capers, drained
2 tbsp pitted black olives
75g mozzarella, torn

1. Preheat grill to high. In a medium bowl, mix the
   flour, oil, a pinch of fine salt and 100ml water to
   make a dough, adding a little water if the mixture
   looks dry. Tip on to a lightly floured surface and
   knead for 1min until smooth and pliable. Roll into
   a ball and leave to rest until needed.

2. For the sauce, mix the tomato purée, passata,
   chilli, garlic and a little seasoning. Set aside.

3. Heat a large (about 23cm) ovenproof frying pan
   over high hob heat until very hot. On a lightly
   floured work surface, roll out the dough to a
   rough 25cm circle (you want the dough to go
   up the sides of the pan a little). Carefully lift the
   dough circle into the frying pan and spread over
   the sauce, leaving a rough 1cm border. Sprinkle
   over the anchovies, capers, olives and mozzarella.
   Cook for 2min until base is starting to brown.

4. Continue cooking under the grill for about
   3–4min until the crust is golden and the cheese
   is bubbling. Transfer to a board and serve.

Hands-on time: 15min
Cooking time: about 10min
Makes 1 pizza, to serve 2

PER SERVING 516cals, 18g protein, 17g fat
(7g saturates), 70g carbs (4g total sugars), 6g fibre

Garlic and Brown Butter Prawn Pappardelle

A simple and delicious seafood supper. Chicken stock adds richness to the sauce, but you can use vegetable stock, or swap it for white or rosé wine, if you prefer.

300g pappardelle pasta
150g unsalted butter, chopped
300g raw peeled king prawns, butterflied and deveined (see GH Tip)
2 garlic cloves, finely chopped
100ml chicken stock
Juice 1 lemon
Handful dill, finely chopped
Handful flat-leaf parsley, finely chopped

1. Bring a pan of salted water to the boil and cook the pasta according to pack instructions. Drain.

2. Meanwhile, melt 25g butter in a large frying pan over medium-high heat. Add the prawns and garlic and cook for 3-4min or until the prawns are opaque and cooked through. Scrap into a bowl and return the pan to the heat.

3. Add the remaining 125g butter to the frying pan. Once melted, increase the heat to high and cook, swirling the pan occasionally, until the butter is golden brown and smells nutty. Carefully add the stock to the butter pan (it will splutter) and bubble for 3-4min, until slightly reduced.

4. Add the pasta to the butter pan with the garlic prawns, lemon juice and some seasoning. Toss to coat, then add the herbs and toss again. Check the seasoning. Divide among 4 bowls and serve.

★ GH TIP
If you're short on time, you can skip butterflying and deveining the prawns. But it does help keep them tender.

Hands-on time: 15min
Cooking time: about 15min
Serves 4

PER SERVING 611cals, 24g protein, 33g fat (20g saturates), 54g carbs (2g total sugars), 4g fibre

16

Ring in the New Year

Vegetarian menu for 6

Roasted Squash and Burrata Salad with Salsa Verde
★ ★ ★
Individual Shallot and Chestnut Galettes with Horseradish Crème Fraîche
Whole Roasted Cauliflower Cheese
Sprout and Green Bean Salad
Hasselback Roots
★ ★ ★
Passion fruit possets

Cocktail party and dinner menu for 6

Rum Twinkle
Salmon Tartare Bites
Parmesan Madeleines
★ ★ ★
Jerusalem Artichoke and Cider soup
★ ★ ★
Individual Beetroot Wellington (Vegetarian)
★ ★ ★
Beef Wellington with Port Gravy
White Winter Salad
Roasted Herby Squash
Chilli and Garlic Romanesco
★ ★ ★
Caramel Banana Cake with Rum Butterscotch
★ ★ ★
Black and White After Dinner Mints

Crowd-pleasing celebration menu for 8

Smoked Salmon Palmiers
★ ★ ★
Fig and Candied Pecan Salad
★ ★ ★
Venison Guard of Honour with Blackberry Gravy
★ ★ ★
Wild Mushroom and Lentil Filo Spiral (Vegetarian)
★ ★ ★
Three Root Boulangère
Speedy Roasted Broccoli
★ ★ ★
Triple Chocolate Mousse Cake with Mirror Glaze
★ ★ ★
Raspberry Jellies

Roasted Squash and Burrata Salad with Salsa Verde

A quick-assembly warm salad is the perfect start to a celebratory meal. Check the burrata is vegetarian, if needed.

FOR THE SALAD
50g blanched hazelnuts
3 x 150g burrata balls
1 medium butternut squash (about 1.5kg), peeled, halved and deseeded
2 tbsp olive oil

FOR THE SALSA VERDE
6 tbsp extra virgin olive oil
1 tbsp red wine vinegar
2 tsp capers, finely chopped
1 small garlic clove, crushed
½ tsp caster sugar
Large handful parsley, finely chopped
Handful basil leaves, finely chopped
Handful mint leaves, finely chopped

★ MAKE IT VEGAN
Leave out the burrata and replace it with small wedges of peeled beetroot, roasted with the butternut squash. Serve the roasted veg with the salsa verde, hazelnuts and dollops of a dairy-free crème fraîche alternative.

Hands-on time: 30min
Cooking time: about 35min
Serves 6

PER SERVING 479cals, 18g protein, 33g fat (11g saturates), 26g carbs (11g total sugars), 6g fibre

1. Preheat oven to 180°C (160°C fan) mark 4. For the salad, scatter the hazelnuts on a small baking tray and toast in the oven for 8min, or until golden. Set aside. Remove the burrata from the fridge and allow to come up to room temperature.

2. Increase oven to 220°C (200°C fan) mark 7. Cut the squash into 1cm-wide wedges and arrange in a single layer on a large baking tray. Drizzle over the olive oil and season. Roast for 25min, or until tender and golden.

3. Meanwhile, make the salsa verde. In the bowl of a food processor, whizz the olive oil, vinegar, capers, garlic, sugar and some seasoning until combined. Add the herbs and whizz again until fairly smooth. Alternatively, mix everything by hand for a chunkier finish.

4. To serve, divide the squash among 6 plates. Drain the burrata, then tear and dot around the squash. Roughly chop the hazelnuts and scatter over the salad, then spoon over some of the salsa verde. Serve with the remaining salsa on the side.

★ GET AHEAD
Toast the nuts up to 4hr ahead. Set aside at room temperature. The salsa is best served fresh but can be made up to 2hr ahead. Cover and set aside. To serve, stir to recombine and complete the recipe.

Individual Shallot and Chestnut Galettes

These tarts have a hint of sweetness from the chestnuts and a salty kick from the olives. Perfect with the horseradish sauce spooned on top.

FOR THE FILLING
25g unsalted butter
2 tbsp olive oil
800g echalion shallots, peeled and halved lengthways
2 tbsp sherry vinegar
250ml vegetable stock
2 tsp light brown soft sugar
6 small rosemary sprigs
200g cooked chestnuts, thickly sliced
100g pitted black olives, roughly chopped
Small handful parsley, roughly chopped, to serve

FOR THE PASTRY
450g plain flour, plus extra to dust
1 tsp caster sugar
225g unsalted butter, chilled and cubed
1 tsp nigella seeds (optional)
1 medium egg, beaten

★ GET AHEAD
Prepare to the end of step 6 up to 1 day ahead, then cover loosely and chill. Complete the recipe to serve.

Hands-on time: 45min, plus chilling
Cooking time: about 1hr 20min
Makes 6 galettes

PER GALETTE 794cals, 13g protein, 46g fat (24g saturates), 79g carbs (10g total sugars), 8g fibre

1. Preheat oven to 180°C (160°C fan) mark 4. For the filling, heat the butter and oil in a large ovenproof frying pan over medium-high heat and fry the shallots and a pinch of salt for 8min, turning once, or until beginning to colour.

2. Stir in the vinegar, stock, sugar, rosemary and chestnuts, then transfer to the oven and cook for 35–40min, stirring halfway, or until golden, sticky and all the liquid has evaporated. Remove the rosemary sprigs, stir in the olives and set aside to cool completely.

3. Meanwhile, make the pastry. In a food processor, pulse the flour, sugar and 1 tsp fine salt to combine. Add the butter and pulse until the mixture resembles fine breadcrumbs. Alternatively, rub the butter into the flour mixture using your fingertips. Add the nigella seeds, if using, and 6 tbsp ice-cold water. Pulse/mix until the pastry comes together (add a little more water, if needed).

4. Tip the pastry on to a work surface and knead briefly until smooth. Divide into 6 equal pieces, shape each into a flat disc, then wrap and chill for at least 20min (up to 24hr).

5. Reheat oven to 200°C (180°C fan) mark 6. Line 2 large baking sheets with baking parchment. Lightly flour a work surface and roll out each pastry disc to a roughly 20.5cm circle (allow the pastry to soften slightly at room temperature before rolling if very chilled).

6. Pile a sixth of the cooled shallot mixture into the centre of a pastry circle, leaving a 3–4cm border, then fold the pastry border over the filling. Repeat to make 6 tarts and place on the prepared sheets, spacing apart.

7. Brush the pastry borders with beaten egg and cook in the oven for 25–30min or until golden.

8. When the galettes are cooked, scatter the parsley over the top and serve with horseradish crème fraîche on the side.

Horseradish Crème Fraîche

In a small bowl, mix **250g crème fraîche**, **50g freshly grated horseradish** (or use 1–2 tbsp hot horseradish sauce, to taste), **1 tsp red wine vinegar** and some **seasoning**. Cover and chill (up to 24hr) until ready to serve.

PER 1 TBSP 54cals, 0g protein, 6g fat (4g saturates), 0g carbs (0g total sugars), 0g fibre

★ MAKE IT VEGAN
Swap the butter for the shallots for oil and use 750g ready-made vegan shortcrust pastry instead of making your own. Glaze with a dairy-free milk alternative and sprinkle with nigella seeds, if using, before cooking. Use a dairy-free yogurt or crème fraîche alternative for the horseradish sauce.

Whole Roasted Cauliflower Cheese

Pale ale and Swiss cheese combine to make a wonderfully rich sauce to drape over a whole roasted cauliflower. A real meat-free showstopper.

1 large cauliflower (about 900g)
40g unsalted butter, softened
Small lemon wedge
25g plain flour
200ml whole milk
200ml pale ale
2 tsp English mustard
75g mature Cheddar, coarsely grated
75g vegetarian Swiss-style cheese (such as Jarlsberg), coarsely grated
1 tbsp chopped chives, to serve (optional)

★ GH TIP
If you prefer not to use alcohol, replace the ale with cauliflower cooking water, or use a good-quality alcohol-free beer or ale.

Hands-on time: 25min, plus cooling
Cooking time: about 40min
Serves 6

PER SERVING 250cals, 12g protein, 16g fat (10g saturates), 12g carbs (6g total sugars), 3g fibre

1. Trim the cauliflower base, creating a flat bottom so it can stand up, then cut/peel away the tough outer leaves, leaving small inner leaves attached.

2. Bring a large pan (that has a lid) of salted water to the boil. Add the cauliflower (floret-side down), cover and simmer gently for 10min, or until almost tender (pierce the stalk with a knife to check). Drain and leave to cool (floret-side down) in a colander/sieve for 20min.

3. Preheat oven to 220°C (200°C fan) mark 7. Put the cauliflower, floret-side up, into an ovenproof serving dish (a 23cm round dish works well) and rub over 20g butter. Squeeze over the lemon and season all over. Roast for 20min, or until just starting to turn golden on top.

4. Meanwhile, make the cheese sauce. Melt the remaining 20g butter in a medium pan over medium-high heat. Stir in the flour and cook for 1–2min, stirring. Remove the pan from heat and gradually mix in the milk, followed by the pale ale, to make a smooth sauce. Stir in the mustard and some seasoning.

5. Return the pan to the heat and cook, stirring frequently, until thickened. Remove from heat and stir in most of the cheese. Check the seasoning.

6. Preheat grill to high. Pour the sauce over the cauliflower and scatter over the remaining cheese. Grill for 8–10min, or until bubbling and golden. Sprinkle over the chives, if using, and serve in slices.

Sprout and Green Bean Salad

When shredded, raw Brussels sprouts make a great base for a wintry salad. You can also toast the pecans in a dry frying pan on the hob.

40g pecans
300g fine green beans, ends trimmed
4 tbsp extra virgin olive oil
½ small garlic clove, crushed
Juice 1 orange (about 4 tbsp)
300g Brussels sprouts, ends trimmed
50g pomegranate seeds

1. Preheat oven to 180°C (160°C fan) mark 4. Scatter the pecans on a small baking tray and toast in the oven for 10min. Set aside to cool before roughly chopping.

2. Meanwhile, bring a medium pan of salted water to the boil and cook the beans for 4min or until just tender. Drain, then rinse under cold water to cool completely. Drain well and tip on to a clean tea towel or kitchen paper to dry.

3. For the dressing, in a large bowl whisk the oil, garlic, orange juice and some seasoning.

4. Shred the sprouts (see GH Tip) and add to the dressing bowl along with beans. Toss to combine. Empty into a serving bowl, scatter over the pecans and pomegranate seeds and serve.

★ GH TIP
The shredding attachment of a food processor will make speedy work of slicing the Brussels sprouts.

★ GET AHEAD
Toast the pecans, blanch the beans and shred the sprouts up to 4hr ahead. Cover the vegetables with damp kitchen paper; chill. Set aside the pecans at room temperature. Complete the recipe to serve.

Hands-on time: 20min
Cooking time: about 10min
Serves 6

PER SERVING 167cals, 4g protein, 13g fat (2g saturates), 6g carbs (5g total sugars), 5g fibre

Hasselback Roots

You can mix and match your root vegetables in this pretty side dish, or opt for a single variety – a tray of golden Hasselback potatoes is a guaranteed crowd-pleaser.

400g carrots, peeled
400g parsnips, peeled
400g medium new potatoes
400g small raw beetroots, peeled
3 garlic cloves
15 small sage leaves
6 tbsp olive oil

1. Slice the carrots and parsnips into pieces about the same length as the potatoes. Make vertical slices across all the vegetables, spacing the slices about 3mm apart and cutting deep into each piece but not all the way through.

2. Preheat oven to 200°C (180°C fan) mark 6. Finely slice 2 garlic cloves and carefully insert the slices and sage leaves randomly into some of the cuts in the vegetables. Crush the remaining garlic and mix with 3 tbsp of the oil.

3. Heat the remaining 3 tbsp oil in a large roasting tin in the oven for 10min. Add the vegetables to the hot tin, turning to coat in the hot oil. Arrange with the cuts facing up. Drizzle over the garlic oil and season well.

4. Roast for 1hr, gently basting the vegetables halfway through, or until golden and tender. Empty into a serving bowl and serve.

Hands-on time: 30min
Cooking time: about 1hr 10min
Serves 6

PER SERVING 253cals, 4g protein, 12g fat (2g saturates), 28g carbs (14g total sugars), 9g fibre

Passion Fruit Possets

With a tangy tropical flavour, these possets make a deliciously light ending to a special meal.

450ml double cream
130g golden caster sugar
1 star anise
9 ripe passion fruits
2 tbsp lime juice
Zest ½ small orange, plus 3 tbsp juice
12 shop-bought madeleines
75g white chocolate
20g pistachio kernels, crushed

★ GET AHEAD
Make possets up to 2 days ahead and keep chilled. Complete recipe.

Hands-on time: 30min, plus chilling
Cooking time: about 30min
Serves 6

PER SERVING (1 posset and 1 madeleine): 779cals, 7g protein, 59g fat (35g saturates), 54g carbs (46g total sugars), 2g fibre

1. To make the possets, put the cream, sugar and star anise into a large, heavy-based pan. Heat very gently until the sugar dissolves, stirring occasionally. Once dissolved, bring to the boil and boil rapidly for 1min, stirring occasionally to ensure it doesn't catch, and then remove from the heat.

2. Meanwhile, halve 7 of the passion fruits, scoop the contents into a food processor and whizz to separate the pulp from the seeds. Push through a sieve over a measuring jug. You should have about 130ml juice. Add the citrus juices to this, then add to the cream mixture along with most of the orange zest – the mixture will thicken. Leave to cool for a few min before straining through a sieve into a jug. Pour into 6 ramekins or small glasses, about 100ml per serving. Leave to cool completely, then cover and transfer to the fridge for at least 2–3hr until set, or up to 2 days ahead.

3. To decorate the madeleines, melt the white chocolate in a bowl set over a pan of barely simmering water. Leave to cool for a few min, then dip the rounded ends of the madeleines into the chocolate and scatter over the crushed pistachios. Set aside on a wire rack to cool.

4. When ready to serve, uncover the possets and spoon a little of the pulp from the remaining passion fruits over each one. Serve with the madeleines alongside.

Cocktail party and dinner menu for 6

Rum Twinkle

Spiced rum adds a glorious golden hue and exotic edge to this simple but potent aperitif.

125ml spiced golden rum (we used Sailor Jerry)
75cl bottle cava, chilled

1. Divide the rum among 6 chilled Champagne flutes/saucers and top up the glasses with cava. Serve immediately.

★ GH TIP
To decorate your Champagne glasses, dip the rims in cold water and let the excess drip off. Then dip into a mixture of caster sugar and edible gold glitter.

Hands-on time: 5min
Makes 6 cocktails

PER COCKTAIL 151cals, 0g protein, 0g fat (0g saturates), 6g carbs (6g total sugars), 0g fibre

Salmon Tartare Bites

As you are serving raw salmon here, it needs to be as fresh as it can be.

FOR THE TARTARE
100g fresh organic salmon fillet, skinned
5cm piece cucumber
60g smoked salmon, finely chopped
½ small shallot, finely chopped
1 tsp Dijon mustard
Finely grated zest and juice ½ lemon
1 tbsp crème fraîche
1 tbsp chopped chives
1 tbsp capers, chopped

TO SERVE
2.5cm squares rye bread and/or ready made croustade cups

1. Wrap the salmon in clingfilm and freeze for 30min (no longer – this just helps to make it easier to slice).

2. Meanwhile, peel, deseed and finely chop the cucumber. Put into a bowl and mix in remaining tartare ingredients and some seasoning.

3. Finely chop the chilled salmon and mix into the tartare no more than 30min before serving. Serve on rye bread or in croustade cups (or a mixture of both).

Hands-on time: 15min, plus freezing
Makes 18 bites

PER CANAPÉ 31cals, 2g protein, 2g fat (1g saturates), 1g carbs (0g total sugars), <1g fibre

Parmesan Madeleines

We've given these traditional French cakes a savoury, herby twist.

75g unsalted butter, plus extra to grease
75g self-raising flour, plus extra to dust
2 tbsp thyme leaves
40g runny honey
2 large eggs
50g Parmesan, finely grated
½ tbsp finely chopped rosemary
2 tbsp natural yogurt

1. Preheat oven to 180°C (160°C fan) mark 4. Grease the holes of a 12-hole madeleine tin and dust with flour, tapping out any excess. Sprinkle half the thyme leaves into the holes. Finely chop the remaining thyme and set aside.

2. Melt the butter and honey in a small pan, then cool for 10min. Meanwhile, in a large bowl with a handheld electric whisk, beat the eggs until pale, thick and doubled in volume.

3. Using a large metal spoon, gently fold the butter mixture into the eggs. Fold in the flour, Parmesan, chopped herbs, yogurt and ¼ tsp fine salt until combined. Divide among the holes of the tin (don't smooth).

4. Cook for 10–12min until risen and golden. Cool in tin for 5min. Firmly tap the tin on a work surface to loosen the madeleines, then carefully invert on to a wire rack and allow them to fall out on to the rack. Cool before serving.

★ GET AHEAD
Make up to 2hr ahead; once completely cool, store in an airtight container at room temperature.

Hands-on time: 20min, plus cooling
Cooking time: about 15min
Makes 12 madeleines

PER MADELEINE 113cals, 4g protein, 7g fat
(4g saturates), 8g carbs (3g total sugars), <1g fibre

Jerusalem Artichoke and Cider Soup

The sweet acidity of cider balances the earthy flavour of Jerusalem artichokes.

FOR THE SOUP
40g butter
1 onion, finely chopped
2 garlic cloves, crushed
1kg Jerusalem artichokes, peeled and roughly chopped
1 medium potato, peeled and roughly chopped
750ml vegetable stock
500ml cider
1 tsp ground white pepper
150ml double cream, plus extra, to garnish (optional)

FOR THE TOPPING
40g sourdough bread, cut or torn into small pieces
1 eating apple, cored and finely chopped
40g mature Cheddar, finely grated
1 tsp olive oil

1. Preheat oven to 200°C (180°C fan) mark 6. Melt the butter in a large pan over medium heat. Add the onion and cook for 10min, stirring occasionally, until softened. Stir in the garlic, artichokes and potato. Cook for 10min, until the veg start to soften. Add the stock and cider, bring to the boil and simmer for 15min, or until the veg are tender. Stir in the pepper and salt to taste.

2. Meanwhile, mix the topping ingredients and some seasoning in a small roasting tin. Cook for 15min, stirring, until golden. Set aside.

3. Cool the soup slightly, then blend until smooth (thin with extra stock if needed). Return to a clean pan and stir in the cream. Reheat if needed, then divide among 6 bowls. Add a swirl of cream, if you like, and the topping. Serve.

★ GET AHEAD
Make the soup up to 1 day ahead, then cool, cover and chill. To serve, make the topping and reheat the soup gently in a pan.

V

Hands-on time: 25min, plus cooling
Cooking time: about 45min
Serves 6

PER SERVING 654cals, 23g protein, 44g fat
(13g saturates), 31g carbs (9g total sugars), 12g fibre

Individual Beetroot Wellington

Beetroot and goat's cheese are a match made in heaven, especially in pastry.

1 medium raw beetroot (about 100g unpeeled weight)
75g baby spinach
½ tbsp Dijon mustard
Freshly grated nutmeg, to taste
Plain flour, to dust
250g puff pastry, from a block
25–40g goat's cheese, crumbled
1 medium egg, beaten

1. Preheat oven to 200°C (180°C) mark 6. Wash the beetroot; wrap in foil. Roast for 1hr, or until you can easily push a knife into the centre. Cool.

2. Put the spinach into a sieve in the sink, then pour over boiled water from the kettle to wilt. Run under cold water to cool, then squeeze out all the excess moisture. Put into a bowl, mix in the mustard, nutmeg and some seasoning. Set aside.

3. Wearing gloves to protect your hands, peel off the skin from the beetroot, then remove a thin slice from the root end so it stands up.

4. Lightly flour a work surface and roll out a third of the pastry to make a rough 16cm square. Transfer to a baking sheet lined with baking parchment. Sit the beetroot in the middle, then make a tight nest of the spinach mixture around it. Top the spinach with a halo of cheese. Brush the visible pastry with beaten egg.

5. Roll out the remaining pastry until large enough to cover the filling. Lay it over the filling (work out any air pockets and press the edges together to seal). Trim excess and crimp around the edge. Brush with the egg. Chill for 20min.

6. Reheat oven to 200°C (180°C) mark 6. Re-glaze with egg and cook for 35min, until golden. Serve. Repeat the recipe, as needed, if you are catering for more vegetarian guests.

Hands-on time: 25min, plus cooling and chilling
Cooking time: 1hr 35min
Serves 1

PER SERVING 761cals, 21g protein, 46g fat (30g saturates), 64g carbs (9g total sugars), 5g fibre

Beef Wellington with Port Gravy

Nothing says special occasion quite like a beef Wellington, and the combination of Parma ham, porcini paste and garlic spinach makes for a taste sensation that's well worth the effort.

FOR THE WELLINGTON

750–800g centre-cut beef fillet
1 tbsp olive oil, plus extra to grease
25g butter
2 garlic cloves, crushed
450g baby spinach, any woody stalks removed
Freshly grated nutmeg, to taste
8 Parma ham slices
2 tbsp porcini and truffle paste (see GH Tip)
Plain flour, to dust
500g block puff pastry
1 medium egg, beaten
Poppy seeds, to garnish (optional)

FOR THE PORT GRAVY

1 tsp olive oil
75g pancetta lardons
1 echalion shallot, finely chopped
3 tbsp plain flour
200ml ruby port
500ml beef stock
1 tbsp redcurrant jelly

★ GH TIP
If you can't find porcini paste, use Dijon mustard instead.

Hands-on time: 1hr, plus cooling, chilling and resting
Cooking time: about 1hr
Serves 6

PER SERVING 797cals, 49g protein, 43g fat (23g saturates), 43g carbs (7g total sugars), 2g fibre

1. For the Wellington, pat the fillet dry with kitchen paper. Heat the oil in a large frying pan over high heat and fry the beef for 8–10min, turning regularly, until browned all over (including the ends). Cool on wire rack set over a baking tray.

2. Melt the butter in same pan, add the garlic and cook for 30sec. Add half the spinach, season with salt, pepper and nutmeg, then cook until slightly wilted. Add the remaining spinach and cook, stirring, until wilted. Drain in a colander in the sink. When cool enough to handle, squeeze out all excess moisture with your hands, then dry thoroughly on kitchen paper.

3. Lay 2 large overlapping sheets of clingfilm on a work surface. Arrange slices of Parma ham, slightly overlapping, in the centre, in a rectangle large enough to completely cover the beef (including ends). Top with spinach, leaving a 2.5cm border. Brush the fillet with porcini paste and place in the centre of the spinach. Using the clingfilm to help, wrap the ham and spinach around the fillet, then roll up into a clingfilm-wrapped log, twisting the ends tightly to secure. Chill for at least 30min (or up to 6hr).

4. Line a baking tray with baking parchment. Lightly flour a work surface and roll out the pastry to a rectangle large enough to completely enclose the beef. Cut a 2.5cm strip from one edge and set aside. Reroll the pastry sheet to its original size and brush all over with egg. Unwrap the beef and place in the centre of the pastry. Fold the short edges of pastry in, then wrap up. Put seam-side down on the prepared tray and

brush all over with egg. Stamp or cut out small shapes (we did stars) from the reserved pastry, stick on top and brush with egg. Chill for at least 30min (or up to 24hr).

5. Preheat the oven to 220°C (200°C fan) mark 7. Heat a sturdy baking tray in oven for 10min. Brush the Wellington all over with more egg and sprinkle over the poppy seeds, if using. Lift on to the preheated baking tray (still on parchment) and cook for 10min. Reduce oven temperature to 200°C (180°C fan) mark 6 and cook for 35–40min (for medium), until the pastry is a deep golden brown (if you have a meat thermometer, it should read 60°C when inserted into the centre of the fillet).

6. Meanwhile, make the gravy. Heat the oil, pancetta and shallot in a pan over medium heat and cook, stirring occasionally, until the pancetta is golden and shallots are tender. Stir in the flour and cook for 1min. Gradually add the port, whisking to avoid lumps, then whisk in the stock. Increase the heat to high and bubble vigorously for 5min until thickened. Whisk in the jelly and check the seasoning. Set aside.

7. Remove the Wellington from oven and rest for 10min. Transfer to a serving plate or board and serve with the gravy, reheated if needed.

★ GET AHEAD

Prepare to end of step 4 up to 1 day ahead. Loosely cover with foil and chill. Make the gravy up to 1 day ahead, then cool, cover and chill. Complete the recipe to serve, reheating the gravy in a pan.

White Winter Salad

Sweet pears paired with bitter chicory make for a tantalising side.

---

3 medium heads chicory, leaves separated
2 ripe pears, quartered lengthways, cored and
   thinly sliced
75g vegetarian Stilton, crumbled

FOR THE DRESSING
2 tsp wholegrain mustard
1 tbsp runny honey
1½ tbsp cider vinegar
4 tbsp extra virgin olive oil

1. Whisk the dressing ingredients in a large bowl
   with some seasoning.

2. Add the chicory and pears and toss. Transfer
   to a platter, scatter over the Stilton and serve.

★ GET AHEAD
Make the dressing 1 day ahead, cover and chill.
Complete the recipe to serve.

Hands-on time: 15min
Serves 6

PER SERVING 157cals, 3g protein, 12g fat (4g saturates),
8g carbs (7g total sugars), 2g fibre

Roasted Herby Squash

We've left the skin on our squash to add texture, but peel it if you prefer.

---

1 large butternut squash, halved and deseeded
1 tbsp runny honey
4 tbsp olive oil
Small handful chopped soft herbs (we used parsley, basil
   and coriander)
Juice ½ lemon

1. Preheat oven to 200°C (180°C fan) mark 6.
   Cut the squash lengthways into rough 1cm thick
   slices, cut some slices in half widthways if very
   long. Put on a large baking tray in a single layer.
   Drizzle with honey and 2 tbsp oil, then season.
   Roast for 45–50min, turning midway, until tender
   and charring at the edges.

2. Mix the remaining oil, herbs and lemon juice
   with some seasoning. Transfer the cooked
   squash to a serving plate and drizzle over the
   herby dressing. Serve.

★ GET AHEAD
Prepare to end of step 1 up to 2hr ahead.
Set aside. To serve, reheat in an oven preheated
to 200°C (180°C fan) mark 6 for 10min and
complete the recipe.

Hands-on time: 15min
Cooking time: about 50min
Serves 6

PER SERVING 143cals, 2g protein, 8g fat (1g saturates),
15g carbs (9g total sugars), 4g fibre

Chilli and Garlic Romanesco

If you can't get hold of Romanesco, use broccoli instead.

600g Romanesco cauliflower florets (about 1 medium head of cauliflower)
1 tbsp olive oil
1–2 garlic cloves, thinly sliced, to taste
1 red chilli, deseeded and finely chopped
2 tbsp flaked almonds, toasted

1. Put the Romanesco florets into a large frying pan (that has a lid), pour in 50ml just-boiled water, cover with the lid and steam over medium heat for 7–8min until the water has evaporated and the florets are just tender.

2. Uncover and add oil to the pan. Fry for 5min, tossing occasionally, until the florets have taken on some golden colour. Add the garlic, chilli and some seasoning. Fry for 1min to soften the garlic. Transfer to a warm serving dish, sprinkle over the flaked almonds and serve.

★ GET AHEAD
Complete step 1 up to 1 day ahead. Transfer to a bowl, then cool, cover and chill. Complete the recipe to serve.

Hands-on time: 20min
Cooking time: about 15min
Serves 6

PER SERVING 83cals, 4g protein, 5g fat (1g saturates), 5g carbs (3g total sugars), 2g fibre

Caramel Banana Cake with Rum Butterscotch

Easy to make, but impressive to serve guests, this is delicious eaten warm or at room temperature.

FOR THE CARAMEL
50g unsalted butter, plus extra to grease
100g light brown soft sugar
2–3 medium bananas, as straight as possible

FOR THE CAKE
100g unsalted butter, softened
175g light brown soft sugar
200g self-raising flour
½ tsp bicarbonate of soda
2 medium eggs, beaten
1 tsp vanilla bean paste
75g soured cream

FOR THE RUM BUTTERSCOTCH
40g unsalted butter
50g light brown soft sugar
50g soured cream
1 tbsp spiced golden rum

★ GET AHEAD
Make the cake up to 6hr ahead. Cool for 5min, then invert on to a plate. Loosely cover with foil. To serve, make the rum butterscotch.

Hands-on time: 25min, plus cooling
Cooking time: about 1hr
Serves 6–8

PER SERVING (for 8) 504cals, 5g protein, 24g fat (15g saturates), 65g carbs (45g total sugars), 1g fibre

1. Preheat oven to 180°C (160°C fan) mark 4. Grease a 900g loaf tin. For the caramel, melt the butter and sugar in a heavy-based medium pan, stirring to dissolve the sugar. Bring up to a bubble, then pour into the prepared tin.

2. Halve the bananas lengthways and trim the ends. Cut into shorter lengths to fit the width of base of tin. Arrange the fruit snugly in a single layer in base of tin, cut-side down.

3. For the cake, in a large bowl using a handheld electric whisk, beat the butter, sugar and a large pinch salt until pale and fluffy. Sift the flour and bicarb into a separate bowl. Beat the eggs and vanilla into the butter mixture. Beat in half the flour mixture, then half the soured cream. Repeat until incorporated.

4. Spoon the batter over the bananas and level. Bake for 55min, until a skewer inserted into the centre comes out clean. Cool in the tin for 5min (no more), then invert on to a plate to cool.

5. Meanwhile, make the rum butterscotch. Heat the butter, sugar and soured cream in a pan, stirring to dissolve the sugar. Bubble for 2min, then remove from heat and stir in the rum. Serve the cake just warm or at room temperature with the sauce poured over or on the side.

Black and White After Dinner Mints

Served straight from the freezer, these mints are utterly tempting. Don't worry about cracks when cutting, as freezing will help keep the filling firm.

100g good-quality white chocolate, finely chopped
200g icing sugar, sifted
1 tsp liquid glucose
1 tsp peppermint extract
150g good-quality dark chocolate (70% cocoa solids), finely chopped

★ FREEZE AHEAD
Prepare to end of step 4 up to a week ahead. Once frozen, loosely wrap in clingfilm. Keep frozen. Complete the recipe to serve.

1. Put the white chocolate in a heatproof bowl. Set the bowl over a pan of gently simmering water (making sure the base doesn't touch the water), then immediately turn off heat. Stir regularly until the chocolate has melted.

2. Line a baking sheet with baking parchment. Spread the melted chocolate on baking parchment into a thin rectangle, about 15 x 20.5cm. Chill until set.

3. Mix the icing sugar, glucose, peppermint extract, a pinch of fine salt and 5½ tsp cold water to make a thick paste. Add an extra drop of water if it's too stiff to make it just pourable. Spread over the set chocolate, then chill for at least 30min (or up to 2hr) to firm up.

4. Melt the dark chocolate following the instructions in step 1. Pour over the mint layer, tilting the sheet quickly so it spreads evenly (it will start to set almost immediately). Freeze overnight.

5. Cut into rough 5cm squares with a large, sharp knife. Return to the freezer on a baking sheet lined with fresh baking parchment. Serve the mints from frozen.

Hands-on time: 20min, plus chilling and overnight freezing
Cooking time: about 5min
Cuts into 12 mints

PER MINT 177cals, 1g protein, 6g fat (4g saturates), 29g carbs (29g total sugars), 0g fibre

Smoked Salmon Palmiers

If you prefer, swap the salmon for Parma ham, using just enough to cover the cheese.

320g sheet ready-rolled puff pastry
100g cream cheese with chives
150g smoked salmon slices
1 medium egg, beaten
1 tsp sesame seeds

1. Preheat oven to 200°C (180°C fan) mark 6 and line a large baking sheet with baking parchment. Unroll the puff pastry and spread the cream cheese evenly over the top.

2. Lay the salmon on top of the cream cheese in a single layer. Roll up the pastry tightly from one long edge until you reach the middle, then repeat from the other long edge, pressing the rolls together. Transfer to a board and chill for 20min.

3. Brush the top and sides with beaten egg, then sprinkle over the sesame seeds. Trim the ends to neaten, then cut across the rolls to make 1.5cm slices. Arrange on the prepared sheet, spacing apart. Chill again for 20min.

4. Cook for 20–25min until golden. Cool for a few minutes on the tray, then transfer to a wire rack. Serve warm or at room temperature.

Hands-on time: 15min, plus chilling and cooling
Cooking time: about 25min
Makes about 16 palmiers

PER PALMIER 117cals, 4g protein, 8g fat (5g saturates), 8g carbs (1g total sugars), 0g fibre

★ GET AHEAD
Prepare to the end of step 2 up to 1 day ahead. Cover and chill. Complete the recipe up to 2hr ahead. Warm through in an oven for a few minutes before serving.

Fig and Candied Pecan Salad

Crumbled Stilton also works wonderfully in this elegant starter.

100g pecans
2 tbsp runny honey
About 200g salad leaves (we used baby kale, lamb's
    lettuce and mixed leaves)
4 figs, each cut into 8 wedges
50g pecorino, shaved

FOR THE DRESSING
1 tbsp wholegrain mustard
2 tbsp balsamic vinegar
3 tbsp extra virgin olive oil
1 tbsp runny honey

1. Preheat oven to 180°C (160°C fan) mark 4.
   Line a small baking tray with baking parchment.
   Mix the pecans and honey on the lined tray and
   cook in the oven for 15min, turning midway
   through. Set aside to cool.

2. Mix the dressing ingredients in a small jug
   with some seasoning.

3. Divide the salad among 8 plates or arrange on
   a large platter. Break up the pecans (or roughly
   chop) and sprinkle over the leaves together with
   the figs and pecorino. Drizzle over the dressing
   and serve.

★ GET AHEAD
Prepare to end of step 2 up to 4hr ahead. Store
the pecans (uncovered) and dressing (covered)
at room temperature. Complete the recipe to serve.

Hands-on time: 15min, plus cooling
Cooking time: about 15min
Serves 8

PER SERVING 198cals, 4g protein, 16g fat (3g saturates),
9g carbs (9g total sugars), 2g fibre

Venison Guard of Honour with Blackberry Gravy

A lean meat with a deep colour and rich flavour, venison is mild enough to not scare off those unaccustomed to game while being special enough for a celebratory meal.

1 tbsp olive oil
2 x 8 bone racks of venison, French trimmed (ask your butcher to do this)
4 tbsp Dijon mustard

FOR THE HAZELNUT CRUMB
75g fresh white breadcrumbs
2 tbsp thyme leaves
Small handful parsley, chopped
2 garlic cloves, crushed
2 tbsp olive oil
50g chopped roasted hazelnuts
1 medium egg yolk

FOR THE GRAVY
1 tbsp olive oil
25g plain flour
500ml beef stock
75g blackberries
2 thyme sprigs
1 tbsp redcurrant jelly

1. Using a small sharp knife, remove any fat and sinew from the ends of rib bones (if your butcher hasn't done this) by carefully scraping down the bones. Season the racks well with freshly ground black pepper.

2. Preheat oven to 200°C (180°C fan) mark 6. Heat the oil in a large frying pan over medium-high heat. Brown the racks well all over, one at a time if needed, for a couple of minutes per side. Lift on to a board and leave until cool enough to handle. Join the racks together so the ribs interlock, tying in place along their length with kitchen string. Transfer to a sturdy roasting tin.

3. Roast the venison for 15min. Meanwhile, whizz the crumb ingredients in a food processor to combine. Remove the tin from the oven and brush the meat with the mustard. Press the crumb on to the meat, keeping the bones visible. Return to the oven for 40min for rare to medium-rare (a meat thermometer pushed into the thickest part in the centre of the meat should read about 62°C) or cook for longer if you prefer.

4. Lift the venison on to a board (reserve the roasting tin for gravy), cover loosely with foil and leave to rest for 20min. Meanwhile, make the gravy. Put the roasting tin on a medium-heat hob and add oil. Heat, then stir in the flour and cook for 1min. Take roasting tin off heat and gradually mix in the stock to make a smooth sauce. Cook, stirring, until the sauce has thickened. Add the blackberries and thyme and simmer, stirring occasionally, for 5min. Strain into a clean pan and stir in redcurrant jelly. Check the seasoning and reheat if needed. Serve with the venison, cutting between the bones and removing the string as you go.

Hands-on time: 30min, plus cooling and resting
Cooking time: about 1hr 10min
Serves 8

PER SERVING 395cals, 55g protein, 15g fat (3g saturates), 10g carbs (3g total sugars), 1g fibre

GET AHEAD
Whizz crumb ingredients up to 3hr ahead.
Cover and chill. Prepare to the end of step
2 up to 3hr ahead. Once browned, cool,
cover and chill. Allow to come up to room
temperature (at least 30min) before roasting.

Wild Mushroom and Lentil Filo Spiral

To make this recipe vegan, replace the cheese with a vegan feta-style cheese substitute or some chopped sundried tomatoes.

Small handful dried wild mushrooms
1 tsp olive oil, plus extra to brush
1 shallot, finely sliced
75g cooked beluga lentils, from a packet
2 thyme sprigs, leaves picked
25g feta, finely cubed
3 sheets filo pastry

YOU'LL ALSO NEED
A wooden skewer

★ GET AHEAD
Prepare to end of step 4 up to 1hr ahead.
Cover and leave at room temperature.
Uncover and complete the recipe to serve.

1. Cover the mushrooms with boiling water and set aside to soften for 15min.

2. Preheat oven to 200°C (180°C fan) mark 6. Heat the oil in a small frying pan and fry the shallot for 5min to soften. Lift the mushrooms out of the soaking water and chop. Add to the pan and fry for 2min. Stir in the lentils and thyme. Take off heat and leave to cool.

3. Stir in the feta and check the seasoning. Brush the top of one filo sheet with oil, then flip and brush again. Lay over another filo sheet, brushing the top with oil. Repeat once more. Arrange the filling in a strip along one of the long edges, leaving a 2.5cm border at both ends. Fold these borders over the filling, then roll up from the long edge nearest the filling.

4. Gently curl the filo sausage into a spiral, being careful to avoid tearing. Secure in place with a skewer pushed through spiral. Transfer to a baking sheet lined with baking parchment.

5. Cook for 25min until golden and crisp, then serve. Repeat the recipe, as needed, if you are catering for more vegetarian guests.

Hands-on time: 15min, plus softening and cooling
Cooking time: about 35min
Serves 1

PER SERVING 529cals, 20g protein, 23g fat (6g saturates), 57g carbs (4g total sugars), 9g fibre

Three Root Boulangère

A hearty accompaniment to any roast, this seasonal side is luxurious without being overly rich.

50g butter, plus extra to grease
2 onions, finely sliced
2 garlic cloves, crushed
2 tbsp wholegrain mustard
½ small celeriac
3 large floury potatoes
3 large parsnips
1 litre strong vegetable stock

★ GET AHEAD
Prepare to the end of step 1 up to 3hr ahead.
Complete the recipe to serve.

1. Preheat oven to 200°C (180°C fan) mark 6 and grease a rough 23 x 33 x 5cm ovenproof dish with butter. Melt half the butter in a pan and gently cook the onions until softened, about 10min. Add the garlic and mustard and set aside.

2. Peel the root veg and thinly slice (a mandoline is best for this). Mix and arrange a layer of the veg into the serving dish. Scatter over some of the onion mixture and some seasoning. Continue layering up the veg, onions and seasoning, finishing with a fairly level layer of root veg.

3. Bring the stock to a simmer, then pour into the dish to just cover the vegetables (you may not need all the liquid). Dot over the remaining butter, cover the dish with foil and cook for 45min, then uncover and continue cooking for a further 30min until vegetables are tender (a knife should go through easily). If there's still too much liquid in the dish, carefully pour it off and return the dish to the oven for 10–15min to dry out a little more. Serve.

Hands-on time: 25min
Cooking time: about 1hr 30min
Serves 8

PER SERVING 184cals, 4g protein, 7g fat
(3g saturates), 24g carbs (7g total sugars), 6g fibre

Speedy Roasted Broccoli

Roasting broccoli adds texture and masks the slight bitterness that some people find unappealing.

2 tbsp olive oil
¼–½ tsp dried chilli flakes
2 medium broccoli heads, cut into small-medium florets (about 600g)
1 tbsp capers (in brine), drained
40g Parmesan cheese, finely grated

1. Preheat oven to 200°C (180°C fan) mark 6. Mix the oil, chilli flakes and some seasoning in a large bowl. Add the broccoli and toss to coat. Empty into a roasting tin.

2. Roast for 20min, turning after 10min, until golden and just tender. Toss through the capers and Parmesan, then transfer to a warmed serving bowl.

★ GET AHEAD
Prepare to the end of step 1 up to 3hr ahead. Complete the recipe to serve.

Hands-on time: 5min
Cooking time: about 20min
Serves 8

PER SERVING 78cals, 5g protein, 5g fat (2g saturates), 2g carbs (1g total sugars), 3g fibre

Triple Chocolate Mousse Cake with Mirror Glaze

The ideal get-ahead finish to a festive meal. Chocoholics beware!

FOR THE CAKE
75g unsalted butter, softened, plus extra to grease
225g dark chocolate, chopped
3 medium eggs, separated
100g caster sugar

FOR THE DARK CHOCOLATE MOUSSE LAYER
150g dark chocolate, chopped
200ml double cream
2 medium eggs, separated

FOR THE WHITE CHOCOLATE MOUSSE LAYER
3 sheets leaf gelatine
100g white chocolate, chopped
2 medium eggs, separated
2 tsp vanilla extract
250ml double cream

FOR THE MIRROR GLAZE
15g sheets leaf gelatine (about 8)
60ml double cream
60g cocoa powder
200g granulated sugar
40g dark chocolate, chopped
Bronze metallic cake sprinkles, to decorate (optional)

★ GET AHEAD
Make to end of step 8 up to 1 day ahead.
Glaze up to 5hr ahead and chill.

Hands-on time: 50min, plus cooling and chilling
Cooking time: about 1hr 20min
Serves 12

PER SERVING 645cals, 10g protein, 44g fat
(26g saturates), 52g carbs (51g total sugars), 2g fibre

1. Preheat oven to 180°C (160°C fan) mark 4 and grease and line a 20.5cm springform cake tin with baking parchment. Line the outside of the tin with a few sheets of aluminium foil (to make the tin water tight) and sit in a large roasting tin.

2. For the cake, melt the chocolate in a heatproof bowl set over a pan of simmering water. Take off heat and set aside to cool for 5min. Meanwhile, in a separate bowl using a handheld electric whisk, beat the egg whites and half the sugar until fluffy. Add the rest of the sugar and continue beating until the meringue is thick and shiny.

3. Whisk the butter into the cooled chocolate, followed by the egg yolks. Stir in half the meringue mixture, then fold in the rest. Scrape into the prepared tin and smooth to level. Pour hot water into the roasting tin until it comes about 2.5cm up the outside of the cake tin. Bake for 40min or until a skewer inserted into the centre comes out clean. Cool in the tin (outside of the water bath), then chill for 1hr (still in the cake tin).

4. Remove the cake from the tin. Wash the cake tin. Reassemble the tin. Lightly grease the sides and line the base and sides neatly with baking parchment. Return the cake to the tin, top down.

Continues over the page...

5. To make the dark chocolate mousse layer, melt the chocolate as before. Set the bowl aside to cool for 10min. Beat the cream in a bowl until it holds soft peaks. Whisk the yolks into the chocolate mixture. Next, with clean beaters, whip the egg whites to soft peaks.

6. Scrape the cooled chocolate mixture into the cream and fold together. Fold in the egg whites, being careful to not over-fold. Scrape into the prepared tin, spreading to level (making sure it touches the sides). Chill for 30min.

7. To make the white chocolate mousse layer, soak the gelatine in cold water for 5min. Meanwhile, melt the chocolate as before. Take the bowl off heat. Lift the gelatine out of the water, squeeze out excess and stir into the hot chocolate to dissolve. Stir in the egg yolks and vanilla. Cool for 10min.

8. Beat the cream in a bowl until it holds soft peaks. With clean beaters, whip the egg whites to soft peaks. Fold the chocolate mixture into the cream, followed by the egg whites. Scrape into the tin and level, then chill to set, about 3hr.

9. Around 30min before you want to glaze the mousse cake, soak the gelatine sheets in cold water to soften, about 5min. Heat the cream, cocoa, sugar and 100ml water in a medium pan, whisking to dissolve. Bring to the boil, whisking, then take off heat, add the chocolate and whisk again to dissolve.

10. Lift the gelatine out of the water and squeeze out excess. Mix into the hot chocolate glaze to dissolve. Strain twice through a fine sieve into a glass jug (this step is important to remove any bubbles). Allow to cool to room temperature, stirring occasionally.

11. Unclip the tin and transfer the mousse cake to a rack positioned over a clean tray. Carefully peel off the baking parchment. Pour on the glaze, making sure it covers the top and drips evenly down the sides, spreading with a palette knife to help. Decorate with bronze metallic cake sprinkles, if using. Chill for 30min or until needed.

12. Transfer to a cake stand to serve.

Raspberry Jellies

A jammy, sweet confection to take you joyfully into the New Year!

600g raspberries
600g granulated sugar, plus extra to sprinkle
60g liquid pectin
2 tsp fresh lemon juice

YOU'LL ALSO NEED
A digital thermometer

1. Line a 20.5cm square tin with baking parchment. Purée the raspberries in a food processor or blender. Strain through a fine sieve into a large heavy bottomed pan, working the pulp well. Discard the seeds. Stir in the sugar.

2. Heat gently, stirring, to dissolve the sugar. Turn up the heat and bubble the mixture, stirring frequently, until it reaches 114°C on a digital thermometer – this takes about 15–20min.

3. Add the pectin and lemon juice and boil for 2min, stirring constantly. Scrape into the prepared tin. Leave to cool and set. This should take about 5hr.

4. Lay a sheet of baking parchment larger than the tin on a work surface and sprinkle generously with granulated sugar. Invert the tin on to the baking parchment, remove the tin and peel off the lining parchment. Sprinkle over more granulated sugar. Slice into 2.5cm squares using a large sharp knife or stamp out small shapes. Working with a couple of jellies at a time, toss in granulated sugar. Serve and enjoy.

⭐ GET AHEAD
Make up to 5 days ahead. Store uncovered (ideally in a single layer) on baking parchment and re-toss in granulated sugar before serving, if needed.

Hands-on time: 25min, plus setting
Cooking time: about 25min
Makes about 64 jellies

PER JELLY 41cals, 0g protein, 0g fat (0g saturates),
10g carbs (10g total sugars), 0g fibre

Slowly
Does It

Pumpkin Stew

If you can't find pumpkin, use butternut squash instead.

2 tsp vegetable oil
1 onion, sliced
2 garlic cloves, crushed
1–2 red chillies, to taste, deseeded and finely sliced
2 tsp each ground cumin
2 tsp coriander seeds
3cm piece fresh root ginger, peeled and finely grated
3 tbsp tomato purée
600g pumpkin or butternut squash, peeled, deseeded and cut into 1cm-wide wedges
400g tin chopped tomatoes
200g full-fat coconut milk
1 vegetable stock cube, crumbled
250g pouch cooked puy lentils
Small handful coriander, roughly chopped (optional)

1. Heat the oil in a medium, deep frying pan over medium heat. Cook the onion for 10min, until softened. Stir in the garlic and chilli(es) and fry for 1min, until fragrant.

2. Add the ground cumin, coriander seeds, ginger and tomato purée. Fry for 1min. Scrape into a slow cooker and stir in all the remaining ingredients, except for the lentils and coriander. Season.

3. Cover with the lid and cook on low for 6hr, or until pumpkin/squash is tender. Stir in the lentils, re-cover and cook for 5min more, or until the lentils are piping hot.

4. Check the seasoning. Garnish with the coriander, if using, and some freshly ground black pepper. Serve with crusty bread, if you like.

★ NO SLOW COOKER? NO PROBLEM!
Cook the recipe in the pan, simmering for 25min in step 3, or until the pumpkin/squash is tender. Complete the recipe.

Hands-on time: 15min
Cooking time: about 6hr 20min
Serves 4

PER SERVING 268cals, 11g protein, 12g fat
(8g saturates), 24g carbs (11g total sugars), 9g fibre

Slow-cooker Mushroom Dumpling Stew

Lentils provide a delicious source of protein and Marmite adds depth, but you can leave it out.

FOR THE STEW
2 tsp vegetable oil
1 large onion, finely chopped
2 garlic cloves, crushed
1 tbsp tomato purée
3 tbsp plain flour
150ml vegan red wine
2 carrots, cut into 1cm slices
300g portobello mushrooms, sliced
2 x 400g tins green lentils, drained and rinsed
700ml vegetable stock
Small handful thyme sprigs
1 tbsp Marmite (optional)
Small handful parsley, roughly chopped

FOR THE DUMPLINGS
100g self-raising flour
40g vegan spread, chilled
1 tsp dried thyme

1. For the stew, heat the oil in a large pan over a medium heat. Add the onion and a large pinch of salt, then cook for 10min, stirring regularly, until softened. Stir in the garlic and tomato purée, then cook for 1min. Stir in the flour. Add the red wine gradually, stirring constantly to prevent lumps forming. Bubble for 1min, then transfer to a slow cooker.

2. Add the carrots, mushrooms, lentils, stock, thyme sprigs and some seasoning. Cover and cook on high for 4hr.

3. Discard the thyme, stir through the Marmite, if using, and check the seasoning. Re-cover.

4. To make the dumplings, in a bowl, rub the flour, vegan spread and plenty of seasoning together with your fingertips, or pulse in a small food processor until the mixture resembles fine breadcrumbs. Stir in the dried thyme, sprinkle over 2–3 tbsp cold water and stir/pulse until the mixture comes together. Divide the dough into 8 and roll into balls. Uncover the stew and arrange the dumplings on top, spaced apart.

5. Re-cover and cook on high for 1hr until the dumplings are cooked and fluffy. Sprinkle over the parsley and serve.

Hands-on time: 10min
Cooking time: about 5hr 15min
Serves 4

PER SERVING 387cals, 16g protein, 9g fat
(2g saturates), 50g carbs (8g total sugars), 11g fibre

Braised Lamb Shanks

Easy to portion, simple to cook and delectable to eat, lamb shanks are a great easy-entertaining option.

1½ tbsp olive oil
6 lamb shanks
1 onion, roughly chopped
4 tbsp plain flour
3 garlic cloves, bashed (leave skins on)
3 rosemary sprigs
2½ tbsp tomato purée
400ml red wine
800ml chicken stock (not too strong)

★ GH TIP
Shanks are a delight served with mashed potatoes and steamed cabbage.

1. Heat the oil in a large ovenproof pan (that has a lid and that will hold all the shanks) or a large, sturdy roasting tin over medium-high heat. Brown the lamb shanks well all over (do this in batches). Set aside.

2. Add the onion to the empty pan/tin, reduce heat to low and fry for 10min (add a splash of water if the onion is sticking). Stir in the flour, garlic, rosemary and tomato purée and cook, stirring, for 30sec. Gradually stir in the wine, followed by the stock and some seasoning.

3. Preheat oven to 180°C (160°C fan) mark 4. Return the shanks to the pan or tin, arranging them so they are covered with liquid as much as possible. Bring to the boil, then cover with a lid or tightly with foil. Cook in the oven for 1hr 45min, or until the lamb is tender and pulling away from the bone.

4. When cooked, transfer the shanks to a large serving dish and cover well with a few layers of foil to keep warm. Put the pan or tin back over high hob heat. Bubble for 20min, or until the liquid is thickened and glossy. Strain into a jug.

5. Pour some of the gravy over the lamb shanks to moisten. Serve with the remaining gravy on the side and steamed greens, if you like.

Hands-on time: 25min
Cooking time: about 2hr 30min
Serves 6

PER SERVING 711cals, 52g protein, 34g fat
(14g saturates), 11g carbs (3g total sugars), 1g fibre

Sweet and Sour Dal

Use chana dal lentils if you can, as they hold their shape well when cooking. Yellow split peas can be used, but will go mushy more quickly, so cook them for less time.

500g chana dal lentils
50g butter
1 onion, finely chopped
1 tsp dried chilli flakes
1 tsp mustard seeds
2 tbsp dried curry leaves
1 tbsp garam masala
3 garlic cloves, crushed
3 star anise
3 tbsp tamarind paste
3 tbsp dark muscovado sugar
4 large tomatoes, roughly chopped
Juice 2 limes, plus extra wedges, to serve

FOR THE BOMBAY PUFFED RICE (optional)
25g puffed rice
1 tsp garam masala
2 tbsp tamarind paste
1 tbsp dark muscovado sugar
2 tomatoes, finely chopped
Juice 2 limes
Handful coriander, roughly chopped
½ red onion, finely chopped

⭐ GH TIP
To make this vegan, swap the butter for 2 tbsp vegetable oil.

1. In a bowl, rinse the lentils in 3 changes of water. Pour over enough water to cover, then leave to soak for 30min.

2. In a large casserole, heat the butter and fry the onion for 8–10min. Add the chilli flakes, mustard seeds, curry leaves, garam masala and garlic and heat for 1min until the spices release their aroma.

3. Drain the lentils, put into the casserole, and add enough water to cover generously (about 1 litre). Add the star anise. Bring up to a simmer, turn down heat and cover. Cook over a very low heat so it is barely simmering for 2hr, stirring occasionally. Remove the star anise.

4. Stir in the tamarind paste, sugar, chopped tomatoes and lime juice. Simmer for 15min, or until the tomatoes have broken down. Remove from the heat and leave to stand for 5min.

5. If making the Bombay puffed rice, toast the rice in a large, dry frying pan. Remove from heat and stir in the remaining ingredients. Sprinkle over the dal and serve with lime wedges on the side.

Hands-on time: 20min, plus soaking
Cooking time: about 2hr 30min
Serves 6

PER SERVING (with Bombay puffed rice) 453cals, 20g protein, 9g fat (5g saturates), 68g carbs (19g total sugars), 9g fibre

Tetuler Mangsho Bengali Slow-cooked Lamb and Tamarind Curry

Check how sour your tamarind paste is before you add it to the gravy, as different brands can vary. We've used mustard oil, which is common in the east of India, but you can use vegetable oil instead.

FOR THE MARINADE
1½ tbsp plain yogurt
1 tsp gram (chickpea) flour
½ tsp mild chilli powder
1½ tsp ground turmeric
1 tbsp ground coriander
600g diced lamb leg (see GH Tip)

FOR THE CURRY
3 tbsp mustard oil or vegetable oil
3 dried bay leaves
6 green cardamom pods
1 large onion, finely chopped
6 garlic cloves
5cm piece fresh root ginger, peeled and finely grated
2 tbsp sugar
½ tbsp tamarind paste
Handful coriander, roughly chopped

★ GH TIP
Traditionally, chopped lamb leg (with bone) would be used here, as the bone adds lots of flavour to the curry. If you can source this, then use 700g. If using boneless lamb leg, try to buy it in one piece and chop it yourself, as pre-diced pieces tend to be small.

1. For the marinade, in a large bowl, mix the yogurt, gram flour and spices. Stir in the lamb, making sure all the pieces are coated in the marinade. Set aside for 1hr while you make the curry.

2. Heat the oil in a large, heavy-based pan (that has a lid) over medium heat. Add the bay leaves and cardamom pods and fry for 10sec. Stir in the onion and fry for 18–20min, stirring frequently, until dark golden brown.

3. Pound the garlic using a pestle and mortar to make a smooth paste. Add to the pan together with the ginger and fry for 1min. Mix in the marinated lamb and fry for 7–8min, stirring frequently and scraping the bottom of the pan. Pour in 250ml water and add some seasoning. Bring to the boil, turn down the heat, cover and simmer for 45–50min, stirring occasionally to make sure the curry thickens and coats the lamb. If it's too thick, add a splash of water.

4. Add the sugar, tamarind paste and coriander. Continue to cook, uncovered, for 7–10min. Check the seasoning and serve with rice or puris.

Hands-on time: 20min, plus marinating
Cooking time: about 1hr 30min
Serves 4

PER SERVING 417cals, 30g protein, 27g fat (9g saturates), 13g carbs (11g total sugars), 1g fibre

Easy Slow-cooker Ham

A ham is an economical and seasonal showstopper. If you prefer a stronger flavour, start with a smoked gammon. Don't waste the poaching liquid; strain it through a fine sieve and chill or freeze to use later. It makes a good base for soups or stews – just check it's not too salty before using.

FOR THE HAM
1.6kg unsmoked gammon joint (see intro and GH Tip)
2 bay leaves
10 black peppercorns
2 tbsp light brown soft sugar
500ml cider

FOR THE GLAZE
1 tbsp runny honey
1 tbsp wholegrain mustard
1 tbsp light brown soft sugar

⭐ GET AHEAD
Cook the gammon 1–2 days ahead, then cool completely in the cooking liquid. Cover and chill (still in the liquid). To serve, allow the ham to come to room temperature and complete the recipe. The finished ham will keep in the fridge, well-wrapped, for up to 4 days. Allow to come to room temperature before serving.

⭐ GH TIP
When buying your gammon, bear in mind the size and shape of your slow cooker bowl, opting for a rounder or more bullet-shaped joint as needed.

1. For the ham, put the gammon, bay and peppercorns into a slow cooker and rub the sugar all over the gammon. Pour the cider around the meat, then top up with cold water to just barely cover the meat.

2. Cover with the lid and cook on low for 5hr or until cooked through. Remove the lid, turn off the cooker and leave the ham to cool in the poaching liquid for at least 30min, or until cool enough to handle.

3. Preheat oven to 200°C (180°C fan) mark 6. Lift the ham on to a board and remove any string. Using a sharp knife, slice off the skin, leaving a good layer of fat. Score a close diamond pattern into the fat (not cutting into the meat). Place fat-side up in a small roasting tin.

4. For the glaze, mix all the ingredients in a small bowl and brush over the ham fat. Roast for 20–30min or until an even golden brown. Serve hot, warm or at room temperature, in slices.

Hands-on time: 20min, plus cooling
Cooking time: about 5hr 30min
Serves 6

PER SERVING 486cals, 69g protein, 19g fat (7g saturates), 10g carbs (10g total sugars), 0g fibre

Sausage Casserole

Super easy and hearty, this recipe relies on good-quality pork sausages. Use your favourite plain variety or try flavoured – pork and apple, Cumberland or a robust Toulouse work well here, too.

1 tbsp olive oil
8 good-quality pork sausages
2 red onions, finely sliced
2 tbsp plain flour
400ml beef stock
3 parsnips, peeled and cut into batons
2 garlic cloves, crushed
3 tbsp onion chutney or marmalade

1. Heat ½ tbsp oil in a large frying pan over medium-high heat and brown the sausages (they don't need to be cooked through). Empty into a slow cooker.

2. Add the remaining ½ tbsp oil to the pan, reduce heat to low-medium and cook the onions for 7min, until softened. Increase heat to medium-high and cook, stirring frequently, until the onions are starting to caramelise.

3. Stir in the flour and cook for 1min, then gradually mix in the stock. Empty into a slow cooker and mix in the parsnips, garlic, chutney/marmalade and some seasoning. Cover with the lid and cook on high for 4hr until the sausages are cooked through.

4. Check the seasoning and serve with mashed potato and steamed greens, if you like.

★ NO SLOW COOKER? NO PROBLEM!
Return the sausages to the pan in step 3 with the other ingredients. Cover and simmer for 15–20min, or until sausages are cooked through and the gravy is glossy and thickened. Complete the recipe.

Hands-on time: 10min
Cooking time: about 4hr 20min
Serves 4

PER SERVING 547cals, 26g protein, 32g fat (11g saturates), 34g carbs (34g total sugars), 9g fibre

Chicken Cacciatore

Meaning 'hunter's chicken', this Italian classic is made with chicken thighs cooked in a rustic tomato sauce.

2 tbsp olive oil
500g bone-in, skin-on chicken thighs
40g plain flour
1 onion, finely chopped
150ml red wine
3 garlic cloves, crushed
2 bay leaves
2 rosemary sprigs, leaves picked and finely chopped
5 anchovy fillets in oil, drained and roughly chopped
400g tin plum tomatoes, chopped
200ml chicken stock
2 mixed peppers, deseeded and sliced
100g pitted olives
Cooked rice or polenta, to serve (optional)

1. Heat half the oil in a large, deep frying pan over a medium heat. Toss the chicken in the flour and add to the pan, skin-side down. Fry until a dark golden brown, then turn and brown the other side. Remove to a plate, skin-side up.

2. Add the remaining oil to the pan and fry the onion until beginning to soften, about 5min. Increase the heat to high, add the wine and bubble until reduced by half. Stir in the garlic, herbs and anchovies. Cook for 2min, stirring. Pour in the tomatoes and stock and bring to the boil.

3. Pour the mixture into the slow cooker, stir in the peppers and set the thighs on top. Cover and cook on high for 3hr.

4. Remove the chicken to a plate and keep warm. Pour the sauce into a wide, shallow pan. Stir in the olives and bubble over a high heat for 10min to reduce and thicken slightly. Return the chicken to the sauce and check the seasoning. Serve with rice or polenta.

★ GH TIP
Chicken thighs remain juicy and tender with slow cooking, but use skin-on breasts, if you prefer.

Hands-on time: 25min
Cooking time: about 3hr 30min
Serves 4

PER SERVING 483cals, 28g protein, 31g fat (7g saturates), 17g carbs (9g total sugars), 5g fibre

Normandy Pork with Apples and Cider

A slow-roast twist on a classic Normandy casserole. Delicious served with mashed potato for soaking up the creamy juices.

2kg boneless skin-on pork shoulder, skin scored
½ tbsp vegetable oil
4 echalion shallots, finely sliced
75g diced smoked pancetta
2 large garlic cloves, crushed
2 tbsp plain flour
500ml cider
250ml chicken stock
3 Braeburn apples, cored and each cut into 8 wedges
100ml half-fat crème fraîche
2 tsp Dijon mustard
200g kale, woody stems discarded and shredded
Small handful tarragon, leaves picked and
   roughly chopped

★ GH TIP
If the crackling still needs a little help, once the pork is cooked through, transfer to a baking tray (skin-side up) and crisp it up under a hot grill – keeping an eye on it to make sure it doesn't burn.

Hands-on time: 30min
Cooking time: about 4hr 55min
Serves 8

PER SERVING 515cals, 35g protein, 34g fat
(11g saturates), 12g carbs (9g total sugars), 2g fibre

1. Preheat oven to 160°C (140°C fan) mark 3. Pat the pork dry with kitchen paper. If the skin is not already scored by your butcher, do so in a diamond pattern with a sharp knife or scalpel. This is important to help the crackling crisp up.

2. Heat the oil in a large, shallow casserole dish over medium-high heat. Brown the pork all over. Remove to a plate. Add the shallots and pancetta to the casserole, then reduce heat to low and cook for 4min, until slightly softened. Stir in the garlic and cook for 1min.

3. Next stir in the flour, followed by the cider, stock and some seasoning. Bring to the boil, then return the pork (and any juices on the plate) to the dish, skin-side up. Season the pork, cover the dish loosely with foil and transfer to the oven.

4. Cook for 3hr, then remove the foil, add the apple wedges to the liquid and return to the oven, uncovered, for 1hr–1hr 30min, or until the pork is tender and the skin has crisped up (see GH Tip).

5. Carefully transfer the pork and apples to a clean plate and set aside in a warm place to rest (uncovered). Skim off and discard excess fat from the sauce, then stir in the crème fraîche and mustard and check the seasoning. Stir in the kale and bubble over medium hob heat for 4–5min until the kale is wilted and tender.

6. Return the pork to the dish, sprinkle over the tarragon and serve with mash, if you like.

Slow-cooker Lamb Tagine

So easy, especially as the slow cooker does all the work. The ideal warming meal to have waiting for you after a long day.

FOR THE TAGINE
1 tbsp vegetable oil
900g lamb neck fillet, cut into roughly 3cm pieces
1 large onion, finely chopped
1 tsp za'atar
1 tsp ground cinnamon
1 tsp ground cumin
1 tbsp tomato purée
400g tin chopped tomatoes
300ml chicken stock
400g tin chickpeas, drained and rinsed
100g pitted green olives
75g dried apricots, chopped

TO SERVE
Small handful mint leaves, roughly chopped
50g flaked almonds, toasted
100g natural yogurt

⭐ FREEZE AHEAD
Prepare to the end of step 3. Cool, transfer to a freezer-safe container and freeze for up to 1 month. To serve, defrost in the fridge and reheat in a pan until piping hot. Complete the recipe.

1. For the tagine, heat the oil in a large pan over medium-high heat and brown the lamb all over, in batches if needed. Using a slotted spoon, transfer the browned lamb to the slow cooker.

2. Reduce heat under the pan to medium, add the onion and a large pinch of salt and cook for 10min, stirring regularly, until softened. Stir in the spices and tomato purée and cook for 1min until fragrant. Transfer the mixture to the slow cooker.

3. Add the remaining tagine ingredients to the slow cooker, stir, then cover and cook on low for 6hr, or until the lamb is cooked through.

4. Check the seasoning, transfer to a warmed serving dish and garnish with mint and almonds. Serve with the yogurt to dollop on top, and flatbreads, couscous or rice, if you like.

Hands-on time: 20min
Cooking time: about 6hr 30min
Serves 6

PER SERVING 540cals, 39g protein, 34g fat
(11g saturates), 17g carbs (10g total sugars), 5g fibre

Slow-roast Ratatouille Lamb Shoulder

An all-in-one roast that's full of the flavours of France. You might want a crusty baguette on the side to dip into the ratatouille.

1.8kg lamb shoulder (on the bone)
4 garlic cloves
4 tsp herbes de Provence (or dried mixed herbs)
1 tsp olive oil
1½ tbsp runny honey
2 red onions, roughly chopped
400g tin chopped tomatoes
500ml vegetable stock
2 x 400g tins cannellini beans, drained and rinsed
1 large aubergine, cut into roughly 2.5cm pieces
2 mixed colour peppers, deseeded and cut into roughly 2.5cm pieces
2 courgettes, trimmed and cut into 1cm rounds
250g cherry tomatoes on the vine, cut into bunches
Large handful basil, leaves picked

1. Preheat oven to 170°C (150°C fan) mark 3. Lay the lamb on a board and slash the fatty side well with a sharp knife. Crush 2 garlic cloves and mix in a small bowl with 2 tsp dried herbs, the oil, ½ tbsp honey and plenty of seasoning. Rub the mixture all over the lamb.

2. Thinly slice the remaining 2 garlic cloves. In a sturdy roasting tin just large enough to hold the lamb, mix the onions, tinned tomatoes, stock, sliced garlic, remaining 2 tsp dried herbs and some seasoning. Lay the lamb on top (slashed side-up) and cover the tin with foil.

3. Roast the lamb for 3hr 30min, then remove the foil and carefully lift the lamb on to a plate. Spoon off any excess fat from the tin, then stir in the beans, aubergine, peppers, courgettes and remaining 1 tbsp honey.

4. Place the lamb on top of the vegetables and arrange the cherry tomatoes around the lamb. Return to oven, uncovered, for 45min or until the vegetables are tender, the lamb is browned and you can shred the meat off the bone with 2 forks.

5. Cover the tin and set aside to rest in a warm place for 20min. To serve, check the seasoning and garnish with basil.

Hands-on time: 25min, plus resting
Cooking time: about 4hr 15min
Serves 8

PER SERVING 477cals, 51g protein, 19g fat (8g saturates), 22g carbs (12g total sugars), 9g fibre

Spiced Beef Brisket with Roasted Carrot Orzo

Melt-in-the-mouth, tender beef and warming Middle Eastern spices are a match made in heaven in this slow-cooked crowd-pleaser. A long, slow braise transforms a great-value cut of meat into a wow-factor main fit for a dinner party.

2 tbsp rose harissa
2 tsp ras el hanout spice blend
1 tbsp pomegranate molasses
Finely grated zest and juice 1 orange
1.6kg boned and rolled beef brisket

FOR THE ORZO
800g mixed heritage carrots, peeled and cut into
    chunky pieces on the diagonal
3 tbsp olive oil
2 tsp ras el hanout spice blend
1 tsp cumin seeds
2 tbsp pomegranate molasses
1 litre fresh beef stock
2 cinnamon sticks
400g orzo
2 onions, sliced
2 celery sticks, diced
6 garlic cloves, finely chopped
Radicchio, shredded
½ small bunch flat-leaf parsley, roughly chopped
Seeds from 1 pomegranate
100g pistachio kernels, roughly chopped

Hands-on time: 30min, plus marinating
Cooking time: about 6hr 30min
Serves 10

PER SERVING 576cals, 51g protein, 20g fat
(5g saturates), 43g carbs (13g total sugars), 8g fibre

1. Make the marinade: in a bowl mix together the harissa, 1 tsp ras el hanout, pomegranate molasses, half the orange zest and 2 tbsp of the juice. Spread this over the beef to coat and set aside to marinate, covered, in the fridge, for at least 2hr or for up to 24hr.

2. Meanwhile, preheat oven to 190°C (170°C fan) mark 5. Put the carrots into a medium roasting tin. Add 1 tbsp oil, the remaining orange zest and juice, ras el hanout and the cumin seeds. Toss together and season with salt and pepper. Cover with foil and roast for 40min. Remove the foil and drizzle with pomegranate molasses. Return to oven, uncovered, for 10–15min, until beginning to char at the edges and turn sticky. Remove from oven and set aside.

3. Pour half the beef stock into a pan, add 500ml boiling water and bring to the boil with one of the cinnamon sticks, add the orzo and cook for about 10min until tender. Drain well, transfer to a bowl and set aside.

4. When the beef has finished marinating, preheat oven to 140°C (120°C fan) mark 1. Heat 1 tbsp oil in a medium casserole (large enough to fit the beef with a little space around it), add the onion, celery and remaining cinnamon stick and cook over a low heat for 10min, stirring occasionally. Add the garlic and cook for a further 10min. Tip on to a plate and set aside.

★ GET AHEAD
Complete the recipe to the end of step 6 up to 1 day ahead. Allow to cool completely, transfer the beef and orzo to separate airtight containers and chill until needed. To reheat, tip both into separate saucepans and gently heat, stirring occasionally, until piping hot throughout (you may need to add a splash of boiling water to the orzo to make sure it doesn't stick to the pan). Complete the recipe to serve.

5. Heat the remaining oil in the casserole and return to heat. When hot, sear the beef on all sides to brown. Return the onion mixture to the casserole. Add the remaining beef stock – it should come about halfway up the casserole. Bring to the boil, cover with a lid and cook in the oven for 4–6hr, turning every hr, until very tender and shreddable.

6. To serve, lift the beef out on to a board and shred using 2 forks. Return the casserole to the hob, bring the liquid to the boil and bubble for 10–15min to reduce and thicken (there should be about 500ml once reduced). Add 100ml of the gravy to the orzo and stir through to dress it. Add the remaining gravy to the shredded beef and toss.

7. Add the roasted carrots, radicchio, most of the parsley, pomegranate seeds and pistachios to the orzo, then toss together and season to taste.

8. Spoon the orzo on to a large serving plate, top with the shredded beef and scatter over the remaining parsley, pomegranate seeds and pistachios.

Meat-free Chilli

We've replaced the meat in this chilli with an array of veggies and protein-rich kidney and black-eyed beans.

2 tsp vegetable oil
1 large onion, finely chopped
½–1 tbsp hot chilli powder, to taste
1 tsp ground cumin
1 tsp smoked paprika
2 garlic cloves, crushed
1 tbsp tomato purée
2 celery sticks, finely sliced
1 carrot, peeled and chopped
1 red pepper, deseeded and finely sliced
1 large sweet potato, peeled and cut into
    roughly 2cm pieces
400g tin chopped tomatoes
400g tin kidney beans, drained and rinsed
400g tin black-eyed beans, drained and rinsed
400ml vegan vegetable stock
25g vegan dark chocolate
Small handful coriander, roughly chopped (optional)
Rice and guacamole, to serve (optional)

1. Heat the oil in a large pan over medium heat and cook the onion for 10min until softened. Stir in the spices, garlic and tomato purée. Cook for 1min until fragrant. Transfer to a slow cooker.

2. Add the vegetables, tomatoes, beans and stock. Cover with the lid and cook on high for 4hr or until the sweet potato is tender.

3. Stir in the dark chocolate until melted and check the seasoning. Garnish with coriander, if using, and serve with rice and guacamole, if you like.

★ NO SLOW COOKER? NO PROBLEM!
Simply add the ingredients in step 2 to the pan with the onion mixture. Simmer for 15min or until the sweet potato is tender. Complete the recipe.

Hands-on time: 10min
Cooking time: about 4hr 10min
Serves 4

PER SERVING 314cals, 12g protein, 5g fat (1g saturates), 48g carbs (18g total sugars), 14g fibre

Warming Venison Casserole

Rich and delicious, venison makes a hearty meal for the winter.

1.2kg venison for casseroling, diced
2 tbsp vegetable oil
1 onion, sliced
250g mixed mushrooms (we used chestnut and shiitake) sliced
1 garlic clove, crushed
150ml dry cider
600ml beef stock
2 bay leaves
Pared zest of 1 orange
1 tbsp cornflour
1 tbsp redcurrant jelly
Small handful parsley, chopped

1. Preheat oven to 160°C (140°C fan) mark 3. Pat the venison dry with kitchen paper and season. Heat 1½ tbsp oil in a large ovenproof casserole (with a tight-fitting lid) over medium-high heat. Brown the venison in batches and set the meat aside.

2. Heat the remaining oil. Fry the onion for 5min until golden, then add the mushrooms and fry for 2–3min until softened. Stir in the garlic.

3. Return the venison to the pan with any juices. Add the cider, stock, bay leaves and orange zest. Bring to the boil, then cover the surface of the casserole with greaseproof paper. Put on the lid and cook in oven for 2hr 15min or until venison is tender (add a little extra stock if the pan looks too dry).

4. Strain the stew, reserving the venison mixture and liquid. Return the liquid to the pan, then bring to the boil on the hob and simmer for about 10min or until the flavour has intensified. In a small bowl, mix together the cornflour and 2 tbsp water. Whisk into the simmering liquid. Boil the sauce for 4–5min, stirring constantly, until the mixture thickens. Stir in the redcurrant jelly, then return the strained venison mixture to the pan and heat through (don't boil or the meat will toughen). Discard the bay leaves, add the parsley and check the seasoning. Serve immediately.

Hands-on time: 20min
Cooking time: about 2hr 45min
Serves 6

PER SERVING 433cals, 64g protein, 16g fat (5g saturates), 6g carbs (4g total sugars), 1g fibre

Chicken Curry

An easy curry that you can adjust to your heat preference. Frying the onion and spices first helps create a deeper flavour.

1 tbsp sunflower or vegetable oil
1 onion, finely chopped
3 garlic cloves, crushed
1 tsp ground cumin
1 tsp ground coriander
1½ tbsp garam masala
1–3 tsp hot paprika, to taste
2 tbsp tomato purée
3cm piece fresh root ginger, peeled and finely grated
400g tin chopped tomatoes
200ml coconut milk
1 tsp caster sugar
650g chicken thigh fillets
Large handful coriander, roughly chopped
Rice and mango chutney, to serve (optional)

1. Heat the oil in a medium pan over low-medium heat and cook the onion for 8–10min until softened. Stir in the garlic, ground cumin and coriander, the garam masala and 1 tsp paprika and cook for 1min until aromatic.

2. Add the tomato purée and cook for 1min, then stir in the ginger, tomatoes, coconut milk, sugar and some seasoning. Transfer to a slow cooker.

3. Trim and discard excess fat and sinew from the chicken. Cut into roughly 5cm pieces. Add to the slow cooker and stir to coat. Cover with the lid and cook on low for 6–8hr until chicken is cooked through.

4. Check the seasoning, adding more paprika to taste. Stir in half the coriander and divide among 4 bowls. Garnish with the remaining coriander and serve with rice and mango chutney, if you like.

★ NO SLOW COOKER? NO PROBLEM!
Add the prepared chicken to the pan at the end of step 2. Simmer on the hob for 15–20min or until the chicken is cooked through. Complete the recipe.

Hands-on time: 15min
Cooking time: about 8hr 15min
Serves 4

PER SERVING 418cals, 31g protein, 27g fat (12g saturates), 11g carbs (9g total sugars), 2g fibre

Spiced Short Ribs

Rich, tender and melt-in-the-mouth, short ribs are a real supper showstopper. Slow braising means the meat almost falls off the bone. We've infused these with classic Asian flavours, but this versatile cut is also delicious cooked in red wine or stout.

2 tsp sunflower oil, for frying
2kg beef short ribs
6 banana shallots, peeled and quartered
2 cinnamon sticks
3 star anise
6 garlic cloves, peeled and bruised
9cm piece fresh root ginger, peeled and sliced
   into matchsticks
1 orange
900ml beef stock
2 tbsp rice wine vinegar
2 tbsp soy sauce
2 tbsp runny honey
250g shiitake mushrooms, quartered
Jasmine rice, black sesame seeds, steamed pak choi or
   seasonal greens and micro herbs (optional), to serve

1. Heat the oil in a large, high-sided casserole and brown the ribs all over (you will need to do this in batches). Set the ribs aside and wipe most of the fat from the pan. Add the shallots and cook for 5min until just beginning to soften. Add the spices, garlic and ginger for the remaining 1min, then return the beef to the pan with any juices, stirring to coat well. Using a vegetable peeler, zest the orange. Add to the pan with the orange juice (about 4 tbsp), stock, vinegar, soy sauce and honey. Bring to the boil, then reduce to a simmer and cover with a tight-fitting lid. Cook for 3–4hr, stirring occasionally, then add the mushrooms and continue cooking for a further hour until the meat is tender and just coming away from the bone.

2. Carefully remove the meat from the sauce, then bring the sauce to the boil and bubble until thickened. Return the beef to the pan and stir well to coat. Serve with steamed jasmine rice sprinkled with black sesame seeds, pak choi or seasonal greens, micro herbs, if using, and extra sauce on the side.

Hands-on time: 15min
Cooking time: about 5hr
Serves 6

PER SERVING 428cals, 44g protein, 24 fat
(11g saturates), 8g carbs (8g total sugars), 1g fibre

Slow-cooker Aubergine and Sweet Potato Jalfrezi

A little preparation is all that's needed before you can relax and allow the aromatic flavours of this curry favourite to develop.

---

1 tbsp vegetable oil
1 onion, finely chopped
2-3 green chillies, to taste
2 garlic cloves, crushed
1 tbsp garam masala
½-1 tsp chilli powder, to taste
1 tsp ground coriander
1½ tsp ground cumin
2 tsp ground turmeric
300g passata
2 medium sweet potatoes, peeled and chopped into rough 2cm chunks
1 large aubergine, chopped into rough 2cm chunks
400g tin chickpeas, drained and rinsed
Small handful coriander leaves, roughly chopped

1. Heat the oil in a medium pan over medium-high heat and fry the onion for 8–10min until softened. Deseed and finely chop 1–2 of the chillies (depending on how spicy you like it), add to the pan with the garlic and spices and cook for a few minutes until aromatic.

2. Transfer to a slow cooker and stir in the passata, sweet potatoes, aubergine, the remaining whole chilli, 300ml water and some seasoning. Cover and cook on low for 5hr 30min.

3. Stir in the chickpeas, re-cover and cook for 30min. Check the seasoning, remove the whole chilli and garnish with the chopped coriander. Serve.

★ GH TIP

Stir through some spinach leaves towards the end of cooking, and finish with coconut yogurt, if you like.

Hands-on time: 15min
Cooking time: about 6hr 15min
Serves 4

PER SERVING 228cals, 8g protein, 5g fat (1g saturates), 33g carbs (11g total sugars), 10g fibre

Hot-or-not Chilli con Carne

This family-frendly chilli comes with an optional stir-in salsa for those that love the heat. If you're feeling bold, try a Scotch bonnet or habanero chilli in the salsa.

2 tbsp vegetable oil
1kg beef brisket or casserole steak, cut into 2.5cm chunks
2 large red onions, chopped
4 garlic cloves, crushed
2 tsp ground cumin
½ tsp ground cloves
2 tsp sweet smoked paprika
2 tsp dried oregano
½ x 90g jar ancho chilli paste
500ml beef stock
2 x 400g tins plum tomatoes
2 x 400g tins red kidney beans, drained and rinsed

FOR THE HOT SALSA (optional)
3 ripe tomatoes, finely chopped
2-3 red chillies, deseeded and finely chopped
1 tbsp lime juice
2 tsp caster sugar

TO SERVE
Spring onions, sliced
Cheddar cheese, grated
Sour cream

1. Preheat oven to 170°C (150°C fan) mark 3. Heat the oil in a large casserole dish (that has a lid) over high heat and brown the beef all over – do this in batches. Transfer the browned beef to a bowl using a slotted spoon.

2. Reduce heat to low, add the onions and cook for 7–8min until softening. Add the garlic, spices and oregano and cook for 2–3min, stirring.

3. Return the beef to the dish with the ancho paste, stock and tomatoes. Bring to the boil, cover with a lid and cook in oven for 2hr. Stir in the kidney beans and return to the oven, uncovered, for 1hr, until the beef is tender. Check seasoning.

4. To make the salsa, mix the ingredients. Serve the chilli with the salsa (if making), spring onions, cheese and sour cream on the side.

Hands-on time: 30min
Cooking time: about 3hr 20min
Serves 6

PER SERVING 587cals, 46g protein, 32g fat (12g saturates), 24g carbs (11g total sugars), 10g fibre

Proper Beef Stew with Dumplings

There's no need to brown the meat for this beef stew recipe, so it couldn't be easier.

2 tbsp vegetable oil
1 onion, roughly chopped
1kg braising steak, cut into 4cm chunks
Flour, to dust
2 parsnips, cut into 2.5cm pieces
2 carrots, cut into 2.5cm pieces
1 large leek, cut into 1cm slices
3 tbsp tomato purée
200ml red wine
600ml beef stock
3 rosemary sprigs

FOR THE DUMPLINGS
125g self-raising flour
60g suet
1 tbsp dried parsley

★ FREEZE AHEAD
Make to the end of step 2 (cooking for 3hr), then cool completely. Transfer to a container and freeze for up to 1 month. To serve, defrost overnight in the fridge. Empty into the casserole and bring to boil on the hob. Make dumplings, place on top of the stew and cook for 30min in an oven preheated to 160°C (140°C fan) mark 3.

1. Preheat oven to 160°C (140°C fan) mark 3. Heat the oil in a medium-large casserole (with a tight-fitting lid) and gently fry the onion for 5min until softened.

2. Meanwhile, dry the beef pieces with kitchen paper and dust with the plain flour (tapping off any excess). Add to the onion pan with the vegetables, purée, wine, stock, rosemary and some seasoning (the meat and veg should just be covered with liquid – if not, top up with more stock or water). Turn up the heat, bring to the boil, cover and put in the oven. Cook until the beef is tender – about 3hr.

3. Half an hour before the beef is ready, make the dumplings. Sift the flour into a large bowl and stir in the suet, parsley and lots of seasoning. Add 100ml cold water and stir to make a soft, slightly sticky, dough.

4. Take the casserole out of oven, remove the lid and discard the rosemary sprigs. Check the seasoning. Pinch off walnut-sized pieces of the dumpling dough, roll into balls and place on top of stew. Return to the oven (without the lid) for the final 30min of cooking, or until the dumplings are lightly golden. Check seasoning and serve with mashed potatoes, if you like.

Hands-on time: 25min
Cooking time: about 3hr 15min
Serves 6

PER SERVING 491cals, 40g protein, 20g fat (8g saturates), 28g carbs (7g total sugars), 6g fibre

Portuguese Fish Stew

We love the smoky paprika in this classic dish from Portugal. It can be made with any fish, so you can choose varieties that are in season and sustainable – look for the MSC logo.

1 tsp rapeseed oil
1 onion, sliced
2 roasted red peppers, from a jar, roughly diced
3 garlic cloves, finely sliced
1 tsp grated fresh root ginger
1 tsp sweet smoked paprika
¼ tsp cayenne pepper
200ml white wine
2 x 400g tins chopped tomatoes
½ tsp caster sugar
2 fresh bay leaves
Pinch saffron
500g clams (see GH Tip)
375g cod loin, cut into 3cm pieces
350g raw tiger prawns
Juice 1 lime, plus extra wedges, to serve
Small handful parsley leaves

★ TO MAKE IN A SLOW COOKER

Prepare the vegetables as in step 1. Add the tomatoes, sugar, bay and saffron, bring to the boil and transfer to the dish of a slow cooker. Set to low and leave for 4–6hr. Using a stick blender, whizz until smooth. Bring to the boil, add the clams and cook for 5min. Add the cod, prawns and juice of 1 lime. Continue as per the recipe, until the fish is cooked through.

1. Heat the oil in a large casserole, add the onion and cook for 10min, until softened. Add the peppers, garlic, ginger and spices and cook for a further 3min. Pour in the wine and boil for 5min.

2. Tip in the tomatoes, sugar, bay leaves and saffron and bring to a simmer. Season, cover and cook for 1hr 30min. Remove from the heat, discard the bay leaves and, using a stick blender, whizz until smooth.

3. Return to the heat and bring to the boil. Add the clams, cover and cook for 5min. Reduce to a gentle simmer and add the cod, prawns and juice of 1 lime, continuing to cook for 5min until the fish is just cooked through and the clams are open (discard any unopened). Season to taste.

4. Divide the soup among 6 bowls, sprinkle with parsley and serve alongside a small bowl with the remaining lime cut into wedges.

Hands-on time: 15min
Cooking time: about 2hr
Serves 6

PER SERVING 231cals, 35g protein, 3g fat (1g saturates), 10g carbs (8g total sugars), 3g fibre

★ GH TIP
Before adding the clams, rinse, tap and discard any that don't close or have damaged shells.

★ GET AHEAD Complete to end of step 3 up to 2 days in advance. Keep in an airtight container in the fridge. Complete the recipe to serve.

18

Fill Your Freezer

Crab Quiche

We've used tinned crab, but use fresh
white crab meat instead, if you prefer.

250g plain flour, plus extra to dust
125g cold butter, cut into cubes
1 large egg yolk
Green salad, to serve

FOR THE FILLING
4 large eggs
275ml double cream
½–1 red chilli, deseeded and finely chopped
2 tbsp chopped chives
2 x 170g tins white crab meat chunks in brine

1. Put the flour and butter into a food processor
   and whizz until the mixture resembles fine
   breadcrumbs. In a small bowl, stir together the
   egg yolk and 2½ tbsp ice-cold water. Add the
   liquid to the food processor and pulse until the
   mixture just comes together. Tip on to a work
   surface, then bring together and form into a
   disc. Wrap in clingfilm and chill for 15min.

2. Preheat oven to 200°C (180°C fan) mark 6.
   Lightly flour a work surface and roll out the
   pastry, then use to line a 25cm loose-bottomed
   fluted tart tin. Chill for 15min in the fridge.

3. Meanwhile, in a large jug, mix together the
   eggs, cream, some seasoning and most of the
   chilli and chives. Next, drain the crab, tip on
   to kitchen paper and pat dry.

4. Remove the pastry from the fridge and cover
   with a large sheet of greaseproof paper. Fill
   with baking beans (on top of the greaseproof),
   then put the tin on a baking sheet. Cook for
   20min, then carefully lift out the beans and
   paper. Return the pastry case to the oven and
   cook for a further 10min.

★ FREEZE AHEAD
Leave quiche to cool completely, then wrap well
in clingfilm and freeze for up to 1 month. To
serve, defrost in the fridge, then serve at room
temperature or warmed in an oven preheated to
160°C (140°C fan) mark 3 for 20min.

5. Lower the oven temperature to 180°C (160°C fan)
   mark 4. Scatter most of the crab into the pastry
   case, then pour over the egg mixture. Scatter
   over the remaining chilli, chives and crab. Cook
   for 30min or until set. Leave to cool in tin for
   5min, then remove. Serve warm or at room
   temperature with a crisp green salad.

Hands-on time: 25min, plus chilling
Cooking time: about 1hr
Serves 6

PER SERVING 647cals, 22g protein, 47g fat (28g
saturates), 33g carbs (1g total sugars), 2g fibre

French Onion Soup

The onions need to cook very slowly here, without catching. Any burning will turn the whole soup bitter. Instead of Gruyère, top with your favourite melting cheese.

FOR THE SOUP
75g butter
8 onions (about 1kg), thinly sliced
2 tbsp plain flour
2 tsp finely chopped thyme leaves, plus extra whole
    leaves, to garnish
1.5 litre hot beef or vegetable stock
2 tbsp cider vinegar

FOR THE CROUTONS
1 garlic clove
100g baguette, cut into 6 x 2cm slices
75g Gruyère, grated

1. For the soup, melt the butter in a wide ovenproof pan or casserole dish over a very low heat. Add the onions and a pinch of salt and cook gently for 2hr, stirring regularly, or until the onions are softened and a deep golden colour.

2. Stir in the flour and thyme and cook for 1min. Gradually stir in the stock, followed by the vinegar. Increase heat and bring to the boil. Reduce heat and simmer, stirring occasionally, for 40min, until slightly thickened. Check the seasoning.

3. Preheat grill to high. For the croutons, rub the garlic clove over both sides of each baguette slice. Remove the soup from heat and arrange baguette slices on top. Alternatively, transfer the soup to 6 x 500ml individual casserole or ovenproof serving dishes, and top each with a baguette slice.

4. Sprinkle the cheese over the bread and grill for 5min or until golden. Garnish with thyme and some freshly ground black pepper and serve.

⭐ FREEZE AHEAD
Freeze for up to 3 months in a freezer-safe container or food bag. To serve, defrost completely, then reheat gently in a large pan until piping hot, adding a little extra stock or water, if needed. Complete the recipe.

Hands-on time: 30min
Cooking time: about 2hr 50min
Serves 6

PER SERVING 334cals, 18g protein, 15g fat (9g saturates), 28g carbs (13g total sugars), 6g fibre

Pancetta and Polenta Muffins

Polenta adds wonderful texture to these savoury muffins.

150g diced pancetta
275g plain flour
1½ tsp baking powder
1 tsp bicarbonate of soda
125g quick-cook polenta
2 rosemary sprigs, leaves picked and finely chopped
125g Parmesan, coarsely grated
150g sour cream
125ml milk
50ml olive oil
2 medium eggs

1. Preheat oven to 180°C (160°C fan) mark 4. Line the holes of a muffin tin with squares of baking parchment or muffin cases.

2. Fry the pancetta until golden. Empty into a large jug and set aside. In a large bowl, mix the flour, baking powder, bicarbonate of soda, polenta, rosemary, 100g of the Parmesan, ¾ tsp salt and plenty of freshly ground black pepper.

3. To the pancetta, add the sour cream, milk, oil and eggs. Whisk to combine. Add the egg mixture to the flour bowl and mix until nearly combined (a few floury lumps are fine – the muffins will be tough if you overmix). Divide the mixture among the cases and scatter over the remaining Parmesan.

4. Bake for 15–20min or until lightly golden and a skewer inserted into the centre comes out clean. Serve warm or at room temperature with a crisp green salad, if you like.

★ FREEZE AHEAD
Freeze the cooled muffins (in cases) in an airtight container for up to a month. To serve them warm, reheat from frozen in a preheated 180°C (160°C fan) mark 4 oven for 20min, or simply defrost to serve at room temperature.

Hands-on time: 20min
Cooking time: about 25min
Makes 12 muffins

PER MUFFIN 271cals, 11g protein, 14g fat
(6g saturates), 25g carbs (1g total sugars), 1g fibre

Duck and Sausage Cassoulet

This hearty dish is deliciously versatile. Serve as a stew once you've stirred the duck back in (reheating on the hob first briefly, if needed) or, as is more traditional, baked with a crispy breadcrumb topping.

4 duck legs
2 tsp olive oil
6 chunky pork sausages
100g smoked bacon lardons
1 onion, finely chopped
1 carrot, finely chopped
1 celery stick, finely chopped
4 garlic cloves, crushed
4 ripe plum tomatoes, about 400g, roughly chopped
Handful thyme sprigs, leaves picked
2 bay leaves
500ml chicken stock
2 x 400g tins haricot beans, drained and rinsed

FOR THE CRUMB
50g fresh or dried breadcrumbs
1 garlic clove, crushed
Handful parsley, finely chopped

★ FREEZE AHEAD
Prepare to the end of step 5. Cool, then freeze the cassoulet mixture and breadcrumbs separately for up to 3 months. To serve, defrost in the fridge, then return the cassoulet to a casserole dish. Reheat on the hob for 10min, adding a splash of water if needed. Complete the recipe to serve.

Hands-on time: 30min, plus cooling
Cooking time: about 2hr 15min
Serves 6

PER SERVING 716cals, 54g protein, 42g fat
(14g saturates), 26g carbs (6g total sugars), 9g fibre

1. Preheat oven to 180°C (160°C fan) mark 4. Pat the duck legs dry with kitchen paper, then season all over and arrange on a wire rack set over a roasting tin. Roast for 1hr 30min, or until the meat is pulling away from the bones. Cool (reserve the fat in the roasting tin).

2. Meanwhile, heat the oil in a large casserole dish (that has a lid) over medium heat. Brown the sausages all over. Remove to a plate. Add the lardons, onion, carrot and celery to the casserole and cook for 8–10min until softened and starting to brown. Stir in the garlic and cook for 2min, until fragrant.

3. Stir in the tomatoes, thyme, bay leaves, stock and some seasoning. Bring to the boil, then return the sausages to the casserole. Reduce heat to low, cover and cook for 1hr, removing the lid for the final 15min.

4. Chunkily shred the duck meat and skin from the bones, discarding any fatty bits. Stir the shredded duck into the casserole, along with the beans. Check the seasoning.

5. In a small bowl, mix the breadcrumbs with the garlic, parsley, 2 tbsp of the reserved duck fat and some seasoning.

6. Sprinkle the crumb mixture over the casserole in an even layer and cook in the oven, uncovered, for 45min, or until bubbling and golden brown. Serve with some cooked greens, if you like.

Pancetta Chicken Parcels with Brioche Stuffing

A timeless dinner party staple, our recipe uses brioche for a decadent, sweet stuffing and can be cooked from frozen.

25g butter
1 small onion, finely chopped
1 celery stick, finely chopped
6 garlic cloves, unpeeled
175g stale brioche
25g dried apricots, finely chopped
1 medium egg
Small handful parsley, finely chopped
Finely grated zest and juice ½ lemon
6 large skinless chicken breasts
18 pancetta slices
1 tbsp olive oil
2 tbsp double cream

1. Preheat oven to 200°C (180°C fan) mark 6. Melt the butter in a medium pan and cook the onion and celery for 10min until softened but not coloured. Peel and finely chop 2 garlic cloves, add to the pan and fry for 1min. Empty into a bowl and let cool.

2. Meanwhile, whizz the brioche in a food processor to make crumbs. Tip the crumbs into the cooled onion mixture. Add the apricots, egg, parsley and lemon zest and juice, and season. Stir to make a stuffing.

3. Cut a slit into the underside of each chicken breast, then use your finger to open into a pocket. Firmly push a sixth of the stuffing into the pocket. Repeat the process with the remaining breasts and stuffing.

4. Arrange 3 pancetta slices side by side, lay on a chicken breast (stuffing-side up) and wrap the ends of the pancetta around the breast, sealing in the stuffing. Repeat with the remaining pancetta and breasts.

5. Put the wrapped breasts (pancetta-seam down) in a large roasting tin. Scatter in the remaining garlic cloves and drizzle over the oil. Cook in oven for 35min until golden and cooked through, basting the chicken with juices after 20min. Remove from the oven, transfer the chicken to a board and cover loosely with foil to keep warm.

6. Mash the roasted garlic in the tin with the juices and a splash of water. Stir in the cream and put over medium hob heat. Bring to the boil and simmer for 1–2min, until it is coating consistency. Check the seasoning, then strain into a small jug. Serve the chicken with the sauce and Boulangère Potatoes (see p482), if you like.

★ FREEZE AHEAD
Make to the end of step 5, then tightly wrap each breast in clingfilm and put into one sealable bag. Freeze for up to 3 months. To serve, unwrap the frozen breasts and complete the recipe, cooking for 1hr and adding garlic cloves halfway. Check the chicken is cooked through before serving (if using a thermometer, the temperature needs to be 75°C).

Hands-on time: 30min
Cooking time: about 50min
Serves 6

PER SERVING 421cals, 40g protein, 21g fat (9g saturates), 17g carbs (5g total sugars), 1g fibre

Turkey Burgers with Onion Rings

Our gourmet-style burgers feature turkey thigh mince, which has more fat than breast mince and makes a juicier burger.

About 200ml vegetable oil, plus 3 tbsp extra
3 large onions, 1 finely chopped
2 cloves garlic, crushed
1 tsp allspice
75g dried cranberries, chopped
4 large eggs
Juice ½ lemon
3 thyme sprigs, leaves picked
450g turkey mince (preferably thigh mince)
75g plain flour
150g fresh breadcrumbs
6 burger buns
Cranberry sauce, to serve

★ FREEZE AHEAD

Brush the burgers with oil on both sides. Freeze in a container lined with baking parchment for up to 3 months. Defrost overnight in the fridge, then follow step 6 to cook. To freeze the cooked onion rings, leave them to cool, then freeze on lined baking trays for 10min until firm. Transfer to freezer bags. To reheat from frozen, put on 2 baking trays in an oven preheated to 220°C (200°C) mark 7 for 3–5min. Swap the trays halfway through.

Hands-on time: 45min, plus cooling and chilling
Cooking time: about 40min
Serves 6

PER SERVING 634cals, 36g protein, 26g fat (5g saturates), 63g carbs (15g total sugars), 5g fibre

1. Heat 1 tbsp oil and fry the chopped onion with a pinch of salt for 8min until softened. Add the garlic and allspice and fry for 2min until fragrant. Spoon on to a plate and spread out to cool.

2. Mix the cooled onion mixture, cranberries, 1 egg, lemon juice, thyme and turkey mince with plenty of seasoning in a large bowl.

3. With oiled hands, form the mixture into 6 patties about 2.5cm thick. Cover and chill for at least 20min while you make the onion rings, or follow the instructions to freeze.

4. Slice the 2 remaining onions into thick rounds and separate out. Gently whisk the remaining eggs in a bowl. Scatter the flour on to a plate and season well. Put half the breadcrumbs into a medium bowl (replace them when they clump together). Working in batches, toss the onion rings in the flour, then dip in the egg, followed by the breadcrumbs to coat. Lay on a baking tray lined with baking parchment, spaced apart.

5. Heat 2cm depth of oil in a shallow pan until the breadcrumbs brown in 30sec. Fry onions rings over high heat in 3 or 4 batches for 2min, until golden. Turn halfway through, then remove and drain on kitchen paper. Set aside.

6. Heat 2 tbsp oil over low heat. Fry the burgers for 10min on each side. Serve in buns with cranberry sauce and onion rings on the side.

Porcini 'Meatballs' and Creamy Mash

Flaxseed is the secret to binding these dairy-free, protein-packed black bean and mushroom balls.

25g dried porcini
3 tbsp olive oil
250g chestnut mushrooms, chopped
2 garlic cloves, crushed
1 tsp smoked paprika
400g tin black beans, drained and rinsed
1 tbsp ground/milled flaxseed
60g couscous (dried/uncooked)

FOR THE SAUCE
½ tbsp olive oil
1 red onion, finely chopped
2 rosemary sprigs
2 x 400g tins chopped tomatoes
250ml vegan red wine
150g baby spinach

FOR THE MASH
900g floury potatoes, peeled and cut into even chunks
1 large garlic clove, peeled
75g dairy-free olive oil spread
4-5 tbsp dairy-free cream (optional)

Hands-on time: 45min, plus soaking and chilling
Cooking time: about 1hr
Serves 4

PER SERVING 692cals, 19g protein, 25g fat
(5g saturates), 78g carbs (13g total sugars), 15g fibre

1. Put the porcini in a heatproof bowl, pour over 100ml just-boiled water and soak for 20min. Heat 1 tbsp oil in a deep frying pan over medium heat. Add the mushrooms and fry for 6–7min, stirring, until softened and golden. Add the garlic, paprika and beans and cook, stirring, for 2min until the mixture looks dry. Put the flaxseed in a bowl with 2 tbsp cold water, stir and leave to soak for 10min.

2. Put the mushroom mixture into a food processor. Drain the porcini (reserving the water) and add to processor with some seasoning. Pulse to a coarse purée. Add the couscous and soaked flaxseed and pulse briefly to combine. Roll into 20 balls with damp hands. Arrange on a plate and chill for 30min.

3. Meanwhile, make the sauce. In the same pan, heat ½ tbsp oil over low-medium heat and fry the onion for 8–10min until softened. Add the rosemary, tomatoes, wine, reserved porcini soaking water and some seasoning, then bring to the boil and bubble for 20min until reduced.

4. Preheat oven to 180°C (160°C fan) mark 4. For the mash, put the potatoes into a large pan with the garlic and some salt, cover with cold water and bring to the boil. Bubble for 15min, or until the potatoes are tender. Drain and leave to steam-dry in a colander for 10min.

5. While the potatoes cook, heat 2 tbsp oil in a separate frying pan over medium heat, add the 'meatballs' and shake to coat in oil. Fry for 10min,

turning regularly, until well browned. Transfer to a baking tray and cook in oven for 12min.

6. Return the potatoes and garlic to the empty pan, mash well with the spread and cream alternative (if using). Cover and keep warm. Stir the spinach into the sauce until just wilted.

7. Divide the mash among 4 plates or bowls. Stir the 'meatballs' into the sauce, spoon onto the mash.

★ FREEZE AHEAD
Prepare to the end of step 6. Cool and freeze the 'meatballs', sauce and mash separately, for up to 1 month. To serve, defrost overnight in fridge. Reheat the sauce and mash separately on the hob, adding a splash of water if needed, until piping hot. Add the 'meatballs' to the sauce (do not stir), cover with a lid and cook for 5min, until heated through.

Duck Ragu

A delicious, warming winter treat that can be made in advance.

½ tbsp olive oil
4 duck legs, excess skin and fat removed
1 large onion, finely chopped
2 carrots, finely chopped
1 celery stick, finely chopped
2 garlic cloves, crushed
150ml red wine
500ml hot chicken stock
400g tin plum tomatoes
2 tbsp tomato purée
1 tbsp dried basil
1 bay leaf

1. Heat the oil in a large pan and brown the duck legs all over, then set aside. Pour away all but 1 tbsp of the fat. Gently fry the onion, carrots and celery for 10min. Add the garlic and cook for 1min.

2. Stir in the red wine, stock, tomatoes and tomato purée, the basil and bay leaf. Nestle in the duck legs. Cover and simmer for 1hr.

3. Remove the duck and, when cool enough to handle, pull off the meat and roughly shred, discarding the bones and skin. Return the meat to the pan. Simmer, uncovered, for 30min until the sauce has reduced and thickened slightly.

4. Serve with tagliatelle, garnished with basil and Parmesan, or with jacket potatoes.

★ FREEZE AHEAD
Make the recipe to the end of step 3, then cool completely. Empty into a freezerproof container and freeze for up to 3 months. Defrost in the fridge overnight, then reheat on the hob until piping hot.

Hands-on time: 25min
Cooking time: about 1hr 50min
Serves 8

PER SERVING (without pasta or potatoes) 311cals, 29g protein, 17g fat (5g saturates), 7g carbs (5g total sugars), 2g fibre

Kedgeree Fishcakes

Inspired by the classic breakfast dish, these can be kept on standby in your freezer.

400g floury potatoes, peeled and cut into small chunks
4 medium eggs
350g undyed smoked haddock, skinned
½ small onion, finely chopped
300ml milk
2 tbsp chopped coriander or parsley
2 tsp curry powder
3 tbsp plain flour
100g fresh breadcrumbs
4 tbsp sunflower oil

1. Bring a medium pan of water to the boil and simmer the potatoes for 15min or until tender. Meanwhile, put 3 of the eggs into a small pan, cover with cold water and bring to the boil. Once boiling, turn down heat and simmer for 7min. Drain the eggs and run under cold water for 2min, then peel and roughly chop.

2. Put the haddock and onion into a frying pan and pour over the milk (add a little water if the fish is not covered). Bring to a gentle simmer and poach for 5min until fish is cooked. Strain into a sieve set over a jug (reserve both).

3. Drain the potatoes and leave to steam dry for 5min. Return to the empty pan with 5 tbsp of the reserved poaching milk (discard the rest) and mash until smooth. Flake in the fish, then add the onions, chopped eggs, herbs, curry powder and some seasoning. Shape into 8 patties.

4. Set up 3 bowls: one with flour, one with the remaining egg (beaten) and one with breadcrumbs. Coat the patties in flour, then egg, and finally the breadcrumbs.

★ FREEZE AHEAD
Cool the fishcakes completely and open-freeze on a baking tray. Once frozen, wrap in clingfilm; freeze for up to 3 months. To serve, cook from frozen on a lightly oiled baking sheet in an oven preheated to 200°C (180°C fan) mark 6 for 20–25mins until piping hot.

5. Heat the oil in a large frying pan and fry the fishcakes for 3-5min on each side until golden and heated through. Serve with peas, lemon wedges and mango chutney, if you like.

Hands-on time: 35min
Cooking time: about 25min
Makes 8 fishcakes

PER FISHCAKE 216cals, 13g protein, 7g fat (1g saturates), 24g carbs (3g total sugars), 2g fibre

Spanish Chicken

Packed with flavour, this lighter stew showcases Spanish tastes. Choose your favourite stuffed olives for the recipe.

1 tbsp olive oil
8 chicken thighs, skin on
175g cooking chorizo, sliced into 5mm rounds
3 mixed peppers, deseeded and roughly chopped
2 tbsp plain flour
1 tsp sweet smoked paprika
350ml Spanish red wine, such as Rioja
300ml chicken stock
2 tbsp red wine vinegar
200g stuffed olives
2 x 400g tins cannellini beans, drained and rinsed
Dash of sherry (optional)
Small bunch parsley, roughly chopped

1. Heat the oil in a large flameproof casserole over medium-high heat and brown the chicken (do this in batches if necessary). Lift out the chicken and set aside.

2. Drain off excess fat from the pan. Add the chorizo and peppers to the pan and fry for 3–5min, stirring often, until beginning to colour. Stir in the flour and cook for 1min.

3. Return the chicken to the pan, add the paprika, wine, stock and vinegar. Bring to the boil, cover and simmer for 30min. Stir in the olives and beans and simmer uncovered for 15min.

4. Add the sherry, if using, then check the seasoning. Sprinkle over parsley and serve with bread to mop up the juices, if you like.

⭐ FREEZE AHEAD
Make to end of step 3, then allow to cool completely. Transfer to a freezerproof container and freeze for up to 3 months. To serve, defrost overnight in the fridge. Transfer to a large pan, bring to the boil and simmer for 30min until piping hot. Complete the recipe.

Hands-on time: 20min
Cooking time: about 1hr
Serves 4

PER SERVING 762cals, 58g protein, 39g fat (11g saturates), 24g carbs (4g total sugars), 11g fibre

Little Salmon Pies

Try a mixture of your favourite fish in this delightful starter — it's a great way to use up any uncooked, leftover fish.

50g butter
40g flour
1 tsp English mustard powder
450ml milk
Small bunch chives, finely chopped
175g salmon fillet, cut into 4cm pieces
175g lightly smoked salmon fillet, cut into 4cm pieces
2 small floury potatoes, about 150g, peeled
Salmon caviar, to serve (optional)

1. In a small pan, melt 40g of butter. Stir in the flour with the mustard powder and cook for 1min. Remove from heat and gradually whisk in the milk, adding a little at a time to prevent lumps from forming. Return to the heat and bring the mixture to the boil, stirring all the time. Simmer for 2min until thickened and the mixture coats the back of the spoon.

2. Mix in most of the chives and season well. Add the fish to the sauce and divide among 6 x 125ml ramekins.

3. Preheat oven to 190°C (170°Cfan) mark 5. Slice the potatoes very thinly, using a mandoline if you have one. Melt the remaining butter, then layer the potatoes to cover the top of the fish mixture (about 4-5 slices on each pie), brushing them with a little butter between each layer. Finish with a little butter brushed on top.

4. Cook in the oven for 30-35min, until the sauce is bubbling and the potatoes are cooked. Sprinkle with the remaining chives and a spoonful of salmon caviar, if you like.

★ FREEZE AHEAD
After baking the fish pies, let them cool before wrapping well in clingfilm and freezing for up to 2 months. Reheat from frozen at 190°C (170°C fan) mark 5 – brush a little melted butter over the pies and cook them for 20–25min.

Hands-on time: 10min
Cooking time: about 45min
Serves 6

PER SERVING 313 cals, 18g protein, 18g fat (9g saturates), 19g carbs (4g total sugars), 1g fibre

Boulangère Potatoes

This French potato gratin will please vegetarians, gluten-free guests and meat eaters alike.

Butter, to grease
1.5kg floury potatoes
40g butter
2 garlic cloves, finely chopped
300ml strong, gluten-free vegetable stock
2 tbsp onion marmalade

1. Preheat oven to 200°C (180°C fan) mark 6 and butter a large ovenproof dish. Peel and thinly slice the potatoes (a mandoline or food processor slicer is ideal).

2. Heat the butter in a large pan and gently fry the garlic for 1min until soft. Stir in the vegetable stock and season. Bring to the boil, add the potatoes, cook for 2–3min, stirring frequently, until hot. Fold in the onion marmalade, put in an ovenproof dish and cook for 1hr until tender.

★ FREEZE AHEAD
Cool completely, then cover with foil and freeze for up to 3 months. Cook from frozen (still covered with foil) at 180°C (160°C fan) mark 4 for 50min, removing the foil halfway, until piping hot.

Hands-on time: 10min
Cooking time: about 1hr 5min
Serves 6

PER SERVING 263cals, 5g protein, 6g fat (4g saturates), 44g carbs (4g total sugars), 5g fibre

Rösti-topped Fish Pie

Use any sustainably sourced fish you like in this crispy pie.

50g butter
2 leeks, finely sliced
2 tsp Dijon mustard
50g plain flour
600ml milk
750g skinless fish fillets, cut into 2cm chunks (we used salmon, smoked haddock and cod)
200g frozen peas

FOR THE RÖSTI TOPPING
750g floury potatoes, unpeeled
2 tbsp cornflour
5g butter

1. Preheat oven to 200°C (180°C fan) mark 6. For the filling, melt the butter in a large pan over medium heat and cook the leeks for 10min until softened. Stir in the mustard and flour and cook for 1min. Remove from heat and gradually stir in the milk. Return to heat and cook, stirring, until thickened. Set aside.

2. To make the rösti topping, coarsely grate the potatoes, then lay on to a clean tea towel. Gather up the corners; squeeze out as much moisture as you can. Empty the squeezed potato into a bowl; mix in the cornflour and some seasoning. Melt the butter in a large, non-stick frying pan over medium heat. Add the potatoes, stir, and fry for 5-10min, stirring regularly, until softened.

3. Stir the fish, peas and plenty of seasoning into the leek sauce, then decant into a shallow 2 litre ovenproof serving dish. Top with the rösti mixture in an even layer.

4. Cook in the oven for 25–30min, until bubbling and golden. Serve with seasonal greens, if you like.

⭐ FREEZE AHEAD
Prepare to the end of step 3, then cool the leek sauce before adding the fish and peas. Cool the rösti topping before assembling. Wrap the dish well and freeze for up to 1 month. To serve, defrost overnight in the fridge. Complete the recipe.

Hands-on time: 30min
Cooking time: about 45min
Serves 6

PER SERVING 496cals, 31g protein, 23g fat (12g saturates), 39g carbs (4g total sugars), 6g fibre

Celeriac and Porcini Soup

Double cream and olive oil give this soup an indulgent edge.

10g dried porcini mushrooms
2 tbsp olive oil
1 onion, finely chopped
1 celery stick, finely chopped
500g celeriac, chopped
900ml hot vegetable stock
2 tbsp chopped fresh sage
2 thick slices wholemeal bread, cut into 1cm cubes
Extra virgin olive oil for drizzling
50ml double cream
Handful curly parsley, roughly chopped

1. Cover the porcini with boiling water and leave to soak for 10min.

2. Meanwhile, heat 1 tbsp olive oil in a pan and fry the onion and celery until soft but not coloured. Drain the porcini, reserving 300ml of the soaking water – make up with boiling water if necessary. Stir the celeriac and porcini into the pan along with the reserved liquid and stock. Simmer for 10–15min until the celeriac is tender. Blend the soup in batches with the sage until smooth. Taste and adjust the seasoning.

3. Gently heat the remaining olive oil in a frying pan, then fry the bread cubes until golden to make croutons. Season. Serve the soup drizzled with a little oil and cream, garnished with croutons and parsley.

★ FREEZE AHEAD
Make to the end of step 2, then cool, transfer to a freezerproof container and freeze for up to 3 months. Defrost overnight in the fridge, then heat in a pan until piping hot and complete the recipe.

Hands-on time: 20min, plus soaking
Cooking time: about 25min
Serves 4

PER SERVING 225cals, 5g protein, 14g fat
(5g saturates), 16g carbs (5g total sugars), 9g fibre

Lamb and Pork Cannelloni

This extra-special cannelloni will become a firm family favourite.

1 tbsp sunflower oil
400g each pork and lamb mince
1 onion, thinly sliced
1 carrot, finely diced
2 garlic cloves, crushed
Large pinch each of chilli flakes and mace
¼ tsp sweet smoked paprika
2 x 400g tins chopped tomatoes
110g tin kidney beans, drained and rinsed
50g butter
50g flour
350ml milk
350ml lamb stock
2 large handfuls spinach
8 fresh egg lasagne pasta sheets
75g feta cheese, crumbled

1. Heat the oil in a large frying pan and brown the minces in batches. Tip each batch into a colander set over a bowl to drain excess fat.

2. In the same pan, gently fry the onion and carrot for 10min until softened but not coloured. Stir in the garlic and spices and cook for 1min. Add the mince and tomatoes and simmer for 30min. Stir in the kidney beans, then leave to cool.

3. Melt butter in a pan and stir in the flour. Cook for 1min. Take off the heat and slowly stir in the milk and stock. Return the pan to heat and stir until thickened. Stir in the spinach, then set aside.

4. Preheat oven to 180°C (160°C fan) mark 4. Lay a sheet of pasta on a board, with the long edge facing towards you. Spoon 3 tbsp of mince along the long edge of the pasta, then roll up. Put into a large ovenproof, freezerproof dish. Repeat with

remaining sheets. Spoon the leftover mince around the edges. Top with the sauce and feta. Cook for 30–35min until golden and bubbling.

★ FREEZE AHEAD
Complete the recipe to the end of step 4, then cool. Wrap in clingfilm, then freeze for up to 3 months. To serve, defrost overnight in the fridge. Preheat oven to 180°C (160°C fan) mark 4; cook for 45min.

Hands-on time: 25min
Cooking time: about 1hr 30min
Serves 8

PER SERVING 427cals, 27g protein, 23g fat (8g saturates), 28g carbs (8g total sugars), 4g fibre

Venison Pie

Diced venison is now available in larger supermarkets, but this rich combination of classic bourguignon flavours will work just as well with the same quantity of beef stewing steak.

150g diced pancetta or smoked streaky bacon
400g shallots, peeled and halved
1.2kg diced venison
2 tbsp oil
2 garlic cloves, crushed
1 tsp juniper berries, lightly crushed
1 tsp allspice
6 tbsp plain flour, plus extra to dust
275g button mushrooms, halved
650ml red wine
450ml beef stock
1 bay leaf
3 sprigs thyme, leaves picked
200g cooked chestnuts, left whole
500g block puff pastry
1 medium egg, beaten

1. In a large pan or casserole dish over medium heat, fry the pancetta (or bacon) and shallots for 10min. Scoop out with a slotted spoon and set aside. Season the venison well. Fry in 2 batches, using 1 tbsp oil for each, until evenly browned all over. Return all the meat to the pan.

2. Stir in the garlic, juniper and allspice for 1min until fragrant. Add the flour and cook for another minute, stirring constantly.

3. Return the pancetta (or bacon) and shallots to the pan with the mushrooms. Pour in the wine and stock, then add the herbs. Bring to the boil, reduce temperature to low, partially cover and simmer for 3hr. Once the meat is tender, stir in the chestnuts, remove from heat and set aside to cool completely. Remove the bay leaf and thyme sprigs and discard.

4. Spoon the cold filling into a 1.3 litre pie dish with a rim, mounding it slightly in the centre and adding enough liquid to come just below the pie rim.

5. Roll out the pastry on a lightly floured surface to £1-coin thickness. Cut off a few strips to fit around the pie dish rim. Brush the rim lightly with water, press the pastry strips on to the rim and brush with the egg. Use a rolling pin to lift the remaining pastry over the pie. Trim away excess, cutting downwards against the edge of the rim. Reserve the trimmings. Tap the blade of a sharp knife against the edge of the pastry, separating the pastry layers slightly: this encourages the layers to 'puff'. Scallop the pie edge with the back of your knife and finger, then brush lightly all over with beaten egg. Pastry trimmings can be used to decorate the pie top; brush these with beaten egg as well. Make 2 small vent holes with a knife. Chill for 20min, then bake or follow freezing instructions.

6. Heat oven to 220°C (200°C) mark 7. Brush the pie again with egg, then place on a baking sheet and cook in the middle of the oven for 30min until the pastry is golden.

Hands-on time: 30min, plus cooling and chilling
Cooking time: about 4hr
Serves 6

PER SERVING 834cals, 60g protein, 35g fat (16g saturates), 49g carbs (5g total sugars), 6g fibre

★ FREEZE AHEAD
Assemble the pie up to the end of step 5. Open freeze for 30min, then wrap well in clingfilm and freeze for up to 2 months. To cook from frozen, heat oven to 220°C (200°C fan) mark 7. Remove the clingfilm. Place on a baking tray in the middle of the oven and bake for 30min, then reduce oven temperature to 180°C (160°C fan) mark 4 and bake for 50min.

Flourless Chocolate Cake with Raspberry Coulis

This soft, truffley chocolate cake is easy to make and delicious. Check the chocolate is gluten-free, if necessary.

250g unsalted butter, cut into pieces, plus extra to grease
250g dark chocolate, chopped
75g cocoa powder, sifted
1 tbsp vanilla extract
6 medium eggs
150g caster sugar
400g frozen raspberries
100g icing sugar, plus extra to dust
Crème fraîche, to serve (optional)

★ TO STORE
The cake will keep up to 5 days wrapped in clingfilm or in an airtight container at room temperature. Store the coulis in the fridge for up to 3 days.

★ FREEZE AHEAD
Make up to the end of step 5. Remove the cake from the tin, leave in its parchment paper and wrap in a double layer of clingfilm. Freeze for up to 1 month. Freeze the coulis in a bag or airtight container for up to 1 month. To serve, defrost both at room temperature and complete the recipe.

Hands-on time: 20min
Cooking time: about 1hr
Serves 10–12

PER SERVING (for 12) 418cals, 6g protein, 27g fat (16g saturates), 36g carbs (35g total sugars), 3g fibre

1. Preheat oven to 160°C (140°C fan) mark 3. Grease and line the base and sides of a 20.5cm loose-bottomed cake tin with parchment.

2. In a medium heatproof bowl set over a pan of simmering water, melt the chocolate and butter together. Remove the bowl from the heat and stir in the cocoa powder, vanilla and pinch of salt. Leave to cool.

3. In a freestanding mixer or using a handheld electric whisk, beat the eggs and caster sugar for 5–8min until thick and pale, and the mixture leaves a trail when a beater is lifted out.

4. Gently fold in the chocolate mixture using a spatula or large metal spoon. Pour into the tin and bake for 50min until the top feels dry and springy, and the cake doesn't wobble when you shake the tin slightly. Leave to cool in the tin on a wire rack.

5. To make the coulis, heat the raspberries and icing sugar in a medium pan until the berries break down and mixture is syrupy, about 8–10min. Strain through a sieve into a jug or bowl and leave to cool.

6. Carefully remove the cooled cake from the tin and peel away the parchment. Transfer to a cake stand or plate, dust with icing sugar and serve with the coulis and crème fraîche, if you like.

Layered Rum and Coffee Parfait

This iced indulgence is ready to serve straight from the freezer and needs no softening time, making it the ideal sweet treat to have on standby for 11th-hour entertaining.

75g amaretti biscuits
3 medium egg whites
150g caster sugar
1 tsp vanilla extract
150g mascarpone
150ml double cream
1½ tsp instant espresso/coffee powder
1 tbsp dark rum
Caramel dessert sauce, to serve

1. Dampen a 900g loaf tin with a little water and line with clingfilm, making sure there is an overhang at the edges. Whizz 50g amaretti biscuits in a food processor to make coarse crumbs. Set aside.

2. Put the egg whites into a medium bowl and beat with a handheld electric whisk until forming stiff peaks. Gradually add the sugar, whisking constantly, until the mixture is thick and glossy. Set aside.

3. In a separate large bowl, whisk the vanilla extract and mascarpone together briefly until smooth, then add the cream and whisk until the mixture holds its shape. Stir a large spoonful of the egg whites into the cream mixture to loosen, then, using a large metal spoon, fold in the remaining egg whites.

4. In a clean bowl, stir the espresso/coffee powder with 1½ tsp warm water to dissolve coffee. Tip a third of the parfait mixture into the coffee bowl and fold gently to combine. Add the rum to the unflavoured parfait bowl and fold gently to combine.

5. Spoon half the rum parfait into the lined tin and level. Scatter over half the amaretti crumbs. Spread over the coffee parfait and scatter over the remaining crumbs, then finish with the remaining rum parfait, levelling it.

6. Wrap the whole tin in clingfilm and freeze until solid (at least 6hr or preferably overnight).

7. To serve, roughly crush the remaining amaretti biscuits. Unwrap the tin to expose the surface of the loaf. Dip the bottom of the tin in cold water for a few seconds to loosen, then dry. Invert the parfait on to a serving plate and carefully remove the tin and clingfilm. Scatter crushed biscuits over the top, drizzle with caramel sauce and serve in slices.

Hands-on time 20min, plus (overnight) freezing
Serves 10

PER SERVING (without caramel sauce) 239cals, 2g protein, 16g fat (10g saturates), 21g carbs (21g total sugars), 0g fibre

★ FREEZE AHEAD
Make to end of step 6 up to 1 month ahead.
Complete the recipe to serve.

Freeze-ahead Mince Pies

Christmas just wouldn't be Christmas without a delicious homemade fruity treat!

450g Bramley apples, peeled, cored and cut
   into 2cm chunks
Zest and juice ½ orange and ½ lemon
200ml medium cider
150g soft brown sugar
1 tsp mixed spice
150g each raisins and currants
75g glacé cherries, chopped
2 tbsp Grand Marnier (optional)

FOR THE PASTRY
400g plain flour, sifted, plus extra for dusting
250g cold butter, diced
100g caster sugar
Finely grated zest 1 large orange
2 large egg yolks, plus 1 egg, beaten
100ml double cream
Icing sugar, for dusting

★ FREEZE AHEAD
Freeze uncooked pies in their tins for up to
3 months, wrapped in clingfilm. Bake from frozen
as in step 4, allowing 5min extra. Or pack cooked
pies (without icing sugar) into freezerproof boxes
and freeze for up to 3 months. To reheat, defrost
overnight in the fridge, then heat for 5–10min at
200°C (180°C) mark 6.

Hands-on time: 1hr, plus chilling
Cooking time: about 45min
Makes 24 pies

PER PIE 264cals, 3g protein, 12g fat (7g saturates),
36g carbs (20g total sugars), 1g fibre

1. Put the apples, citrus zest and juice, and cider in
   a pan. Bring to the boil, then simmer for 10min.
   Add the brown sugar, spice, raisins and currants
   and stir over a low heat until the sugar dissolves.
   Simmer for 15min. Remove from the heat, add the
   cherries and liqueur, if using, and cool completely.

2. For the pastry, put the flour into a food processor
   with the butter and whizz until the mixture
   resembles breadcrumbs. Briefly whizz in the
   sugar and zest. Combine the egg yolks and cream
   and, with the motor running, pour in the flour –
   stop when the mixture clumps together. Knead
   briefly, then wrap in clingfilm and chill for 30min.

3. Dust the worktop with flour and roll out pastry
   to 3mm thickness. Stamp out 24 rounds with a
   9cm cutter and line 24 deep bun tin holes. Fill
   each with 2 tsp mincemeat.

4. Preheat oven to 190°C (170°C fan) mark 5. Stamp
   out 12 circles with an 8cm cutter and 12 stars
   with the same size star cutter. Brush the base
   rims with water and top the pies with a star or
   circle (cut a slit in the circles), then brush with
   beaten egg. Chill for 30min. Bake for 15–20min
   until golden. Leave in the tins for 5min, then
   turn out on to wire racks to cool. Dust with icing
   sugar. Serve warm or cold.

Pecan and Cranberry Freezer Cookies

These cookies can be cooked from frozen, so are convenient to keep on hand for unexpected guests.

225g softened, unsalted butter
75g caster sugar
2 large egg yolks
Finely grated zest 1 orange
75g pecans, chopped
75g dried cranberries, finely chopped
½ tsp ground cinnamon
200g plain flour

★ FREEZE AHEAD
At the end of step 2, freeze the cookie logs for up to 1 month. Transfer from the freezer to fridge 20min before baking, to soften them slightly for easier slicing. Put the sliced rounds on baking sheets spaced about 4cm apart and bake on the top and middle shelves of the oven at 180°C (160°C fan) mark 4 for 15min until golden. Leave on the baking tray to cool for 10min, then transfer to a wire rack to cool completely.

1. In a large mixing bowl, beat the butter until softened, add the sugar and beat until light and smooth. Beat in the egg yolks and a pinch of salt. Fold in the orange zest, pecans, cranberries and cinnamon, followed by the flour until just incorporated. Divide the mixture in 2 and spoon the dough on to 2 large squares of clingfilm. Form into 2 disc shapes, wrap and chill for 30min to firm slightly.

2. Remove from the fridge. Unwrap the dough and roll into 2 logs about 5cm thick. Re-wrap in clingfilm and chill for 20min or follow the freezing instructions.

3. Preheat oven to 180°C (160°C fan) mark 4. Line 2 baking sheets with baking parchment. Unwrap the chilled cookie logs and slice into 1cm rounds.

4. Transfer the rounds to the baking sheet, spaced about 4cm apart. Bake for 12min, then leave to cool for 10min on the sheet before transferring to a wire rack to cool completely.

Hands-on time: 20min, plus chilling
Cooking time: about 15min
Makes 32 cookies

PER COOKIE 113cals, 1g protein, 8g fat (4g saturates), 9g carbs (4g total sugars), 1g fibre

Salty Pistachio Ice Cream with Berry Compote

An indulgent dessert, layered with flavour.

275g salted pistachio kernels
150g caster sugar
4 large egg whites
400ml double cream
2 drops almond extract

FOR THE BERRY COMPOTE
300g frozen blueberries
2 tbsp ginger wine
25g caster sugar

1. Pulse 100g of the pistachios and 25g of the sugar in a food processor until finely ground. Add the remaining pistachios and pulse once or twice to break up roughly.

2. Using an electric hand whisk, whisk the egg whites in a clean bowl until they hold their shape and form peaks. Gradually add the remaining sugar and beat until stiff and glossy.

3. Whip the cream in a bowl with the almond extract until just holding its shape – it's important not to overwhip. Using a metal spoon, fold the egg whites into the cream, then fold in the pistachios. Pour into a freezerproof dish, then cover and freeze for at least 5hr or overnight.

4. To make the berry compote, gently warm the blueberries in a pan with the ginger wine, caster sugar and 2 tbsp water for about 5min until the berries release their juice.

5. Transfer the ice cream to the fridge and soften for 10min before serving with the compote.

★ FREEZE AHEAD
The ice cream will keep for up to 1 month. You can freeze the berry compote, too – once made, cool completely, then transfer to a freezerproof container and freeze for up to 1 month. Defrost the compote in the fridge and serve with the ice cream as in step 5.

Hands-on time: 25min, plus freezing
Cooking time: about 5min
Serves 8

PER SERVING 475cals, 8g protein, 38g fat (18g saturates), 30g carbs (28g total sugars), 1g fibre

Frozen Christmas Bombe

This iced, tipsy pud makes a refreshing alternative to the traditional version.

50g dried cranberries
175g mixed dried fruit
Finely grated zest 1 orange
Finely grated zest 1 lemon
60ml brandy or rum
1 tsp mixed spice
300ml double cream
75g icing sugar, sifted
500g tub chilled fresh custard
50g pistachios, roughly chopped

TO DECORATE
100g plain chocolate, finely chopped
Silver dragées, gluten free, if required (optional)

1. Put all the dried fruit into a large bowl and mix in the citrus zests, brandy/rum and mixed spice. Set aside to soak for 15min.

2. Line a 1.3 litre pudding basin or freezerproof bowl with a double layer of clingfilm, ensuring excess hangs over the sides.

3. Whip the cream and icing sugar until it holds its shape, then fold in the custard, soaked fruit and pistachios. Spoon into prepared basin/bowl and level the surface. Cover with overhanging clingfilm and freeze until solid – about 4hr.

4. To serve, remove from freezer and let soften at room temperature for 15min. Meanwhile, melt the chocolate in a heatproof bowl set over a pan of barely simmering water.

5. Remove the clingfilm from the pudding, then invert on to a serving plate. Lift off basin/bowl

and peel off the clingfilm. Spoon the melted chocolate on top, then decorate with dragées, if using, and serve in wedges.

★ FREEZE AHEAD
Make to end of step 3 up to 1 month ahead. Complete the recipe to serve.

Hands-on time: 20min, plus soaking and freezing
Cooking time: 5min
Serves 10

PER SERVING 404cals, 4g protein, 25g fat (14g saturates), 37g carbs (34g total sugars), 2g fibre

Index

mangetout: king prawn and pineapple fried rice 390

mangoes: deluxe mango chutney 300

mango and Scotch bonnet hot sauce 299

tropical vegan coconut ice 279

maple bacon Brussels 173

margarita: clementine and vanilla margarita 62

mulled wine margarita 69

marinara sauce 53

marmalade: chunky cranberry and orange marmalade 302

marmalade and bourbon glazed ham 344

marmalade and chocolate mince pies 230–1

sausage and marmalade plait 343

marshmallows: hot chocolate mix 295

hot chocolate stirrers 274

rocky road 279

martini, dirty chai latte 70

marzipan 328–9

masala sauce 372

mascarpone cheese: brandysnap and coffee cups 196

chestnut and chocolate macaroon 242–3

clementine and Prosecco trifle 212–13

layered rum and coffee parfait 490

mayonnaise: beetroot prawn cocktail 87

celeriac and pear remoulade 77

coronation chicken bites 40

fish finger tacos 365

meat-free chilli 458

meatballs: cauliflower 'meatballs' 372

lamb and oregano meatball traybake 397

meatball subs 52

mozzarella stuffed meatballs 402

porcini 'meatballs' and creamy mash 476–7

Melba toast 87

meringue: Black Forest mess 191

chestnut and chocolate macaroon 242–3

Christmas tree meringues 278

meringue buttercream 324–5

mini meringue mince pies 56

mulled clementine meringue wreath 353

tropical baked Alaska 211

Mexican buñuelos 327

milk: Danish risalamande 320

eggnog latte 63

milk (plant-based): chai and dark chocolate rice pudding 209

millefeuille, salmon 94

mince pies: baked mince pie apples 268

freeze-ahead mince pies 492

marmalade and chocolate mince pies 230–1

mince pie and cranberry brownies 269

mini meringue mince pies 56

ricciarelli mince pies 292

mincemeat: marmalade and chocolate mince pies 230–1

mincemeat tart 200

mini meringue mince pies 56

PX and pear mincemeat 215

ricciarelli mince pies 292

mini BLTs 47

mini bûches de Noël 322–3

mini meringue mince pies 56

mini mushroom crackers 188

mint: salsa verde 118

see also peppermint

mirror glaze 438–9

miso butter roast potatoes 168

mixed peel *see* candied peel

mocktails 72–5

apple and ginger alcohol-free twist 75

beetroot zinger 74

cucumber spritz 73

green power daiquiri 75

mulled cranberry and raspberry punch 74

pear sipper 72

tropical teaser mocktail 73

warming ginger soda 72

mojito, merry 70

monkfish: wrapped roast monkfish with Champagne sauce 126–7

mousse torte, vegan chocolate 202

mozzarella stuffed meatballs 402

muffins: pancetta and polenta muffins 471

raspberry and yogurt breakfast muffins 21

mulled berry trifle 354

mulled clementine meringue wreath 353

mulled cranberry and raspberry punch 74

mulled cranberry sauce 182

mulled pomegranate gin 283

mulled wine glazed devils on horseback 35

mulled wine jelly 192

mulled wine margarita 69

mushrooms: celeriac and porcini soup 484

chestnut and artichoke en croûte 144

coq au vin 346

giant savoury mince pie 140

kimchi and tofu cabbage stew 364

luxury vegan Wellington 146–7

mini mushroom crackers 188

mushroom molletes 29

mushroom, walnut and chestnut soup 249

mushroom Wellingtons 158–9

onion and porcini gravy 183

porcini 'meatballs' 476–7

pork stroganoff 396

roasted squash with porcini mushroom and dolcelatte risotto 362–3

slow cooker mushroom dumpling stew 444

speedy coq au vin 391

spiced short ribs 461

squash and mushroom lasagne 151

venison pie 486–7

warming venison casserole 459

whole stuffed celeriac 142

wild mushroom and lentil filo spiral 434

wild mushroom, cranberry and hazelnut sausage plait 336

wild mushroom soup 78

mussels: 'nduja and mussel spaghetti 383

Thai-style mussels 395

mustard: dill and mustard sauce 306

N

'nduja and mussel spaghetti 383

negroni, winter spiced 61

noodles: 'chicken' noodle soup 403

chicken yakisoba 398

quick Thai drunken noodles 379

spicy chicken peanut noodles 361

turkey pad thai 254

Normandy pork with apples and cider 452

Norwegian julekaka 312

nougat, best-ever 290

Nutella and Baileys cheesecake brownies 237